IN COLD TYPE

IN COLD TYPE

Overcoming the Book Crisis

Leonard Shatzkin

Houghton Mifflin Company Boston   1982

To the Reader:

It is not often that Houghton Mifflin adds a statement to a book it has published. Any book bearing our imprint is obviously one that we feel is worthy of being brought before the public. For nearly 150 years we have published books in the belief that each would find its proper place in the world of letters. In most cases, no discerning reader would assume that an author's book represented the opinions of the publisher. Indeed, many books that we have published held opinions that were contrary to those of the editors and, at times, to the prevailing sentiments of the era. To a certain extent, it is an American publisher's duty to seek out such books.

However, when a publisher presents a book containing strong opinions about the present circumstances of American trade publishing, it may be thought that such a book represents, in some measure, the philosophy of the publisher as well as that of the author.

We feel that Leonard Shatzkin has written an important book. We hope that it will interest all those who care, as we do, about the health, role, and prospects of books in American society. Mr. Shatzkin's evaluations of the present condition of publishing, together with his recommendations for change, are the fruit of his long career and have not been altered by us. We believe that this book, like all our books, will stimulate, entertain, inform, and contribute to the exchange of ideas.

HOUGHTON MIFFLIN COMPANY

Copyright © 1982 by Leonard Shatzkin

Library of Congress Cataloging in Publication Data
Shatzkin, Leonard.
  In cold type.
  1. Book industries and trade — United States.
2. Publishers and publishing — United States. I. Title.
Z471.S44   1982   070.5′0973   82-7701
ISBN 0-395-32160-3   AACR2

Printed in the United States of America

V 10 9 8 7 6 5 4 3 2 1

Diagrams by Celie Fitzgerald

For Elky

a small token
in appreciation for so much,
especially
three fantastic kids

Contents

9. Mass Market Publishing: An Industry in Trouble 193

The reasons for mass market's early and unexpected success · the role of the magazine distributor · the reasons for the recent deterioration in mass market publishing · how the mass market publishers' solutions have made matters worse · the increasing unhappiness of mass market distributors · the accelerating trend toward category publishing · the probable disappearance of mass market publishing in its present form · why mass market publishers are "invading" trade publishing and the probable results · one way to rescue mass market publishing from itself.

10. Editorial 217

The ambivalence of publishers toward the editorial function · how editorial productivity can be encouraged and controlled · developing the publisher's list · why editorial committees produce bad results · why editors produce better sales results when given independence and freedom.

11. Don't Forget the Author 239

The unequal negotiation between author and publisher · what the author should know about publishing skills · the role of the agent · the publisher's moral obligation to publish well · publishing "malpractice" · recognizing a publisher's specific talents · advance payments and royalty rates · the trend toward lower royalties · some other contract problems · the author's participation in selling his book.

12. The Economics of Publishing 262

Fallacies promoted by publishers' accountants · a financial model of a book publishing business · how to evaluate the economic effects of business policy · when to cut costs · when to expand editorial or sales departments · some common business mistakes resulting from accounting misconceptions · the flaws of "unit cost" accounting · how to choose retail price for maximum profit.

13. Production Management 299

Book production, the area publishing management understands least and that costs the most · the wastefulness of the usual approach to production · why buying cheap costs more · why producing a book takes months instead of weeks · why proofreading is wasteful and silly · how to reduce costs and speed up production · the proper role of the book designer.

14. How Many Books and When? Printing Quantities and Inventory Control 337

The cost of imprecise determination of printing quantities · the difference between new book and backlist printing decisions · mathematical prediction of sale by title · the Economic Order Quantity calculation · determining when to reprint and when to drop a book from the list.

15. Computerization, Management Information, and Odds and Ends 353

Using the computer for analysis and operational control · predicting sales, title by title, store by store · measuring sales force effectiveness · use of the "control chart" · why market research doesn't work for books · more sophisticated computer use in order fulfillment · reducing cost by combination shipping.

16. Conclusion 374

A developing crisis that demands response · the probability of many business casualties · some possible directions of industry change · the stake of authors and the public in finding better solutions.

Preface and Acknowledgments

It is not possible to thank, or even to name, all the friends and coworkers who, over the years, stimulated and challenged my own thinking or provided opportunities for testing some unconventional hypotheses. They have all helped me develop the ideas presented here.

It is one thing to discover that you have what seems to be a coherent outlook on the field in which you have spent your life; it is quite another matter to set it down beyond the reach of apologies, amendments, or second thoughts. And one who finds that his outlook is, generally speaking, at variance with that of many others, at least as intelligent, who have spent equivalent lifetimes arriving at different conclusions, must feel especially apprehensive.

If this book were less of a "minority report," I would, perhaps, have felt less need to test my convictions actively by defending them against arguments of experts who disagree and refining them in conversations with experts who do not. In the two years that this book was being written, rewritten, and re-rewritten, I have had the benefit of help from many friends and experts.

I owe a particular debt to Dan Melcher, who read the manuscript in an early and a later draft and spiced his encouragement of my efforts by challenging every place he felt that my statements were unsupported or at variance with his own extensive experience. I could not have found a sharper or more knowledgeable critic.

Bram and Ruth Cavin's reading of early drafts led them to demand that I make this a book for book readers, of value for every literate American, raising it above the parochial arguments of interest to "the trade." Whether I have been able to do that, only the reader can judge.

To test the interest of the book for the nonspecialist, several people outside any aspect of publishing read some or all of it and gave me a "layman's reaction." In particular, an early draft was carefully read and very ably criticized by Jack Litewka and by my daughter, Karen Shatzkin. If I have not achieved that aim after the help of their extensive comments, I can only blame myself.

Others who read early drafts and helped me with sound advice, and particularly with their encouragement, were Judy Applebaum, George Blagowidow, Larry Dietz, Austen Ettinger, Bob Hagelstein, Caroline Latham, Martha Moran, Marg Melcher, Hilda Rogin, Len Schwartz, Tim Seldes, Roysce Smith, Nat Sobel, and Vance Weaver.

Many of the concepts were refined in conversations with my son, Mike, who also read early versions. It is rewarding to throw ideas at Mike because they usually bounce back somewhat improved.

There are a number of people who were kind enough to discuss with me the areas in which they were particularly expert. Among the ones I owe thanks are Jay Acton, Rob Bartles, Mort Berke, George Brockway, Marvin Brown, Dwight deGolia, Bob Diforio, Eliot Fremont-Smith, Jerry Garbacz, Lew Gillenson, John Hersey, Larry Hughes, Peter Israel, Howard Kaminsky, Jack Kendig, Igor Kropotkin, Eliot Leonard, Mort and Doris Levin, Tom McCormack, Bernard Malamud, Alan Mirken, Michael Mirsky, Paul Ohran, Jack O'Leary, Eliot Paris, Stan Rice, Leonard Riggio, Andy Ross, Herb Schnall, Tony Schulte, Dick Seaver, Nance Shatzkin, Ed Stoddard, Roger Straus, Jr., Larry Todd, Sy Turk, Sam Vaughan, Hy Weintraub, Sam Weller, and Ivor Whitson.

Thanks are certainly due my very competent and patient secretary, Lorraine Morris, who typed every part of the original manuscript, evenings and weekends, and did most of the correcting. The work was done on an IBM Magnetic Card A typewriter (for easy revision), made available to us by Larry Silverman and Dick DeLorenzo, attorneys in our village of Croton-on-Hudson, who put up with considerable inconvenience once we wriggled our way inside their tent.

Of course, behind every published book there is a publisher. I consider myself fortunate that David Replogle felt *In Cold Type* to be a useful contribution to a broad discussion of the problems evident in trade publishing. Neither he nor any of the editors at Houghton Mifflin, by even the slightest hint, ever suggested that any ideas should be revised or amended, although there are many points on which they and company policy disagree. David Replogle made useful suggestions for restructuring an earlier version to present my point of view more effectively, and Gerard Van der Leun patiently improved the manuscript line by line to help me say it better.

Finally, this book would never have been were it not for the generous and exceptionally competent help and guidance of my wife, Elky. She protected and pampered me so that I could "work"; she read and questioned every draft. She organized the procedure for typing and correcting on the Mag Card and did much of the correcting and "playing out." She gave up her evenings, weekends, and more, in a way that made this project take on an importance far above what it deserves. It was very flattering, particularly from the person whose opinion I value most.

None of the people who have helped, by discussing or challenging my ideas, by attempting to improve the presentation of these ideas, or in any other way, should be considered identified with or endorsing anything in these pages. I am solely responsible for any errors, which, if the public and the distribution system are kinder to this book than they are to most, will be addressed in a revised edition.

Introduction

This book appears as the trade book industry in the United States is entering a profound crisis. Some of the effects — just the beginnings — are already being felt. Publishing houses are generally reducing staff and publication lists; author's agents are expressing frustration at the failure to get contracts for manuscripts that, perhaps a year ago, would have routinely been granted advances of $7500 or $10,000; publishers are expressing vexation with high returns of unsold books from retailers and the royalty rates demanded by authors. Some publishers, notably Rawson Wade, E. P. Dutton, and Dodd Mead, have been sold or "merged," and it is clear from the general nervousness that many more publishers, including some old and prestigious houses, are sliding toward the edge.

The surest evidence for this sad prediction is the almost total absence in book publishing — industry seminars, press releases from leading houses, the pages of *Publishers Weekly* or the *American Bookseller* — of the inclination to probe the situation to find causes or look for anything more innovative than budget-cutting to deal with the crisis.

The immediate cause of the economic pressures within trade publishing is the drying up of royalty income from mass market publishers. In recent times this income, amounting to more than the total final profit from original trade publication, has enabled the entire industry to survive even though it operated at a net loss. Purchases of reprint rights by mass market paperback houses are now approaching zero, and the industry is being weaned without warning.

To make matters worse, the paperback publishers are, in response to their own difficulties, compounding the damage by entering the trade book field in direct and rather powerful competition with the very houses suffering this loss of income.

It is the kind of one-two punch that only the very healthy can survive.

Any misfortune for book publishing is a misfortune for all Americans. Books are too important to our lives; we cannot be indifferent, or even casual, about what happens to the industry that produces them. This, then, is a report to those inside and outside book publishing on the nature of the industry's difficulties and, more particularly, on how these are exacerbating the problems with which the industry has lived in the past. Although the new developments create pressures of unusual severity, it has been true for a long time that books cost too much, they are sold in too few places, the title one wants is too hard to find, the sales life of a book is distressingly short, and that authors earn a pittance for their creativity and, even so, find it tremendously difficult to get their early work published.

Fortunately, the problems in publishing are not only important, they are fascinating. People in publishing may not like what they read here, but they will know it is true. I expect that outsiders will be skeptical and will look to their friends with some connection to publishing for confirmation. They will find it hard to believe that an industry manned and directed by our intellectual elite can function so poorly.

It is purely by chance that *In Cold Type* appears almost exactly fifty years after the *Cheney Report,* which, although it was commissioned and paid for by the book industry, soundly condemned publishers for a long laundry list of failures. Fully 75 percent of the practices criticized by Cheney remain in the industry, some (such as selling new titles in advance) even more destructive than when Cheney first identified them. Yet, although I believe this report is the first since Cheney's to range as broadly over the practices and problems of the industry, it is by no means a repetition of his criticisms, nor of his remedies.

One of the weaknesses in Cheney's prescriptions (aside from his failure to diagnose the illnesses correctly) was his demand that the publishing *industry* act in some concerted fashion. Fortunately for all of us, publishers are much too individualistic to act like a cartel, even if they did not fear (as they do) the antitrust arm of the Department of Justice.

Concerted action by publishers as an industry is virtually impossible. Happily, it is completely unnecessary. As, I think, the reader will agree, corrective action may be taken by any publisher (though the larger publisher has marked advantages) if he is prepared to question the axioms that are endlessly repeated to justify the present state of affairs.

My own thirty-five years in publishing have been much more fun and, I hope, more productive because I did question the axioms. I have been more fortunate than most because I have been involved in a great variety of activities — book production, editorial procurement, sales and sales management, warehousing and shipping, order processing and customer service, computerization, book retailing — and in large organizations. I have also had the good fortune to help design advanced printing and binding machines and to be issued patents on new printing plates, stronger book bindings, and even on a new printing process used in the separation of uranium isotopes.

Book publishing has been a wonderful world for me in which every minute, it seems in retrospect, brought new pleasures and new excitement. It has been exciting for itself, for the wonderful things it does, and for the even more wonderful things it can do. I cannot imagine anyone being in publishing without striving constantly to find ways to improve it.

I hope this book will contribute toward that end.

1

Book Publishing

Its Present Condition

BOOK PUBLISHING is a small industry that comprises many even smaller industries. Despite their physical resemblance, books differ widely in function and potential market. The publisher of medical texts is in a completely different business from the publisher of hardcover fiction. Each broad field of publishing is an industry unto itself, distinctly different in the way the product—the editorial content of the books—is contracted for, produced, priced, and marketed. Because of the differences in markets and marketing methods, the economic rules are different in each publishing field. Some, like encyclopedia publishing, can tolerate only large organizations with strong financing. Popular fiction and nonfiction can support minuscule companies competing with the larger ones.

Industry statistics are not very precise. A reasonable estimate of the total sales of the entire book publishing industry for the year 1980 would be a mere $6 billion, less than the sales of the Philip Morris Company alone (about $6.2 billion)—and there are some forty to fifty American companies bigger than Philip Morris. Interestingly, Philip Morris has approximately the same number of employees (65,000) as the entire book publishing industry.

Of the book industry total of $6 billion, reference books, encyclopedias, and professional books aimed at the technical, scientific, business, legal, and medical fields accounted for about $1.2 billion; elementary, secondary, and college textbooks, $1.5 billion; book clubs and direct mail sales, almost $1 billion; and mass market paperback sales, approximately $660 million.

Books intended for the general public, the category on which we will concentrate, reached a sales level of only a little more than

$1 billion. The titles produced in such great variety for this broadest of all book markets are called "trade" books because they are distributed to the public through the "book trade," the network, such as it is, of retail booksellers.

Although probably more international than most of the other publishing "industries," trade book publishing is still, considering world commerce in ideas and in the *rights* to publish, remarkably provincial. In the English-language world, American publishers publish for American readers, British for British. They may buy rights from each other, but rarely do they invade each other's markets with actual books.

The basis for a profound change in this situation was laid a few years ago, when the U.S. Department of Justice forced British publishers to release their hold on the British Empire market. The result was to create one competitive arena for English-language publishing encompassing the world. How quickly this change will be translated into truly international English-language publishing is hard to say. Such changes tend to occur slowly, though the current serious economic crisis among publishers in England is undoubtedly, in part, the first manifestation of such a development.

While this trend may cause trade book publishing to grow, for the present the industry remains tiny (to the extent that sales are a valid measure).

Blue Bell, an American clothing manufacturer, reached a sales level approximately equal to the total reached by the hundreds of U.S. companies actively publishing trade books, and there are about 275 other companies in the country larger than Blue Bell. The trade book industry reaches that modest sales level by publishing approximately 20,000 new titles each year and continuing to sell about 200,000 old ones.

Some figures suggest that trade publishing sells each U.S. inhabitant one and a half books per year (made up of three quarters of a paperback and three quarters of a hardbound book), but that is surely an overstatement. The correct figure is probably closer to one copy per person, which suggests that each of the 220,000 titles available sells an average of about 1200 copies each year.

In addition to being small, book publishing is a very complicated industry, so it is difficult to discern patterns amid the confusion of seemingly chance events.

For example, in publishing there is a much larger number of producing units (publishers) in relation to distribution units (bookstores) than is typical of other consumer products. In publishing, hundreds of publishers supply thousands of bookstores; in other industries, tens of producers supply tens of thousands of outlets. Publishers (except in mass market publishing) have very little direct influence over the distribution system. Sales vary erratically, seemingly at random, and it is extremely hard to forecast accurate market trends.

There is virtually no trademark identification in trade book publishing. A consumer who has enjoyed a Sara Lee cake or had a good experience with a GE washer is well disposed to try another Sara Lee product or GE appliance. The consumer who has been up all night reading an exciting novel will not look for "another Random House book" (if he is even aware of its publisher), though he may search out other books by the same author.

There is limited replenishment business in publishing. A reader, having just finished and thoroughly enjoyed *Gone With the Wind,* does not rush out to buy another copy so he can have more of the same pleasure.

No other consumer industry produces 20,000 different, relatively low-priced products each year, each with its own personality, requiring individual recognition in the market. In very few other consumer industries does the product have so short a life. The average book is dead in days or weeks; 90 percent are dead, in their original editions, within a year.

Because of the large numbers of new books poured out by the industry, and because of limited retail space (and even more limited patience among retailers), the battle to get his books into the distribution system consumes a great deal of the publisher's energy. This battle reaches a crescendo twice a year with the new lists, and in spite of a great effort, most titles never do get satisfactorily represented. The simple fact that most books are not available in most stores is merely another indication that the distribution system cannot cope with the burdens imposed on it.

Another condition that is peculiar to trade book publishing and that creates pervasive problems is the very nature of book wholesaling.

In other industries, the retailer typically buys directly from the manufacturer (automobiles, greeting cards) or through a wholesaler (ethical drugs). In the book industry, the retailer may buy some copies directly from the publisher and other copies of exactly the same title from a wholesaler. The publisher sells to the wholesaler and then competes with him (and, as we shall see, *must* compete with him), offering favorable discounts to entice the bookseller's business.

Paradoxically, the book wholesaling business, which is so precarious as a result, is kept financially secure by the large volume of business it does that is not truly wholesaling, such as supplying books to libraries. Since the books will not be sold again, this is really an entirely different business from wholesaling. (And, even more paradoxically, the financial security of wholesalers has been gained at the expense of that of the retailers, who used to supply libraries until publishers increased wholesalers' discounts to the point that wholesalers were able to take the business away from the retailers.)

The peculiarities of book publishing make it extremely doubtful that wholesaling (despite the outstanding performance of one company, Ingram) can achieve stability and decent financial returns.

Book publishing also differs from other consumer industries in having what appears to be methodically created confusion in its distribution network. Publishers are so sensitive to the possibility of federal antitrust suits that they go to exaggerated lengths to avoid any possible accusation of collusion in setting retail prices or establishing discount schedules or conditions of sale. Each one seems to try to make his business practices sufficiently different from any other publisher's that no one will suspect that they even know each other. The result is a nightmarish obstacle course for the retailer. A reasonably conscientious small bookshop may be doing business with several hundred different publishers; it must remember how different quantities of books qualify for different discounts, how soon books lose their eligibility for return, what percentage of the original purchase price will be refunded, and on and on.

Each book needs to be called to the attention of the reading public, but it is precisely the plethora of titles, and their short life, that makes advertising and publicizing them more difficult and more expensive.

All this frequently leads to overstocks of dead or moribund titles, each approximately a year old, in which the publisher has invested money that could be put to better use. He sees no alternative to selling excess book stock as "remainders," at a fraction of their original prices, which tends to steal sales from new titles and to undermine the verisimilitude of the original pricing.

Books are, of course, more than a medium of communication. As a boy I was taught that "printing is the art preservative of all arts," and it is in the form of books that printing performs this role most effectively. Whether for information, argument, or entertainment, the book is considered a repository. One expects that the contents of a book will be available beyond the immediate moment—for days or years or generations into the future. Not all that goes into books should be preserved—much between the covers, hard or soft, deserves no more than passing attention, some not even that—but if it *is* to be preserved, a book is where to put it.

Because books in general reach a special kind of audience—more accurately, many audiences—they have a special role to play. People who read books, even trivial books, are, on the average, more educated, more sophisticated, more affluent, more influential, and more concerned than those who do not. This attracts to books the writer who feels he has something to say to such people.

People who buy and read books are as varied as the population of the country. There is no "broad, general market" just as there is no "hard-core book buyer." There are numberless large, small, and medium-sized constantly changing and shifting submarkets. There are people who are frequently in bookstores and those seldom there; people interested in numerology and haute cuisine, those interested in numerology and gardening, and those interested in gardening only— and so on through all the permutations and combinations of all the subjects imaginable. There are people with plenty of money, for whom the price of a book is no obstacle; for others, that very same book is a major purchase. There are people with much leisure and those with almost none at all. Some of these markets are sharply defined— apprentice electrical engineers, for instance; others—people unhappy with their appearance or looking for a gift for a sick aunt—are vague and constantly shifting. The same title may be bought by thousands of people for hundreds of different reasons.

Books are a fantastically convenient way to package information or entertainment. They are portable, easy to store, inviting to pick up for a moment or for hours, and much of the time absorbing when in use.

Aside from conversation itself, books are the most practical way for anyone to communicate with a small group. An edition of 5000 is perfectly practical for a trade book, and in professional or university press publishing, even smaller editions can be economically supported, thus making possible the tremendous diversity of book publishing. It means that virtually anyone with something significant to say can (or should be able to) say it in a book, and anyone looking for information on any significant subject should be able to find it in a book.

Books are made by human beings, so they are not always a force for good. One need only mention *Mein Kampf.* Other examples have not been so outstanding. But there is no doubt, probably because the writers and the readers of books tend to be somewhat special, that the contribution of books throughout history has been profoundly influential and beneficial. Books have so many different qualities, so many of them wonderful, that we do not consider it the least bit peculiar to hear someone say, "I love books." There is a great deal to love.

The tiny book publishing industry is like a trust held by those who print and publish and sell books for those who love books. They are the custodians of an instrument that makes itself felt far beyond the narrow circles of publishers. They have an obligation to the writer, who has an audience somewhere out there he can reach only through a publisher, and an equivalent obligation to the reader, who looks to books for information, guidance, amusement, and escape.

So book publishing is more than a matter of making money. It has a very strong element of service, and a few minutes spent among publishers will reveal to anyone how clearly that responsibility is recognized.

Robert S. Lynd, reviewing the *Cheney Report* on book publishing in 1932, said, "The book industry is not the private concern of the little group of business men engaged in it, but a public utility." Although publishers may echo that sentiment from a somewhat different viewpoint when they appeal for special postal rates or tax privileges they do recognize their obligation to society suggested by Lynd's phrase "public utility," and their devotion to freedom from censorship, to opening their lists to unpopular ideas (with which they themselves may disagree), and to publishing new and untried writing talent is in fulfillment of that obligation.

This sense of service to both readers and writers cannot be measured in dollars. Indeed, one could argue (and we shall) that the reader is charged more than he should be for what he gets, the writer rewarded less than he should be for what he gives. Even if that is all true, the publisher gives the writer the priceless gift of an audience and the reader the satisfaction—spiritual, emotional, and intellectual— that is unique to books.

But this role, which gives publishing a position of honor among the varieties of private enterprise in our society, implies some responsibilities that are equally special.

In a sense, all of us have a stake in how well the managers of this public utility, the publishers, are exercising the informal trust that society has placed upon them. How well are publishers supplying the author with a chance to reach an audience; how well are they supplying the public with a wide range of books?

It is not sufficient to know that publishers themselves may be well satisfied with the results or may feel that any shortcomings are due to circumstances beyond their control. We want to know in detail what is being done, how well it is being done, and how it might be done better. No one would suggest the kind of interference with publishing that one might advocate with the steel industry if it were unnecessarily polluting the atmosphere or with automobiles if they were unnecessarily hazardous. The greatest contribution of book publishing is in promoting freedom of expression, which is possible only if publishers are allowed to publish whatever they choose, whenever they choose, and however they choose. However, advocating noninterference is not advocating indifference.

Some of us have felt for a long time that trade book publishers have fallen far short of their potential, that they have failed themselves, their authors, the network of booksellers, and the American public. The most important failing has been in the costly and haphazard method by which books move from publisher to consumer. That failure has by no means been willful. Publishers, writers, booksellers, and readers are all the victims of a kind of cultural lag, the persistence of a method of distribution that was once the only method available for all consumer products. Even in the good old days, it was a method much better suited to pots and pans, soda crackers, furniture, and ladies' underwear than to books. Yet, whereas many commodities have changed to more sophisticated, less expensive, and more effective methods, books still struggle under the burden of a costly and wasteful distribution system made even more costly and more wasteful by the heightened demands made on it by the growth of publishing, the greater discrimination of a more affluent and better educated public, and by the growth in the number of eager and talented writers pleading to be published. Even more unfortunate is the threat of new difficulties over the next several years, which are likely to exacerbate further the existing problems.

Survey after survey confirms that half the people going into bookstores walk out disappointed. These surveys are almost invariably conducted along the stretch of Fifth Avenue in New York that houses the greatest concentration of titles available for sale in the English-speaking world. The ratio of disappointment is higher almost everywhere else, because there are even fewer books available. In the skimpily stocked stores that make up the majority of retail shops, the selection may be so limited that at least part of the potential clientele has learned not to bother coming in at all.

□ *I do not know, of course, how this book got into your hands.*
But if you think I exaggerate the narrowness of the choice in

bookstores, try this experiment. Look for this title in three retail stores, preferably of "average" size. The chances are very good it will not be in two of them, moderately good that it will not be in any of the three. Try the same experiment with last year's best-seller list.

Another symptom is the general lack of bookstores themselves. Except in a few favored locations, a full-range bookstore is hard to find. According to the U.S. Department of Commerce, there is (or was in 1972) approximately one bookstore per 27,000 people; this figure included religious stores and college stores selling only textbooks and school supplies. Considering only general bookstores and book sections of department stores, no matter how small or sparse, we had one bookstore for each 50,000 people—and one drugstore for each 4000 and one auto supply store for each 10,000.

Books are much too expensive.

Publishers like to tell each other that book prices are not high; quite the contrary, they say, comparing book prices with the overall rate of inflation or with the price of theater tickets or with some other comforting index that suggests that the public is benefiting from the publishers' forbearance. The opinion is often expressed in publishing circles that all the industry's problems would disappear if publishers had the courage to increase prices still further. I think neither the consumer nor the author would agree.

Book prices increased faster than the Consumer Price Index between 1967 and 1979. That does not necessarily indicate that books are too expensive. A much more convincing indication is in a study conducted for the Book Industry Study Group by Yankelovich, Skelly and White, Inc., which found that prospective book purchasers were more and more deferring the purchase of the hardbound book on the assumption that it would soon be out in paper.

The high retail prices are only partly due to the high costs of distribution. They also result from antiquated book production methods. The combination of poor distribution and poor production makes high retail prices unavoidable. I believe very strongly that in a more rational distribution system, with better use of available production technology, retail prices could be, on the average, half their present level.

Alongside the high-priced book, the canny shopper will find the remainder, labeled "publishers' overstock," selling at one fifth or one tenth of the list price that was demanded last week—or even yesterday. For every copy of a hardcover book sold at its retail price, one book is sold as a remainder—a book that goes from the publisher

to a remainder dealer for less than the cost of producing it and with
no income to the author. No other industry can make this claim.

The stores specializing in remainders and their imitations, carrying
only a sprinkling of legitimate titles (and those usually at discounts),
are tough and frequently fatal competition for the independent
booksellers trying to carry a broad assortment of titles at list prices.
But the independent booksellers and the full-service book sections of
department stores have even more formidable competition from the
bookstore chains, two of which, B. Dalton and Walden, have exploded
in size over the last twenty years and now represent about one out of
three general bookselling locations.

The growth of the chains, in contrast to the general stagnation
among independent booksellers, has been fueled largely by the higher
discounts allowed the chains by publishers. Publishers give the higher
discounts, even though these cut their margins severely, because the
chains seem to provide relief from the frustration of dealing with the
inefficient, recalcitrant, incomprehensible distribution network of
independent stores. And dealing with the chains seems so much
simpler and less expensive.

Those are all symptoms that everyone can see. There are others
that are less obvious, but certainly not the least bit hidden from those
in and around the publishing industry.

The most glaring symptom is the simple lack of profitability in trade
book publishing and retailing. Publishers have become accustomed to
the idea that publishing itself, on the average, is *un*profitable.
Publishers generally lose money on the original editions of their books.
The deficit is made up, with a little profit added on, by the sale of
subsidiary rights, principally the right to a mass paperback edition.
What is most disturbing is that this precarious profit margin is, as we
shall see, in very serious danger.

The bookseller's profitability is no more attractive. Most bookstores
operate close to the break-even point, and many are below it. The
most recent reliable survey by Booz, Allen & Hamilton, in 1977, puts
the average profit at 2.5 percent of sales and concludes that half the
bookstores are actually unprofitable "when measured by a reasonable
standard of financial performance."

Their frustration with distribution problems has inclined publishers
to put more and more emphasis on the "blockbuster," the book that is
more likely to be a best-seller, the one for which heavy advertising
and promotion expenses are more likely to be justified. Such titles
suffer much less from the deficiencies of the distribution system—in a

sense, they rise above it—so they can actually be put within reasonable reach of the public, and they still have the additional attraction of the promise of spectacular rights income from the mass paperback edition.

Although exasperation with the distribution system supports the widespread notion that "we publish too many books," authors know better. There is hardly a published author who has not suffered rejection after discouraging rejection before finding a publisher willing to take the relatively minor risk of publishing his work. Many writers, of course, give up before they achieve the happy ending.

The rebuttal to "we publish too many books" was dramatized, if somewhat overstated, by a story on the front page of the *New York Times* on April 14, 1981, which carried a two-column headline:

POSTHUMOUS PULITZER GIVEN WRITER
WHO COULDN'T GET NOVEL PUBLISHED

The first sentence reads: "The comic novel, *A Confederacy of Dunces,* whose author, John Kennedy Toole, committed suicide 12 years ago after failing to find a publisher, won the 1981 Pulitzer Prize for fiction yesterday."

Extreme? Yes. It would be foolish to suggest that publishers selectively decline books of great merit or that all disappointed authors end so tragically. But it is true that there is a widespread reluctance among publishers to publish, which is largely the disappointed publishers' reaction to poor book distribution.

Allowing that Toole's experience is exceptional, it is nevertheless true that publishing falls far short of giving writers the opportunities for publication one would expect based on the size, level of education, and affluence of the population, the available leisure time, and on the need for such a wide range of information.

And, as those who finally achieve publication know very well, the average *published* author realizes a pitifully small income from his work. Statistics to buttress this sad truth were recently provided by a survey of published authors conducted for the Authors Guild. Despite the high income of a few prominent writers continually in the public eye, the survey concluded that "writing income places most authors below the poverty line." The reason is embarrassingly simple: Publishers do not distribute and sell enough copies of their books.

One factor contributing to the poor sales record of many titles, which encourages the publisher to send his excess stock to the remainder dealer, is the short life of the trade book. Contrary to the idea that "books are forever," the distribution system assures that 90 percent—perhaps as many as 95 percent—of the books published are stone cold dead by the end of their first year of life. Most books die quietly, without a struggle. The death of that small number of titles that actually manage to get a fair representation in bookstores is usually underscored by the bookseller's return of unsold copies. One out of every three new books is returned to the publisher unsold, a heavy cost imposed on both by the antiquated distribution system.

Yet another sign that trade book publishing may be more rusty than seaworthy is the eagerness with which some of the conglomerates are trying to unload the publishing houses they acquired at great cost only a few years ago. When they were competing to buy the publishers, the conglomerates let it be known that they were going to revolutionize this backward industry by introducing methods right out of Harvard Business School. None of the takeovers resulted in any notable improvement, some managed to do no particular damage, and most resulted in deterioration, sometimes outright disaster.

One symptom that seems to me a failure of book distribution to reach the general public is the disturbing fact that approximately one out of every three trade books sold goes to a library. If one of every three cars sold in America went to Hertz or Avis, the sales managers of Datsun and General Motors would be called upon to explain their failure.

Sales to libraries are largely independent of the distribution system. Libraries depend very little on publishers' sales organizations or on the general availability of books. Library sales are, in a sense, sales made in spite of the inadequacy of the publishers' own efforts and of the distribution system itself.

These are some of the symptoms of deep-seated difficulties in trade book publishing. Most of these symptoms have existed for a long time, suggesting that publishing has accepted its difficulties for all these years.

But trade publishing is rapidly moving toward a crisis. The strains under which the industry functions are about to be multiplied. What changes will be made to accommodate the developing difficulties are hard to predict. One should expect to see a number of respected publishing houses quietly expire. There has already been some preliminary movement in this direction: T. Y. Crowell, Hawthorne, and Lippincott have left only their names for use by others. A number of others are on shaky ground. Many are apprehensive.

Trade publishing has grown significantly in the years since World War II thanks to the parallel growth of mass market paperback reprint publishing. It has now reached the point that each year, the mass market publishers pump royalty income into original hardcover publishing greater than the *entire profit* otherwise realized by the publishers. This seemingly unending flow of easy money has enabled publishers to be casual about the fact that, on the whole, they were making no profit from their own publishing.

That happy era is clearly drawing to a close. Paperback publishing is going through its own crisis, and its own future is somewhat murky. In response to their own new problems, paperback publishers are contracting directly with authors for an increasing percentage of their titles. They are increasingly less interested in buying reprint rights from the trade publisher. If the trade publisher does not learn soon to make a profit from his product, he will have no profit at all.

Ominously, paperback publishers, for many reasons, are invading the trade field, competing for authors, for bookstore space, and for budgets, compounding the traditional publishers' problems still further. The mass market publishers have so far demonstrated no superiority over the existing practitioners in judgment or methods of trade publishing. Simply their entry into the field is sufficiently damaging.

These changes may encourage a more careful and critical look at the problems of trade publishing, which have been accepted as inevitable.

Predominant among the causes of the malaise in publishing is the distribution system itself.

Books get from the publisher to the retail bookseller through a process of negotiation, usually between the publisher's sales representative and the bookseller, in which each title is "presented" by the sales rep and the bookseller makes his decision, title by title. This negotiation always takes place before the book is published (so there is not yet any critical or popular opinion to serve as a guide), usually before it is printed (so neither sales rep nor bookseller can read it), frequently before it is set in type, and sometimes before the manuscript has been completed. In this negotiation, the bookseller knows nothing (except in rare cases) and the sales rep knows what he can remember of the one or two minutes given each title in a presentation of hundreds of titles some months earlier. Since this is the rep's one chance to get his important titles into the store, and since the bookseller has neither the time nor patience to hear about every title nor the budget to buy every one, the rep is happy to take orders for fewer copies than the bookseller needs (usually zero) on many titles in order to get orders for more copies than he needs on a few of them.

These negotiations occur twice a year, in the spring and fall, corresponding to each publisher's two lists. Even though we suffer from too few bookstores, and all the stores in any chain are covered in a single session, it takes four to five months for each season's hundreds of thousands of individual negotiations to be completed as the reps make the rounds of the country's booksellers, frequently waiting in line to be seen.

This "distribution-by-negotiation" has unfortunate results far beyond the very obvious one that decisions made under pressure, with little objective information, and strongly influenced by fleeting subjective factors, are not likely to be very good decisions. To encourage a favorable decision, the publisher agrees to accept the return of any unsold copies.

The drive to get large advance orders on the important books leads, where it is successful, to heavy and extremely costly returns of unsold stock. Since publishers typically refuse returns after one year from publication, booksellers must pack up their unsold books when the calendar registers eleven months.

Because it takes so long for the sales reps to make the circuit of booksellers, the publisher cannot wait until he has all the orders in hand before printing the book. So he has to guess how many to print, usually on the skimpiest of evidence. As a result, approximately one out of every four new books manufactured never gets to the bookstore, but goes directly from the publisher's warehouse (together with the returned copies from bookstores) to the remainder dealer.

Though weakness in distribution is the principal cause, it is not the only cause of problems in publishing.

The folklore of publishing, which exaggerates beyond all possible value the very obvious fact that every book is different, argues against an overall editorial plan. As a result, most publishers have no particular program to guide them in the search for new manuscripts. The decision to publish or not is made book by book, each decision largely unrelated to any other. This disposition to consider each book in isolation is reinforced by how the editorial department usually meets publishing possibilities—one at a time. The proposed manuscript may come directly from the author or through an agent, but it comes by itself, almost never as a part of a broad publishing plan.

Such editorial decision-making not only discourages the development of an editorial plan or publishing strategy, but also tends to make the publisher's editorial (or product development) role more passive than it should be. Publishers do much less than they should to stimulate writers and very little to stimulate work that fits a coherent editorial program.

This lack of coherence or overall purpose in most editorial departments, though it may seem to encourage diversity, does not help sort out the better manuscripts. Except for the obviously publishable project, the fate of the author's submission is decided much too often by luck rather than merit.

The difficulties of editorial selection are compounded by the obstacles that publishing management frequently puts in the way of editorial freedom. The experience of every publisher convinces him that this is a "gambling" business. Tens of thousands of titles published into an unstructured distribution system, millions of unpredictable negotiations between sales reps and booksellers, the happenstance of a book getting into a particular store, together with unforeseeable outside influences—reviews, attention by celebrities, quirks of public taste—lead to results in which chance is the dominant factor. The publisher's reaction to the pervasive influence of chance is frequently to place all sorts of hurdles in the way of each editorial project to try to accept only those that seem to have exaggerated odds in their favor. It doesn't work, but it does set up a conflict between the business side of the publishing house and its editorial side, which does no one any good.

Because an editorial plan is usually lacking and because the defenses many publishers have erected against bad book selection work so poorly, most publishers show a mediocre "batting average" in choosing profitable titles. This limited and uncertain success contributes to instability, inhibits growth, and frustrates authors of perfectly publishable manuscripts.

With very few exceptions, the production of books is extremely wasteful both in time and money. The production cost of books can be reduced (except for a handful of well-organized publishers) by something like 25 percent without any reduction in physical quality. In the process, the time required to put out the typical book can be reduced from months to weeks, making possible further economies and reductions in staff.

A publisher's inventory of finished books is ridiculously high by the standards of most other industries. The figures of the Association of American Publishers suggest that, on the average, each publisher's warehouse holds at all times as many books as the firm will sell in one year. That would be the equivalent of Kellogg keeping as many boxes of corn flakes as will be sold in one year or Arrow's warehouse having a year's supply of shirts at all times. The cost of money (and space) being what it is, such inventory management would drive Kellogg and Arrow out of business pronto.

The recent cries of anguish from publishers when the Internal Revenue Service ruled that the inventory value of books could not arbitrarily be marked down (the so-called Thor Decision) indicate how serious this inventory problem really is. Senator Daniel Patrick Moynihan of New York introduced a bill to permit publishers to continue to take inventory markdowns on the theory, one must suppose, that publishers need this relief because the nature of publishing makes sensible control of inventory impossible. Not so, of course.

One could argue that Senator Moynihan would be doing the publishers a favor by letting the IRS ruling stand, forcing publishers to look at how they put (and keep) themselves in this fix. The right to take the markdowns, while it results in some tax relief, does not correct the mistake (or the cost) of printing huge numbers of books that are not immediately (or ever) needed.

Bad inventory practices are related to and partly the result of bad accounting practices. The accounting system, which should supply the company's captain with the map and nautical chart by which he plots a course, is, in publishing, generally not very helpful. By obscuring the real situation, by offering little guidance and sometimes being downright misleading, accounting practices contribute to the present situation in which publishing executives, as bright and devoted as their peers in other industries, can, year after year, show results hovering at the zero profit level, being rescued continually by the subsidy from paperback publishing.

I have suggested some of the symptoms of malfunctioning in trade book publishing and some of their possible causes. I would like to examine these and other aspects of publishing in more detail. Out of this will come suggestions for improving the publishing of books and for responding to the sharpening of publishers' difficulties due to the changes in mass market paperback houses.

The publishing of books is perhaps more complicated than the production and distribution of any other consumer product, but it is not mysterious. Its complications may require more sophisticated solutions than have been effective in simpler industries, but we have the benefit of seeing how those solutions work in simpler situations.

The success of publishing is of interest not only to publishers. Society needs a healthy book publishing industry. Those who read and write books want to know more about the industry that serves them.

This report, to those inside as well as outside publishing, will be successful if it stimulates the search for better methods.

2

The Role of the
Trade Book Publisher

IN A BROAD SENSE, publishing is the variety of activities that take
place between the author with a manuscript and the reader of a book.
Once the publisher himself performed all these activities: copyediting,
typesetting, printing, binding, and bookselling—even, long ago,
papermaking.

Bookselling separated from publishing as the world of readers
expanded in number and geography and it became clear that they
could not be supplied from one central point efficiently. Besides, as
booksellers know well, offering customers the greatest possible variety
is essential to retailing success, and that is best achieved by freely
combining the wares of many publishers.

Printing and publishing separated somewhat later. Advances in
printing techniques sharply increased the capital investment required.
Higher labor costs and labor's demand for steady, year-round
employment placed additional financial demands on the printing
function. The erratic production needs of each publisher, varying by
season as well as by the luck of finding oneself with a best-seller, made
it difficult to justify such high costs. With rare exceptions (Doubleday
being the outstanding example), publishers contract their books to
commercial printing and binding establishments, which can amortize
equipment costs over a much larger volume of business and match
some publishers' peak demands to other publishers' troughs. For
similar reasons, the publisher no longer sets the type, though changes
in that technology may bring larger publishers back into typesetting.

Today, the publisher functions as the *organizer*, making sure that
the independent activities are performed well and are coordinated
with those that still remain his direct responsibility. Publishing is

variously looked upon as an industry, a business, or, by many publishers, as a profession. It is probably all of these, and more, because the word describes a great many combinations of activities, combinations frequently different from each other in different companies and usually reflecting the personality, as few other businesses do, of the owner or the head of the house.

No two publishers are truly alike. Each publishing house—and within the larger houses, each trade division—tends to have its own personality and its own notion of the role it wants to play. The types of publishing within each house also frequently differ, perhaps including trade, mail order, book clubs, textbooks, reference, and so on, to provide additional income and stability, and the mixture is usually unique.

In view of the publisher's importance in the literary process, it is curious how anonymous he is. If I were to ask the readers of this book who published it, probably four out of five would have to turn to the title page or jacket to see. Yet the publisher's role is vital. In spite of the occasional success of someone who has published his own manuscript, the chance of reaching any significant part of the potential market (except for titles particularly well suited to selling by direct mail) without the help of a publisher is very close to zero. And, of course, the publisher does much more than offer the book for sale.

The publisher must identify the authors and the themes to which a large enough section of the public will respond. The publisher may have to develop the original, perhaps tentative, manuscript into the form that is—editorially and physically—most suitable to the market. Since we live in an era of multimedia and subsidiary rights, the publisher must actively explore, from the very start of the project, possible auxiliary uses and sources of income. The possible sale of rights to a book club or paperback reprint house is not likely to be overlooked, but additional income may be sought in special sales of books to unusual customers—tie-in arrangements with manufacturers of toys, or hair sprays, or whatever the content of the book suggests, or in outright subsidy, for that matter, if that is indicated.

The book must be physically produced by suppliers engaged and supervised by the publisher and in a quantity related to the publisher's estimate of demand. The publisher must establish a retail price that somehow balances the projected income against the costs, with a satisfactory margin in addition. And the book must be promoted and distributed so that it will be available to the market the publisher has identified. All of this activity is, of course, financed by the publisher until the selling activity creates actual cash flow. If he performs well in all these areas, the effort will return a profit to him as well as income to the author, the agent, the booksellers, and the wholesalers, each of whom is essential to the publishing process.

The publisher is concerned not only with this crucial early period in the life of the book but also, for those books that should have a long sales life, with keeping the public aware of its existence and persuading booksellers to keep it in stock and on display long after the more intense early interest has waned. That is by no means easy and requires continuous reinvestment of time, money, and, above all, persistence.

Although one must never discount the contribution of the author to the success of his own work (and a diplomatic publisher will take great pains to exaggerate it), it should be clear that the publishing activities play their role. Whether it is something the publisher actually does or organizes or orchestrates, his influence on the fate of the book can be critical. I do not suggest that the publisher is the complete master of the situation. Actually, I feel he is much less a master than he should be. Chance is, unfortunately, a very large ingredient in publishing as it is now constituted. But some of the elements we sometimes mistake for chance are amenable to a little encouragement, expertly applied.

Going from the manuscript in the hands of the author to the book in the hands of the reader may seem a sufficiently broad span of responsibility, but the publisher may actively search for suitable material and initiate or encourage the process that brings it into existence. This may mean identifying the ideas that find a welcome readership, the points of view that will sell or that should be aired, new developments in any field that could become a focus of public interest, and finding the writers who can best translate those suggestions into manuscripts worthy of publication. Along the way, it means working with each writer to give him the benefit of experience, an understanding of popular taste, or the editorial skill to help improve the final product. He also maintains close contact with authors he has already published to encourage them to continue their work, to suggest appropriate subjects or themes, and to help develop projects in process.

From whatever inspirational source the manuscript originates, with whatever broad guidance it may receive along the way, there will take place, in the publisher's office, that final editorial polishing and finishing—checking facts and dates, searching for anomalies or inconsistencies—that will make the book just a little bit better than it might have been.

The publisher should stimulate the creation of publishable material, and many do. He cannot assume that without his intervention and encouragement a sufficient number of acceptable manuscripts will arrive on his desk at regular intervals. As in any business, the publisher must maintain a flow of production sufficient to assure the health of the company.

The shape of the publisher's "list"—the books he offers for sale— may be determined by the personal interests and expertise of the management, by the determination that certain subjects or certain types of books will find a ready market, by the record of the publisher's own sales organization, or, as it very frequently is, by happenstance. The wise publisher searches for his books according to some sort of plan, flexible out of necessity, but reflecting his judgment of what the overall list should be like.

The publisher may search for and find authors in a variety of ways. He may employ scouts, with contacts among established and budding writers, to find likely candidates. His editors watch newspapers and periodicals for a hint of a possible book or writer. College campuses are a fruitful source. Rarely, very rarely, does he find anything useful in the steady flow of "unsolicited" manuscripts in each day's mail. Some publishers have decided that the cost of reading and evaluating these voluntary submissions is not worth the off chance of finding a gem, and they routinely return such manuscripts unopened.

The most productive source for trade book publishers is the author's agent. The agent is, after all, paid by the author (usually 10 percent of the author's income) partly according to his success in finding a publisher. Although his primary loyalty is to the author, the agent acts in many respects as an extension of a publisher's editorial department. He not only directs the projects of his authors to the publisher he feels is appropriate, but also scouts for the kind of manuscript he knows a particular publisher is seeking.

When I came into publishing after World War II, it was the exceptional author who was represented by an agent, and an agent's "intervention" was usually resented by the publisher. Today, perhaps 75 or 80 percent of trade books are agented, and agents and publishers have learned to live and work together.

□ *It is my opinion, shared by some agents, that the growth of paperback reprint royalties during this period attracted authors' agents to trade publishing and provided the additional money to support them. If changes in mass market publishing cause these royalties to dry up and publishers do not find ways to make the original editions produce more income for authors, agents may find trade book authors to be much less attractive clients. The possible beginnings of this may already be seen in the increase of some agents' fees from 10 to 15 percent.*

Whether the project is initiated by the publisher, is brought in by a scout, or submitted by an agent or the author himself, at some point the publisher must decide whether he wishes to publish the book and under what conditions. A positive decision is predicated on the conviction that the manuscript as it exists is suitable—or that the idea or partial manuscript will be made suitable—and that a reachable market exists of sufficient size and with sufficient interest to buy enough copies at a reasonable retail price.

To make this decision, the publisher must know (at least with good approximation) how much it will cost to produce the bound book, how many copies he may expect to sell at what price, how much it will cost to promote the book, how much he will pay the author, the probable income from subsidiary rights, and anything else that will help him determine what it will cost to publish the book and what income is likely to result.

If it is expected that publication will result in a loss, the decision will be negative except in those extremely rare cases when some other powerful consideration exists: an important intangible benefit, perhaps, or an obligation to an important and profitable author.

If the figures suggest that publication will be profitable, the proposal is then measured against other criteria that differ with each publishing house. They may involve the nature of the book. A project that does not "fit" the list may be discarded if the anticipated profit is small, though it may be considered more favorably if it is large. The degree of risk in the financial forecast may be a factor. Available budgets may dictate selecting among projects even if all of them appear highly profitable.

Publishing houses differ also in how they make this decision. In a small publishing house, where the editor and the business manager (and perhaps even the sales manager) are the same person, the process is simple. As the size of the house increases, it tends to become more complicated and certainly more varied.

In a larger publishing house, the project is usually initiated by a single editor but may require the approval of the editor in chief or an editorial review committee. That approval may then be subject to review by a business manager or "publisher," who may seek the opinions of the sales manager and perhaps the subsidiary rights manager before deciding. In some houses, a series of preliminary recommendations are required before submission to an overall publication board for final approval.

Whatever the mechanism, the purpose is to have the best possible assurance that the published book will meet, not only the literary, intellectual, artistic, and social standards of the house, but its financial standards as well.

Among some people outside publishing, one may find the notion that profit is somehow secondary, or perhaps even completely foreign, to the world of books. This fallacy is reinforced, in part, by the statement frequently heard among publishing people themselves, that "the profitable books underwrite the publication of the unprofitable ones." Although that may explain the ultimate result, it suggests a completely misleading picture of the decision criteria. Unprofitable books happen; they are not planned. Not one book in a hundred is published in the expectation that it will actually be unprofitable. Only a subsidized publishing program, like a university press, can lose money deliberately.

It could not be otherwise. Our economic system has foolproof methods of eliminating enterprises that do not produce a profit with reasonable regularity. Where there is no profit, there is no publishing. The fact that publishing profits tend to be low is neither deliberate nor desirable.

The publisher's decision to publish is not, of course, unilateral. Essential to publication is a contract to which the author and the publisher must agree, specifying the terms under which the author gives the publisher the right to publish the book.

As I have said, most trade authors employ agents who negotiate with the publishers on their behalf. The agent's share of the author's income is usually 10 percent (rarely 15 percent) and payments by the publisher are usually made to the agent, who deducts his percentage before passing on the author's share. The agent's principal role (in addition to the critical one of getting the most desirable publisher to do the book) is to protect the author's interests in the contract negotiations with the publisher. Even as he does this, the agent, as a professional who understands what the publisher can concede, usually contributes to smoother and more expeditious negotiations.

Except in the case of an extremely successful author, very much in demand, the contract is usually the printed version, perhaps slightly amended, offered by that particular publisher. Although these "canned" contracts differ in detail—and sometimes very significant detail—from one publisher to another, the essential elements are similar.

Under the copyright laws of the world, all rights in the manuscript belong to the author. The publishing contract serves to convey some of those rights to the publisher in exchange for the publisher's services and a share of the income. The author agrees to deliver a satisfactory manuscript before a stated deadline. Generally, the author gives the publisher the exclusive right to publish the book in an original edition (which may be hardcover, paperback, or both) in the United States (and perhaps in Canada and other countries), which the publisher agrees to do within a specified time after receiving the manuscript. The contract spells out what the publisher will pay the author on each copy sold and how much will be paid as an "advance" in anticipation of royalty earnings. The contract also specifies whether the publisher or the agent will be responsible for selling other rights—such as book club editions, paperback reprints, movies or television, and translations —and how the income from each of these is to be divided.

The concession of rights by the author to the publisher is usually for the duration of the copyright unless the publisher fails to keep the book in print (available for sale), in which case the author can have the rights "revert" to him.

With a signed contract and the author's manuscript in hand, the publisher is in a position to get on with the business of publishing. Depending on the nature of the book—its possibilities for book clubs or magazine serialization, for instance, or the need for a long period of advance publicity—the publisher may put his subsidiary rights and promotion departments to work with photocopies of the manuscript before the editorial work is completed.

The preliminary consideration of the project in the publishing house normally requires estimates of how much it will cost to produce the book, so that when any project is approved, some of the design and manufacturing decisions have been made, at least tentatively. These may include the size, number of pages, the printing process, type of paper, style of binding, and so on, as well as the specific suppliers of these services, from whose cost schedules the estimates were created.

A tentative publication date may be selected on the basis of the production manager's estimate of how long it will take to manufacture the book from the time the manuscript is ready, or because the date (Mother's Day, the anniversary of the battle of Waterloo) has some newsworthy relation to the book, or for some arbitrary or whimsical reason. The target date for finished books is usually two months before the publication date. When the date the manuscript will be ready is known, the production manager can prepare a schedule that projects when each of the steps in the production process should take place to assure finished books on time.

Depending upon the policy of the publisher, the manuscript may spend some time in the editorial department or may shuttle to the author and back to settle any problems with style or content.

The first production stop is the copyeditor, who goes over the manuscript to correct errors (or at least query the author), assure conformity in style, identify possible legal problems for referral to counsel, label elements of the manuscript and particular passages that need special treatment from the designer, and do all the things that one last effort at improvement can accomplish. After copyediting, and perhaps a review by the book's editor or by the author himself, the manuscript goes to a designer, who decides how the book will look. The choice of type and the way it will be used for the text, headings, charts, footnotes, bibliographies, and the like may depend on the idiosyncrasies of the particular manuscript or may follow styles that are part of house policy. The method of type composition—hot metal, film, CRT—and the compositor must be chosen and a detailed schedule worked out, from the initial keyboarding of the manuscript through galley proof and page proof to the availability of film for platemaking and printing.

If the production manager can possibly do it, he will hide enough time in the schedule to protect himself from the unpredictable but inevitable delays that may be caused by the author, editor, or compositor, or, later, by the printer or binder—or by unforeseen factors. Even with a minimum of such allowance, the production schedule is likely to run five, six, or seven months from manuscript to finished book (except for a rare "rush" project), totaling as much as nine months to publication date.

A copy of the manuscript, or sections of it, may be simultaneously given to an artist to inspire a jacket design. This may be the production manager's responsibility or, in larger houses, there may be an art director to deal with all matters of design. The sketch submitted by the artist may then make the rounds of those responsible for approving it. They will vary with the house, but will almost always include the editor and sometimes the author, the sales manager, and others.

From the book designer, the manuscript then goes for text composition. Galley proofs (and sometimes page proofs) are usually supplied to the author to be proofread, but the publisher does not depend on the author to catch typographical errors. Proof is almost invariably also read by the compositor and by the publisher's own proofreader.

After the type has been set, the pages made up, and the index, front matter, and other auxiliary material completed, the book goes (usually) to another plant to be printed (normally, these days, by offset lithography) and bound, then delivered to the publisher's warehouse for dispatch to retailers and wholesalers.

These production processes, from copyediting to delivery to the warehouse, are scheduled carefully. If all goes well, the bound copies will arrive at the warehouse about five weeks before the announced publication date, to allow time for reviewers to receive, read, and review the book and for copies to reach the West Coast bookstores before reviews and public comment create demand.

But before the books can be shipped, to the West Coast or anywhere, the publisher must have orders. So the publisher has a sales force, or uses the services of independent sales representatives, to call on bookstores and book wholesalers to describe the forthcoming titles and to solicit advance orders. The sales reps usually have samples of the book jacket or cover, the publisher's seasonal catalogue with a description of the book, and details of the projected promotion campaign. If all goes as planned, the major portion of the orders are in hand from the sales force when the books arrive from the bindery.

Just as the publisher cannot passively count on the right manuscripts simply coming to him, he cannot count on the readers finding and buying his books simply because they are offered for sale or even because he has persuaded booksellers to stock them. Stimulation is required here too.

The publisher believes, when he decides to publish a book, that there is a sufficient market for it. But that is only the beginning of the marketing responsibility. The publisher uses his sales force to be sure the book is placed where potential buyers can get it, but he must also be sure that those potential buyers know about the book and are given some reasons to buy it.

Enter the twin activities of promotion and advertising. Advertising costs more and is probably less effective. The opportunities for promotion—free advertising—depend on the nature of the book as well as the ingenuity of the publisher. Free copies are sometimes liberally distributed—to booksellers, newspaper columnists, TV commentators, public personalities—in an attempt to encourage public comment that will stimulate a potential buyer's interest. Where the promotion budget does not permit such extravagance, press releases and descriptive literature may be used instead. The promotion campaign may, when appropriate, include public and TV appearances by the author to discuss the book.

If these marketing efforts are successful, the book will be available for sale in bookstores throughout the country on publication date, with additional stocks in reserve at wholesalers; reviews will appear as widely as the limited media facilities permit; commentators in newspapers, magazines, radio, and television will be discussing the book—and copies will begin to be bought by readers. Once this process starts, the publisher will be watching reader reaction to guide any subsequent activity. Advertising and extra promotion effort may be indicated for those parts of the country where interest seems to be building. Another printing may be needed to avoid going out of stock. It may be necessary to inform booksellers in areas where the book is moving slowly about its success elsewhere.

That, briefly, is the publishing process. Does this description seem a little too simple, too contrived, too free from worldly slings and arrows? It is, as we shall see when we examine each of these publishing activities in detail.

There are hundreds of publishing houses, at least scores of which have sufficient stature to be known to the general public. Though publishing is becoming steadily more "capital intensive," it continues to be very much less so than many other industries. Unlike steel, or even bread baking, publishing requires little financial investment. One can be a publisher with truly modest resources; there is no need to invest in machinery or warehouses or equipment of any kind. Growth tends to be slow, except if struck by the lightning of a best-seller, because, as the discussion of the economics of the business will show, the return on money invested in each book comes in slowly and profit margins are modest.

Because publishing is so easy to enter, because there is such a large number of small firms actively publishing, and because the typical author's personality is more comfortable in a person-to-person rather than a person-to-corporation relationship, there is a widespread notion, particularly among authors, that smallness in book publishing is an advantage. In fact, that is true only in the sense that size tends to dull the sharpness of management and its speed of response—in *all* kinds of business—and publishing is no exception. But smallness is far from being an advantage in itself.

Those who like smallness in publishing are undoubtedly thinking primarily of the editorial function. Size certainly adds nothing to judgment, and judgment is the heart of the editorial process. But that simply argues that as a publisher grows, he must find ways to preserve the freedom of each individual editor to make decisions independently, without the need for corporate review or approval. I don't know any large publisher who has done that, but it would be a simple and effective way to preserve smallness where it truly counts.

In virtually every other aspect of publishing, increased size can be a tremendous advantage. The publisher with a larger list, getting more dollars per sales call, can afford to have his sales force cover more remote bookstores as well as independent bookstores close to home, which are beyond the reach of the smaller house. Greater size provides the new titles and the backlist to enhance the importance of the publisher in the retailers' minds, and actually in their fortunes, so that his sales rep is a somewhat more welcome visitor. It can support larger, more versatile computer installations, which can process orders faster and provide management with more comprehensive analytical tools than anything that can be produced manually.

And because increased size provides the means (though not the assurance) for producing greater sales and visibility, title for title, it creates an appeal for authors (and the basis for offering larger royalty advances), which can make the editor's judgment more effective by giving him more to choose from.

If the publisher does not use his greater size to advantage—if he lets himself be tied in bureaucratic knots that seem only to cause slower shipping, create computer "black holes," stall editorial decisions, and sharply reduce their quality—it is not because his size is a disadvantage. If you grab the sword by the wrong end, what do you blame?

It is true, however, that the existence of a large number of independent publishing houses, and therefore many small ones, and the ease of entry for newcomers have a positive social value. Their existence contributes to maintaining the great diversity of ideas, of style, of personality, of political and social attitudes, that characterizes the world of books; this variety is very much narrower on the radio and in magazines and has largely disappeared in newspapers and on television.

We are lucky that books still jealously protect that opportunity for diversity, including the commitment of publishers to issue titles (witness this one) expressing views at variance with their own.

There has been a tendency in recent years toward mergers, which has left the impression that trade publishing is being concentrated in fewer hands. Where the publishers themselves have been left in control, there has not been any discernible, deliberate tendency toward greater uniformity, though the hamstringing effect of additional layers of management has sometimes created that feeling.

Nor do the occasional statistical analyses of the industry suggest that publishing is becoming more concentrated. The largest eight companies, for example, published 28 percent of the new titles in 1954, and 27 percent in 1972. Studies indicate that publishers just entering the field and small publishers growing in size tend to keep the overall industry profile steady as the number of publishers grows steadily. The danger of an increase in relative strength of the large publishers is, at the moment, more apparent than real.

There is also a growing concern, particularly among writers, that nonpublishing, "foreign" management, through the recent wave of giant conglomerates taking over publishing houses, may represent a more serious danger.

While I believe our concern for our democratic rights should keep us alert to the danger of concentration and particularly to the control of editorial content by management, I do not see this danger arising from the conglomerates, with their almost comic pratfalls of performance.

The most successful publishers operating under the aegis of conglomerates have been Random House and Simon & Schuster; these are clearly cases in which the "parents" have had the good sense to resist the temptation to "help" and have left their publishing subsidiaries very much alone.

Where the conglomerate has become "helpful," either because profit margins were not "satisfactory" by some arbitrary standard or because someone in authority thought it would be fun—or for some other reason—the "help" has usually consisted of an invasion by accounting types. Accountants' solutions almost always depend on cutting costs rather than on innovative improvements. Without real improvements, cost cutting leads only to more cost cutting and eventual disaster.

Though some conglomerates' accounting departments stumble over the publishing terminology, others are familiar with publishing, but that doesn't seem to help much. Bantam, for example, has been bought by the most successful book publisher in the world, Bertelsmann, who has been innovative in other publishing areas. It does not take much reading between the lines of the 1980 Bowker Memorial Lecture delivered by Oscar Dystel, who ran Bantam until it was bought out, to see that Bertelsmann is destroying Bantam faster than unhappy objective circumstances would do of themselves. Bertelsmann, too, seems to have made the mistake of sending in the accountants.

Elsevier, the Dutch publishing giant, bravely invaded the U.S. trade field when it acquired E. P. Dutton only a few years ago, and it has recently disposed of the wreckage it made of that proud imprint. What, then, can one expect of managements that have *no* pretense of knowing about publishing?

When the conglomerates began to move into publishing, buying up established independent houses, it was widely expected that the methods of "big business" would lead to explosive growth and would sweep the traditional publishers away like a whirlwind. The sophisticated types were going to show the ivory tower fuddy-duddies how it should be done. Nothing of the sort has happened. The conglomerates did bring money, which made some rather ridiculous advance payments to authors possible and which served to introduce a wilder competition from which some popular writers profited nicely. It also resulted in sharp increases in the salaries of publishing executives to make them more consistent with salaries throughout the conglomerate.

Now that some time has passed, it is generally accepted that the "know-how" the conglomerates brought to publishing has produced nothing very visible—except, possibly, a great deal of bureaucratic red tape. It is clear that many of the conglomerates wonder what they ever saw in publishing and would like to get out, as some have.

I do not claim that conglomerates, per se, cannot succeed in trade book publishing. It could be very different if Hallmark or National Biscuit Company, or any company with a cadre familiar with retail distribution, comes into the field. In that case, there would be a real danger of explosive growth and the elimination of competition. But the accountants—paper tigers!

However, the conglomerates have the resources to mount sustained, powerful, and effective competition, which can make things tough for independent publishers. Nor is their list-cutting very helpful to authors. Although a few authors may benefit from the intrusion of conglomerates because large sums are available to buy the "blockbusters," the reduction in publishers' lists, however temporary, cuts off opportunities for many, and the accountants' fishy-eyed view of literary endeavor cannot make the publisher's bosom a warm place for the few lucky authors.

But the danger that some authors and critics see in the degradation of the literary climate from the growth of conglomerates is another matter. Bernard Malamud, for example, feels that there can be little understanding between serious writers and the corporate managements that he and other authors see controlling increasing areas of publishing in America. To Malamud, writing is more than earning money: It is the essence of his life. He feels that it helps him— and his readers—find more meaning in life. He gets pleasure in seeing his work become a part of our contemporary culture, whereas corporate management seems interested only in dollars.

Malamud acknowledges that for many authors the dollar *is* important, and he respects their right to feel that way. For such writers, conglomeration and concentration may even be to their advantage, for they create publishing units large enough to supply big advances and big promotion campaigns, even though they cannot supply understanding.

The PEN American Center, of which Malamud was then president, recently lobbied successfully for a Senate hearing at which American writers expressed their concerns at the dangers they saw in this growing concentration of American publishing, which would lead to fewer authors being published and a homogenization of literary production.

That long-term threat from conglomerates may be real enough, and whether they become more powerful or not, they are certainly not a hospitable home for writers who feel as strongly about their life's work as Malamud does. But conglomerates do not immediately threaten to dominate trade publishing. It is not even a question of competence; not a single one shows the desire or ambition.

On the contrary, the corporate accountants seem all to arrive at the same recommendations for their publishing subsidiaries: "Cut back. Reduce costs." It is hard to find an exception to the general big-business doctrine that retreat and retrenchment are the best ways in which to respond to the mysteries of book publishing. Publishing is a little too involved to be run with a business school textbook in one hand and a bankroll in the other. That, quite frankly, is another one of its charms.

Nevertheless, publishing is certainly ripe for change. To be effective, any attempt at change must address the peculiar nature of trade publishing and its complications. And it must also consider the forces that are currently at work, making changes in publishing whether we will it or not.

3

Getting Books to the Public

IN GENERAL, the distribution of titles through the book trade is inefficient, costly, and wasteful. As a result, not only do far fewer books reach the public, but alternate methods for reaching book buyers further undermine the bookseller. Of these, the two major alternatives are selling books by direct mail and the book clubs.

Selling books by direct mail is expensive. It is the rare title that has broad general interest and can command the high retail price that provides the margin to pay for elaborate mailing pieces. The best-selling novel that has large bookstore sales and may be of interest to mail-order patrons is not a likely candidate for this type of selling. The margins above cost are usually moderate for such a book and a large number of respondents is necessary to cover the cost of the sales effort. Furthermore, this sort of book, which is likely to be widely available and can be examined in a bookstore instead of being bought sight unseen, offers no compelling reason for responding to a mail-order appeal.

Books that have a greater margin above actual cost tend to be directed to limited audiences—electrical engineers, business managers, art collectors. These audiences are more precisely defined and mailing lists for them are available. Since more specialized books are less likely to be found in bookstores, the prospective buyer has more reason to order by mail. To encourage him to "act now," the publisher frequently offers a discount from the "list price" (sometimes genuine). A great many titles sold to the engineering and business community can be legitimately charged as a business expense or purchased directly by the employer. Their prices can therefore be somewhat elevated, making it easier to cover the cost of mailing campaigns.

Book clubs, whose members number in the millions, offer their members two advantages: savings and convenience. The choice of titles is restricted, with a club offering a "main selection" each month along with a modest number of "alternate selections." In practice, the member automatically receives the selected main title unless he refuses it in advance or specifies an alternate. This condition of membership, called "negative option," depends heavily on the lethargy of the member in returning his refusal on time and on his honesty in paying the monthly invoice, and it has led to the successful growth of the clubs.

The clubs' bargain appeal takes various forms. Some clubs offer free books, or books at token prices, on joining and additional "bonus" books that depend on the number of selections purchased. Other clubs simply offer their selections at a substantial reduction from the retail price. The Reader's Digest Condensed Book Club offers a unique time saving as well as a money saving by condensing each book so that several titles can be combined in one volume.

Thus the club member may be sure that he is getting more, dollar for dollar, than he would if he purchased the same books from a retail bookseller. In addition, his purchasing is done at home, and frequently automatically. Going to a bookstore would give a buyer a greater choice of books. But even readers who want the opportunity to choose may find it a happy combination to get some books from a club at great savings and buy additional books at retail price from a bookstore.

The book clubs (the Literary Guild and the Book-of-the-Month Club were the early ones) started by making themselves attractive to the largest possible readership, offering books of wide appeal. As the idea became more firmly implanted, clubs were established that catered to narrower, more particular interests—mystery and adventure, American history, psychology, military science, computers—with smaller but perhaps more loyal membership rolls. For members of these specialized clubs, the club performs the additional service of selection, since it keeps in closer touch with forthcoming books on the subject than most members can.

The clubs make their choices by examining photocopies of manuscripts or galley proofs. They buy from the publisher the right to produce their own editions (usually identical to the publisher's and frequently manufactured with his) and pay a royalty for each copy used. It is generally believed that book club sales do not reduce the bookstore market (though this is clearly not always the case) and may actually increase bookstore sales because of the visibility of book club advertising and the word-of-mouth publicity stimulated by book club readers. But the one solid attraction for the publisher is the royalty payment—not much per copy but ultimately impressive because of the large number of copies. A frequent additional attraction to the publisher is the possibility of saving money by producing the club's and the publisher's editions together.

To a large degree, the dual attractions of savings and convenience are underscored by the prevailing system of distributing books through the trade, a system whose costliness and inefficiency contribute to high retail prices, a scarcity of retail outlets, and a narrow selection of titles in the bookstores. To understand why it fails to work well, we should look at the book distribution process in detail.

It is essential that the publisher have his book easily available to possible purchasers by the day of publication (the official debut for the book), when advertising will announce its existence, publicity will begin to surface, and, if the publisher is lucky, reviews will appear. To be sure that books are in the stores by publication date, the publisher must ship them early enough to allow for the vagaries of the postal service, which means about four weeks for points on the opposite coast and not much less for points in between. Books are shipped to stores (or wholesalers) according to the orders that were collected by the publisher's sales reps. Since it takes three to four months for the sales reps to cover all the wholesalers and retailers, the sales tours must start four or five months before publication date. In order to sell any book so far in advance, the sales rep must have enough information about the book to be able to try to convince the bookseller that it is a profitable place to put part of his limited buying budget.

Clearly the publisher cannot inform the sales reps one title at a time, nor can each rep make the round of stores each time an individual title comes up. To make the problem manageable, each publisher's titles are grouped into selling seasons, usually two a year. This enables the publisher to impart the information on an entire season's titles at one time and enables the rep to sell an entire season's titles in one visit to each bookseller. Of course, this also moves the start of the selling operation back even further.

To inform the sales reps about each season's forthcoming titles and to rekindle their enthusiasm for an often demanding and lonely job, publishers have devised the semiannual sales conference, which brings together all the sales reps to hear from the editorial, promotion, and advertising departments about the wonders of the new season. In most publishing houses, every other activity short of the warehouse itself seems to come to a standstill during the few days, and sometimes a full week, of sales conference. And well it should, because a great deal rides on the success of the conference.

Publishers operating on a two-season publishing program are likely to have their sales conferences sometime in May for "fall" books and sometime early in December for "spring" books. The May date is dictated by the fact that the American booksellers usually gather for their annual convention on Memorial Day weekend. Part of that meeting is an exhibition area where each publisher displays his wares, and the fall's books must be unveiled for booksellers at that time. The December meeting date, usually the first or second week, is considered dead selling time, and publishers hope that their reps will resume active selling early in January.

□ *The timing of sales conferences would no doubt create problems no matter when they were held, but it is interesting to examine the effect of these two periods, which are used by 90 percent of trade publishers. The May conference occurs before the booksellers' convention, which disqualifies from sales activity the weeks during which booksellers are preparing to go, are at the convention, and are returning via partial vacation. The weeks after the December conference are disqualified because booksellers are busy with the Christmas selling period and with taking inventory and making returns directly after Christmas. These weeks of inactivity allow time for the presentations so carefully made at the sales conference to become fuzzy in the reps' memories before the selling effort begins.*

Publishers who have their own sales force can, of course, schedule their sales meetings at will. However, the typical small or medium-sized publisher may have one or two of his own reps and cover the bulk of the country with "commission reps." Since the commission rep in one area is independent of the rep in any other area, the commission sales force for one publisher is not likely to be the same as the commission sales force for another publisher, even though they may have representatives in common in several parts of the country. As a result, these publishers have to conform to the period of approximately two weeks in May and two weeks in December, when all commission reps are available to attend conferences. Any attempt to hold a sales conference at another time would find at least some of the commission reps busy making their rounds with the lists of the publishers who conform to the seasonal sales conference pattern.

No matter how the publisher determines his sales conference dates, these dates determine, in turn, a whole series of other activities.

The publisher's catalogue for that season must be ready in time for the sales conference. That means, depending upon how elaborate the catalogue will be, that at some point, weeks before the meeting, the list for that season must be "closed" so the catalogue copy can be written, photographs or other illustrations made available, and the final, proofread and corrected material delivered to the printer.

This, in turn, makes it necessary that cover or jacket artwork, and preferably printed proofs of this artwork, be available in time to be photographed for inclusion in the catalogue. Depending on the publishing house, this artwork may require the approval of several people, which, in turn, requires that the artist for each jacket or cover be selected early enough to supply rough sketches so that all the necessary approvals can be collected in time for material to be ready for the catalogue.

The catalogue requires not only illustrative material but also descriptive copy for each book. This cannot consist entirely of canned, nonspecific superlatives. Some hard information about the book must be communicated to the person preparing the catalogue copy. Also required is specific bibliographic information, such as the trim size of the book, the number of pages, and the retail price.

As a result of such procedural requirements, the possibility for including a book in the catalogue for the May sales conference may be foreclosed as early as February or March. This means that if a book is accepted for publication in March, it is too late to be included in the May sales conference catalogue, so it cannot be published until spring of the following year. (That is precisely what happened to the book you are now reading.) While it is not unknown for a publisher to make a special effort to accelerate the process in the case of a particularly important or timely book (or if he is desperate for additional revenue), the schedule restrictions are very real.

The primary (and frequently the only) purpose of the sales conference is to give the editorial department an opportunity to arm the reps with enough knowledge about each title to enable them to pursue their sales efforts. For this purpose, the publisher prepares a presentation for each book that includes information about the book itself and (when there is anything impressive to say) about the advertising campaign being planned and the publicity the book is expected to get in the period around publication date. In most houses, this information is presented by the sponsoring editor, who is overseeing the fortunes of that title. In some of the larger houses, the publicity and advertising information may be delivered separately by the person in charge of that activity.

The importance to the publisher of new titles becomes steadily greater as the average life span of each title becomes shorter. Accordingly, the pressure to sell new titles grows steadily more acute as the percentage of books that survive their debut season declines and as publishers feel the need to squeeze as many dollars as possible out of them as quickly as possible.

The sales conference becomes, therefore, more and more the focus of the publisher's sales activity, and the forthcoming books, always the centerpiece, become more and more the entire emphasis of the meeting. Very little time is devoted to the backlist, the titles published in previous seasons, except for almost ritual exhortations to sell it and sometimes to announce a special deal that will be offered to booksellers in the form of additional discounts or deferred payment for ordering from the backlist. Very few publishers use the sales conference as a sales training opportunity in the way this is done in other industries.

A publisher's rep may hear about one hundred, two hundred, or three hundred titles at a sales conference lasting two, three, or four days. The commission rep may attend six or eight conferences in the course of a week or ten days, listening to presentations on three or four hundred titles in all, frequently more.

Preparation for the sales conference is taken very seriously in every publishing house. It is the most significant moment in the life of each book on the list. Once the reps leave for the field, it is too late to add a selling point or a bit of interesting background for a title. Knowing this, the editors work hard at getting the maximum said in as little time as possible.

The book's editor will probably never speak to any of the booksellers directly. The only way he can present the case for a particular book to the bookseller is by saying, in five minutes or less, whatever will make each of the reps sitting before him into an accurate and convincing surrogate. In his presentation, he tries to create a favorable attitude that will result in successful negotiations with the hundreds, or in some publishing houses thousands, of bookstores around the country on whom the reps will call. These extremely brief statements at the sales conference and the highly condensed material in the catalogue are all the information on which the sales rep will base his own attitude toward the book.

Inevitably, the few titles for which impressive sales are projected are made the centerpiece of the sales conference. It is clearly understood that the orders for these few titles will be watched (and probably tallied) as they come in. They are the titles by important authors who need to be impressed and that have possible subsidiary rights income that depends on sales, titles on which much has been spent in authors' advances and on which more will be spent in advertising. It does not need to be said that a poor sales performance on the lesser titles will be forgiven (if it is even detected), but "we're counting on you to put the 'big one' over the top!"

The need to assemble the entire sales force twice a year to attempt the impossible job of cramming enough information into them about each of hundreds of new products is probably unique to the publishing industry. The present structure of the sales conference results from the fact that in book publishing, in contrast to most other industries producing consumer goods, the selling effort is still almost entirely directed to *getting the product into the store.* The publisher's representative is essentially a Yankee peddler selling to the retailer. He comes rattling in with his horse and wagon, displays and extols the virtues of every pot and pan, knife, fork, and spoon, and odds and ends of tinware that he carries, and pleads with the retailer to take some of each item. Most other industries have reached the point where, because it is no longer necessary to negotiate every single unit of every single item, the selling job is to *move the product through the store.*

From the sales conference, armed with proofs of jackets and covers, catalogues, and recollections and notes of the rapid-fire "selling points," each sales rep sallies forth to solicit orders from his accounts, the retailers and wholesalers in his geographical area.

How many accounts each sales force covers each season depends on its size and on the quality of its supervision. For most serious trade publishers, it will range from about 1000 to about 2500 accounts. These include the smaller chains, department stores (which may comprise several locations), and the independent booksellers. Walden and B. Dalton, the two huge retail chains, are usually covered by a visit to each headquarters office. Since they operate approximately 1200 stores between them, and some of the other accounts represent multiple locations, the number of sales locations covered by the sales reps may range from 2500 to 4000. The simple fact is that, on publication day (or any other day), a book not in the store has virtually zero chance of being sold. It is a fact confirmed over and over again by surveys and over and over again by the publisher's own experience.

Although it is theoretically possible for a store to "special order" any book it does not happen to have when a customer insists on it and is willing to wait, such sales occur very infrequently. First, such customers are rare, particularly because the wait may be three weeks or three months; second, booksellers don't enjoy the necessary clerical red tape or the prospect of responding to the customers' repeated queries during the long waiting period; and third, publishers generally discourage booksellers from offering this service by imposing penalties on orders for one copy of a book. Of course, a bookstore may combine its special order with other purchases to avoid a penalty or, in the case of some titles, obtain the book from a local wholesaler.

It is true that the sales rep's intervention is not *absolutely* essential to getting books into the store. Booksellers may place orders on their own, particularly for titles that are selling very actively. But perhaps 90 percent of trade sales are made or stimulated by sales reps. All in all, the publisher, "covering the trade" through sales reps' visits to booksellers and wholesalers, with the paraphernalia of catalogues, sales conferences, and advertising in *Publishers Weekly* to back up the sales reps, represents the supply side of the present trade book distribution system.

The demand side is, of course, the bookseller. The bookseller's role in distribution is both very difficult (witness how few of these valuable people there are) and, unfortunately, often insufficiently understood or appreciated by publishers. Bookselling is considered in some detail in the next chapter. For now, it is sufficient to consider the relation of the bookseller to the publisher's sales force.

The bookseller needs to have the right books in the right quantities. Every copy of every book represents an investment. Since investment involves the cost of money, books that do not sell quickly enough place a drain on the store's resources. On the other hand, the bookseller needs as wide an assortment of titles as possible to attract customers, to avoid having browsers leave empty-handed, and to create the volume of daily sales to cover expenses and assure some profit. Selecting books is therefore the most critical activity for any retail bookstore.

Because it is so critical and because there seems to be no alternative, the bookseller maintains tight control over this selection. Every copy of every title in a bookseller's stock is there as a result of his decision.

The pattern of negotiation is remarkably similar for all sales reps and booksellers. The rep arrives with his sample covers arranged in the order in which he has decided to present the list. If it is an important bookseller, he will have made an appointment in advance.

In many cases, he will simply wait his turn while the bookstore buyer sees the reps who arrived first.

□ *For convenience, I have been referring to sales reps as "he." At one time, not so very long ago, only men held such positions. I believe I hired the first female rep in about 1957 at Doubleday to cover what was considered the very unladylike territory of Southern California, Arizona, and New Mexico. The selection was made in the face of very determined opposition from the sales management and from most of the reps on the staff. I was warned of the dangers to a woman traveling alone, of the opportunities for sexual harassment by booksellers, and all the other nonsense familiar to women denied equality. The female rep became one of the stars very quickly.*

When he does have the attention of the bookseller—sometimes in the middle of the selling floor, interrupted by customers seeking help —the rep tries to go through his list systematically, title by title.

Although reps invariably come with several hundred titles to sell, only a few of the largest publishers can claim enough of the bookseller's time for a reasonably complete review of the list. These sessions may last all day, starting in the morning, continuing through lunch, and perhaps going on past the usual store closing hour. Others must move through their wares more quickly, skipping many (frequently most) titles altogether.

The rep shows the proof of the jacket, describing the contents in a sentence or a phrase, recalling the success of a previous title by the same author or a book on a similar theme, and, if any substantial promotion budget is planned, outlining what the publisher will be doing to support the book. To help convince the bookseller, the rep has two selling instruments (in addition to his own persuasive powers).

The first is the discount. The bookseller receives a discount from the retail price that is related to the size of the order. The more books he buys, the less it costs him per dollar of retail price, and the greater his profit. A skillful rep watches the order as it builds up and is alert to point out how many additional copies (or how few) will bring the order to the next discount level.

The second is the "returns" policy. To encourage the bookseller to take some risks and to accept some books about which he is being told very little because the rep, in truth, knows very little, some genius (unknown to me) invented the return privilege, which permits the bookseller to return any unsold copies to the publisher for credit. The bookseller pays the postage for these books, both to receive them and return them, and some publishers hedge the privilege with restrictions, but it nevertheless serves its essential purpose: to reduce the bookseller's risk in buying books.

The concept of the return seems to be a peculiarly brilliant American invention. Unfortunately, it is misused badly in practice, as will be discussed further in Chapter 5.

The discount schedule and returns policy are supposed to help the sales rep get the most desirable order for each title on the list. No doubt they are frequently of great assistance, but the overall results are disappointing: One out of every three copies of a new title is returned to the publisher. These are, for the most part, the more promising titles on the publisher's list, the ones on which the publisher put the greatest emphasis at the sales conference, the ones on which each sales rep's performance will be judged. These very titles, returned in large quantity by some booksellers, may be out of stock at others.

The lesser titles, perhaps 75 percent or more of the publisher's list, are rarely oversold. The problem with these books is that they do not get into most stores in even token quantities. The reasons may become evident if we take a closer look at the difficulties in the rep-bookseller negotiation.

The first difficulty is one of time. There are approximately 40,000 new titles published every year. Of these, perhaps 20,000 should be considered by a serious trade bookseller. Except in the chains or the largest retail stores, where the administrative budget can support individuals who spend their entire time selecting books, the bookseller must combine his buying, important though it is, with all the other responsibilities of running a store. Hence the bookseller is usually trying to make the sales interview as short as possible.

The second difficulty is the atmosphere in which the negotiation is conducted. Frequently it is on the selling floor itself, which invites interruption, and sometimes with the bookseller rearranging stock and performing other chores as he listens. Even when the meeting occurs in a cluttered back room, interruption by clerks and phone calls is common.

The third difficulty is the lack of reliable information on the part of both parties. The bookseller only knows what the rep can tell him in one or two minutes. The theory that justifies this sales method is that the bookseller knows his clientele and can judge how well each title will appeal to them. In fact, his knowledge of the store's customers, even in personal, neighborhood bookshops, is extremely vague. In stores in shopping malls or busy urban locations, the clientele depends significantly on whoever is passing by, and one bookseller's customers are not likely to differ from those of any other in a similar spot. In such cases, the bookseller's impression of public taste is not any better than the publisher's or the rep's. The value of vague notions of what will and won't sell can be judged from the fact that the vast majority of orders are for one or two copies of a given title.

The publisher's rep contributes very little reliable information. It derives from a long gone sales conference at which hundreds of titles were presented over several hours of steady lecturing. In some cases, the editor who described the book had not read it; in others, the manuscript may not have been completed. I have observed negotiation sessions with a number of different reps from the same sales conference, selling the same list; sometimes I did not believe the same title was being described. Furthermore, the sales rep's understanding and presentation are colored by his own interests. The rep who likes baseball will sell larger quantities of a baseball book than one who doesn't, regardless of the intensity of local interest in baseball.

The fourth difficulty is the attitude of each party in the negotiation. The bookseller has a limited budget. He assumes that, since he cannot have every new title in his store, the best buying strategy is to select the "best" titles from each large publisher's list and perhaps ignore the small publishers altogether. The best titles will be those that the publisher is printing in large quantities with the largest advertising budget. And since even the best books cannot each be bought in large quantity, the next problem is to identify the titles for which there will be a strong buying surge on publication day.

The bookseller wants his money tied up in inventory for the shortest possible time with a minimum danger of running out of stock. If a book is likely to sell slowly, he would rather buy small quantities at the beginning.

The rep, on the other hand, wants to get the largest order for a number of reasons, the first being that that is what the publisher wants. At the home office, the sales manager, the editors, and perhaps the head of the house are watching the orders for the lead titles. In most companies, orders for these titles are tallied and memos circulated to all concerned, showing the current week's position for each title. Any single outstanding order will trigger phone calls around the office and possibly a congratulatory note to the sales rep. Rarely, very rarely, will a rep be told that an order is too large.

Congratulations on a large advance order on a lead title are almost never marred by any reference to titles that were skipped altogether. It is expected that some books will be sacrificed to get quantity on the titles that "really" matter.

A sales rep soon realizes that heavy returns of unsold books are almost never blamed on bad selling—though they are frequently blamed, amazingly, on bad buying. Usually, it is simply seen as one of the inevitable misfortunes that publishers are doomed to suffer. In trying to get the largest possible orders for a few leading titles, even at the expense of the lesser books on the list, the sales rep is doing what he believes his management wants him to do.

By placing so much emphasis on a large advance sale, publishers confuse shadow with substance. Advance orders determine what books will be available "out there" on publication day, when the sales life of the book officially begins. It is easy to understand that an advance (the total of all the advance orders) of 15,000 copies is considered better than an advance of 10,000 copies.

The number—10,000, 15,000, 100,000—representing the total of the advance orders is the quick way of expressing the sales condition and prospects for a title on publication date. The sales manager will say at the conference, "We need an advance of 20,000 to give this book the start it needs." Every rep will mentally divide that total by the appropriate figure to estimate how much he is expected to contribute. As the orders come in from the field, the editor will be watching the total, and the author may be told from time to time how the advance projection stands. This number is always taken to express the essence, character, and quality of the sales force's performance, hence the pressure to achieve the largest possible advance sale.

But the advance is a shadow that may not reflect actual sales substance. Accessibility to the public does not depend on the number of *copies* available but rather on the number of *places* copies are available. Yet it is the rare publisher who considers the number of orders rather than, or in addition to, the number of copies ordered. The number of orders is never mentioned as a goal at the sales conference, and neither the sales manager nor the editor is likely to translate the meaning of an advance of 10,000 or 20,000 copies by asking how many stores that represents, even though it is clear that the book with a 10,000-copy advance from 3000 stores is getting a better start than one with a 20,000-copy advance from 500 stores.

There is another side to the advance sale. The 20,000-copy advance represents an investment by the publisher in manufacturing 20,000 copies to reach a particular level of market penetration. If the same degree of penetration can be achieved with 10,000 copies, the investment required will be substantially lower.

Ignoring such considerations, virtually every publisher drives his sales force toward the big advance without closely examining its quality.

□ *I grant that this is an extreme example, but I have sat beside the sales manager of a large and respected publishing house while he arranged, over the phone, to increase a national wholesaler's order by 2000 copies that he knew, and they knew, they would never use, "because I promised [the editor] we would get an advance of 30,000, and we are running short." The wholesaler understood he was buying future favors from the publisher.*

What the sales manager did on that book (and others) was only the last step. His reps had already done the same thing on a smaller scale with local accounts.

And though the editor did not know the specific details that made the advance sale phony, he knew it was in large part phony. But he, and the house, now looked very good to the author, who enjoyed hearing the big number without knowing what it meant.

Very few sales managers or reps ever conspire to place completely phony orders, but some are happy to take orders that are clearly higher than they should be.

The major reason for getting an impressive advance is to boost the book to higher sales levels. But there is frequently another motive, completely unrelated to the immediate sales of the book. A high advance is very useful to the subsidiary rights manager in selling the paperback rights. The paperback publisher is not in a position to look beyond the numbers at the quality of the advance, and, accepting the mystique of numbers that pervades publishing, he usually accepts the shadow of the advance to be reality.

In the dickering over a reprint contract, an advance of 20,000 is more impressive and worth a higher bid than an advance of 10,000. And if the reprint rights do, in fact, go for a high price, the publisher will have justified to himself the extra cost of putting out some thousands of useless books.

There are more defensible reasons for pushing for a large advance. Both publisher and rep are aware that, 95 percent of the time, the advance order is likely to be the only order the bookseller will ever place for that book. It is true that if a book sells extraordinarily well and the initial supply of copies is exhausted, some booksellers may reorder from the publisher or the wholesaler. They may, but because they are busy or short of funds or on vacation they probably won't. And the book may not sell dramatically fast, but sell steadily enough to exhaust the bookseller's supply and to cost the publisher lost sales because the bookseller does not consider a reorder urgent. Or the bookseller may not notice soon enough, or at all, that a book has sold out, or is about to. The object, therefore, is to get an order large enough to last the bookseller for the life of the book.

Because neither the rep nor the bookseller knows the optimal quantity for each store, the rep tries to get in as many copies as possible of his lead titles. He realizes he cannot try to do this for all the books on his list, and he doesn't try. The balance of the list will be represented by a title here and there in modest quantity with a large number of titles totally ignored.

□ *You may wonder why, if the orders obtained by the sales rep are unsatisfactory, sales management does not, with the help of the editors, supply each rep with a copy of the order it considers most desirable from each account. I will have more to say about such helpful guidance, which any sales rep might reasonably consider to be an obligation of management. It is curious that not a single publisher provides such guidance at the present time—despite the obvious cost in millions of dollars year after year because the orders are wrong.*

I was well into writing this chapter when the *New York Times Book Review*, by pure good fortune, ran a piece by a reporter who spent a day making the rounds of New England bookstores with a salesman for William Morrow. The salesman showed the reporter how a rep can destroy titles: He destroyed three. To quote the reporter: " 'Quite forgettable' is his summation of one book. Another: 'I'm sorry. I don't know why this is being published.' Still another: 'I hope it vanishes from the face of the earth.' " The *Times* went on to quote the Morrow salesman: "I think it's psychologically important to have a few skips on a list. It builds trust. It's something you can giggle over with the buyer! Hey, look at this dud!"

The reporter did not have the benefit of traveling with other Morrow sales reps in other territories during the same season. If he had, he would have discovered that different reps have different tastes and find different titles "quite forgettable." Of course, for each rep there is the whole scale of values between the top title and the three or four or seven "quite forgettable" ones. The titles between the very top and the very bottom are not killed; they are merely tortured.

□ *Since the Morrow sales rep's technique is widely used in other publishers' sales forces, publishers might improve our present negotiation system and introduce a lighter touch by adding to each*

*list three or four deliberate "skip" titles to be used by all the reps.
The authors of these "quite forgettable" books, in recognition of
their contribution, could be paid a royalty on the number of copies
that are* not *sold instead of the number sold.*

The *Times* reporter went on:

> Speed is the operative word in bookselling. The essence of the profession is
> to come up with a "handle" for each title—a succinct phrase or two that
> will capture the flavor of the book . . . [The sales rep] has scant seconds—at
> best a minute—to present a work that may have consumed grueling years
> of an author's life. "Authors seeing this would probably go through the
> wall, they would buy guns," [the sales rep] says, and he is at times
> reproofed (sic) ad nauseam by authors who fail to comprehend why their
> books are occupying de facto Worst-Seller lists . . . books have never been
> sold any differently, and although publishers and booksellers perpetually
> grouse about the manner in which books are gotten to the public, no one
> has yet come up with a better way of doing it.

□ *Quick, what was that "handle" for* War and Peace . . . Gulliver's
Travels . . . The Divine Comedy? *The handle, it should be noted, is not
to sell the book to the reader. It is just to get the book into the store.
If the author only knew how thin is the thread on which his hope for
sales hangs!*

Distribution-by-negotiation imposes costs and handicaps upon
publishing simply because procedures make inordinate delays
inevitable in getting the book from author to reader. A book to be
published in October or November must be on the publication
schedule by January or February to be sure it is in the May catalogue
and sales conference. This not only imposes a financial burden on the
publisher because money invested is so very slow coming back, it also
imposes a social cost and reduces the scope within which the book can
usefully function.

A seven- to ten-month delay will not make every statement in a
book on current events out of date, only some. To a lesser degree, it is
likely to do the same for any book in economics, psychology,
international affairs, and so on. A discussion of nuclear energy or
environmental pollution can become studded with embarrassing
archaisms over a period of seven months.

□ *I apologize for anything in these pages on the subject of publishing
that no longer applies.*

It is indisputable that a ridiculously long time elapses between the
moment that the author hands over the finished manuscript and the
date the publisher hands back a copy of the book. The layman might

imagine that the technology of book manufacture imposes this limitation on the speed with which even the most eager of publishers can bring his wares to market. Not at all!

Most trade books (as I will discuss in Chapter 13, on production), which take five to eight months to produce after they are edited, could be produced, like clockwork, and at lower cost, in five weeks. With a little practice, the five weeks could be reduced to three weeks. The technology is not mysterious. It sits there waiting to be properly used. And using the technology properly would simplify internal procedures, cut manufacturing costs, and reduce staff.

But publishers would not know what to do with the books if they produced them faster. They need time to put together a catalogue, have a sales conference rehearsal, a sales conference, and months for the reps to go from store to store, slowly building up the advance sale. To cope with simple, direct, speedy manufacturing would require simple, direct, speedy distribution as well.

Imagine the *New York Times*. Each night after the contents of the issue have been decided and a mock-up of the front page is ready, a "sales conference" is called to tell the delivery staff what a great and exciting issue it is going to be. They go out (with photostats of the front page, of course) to negotiate with each newsstand operator, who then tells them how many copies he would like (full return privileges). They bring the orders back so that newspapers can be dispatched to the stands a few weeks later. In the meantime, the trucks are delivering the issue of several weeks before for which the orders are on hand and have been processed through the fulfillment department.

I know. Books are not newspapers, just as they are not soap or baked goods. But neither are they wine. So what is the advantage of carefully aging each book before letting the lucky reader have it?

However successful the publisher may be in collecting advance orders, it is, though the most critical part of the book marketing process, only the beginning. All the effort and expense incurred so far have been directed toward getting books *into* the stores. Though this effort represents the major portion of the sales budget for most publishers, there remains the task of helping to move books *out* of the stores.

In publishing, the opinion is widely (and I believe soundly) held that the most powerful factor in the sale of books is "word of mouth." The advertising and promotion efforts of the publisher, or the good luck of a publicity break, may create interest that results in sales. People who are carrying a copy may be asked how they like it.

Cocktail or bridge table conversation may prompt an informal report about a book another person may be reading or has heard about. Each purchase thereby can stimulate further purchases.

But if books are not available to a prospective purchaser because the store is out of stock or because there is no convenient bookstore, the word-of-mouth reaction slows down and may stop altogether— another reason for placing advance orders in as many *places* as possible.

Much of what the publisher does to encourage the sale of a book is aimed at initiating, stimulating, and maintaining such word of mouth. The simplest, least expensive, and most direct way to do this is to send free copies to reviewers and to public figures who are likely to be interested and whose opinion is influential. Frequently, depending on the book, the review copy will be accompanied by background material, which may include some information about the author, laudatory statements by people who have read the book in manuscript or galleys, perhaps a press release in the form of a favorable book review ready to run, and, where appropriate, some photographs or other illustrative material. This material is intended to stimulate the recipient to dip into the book and to provide ideas and even phrasing that can be used in commenting on the book.

The number of review copies, and the impressiveness of the auxiliary packet going with them, varies with the nature of the book and the money the publisher feels he can spend on that title. As titles go up the scale of importance (usually meaning the publisher's estimate of potential sale), a larger budget allows a variety of options. The more modest of these include a cocktail party to permit the author to meet people whose interest may be helpful, "reading copies" of the book supplied to bookstore clerks, or small announcement ads in the appropriate media.

For the lead books, the budget will be larger, the promotion plan more ambitious and elaborate, and the planning more precise. Booksellers will be informed in advance of such campaigns, usually by the sales rep and perhaps through follow-up mailings. The reason for letting the bookseller know in good time is partly to justify a large advance order, but also to encourage him to plan to tie his own promotional activity—window displays, co-op advertising, mailings—to the publisher's campaign so as to achieve a synergistic strengthening of both. Sometimes booksellers are encouraged to cooperate when they are given poster material or props for window displays and perhaps substantial prizes for the displays judged most effective.

□ *Unfortunately, the concentration of the sales rep on getting the advance order, in the present archaic distribution system, effectively prevents his helping to ensure timely and effective cooperation by the bookseller in any promotion campaign. By the time the book arrives, the rep's suggestions have been forgotten or have lost much of their force. In the sale of soap and shoes and sealing wax, it is well known that the greatest impact of any advertising campaign is in the repetition of the campaign themes in the retail stores around impressive merchandise displays. All of us who go to supermarkets are familiar with this cooperation between retailer and producer. Nothing like that happens in bookstores at the present time.*

If first or second serial rights are sold to allow excerpts from a book to appear in newspapers or magazines before or just after publication, the promotion department may publicize that use. If rights are not sold, the promotion staff may prepare material from the book or relating to it to be offered free to publications that can use it.

Although the publisher cannot control the timing or even the actual appearance of reviews or news releases, he can control his advertising. If the budget is generous, it may be planned far in advance, with the ads actually prepared. Advertising budgets in book publishing are limited and, in the nature of things, very small compared to budgets in other consumer industries. The publisher may plan, therefore, to concentrate the campaign where there is hope of getting some word of mouth started for that particular book.

The advertising campaign is usually timed to take effect around publication date, shortly after the books arrive in the stores. It is important that stores sense the momentum of sales so that they keep the book prominently displayed and so clerks are conscious of popular interest in it. There is always the danger, particularly for a title taken in quantity, that an apparent lack of movement in the first weeks after publication may cause some booksellers to curtail its display space, even to make premature returns. To forestall this danger, particularly since sales are frequently much stronger in some places than others, the publisher will try to let the trade know as soon as strong sales are detected anywhere.

□ *As we shall have occasion to remark frequently elsewhere, publishers have generally failed to develop techniques for* measuring *the many things for which a precise notion is much more useful than a vague approximation. One of these failures is to know how well a book is selling in the stores before, during, and after an advertising campaign, so that the publisher can know whether his money was spent wisely and whether more should be spent. One technique for doing this, commonly employed in many consumer industries, is described in the chapter on sales management. I am embarrassed to say that I do not know of a single publisher, including those who spend hundreds of thousands of dollars annually on advertising, who measures how these expenditures affect the rate of retail sale.*

A particularly useful promotional device, when appropriate, is the author tour. The publisher may use his own publicity department or a professional agency to plan the tour, to book the author on radio and TV programs, and to arrange university lectures, convention appearances, newspaper interviews, and the like, along the way. The time in a city between such appearances can be devoted to visiting bookstores, possibly for planned autographing appearances, more usually to meet the clerks and thank them for their help and to autograph whatever copies are in the stores. This technique works well when the author is a well-known personality to whom television audiences and autograph seekers will respond or when the book is controversial or on a subject of intense current interest.

Bookstore clerks, by the way, are a powerful resource, largely overlooked by publishers, for selling books. Although bookselling has become much more of a self-service operation than when I was a boy, clerks still help many customers. If someone asks, "Do you have anything particularly funny for my sick aunt in the hospital?" it would be nice to have the clerk say, "No, but I've got a terrific new book by Leonard Shatzkin that will make her an expert on publishing before she gets home."

A little time spent cultivating store clerks, especially in giving them information about current books, would be well spent by any sales rep, but it is rarely done. Although the rep could carry extra copies of the catalogue and other material, distribution to the clerks seems pointless since it will be months before the books actually arrive. The rep might, theoretically, carry material supporting the books he sold previously that are just then arriving, but generally he doesn't. His function is to "get the order."

The author tour device itself is severely handicapped by the cumbersome workings of distribution-by-negotiation. The appearance of the author in Buffalo or Detroit or Atlanta is expected to stimulate the sale of copies in that city. It is therefore important to have copies in as many places as possible in that city when the author is seen on local TV. But since the books can be in the store only if the bookseller has ordered them, this would require the publisher to get his sales rep there four or five weeks before the author's appearance (to allow time for orders to be processed, shipped, travel, and to be unpacked) to persuade the booksellers that the author will actually be there as scheduled and that his appearance will result in increased demand for the book. This almost never happens. Though the tour cities may possibly be (but are usually not) precisely mapped in advance, it would be expensive and disruptive to have the sales rep, even if on the publisher's payroll and certainly if an independent sales agent, interrupt his planned itinerary to rush to the city in his territory that is included in the tour.

□ *Even where it is possible, it is frequently overlooked because in many publishing houses (as I discuss in the chapter on sales management) there is poor coordination between the promotion department and the sales force in the field. Moreover, in most publishing houses the sales rep controls his own itinerary, and interfering with it would be unusual for sales management.*

As a result, some of the benefits of the author tour are often lost because too few copies, or none at all, are in the stores. In the process, the author becomes exasperated with the publisher, although his annoyance should be with the distribution system itself, of which the publisher, the bookseller, and the author are all victims.

We have so far discussed the distribution and promotion of new titles, the publisher's "frontlist." There is also the "backlist": those titles, perhaps 100,000 or more among all the publishers combined, that continue to sell and that must (it might be more reasonable to say "should") be continually reintroduced into the distribution system. Backlist titles are rarely promoted. Even such perennial best-sellers as Kahlil Gibran's *The Prophet,* which sells thousands of copies a year, year in and year out, depend upon word of mouth and the public's and booksellers' familiarity with them. There are exceptions, but it is fair to say that, even more than is true of frontlist titles, the backlist depends upon a copy being in the store for the sale to happen. Virtually every copy of every book in a store is there because of a deliberate decision by the bookseller. That rule applies to the backlist as well as the frontlist, even though the method of selling the backlist and the nature of the negotiation differ greatly from those for the frontlist.

In the frontlist negotiation, the rep has the advantage of knowing virtually all of whatever information about the titles may exist between the two parties. It is also far more interesting for both of them to talk about the future, with the tantalizing promise of "big" books that may catch the public's fancy and sell in large quantity, than to deal with familiar, routine backlist titles that have lost their mystery and excitement. Although the bookseller may be cautious in accepting recommendations, the rep can suggest quantities on new titles with little inhibition; there is no sales record against which to judge. In the case of the backlist, there is a record of sorts, and it tends to be unexciting.

The negotiation process is also slower and more laborious. Arriving at some idea of the sales potential for each title is only part of the problem. To do that, it may be sufficient to consult the store's sales figures, when they exist. They may be in a card file or, in a few of the wealthier and more modern stores, on the computer. That tells at least part of the story. It does not record, however, the sales that might have been had the store not been out of stock for a period—which, chances are very good, it was. Nor does it suggest what the sales might have been had the book been better displayed or had a fresh jacket, and so on.

Then there are the backlist titles on which even the most meticulous store records show no sales history because there were never any copies in the store. The bookseller's attitude is likely to be: Since "we had no calls for that title," there is probably no market for it in his store. That is a challenge to the sales rep to argue that other, luckier, but otherwise similar booksellers are selling that title in attractive numbers.

But whatever figure is established as a sales potential, the bookseller cannot place an order for any backlist title without knowing how many copies are in the store at that moment. For that information, neither file cards nor computer records are reliable. An essential preliminary step to any discussion with the bookseller is a careful inventory of that publisher's titles, taken by the sales rep.

With the bookseller, the rep can then go down the list, title by title, pointing out the books he considers eligible. The orders, when placed at all, are typically for quantities much lower than those he gets on new books. Including the time spent taking inventory, analyzing the numbers to prepare recommendations for an order, and negotiating with the buyer, he is probably spending considerably more time per dollar of books ordered than he expends on selling the frontlist, and he has had a lot less fun doing it. The buyer, if anything, finds the whole process even more boring.

Except for caring about the few highly visible books that sell in respectable quantities and are likely to be asked for specifically, the bookseller can be very relaxed and only mildly interested in the backlist. Among the thousands of lesser titles, of which he knows he must carry several hundred, how can he distinguish between the one that will sell two copies and the one that will sell three copies a year? A representation of such titles is needed in each subject category, but doesn't the store already have that? And if not, the next rep may have something a little better. Getting in a few more backlist titles in ones and twos may be important to the publisher (it *certainly* is to the author), and he may try to make it important to his sales rep, but it is of no great moment to the bookseller.

The fact is that selling the backlist in the manner demanded by the present distribution system *does* impose an unpleasant burden on the sales rep. It *does* take a great deal of time. It *can* be tedious for both rep and bookseller. And it *doesn't* do a very good job of selecting the titles with somewhat better sales prospects from the entire list. As a result, the sale of the backlist is extremely sensitive to the effort invested in it by the sales force and, hence, to the supervision and motivation contributed by sales management. The sales rep who checks stock whenever he is in a store, takes the time to suggest a few additional titles on each occasion, and diplomatically presses for more favorable display will be rewarded by getting far more than his proper share of backlist business.

One of the penalties of using a commission sales force of independent entrepreneurs is that they almost unanimously refuse to spend any time on selling the backlist—except for the truly outstanding titles that can be handled in a few moments. Publishers who use commission reps find that their backlist sales suffer drastically as a result; and, in fact, fewer titles survive to make the backlist.

□ *It is interesting to hear some publishers who sell through commission reps complain that "we can't seem to build a backlist. We seem to publish the wrong books." Frequently, they publish a mix of titles similar to those of publishers (with different sales forces) who do build a backlist. Obviously, you don't increase average life expectancy if you're too quick with euthanasia.*

But even with a proprietary sales force, the members of which are, within rather broad limits, prepared to do what management asks, the cost in time and drudgery is not the only selling difficulty. Even more than in the case of the frontlist, the publisher must cope with the sales reps' own prejudices and limited knowledge.

Even if the sales rep were willing to go through each title on the backlist, the bookseller would not permit it, so the rep must choose a fraction of the titles to discuss. Even a quick survey of sales of individual titles by territory will reveal that the top titles, perhaps four or five, will be the same in every territory, but after that, the ranking of titles varies from one to another. And a little closer study will show that the variation in sales corresponds not to the nature of the territory but to the nature of the sales representative.

If you talk to the sales rep, you will discover that he happens to like, or perhaps is simply more aware of, particular backlist titles. They are the ones he tends to suggest to booksellers, and the fact that they sell well in his territory confirms his judgment. Another rep chooses other titles, with the same result. Imagine Kellogg allowing one sales rep to push backlist sales of corn flakes rather than Rice Krispies because he likes corn flakes or has never tasted Rice Krispies, without any regard for the public's taste in breakfast cereals! When distribution-by-negotiation prevailed in the food industry, that is exactly what happened.

This subjective influence of the sales rep seriously affects sales. Some publishers, conscious of how much they are at the mercy of the awareness of each sales rep, go to elaborate lengths to review backlist titles at sales conferences so the reps will feel confident in suggesting more of them to the bookseller.

The weakening sale per title on a large backlist can be softened by a large sales force. Selling to any one bookstore account may not be more efficient (though the rep can sell more by visiting more often), but since each rep has a slightly different backlist in mind, more titles get at least the minimum orders necessary to keep them alive.

Within the disorder and confusion of this backlist selling by negotiation, the truly outstanding titles do reasonably well, depending on the sales force, though never as well as they should. Titles one level below "outstanding" suffer terribly. Below that, it is strictly Russian roulette.

The cost of covering bookstore accounts is high, and because results are poor, publishers, by and large, are inclined to have a (mistakenly) low opinion of the effectiveness of bookstore coverage generally. As a result, many publishers are inclined to economize on sales reps' personal visits to bookstores. They welcome the growth of bookstore chains because a larger segment of the market can be covered by visiting one location. One often hears, "We get 80 percent of our business from 20 percent of the accounts," as justification for giving less attention to the other 80 percent of the accounts.

The publisher who is seduced into reducing his sales coverage by the idea that only a small number of accounts deserve his attention and by the lure of lower selling costs loses more than just sales. He loses a proper perception of the market, which seems to him much less elastic than it really is.

I know one large publisher ($8 million range) who saves on both fixed costs and management headaches by having another, larger publisher do his selling, warehousing, and distribution. He put it to me this way: "I get 75 percent of my sales from eight large accounts. I keep in touch with them personally. I know the sales force is not very good, but it doesn't much matter what they do because I see to it that respectable quantities go into Walden, B. Dalton, Ingram, Baker & Taylor, Brentano's, Doubleday, and a few other big ones."

That publisher fails not only to see how valuable the market outside his "eight large accounts" could be; much more seriously he fails to see what the sales in these very "eight large accounts" could be if he looked at and *beyond* them in more detail. A sales force covering the retail accounts more thoroughly would multiply the volume going through wholesalers like Ingram and Baker & Taylor. A sales force covering the branch stores would multiply the volume going through chains like Walden, B. Dalton, Brentano's, and Doubleday—*and reduce the returns!*

Because this publisher sees the market as essentially restricted and rigid, he conceives his business strategy to be limited simply to choosing better titles. And because he is concerned with the danger of wearing out his welcome in the "eight large accounts," he sees himself doing better by keeping his list small, restricting his publishing to a few carefully selected titles.

The distribution system into which each publisher must put his books is, in fact, weak, diffuse, and extremely varied in competence and responsibility, presenting a frustrating and difficult hodgepodge of problems for any publisher. And this tends to encourage a lack of patience for, or interest in, the bookseller's problems, particularly those of the smaller bookseller.

Only a few publishers are service oriented. Rarely is there a sense of urgency in replying to booksellers' queries and requests. Few publishers ship books the day, or the day after, orders arrive. Many publishers put books in the mail as late as two weeks after receiving orders; then they are subject to the further unpredictable delays of our primitive mail system. A recent survey by a California bookseller showed that more than half the orders he placed with publishers took three weeks or more to arrive, and 11 percent took more than five weeks.

Why don't publishers (in general) ship books more promptly (in general)? The principal reason is probably that they think faster service is more expensive. Not so, of course. One could argue that slow service, which results from involving more people and more steps in the process and more places for the order to sit, killing time, is likely to be more expensive than faster procedures, which are likely to be more direct. Certainly faster shipping, which is nothing more than using simpler routines that avoid the bureaucracy, should not be more expensive.

Another reason may be the general feeling that speed doesn't matter. *This is a serious misconception.* The real cost of slow shipping is not in the cost of the people or the procedures but in the cost of the result: delay in getting books to the store. Those costs are not obvious. They are rendered less obvious because, whatever the costs of delay are, they vary with every order, every title, and every circumstance. No income will be lost if a special order for a store's customer (who may have already paid for the book) is delayed a few days. The customer's unhappiness with the delay will not affect his attitude toward that publisher or that publisher's titles that he may consider buying in the future. But the delay on an order for ten copies of a current best-seller could be costly; if the store is out of stock, customers are walking into and out of the store without the copy they would buy if it were there. An order for a large number of titles is almost certain to include some that are out of stock, but how many, and which ones? My own experience suggests that the loss in sales due to the absence of titles from the store's displays is substantial, even if it varies greatly and is impossible to determine with any precision.

To the extent that the bookseller shifts his buying to the wholesaler because of the publisher's lethargic service, the penalty to the publisher may be reduced, but not by much. Every dollar of business the publisher diverts to the wholesaler costs the publisher approximately 15 cents in discount differential—15 cents directly out of profit. And if the wholesaler happens not to have the title in stock, the publisher (and the author) lose much more because the order is automatically canceled.

Another consideration is the cost of money, which is currently in the neighborhood of 20 percent annually or 0.4 percent per week. For a publisher doing $5 million worth of sales, speeding up order processing and shipping by five working days (there *are* publishers who are that slow) would reduce interest costs by $20,000.

   □ *Few top publishing executives are aware in any precise way of the speed with which orders are processed and shipped. Some publishers do keep track of how long, on the average, an invoice will sit in trays in the warehouse before it is picked, packed, and shipped. What many publishers do not observe as carefully is what happens to these orders before they appear as invoices at the warehouse to be picked. Some sales departments like to "see" orders before they are released for processing. Another common source of delay may lie in archaic credit procedures, which call up many more orders for review than necessary, or ineffective collection procedures, which result in more booksellers than necessary on the "hold" list.*

We have not even considered how much order-processing delays drive business to another publisher who may be "a pleasure to do business with," whose Italian cookbook, rose gardener's guide— whatever—may become relatively more attractive simply because its arrival is likely to be earlier and more predictable.

The value of speedier shipping in the areas in which we cannot even assign approximate numbers is likely to be several times greater than those in which we can. A publisher with sales of $5 million would probably improve profits on the order of $100,000 to $200,000 (in addition to what he would gain in goodwill) if he could reduce processing time for orders by four or five days on the average.

Any communication between bookseller and publisher on the subject of the economics of book retailing is largely restricted to the bookseller's demand for higher discounts or for the publisher to pay the postage—and the publisher's response that he can't afford it. There is no very compelling reason for the bookseller to understand the publisher's problems, but it seems elementary that the supplier would want to know more about his customers. Few publishers make any attempt to understand the retailing business, the significance of stock turnover to the store's economic well-being, the use of open-to-buy budgeting methods, or, indeed, any aspect of retail store management.

This general lack of sensitivity among publishers to the difficulties in bookselling, many of them created by the publisher, is hard to understand. One simple example, the treatment of the western bookseller, will illustrate the point. (Most publishers are in the East, but the principle applies as well to the treatment of eastern booksellers by western publishers.)

Booksellers in the western part of the United States complain that, because it frequently takes three weeks or more for books to reach them from the publisher's warehouse on the East Coast, they are being dunned for payment on some shipments before they have even unpacked the books. It is a legitimate complaint. The publisher certainly does not want to put western booksellers under more stringent credit terms than eastern booksellers, but that is the result. Virtually every publisher has computerized his billing procedures, so adjusting the date on the invoice according to the distance of the store from the publisher's warehouse is no more complicated than setting a dial. But no publisher does it.

That is not all.

The publisher establishes the retail price—the usual and *maximum* price—for each book and prints it on the dust jacket. The law forbids him to enforce it, which simply means that the bookseller is free to sell the book at a lower price. The publisher also determines the discount from the retail price that he grants the bookseller, thereby determining the maximum amount the bookseller can realize on the sale of the book. The retail price and the discount are the same whether the bookseller is in New York City, a few short miles from the publisher's warehouse, or in Los Angeles, a continent away. But the cost of shipping the books (except those going via slow U.S. mail)—a cost the bookseller must bear—is not at all the same, with the simple result that the western bookseller operates on a smaller margin than his eastern colleague.

Our system of book distribution was not planned. It did not come into being because a careful study of alternatives revealed it to be the best approach. It simply evolved as the methods for distributing other products also evolved. Actually, distribution-by-negotiation in one form or another was the forerunner of the present, more efficient methods used to sell greeting cards, baked goods, automobiles, and virtually every consumer product. Although publishers did not create the system, they tend, as all human beings do, to pretend there is logic in what exists, to find reasons that make it right because it's there.

The concept of distribution-by-negotiation—the supposed pooling of the wisdom of the rep and the bookseller—is simple, but it has a singular flaw: The concept does not work.

It does not work, most important of all, because the resulting decisions are very bad. One new book in every three bought by the stores is returned unsold. For every copy sold, another copy is remaindered as publisher's overstock. Sales are lost right and left because books that should be in the stores are simply not there. In spite of the size of the country, with a population clearly receptive to the idea of buying and owning books, one out of every three trade books sold goes to libraries, essentially outside the distribution system.

It also does not work because it is horrendously expensive, even over and above the expense of returns and lost sales. The cost of a sales force in salaries, commissions, and expenses is a huge burden for any publisher, and to that direct selling cost must be added the catalogues, the conferences, the editorial time preparing sales materials, attendance at the ABA convention, and so on.

In the negotiation process between rep and bookseller, each of them with inadequate preparation and information, chance governs at the expense of wisdom. This would probably be true even if there were unlimited time, instead of discussions being conducted with both parties on the run.

Accidental factors, which have no relation to the merits of any of the titles on the new list, influence the discussion between rep and bookseller in all sorts of ways. Much depends on the skill of the sales rep—on how he understood the presentation at the sales conference, on how well his visual exhibits are organized, on how rushed he is— and on what is happening in his personal life. How attentively is the bookseller listening? What are his immediate personal and professional problems? Which rep preceded this one and how did that negotiation go? Is the bookseller over or under his budget at this particular moment? How often is the presentation interrupted? Has the last return from the store been accepted and credited?

So, as with all the publishing industry practices that have evolved over the years and have taken on the patina of profound wisdom, the selling of books does not happen the way folklore describes it.

Suppose, at some point earlier in publishing history, every book published was presented by every sales rep to every buyer with all the pertinent facts and with enough time to give the bookseller a chance to check his records, or just to lean back, contemplate the title, and imagine the customers who would be interested. Going through the hundreds of thousands of such presentations, contemplations, and decisions would take a finite amount of time. Now imagine increasing the number of titles by 50 percent (the difference in production between 1963 and 1973). Would the sales rep talk 50 percent faster and the buyer listen and contemplate 50 percent faster?

Of course not. The only solution would be to skip some books. And the books to be skipped would be the ones that require some extra effort to explain, or those the rep doesn't understand or doesn't like, or those on the list of a publisher who has no sales force, or titles that make a pleasant buying meeting tedious, such as the lesser books on a larger publisher's list. In other words, we would have the situation that prevails *today.* And this is perhaps how it evolved.

The deadening effect of distribution-by-negotiation, the degree to which it inhibits the growth of publishing, the ways in which it reduces the importance of the book itself, can be imagined by considering how it puts a real (though subtle) ceiling on the growth of any one publisher. That ceiling is imposed by the limit on each sales rep's ability to keep a growing number of titles straight in his head and by each bookseller's patience as a listener.

This is not true of other consumer products—cereals, soap, cosmetics, house paint—where more products from one supplier tend to *increase* the sale of each item because the sales and promotion organizations can grow correspondingly and the manufacturer can reach a larger public. In books, distribution-by-negotiation *decreases* the sales potential of each title as the list grows.

The weakness of the distribution system also helps to reduce the special advantages the book is supposed to have as a communication medium. Although the book is traditionally held up as the repository of human thought and wisdom, the strong forces described earlier that have been operating in publishing in recent years have been undermining its longevity. The drive for large advance sales and the early appearance of mass market paperback editions (which promote a short sales life and early returns), the general practice of refusing to accept returns later than twelve months after publication (which encourages booksellers to kill a title at eleven months), the increasing difficulty of selling title by title as the number of titles continues to grow (forcing publishers to purge their lists to keep their catalogues and sales effort manageable)—these are among the factors that are tending to make the book, with the exception of a few titles each year, an "annual," with serious and unfortunate implications for the future of trade book publishing.

The increasingly evident short life of the book in its original (and frequently only) edition, which is soon sold as a remainder, and the early appearance of a paperback edition of any reasonably popular title encourage bookstore browsers to pass up the original edition at full price. This trend has not reached such proportions as to be obvious to everyone; nor has it affected sales dramatically enough for publishers to feel the pinch. The effect is subtle and insidious, but it is there.

The selling practices that result in excessive returns, the difficulty the publisher finds in determining printing quantities accurately, the publisher's failure to quantify the actual movement of books out of the stores as a guide to sensible reprinting—all these factors leave the publisher with overstock on many titles. After the returns signal that the short bookstore life of the typical trade title is over and the pressures on the publisher for fresh capital to invest in new titles continue, one cannot blame the publisher for converting useless warehouse stocks into useful dollars by remaindering them at a fraction of their value.

With all this confusion and uncertainty created at a ridiculously high cost, with the large number of returned copies of the more popular books, and with the pathetically low sales figures for all the rest, it is not too surprising that there is some unhappiness. The authors, the publishers, the booksellers, the wholesalers—all agree that the situation could stand improvement. It is perhaps also not surprising that they don't blame the distribution system itself but simply see it as overloaded. They believe the system could move the books if there weren't so many trying to crowd into this distribution system.

It is so widely held an article of faith that "we publish too many books" that no commentator on American publishing practice can ignore it. The complaints do not cover *all* books and *all* publishers. There are no complaints that too many medical books or engineering books are published; the perpetrators are not the professional and educational publishers. The damage is being done, it is alleged, by and to trade publishers. Publishers who avoid the book distribution system are not suffering from overproduction; it's just the ones who try to reach the public through bookstores, just the ones who use distribution-by-negotiation.

That's a bit of a giveaway in itself.

The inefficiencies of this distribution system are recognized by the participant-victims. It would be painfully hard to ignore them, and everyone smiles bravely through the pain. The publisher tends to blame the shortcomings on the bookseller, the bookseller sees the whole publishing industry at fault, and the author blames fate along with the publisher's reluctance to spend his way to the author's success. No one seems to blame the *system* itself, so the explanation that too many books are published has a deceptive plausibility.

But, except for the unmistakable strains on the distribution system and its sad performance, what support is there for the "we publish too many books" notion? Should the number of books be related in some way to the size of the educated and literate population? Should the fact that there are more people available to write and to read result in making more books available? Does available leisure time or money have anything to do with it?

How many books are "too many"? No one person is expected to read them all. If half the people looking for something to buy in a bookstore fail to find it, is that a sign that we publish too many books?

If successful author after successful author recounts how his first manuscript was turned down by many publishers before the lucky accident of his first acceptance, is that a sign that we publish too many books? And what about the writers who became discouraged after the fifth or eighth rejection, so we don't know how successful they might have been?

While comparative title statistics are unreliable, they are nevertheless interesting. In 1978, according to UNESCO, the United States published one title per 2324 inhabitants. Not bad, and better than Canada, which published one title for every 2983 Canadians. But Israel published one title per 1671 inhabitants; France, one for every 1680; Germany, one for every 1258; and nearly bankrupt Great Britain, one title for every 1542 inhabitants.

Measured by titles per capita, or titles per college graduate, or titles per level of income, we publish too *few* titles. Measured by the frustrations of our would-be authors, who have been educated to be able to express themselves in writing but cannot find publishers, and by the would-be readers educated to appreciate the printed word, who walk out of bookstores empty-handed, we certainly publish too *few* books.

In absolute numbers, the rate of new book production is unquestionably high, but certainly one cause of the high birth rate of books is their high death rate. (In human—and most other animal—societies, a high death rate is invariably accompanied by a compensatory high birth rate.) Perfectly good books are dead after three months, or six months, and almost certainly after twelve months of bookstore life. So this year's Italian cookbook (from Publisher A) replaces last year's Italian cookbook (from Publisher B), which replaced the previous year's Italian cookbook (from Publisher C)—and so with subject after subject. Each book is on the scene for one year (two if it's very lucky), and its destruction by the distribution system creates the opportunity for a successor. The new versions are usually published by someone other than the publisher of the title being replaced. The publisher of the Italian cookbook will be busy planning a child care book, a home improvement guide, and twenty other titles to replace the revenue previously supplied by his Italian cookbook and the fifteen or twenty other new titles on his list that he knows will be dead in a few months.

The simple truth is that if more of each year's lists survived, there would be considerably less pressure on each publisher to supply new titles (because the old ones would still be selling and earning money) and considerably more competition, suggesting caution in producing new titles. (In this narrow sense, one could argue that we do produce too many titles, and very wastefully.)

The need to replace titles ground to bits and discarded by the distribution system is, in a sense, another cost of distribution: financial to the publisher, psychological to the author, and social to all of us.

We are certainly entitled to better and more effective book distribution. We shall have a great deal to say about such distribution in detail in the chapter on the merchandising plan, but some of its characteristics can be summarized here.

Distribution should put books into stores in relation to their prospect for sale, which should be determined in some objective way. The risk riding on this estimate could be minimized by putting books into stores more frequently, in smaller quantities, adjustable as experience varied from prediction, instead of the present single, large indigestible advance order.

Since the publisher knows his titles and knows how well they sell elsewhere, the publisher should be responsible for selecting the titles and for their sales performance in the store, being rewarded if the results are good and punished if they are bad. This will free both sales rep and bookseller from the burden of negotiating and allow both to devote their time and energy to moving more books out of the store.

Being freed of the uncertainty of negotiation and of the need for large advance orders (knowing how many copies will go to each selling location), the publisher should produce books in quantities corresponding to actual, predictable need. Publishers' overstocks should be a fraction of what they are today or disappear altogether.

The simple change from large shipments lasting a long time in the store to small shipments lasting a short time should make the bookseller's inventory investment more productive and result in many more titles being available with the same or an even smaller investment. The same change will contribute to a reduction in the bookseller's overstock and, hence, in returns.

Since the publisher decides how many copies to put into a store on the basis of some objective measure of sales expectations, and he sells only a few copies at a time, a time limit on the eligibility for returns makes no sense. If that is eliminated, and remaindering is sharply reduced, the pattern of terminating the sales life of a book at eleven months should be broken, and each title should go on selling for a much longer time. The possible effect of a paperback reprint will be strictly theoretical because the way things are rapidly moving (see the chapter on mass market publishing), there won't be very many paperback reprints. And even if the reprint publisher remained willing, the hardcover publisher would be enjoying the continued sale too much to consider it.

These suggestions no doubt seem utopian. They seem absolutely wild to most publishers and booksellers, who have grown up in the present system and find it hard to imagine a different life. But it is not in the least impractical, as the fuller discussion in the merchandising plan chapter will demonstrate. It is simply an application to books of what has already taken place, with spectacular results, in other industries. Fortunately, these suggestions do not require an entire industry to agree to change its ways. It is much better done by a single enterprising publisher, whose immediate success will cause others to rush to follow. Hallmark did not wait for the industry when greeting cards moved from distribution-by-negotiation to a merchandising plan. Who remembers the greeting card publishers who failed to follow?

Perhaps more publishers would look for ways to improve their own position in book distribution if they were more aware of how competitive publishing truly is, and of how important it is not to drift with whatever may be the industry tide.

How competitive is book publishing? Very.

Except in the obvious, but relatively rare, confrontations when publishers are forced to bid against each other for original or reprint publishing rights (at levels occasionally reaching into the millions of dollars), publishing is considered, popularly and within the industry, relatively noncompetitive. Where competition is acknowledged, it is assumed to be in acquiring authors. Between the open auction, in which there is no question that the decision is being made strictly on the basis of money, and the assumed idyllic, spiritual relationship between author and publisher, with no crass material intrusions, everyone knows that there is a whole range of situations in which money is of some importance to the author in his decision of where to go, or where, for that matter, to stay. Competition for authors is certainly increasing as the activity of authors' agents tends to reduce author-publisher relations more and more to a matter of simple dollars.

In the competition for authors, the publisher may pay high advances and may advertise the outstanding titles—his lead books— heavily (with the author's picture prominent in the ads) to show how well he supports important authors, and he may lure editors with a following of important authors from other publishing houses.

The laws of copyright—which give the publisher of any title the exclusive right to sell that title and free him from the danger that anyone else can offer that title once the author has signed over the rights—tend to obscure the fact that competition for authors is only the beginning.

The competition among publishers that is far more critical to their success (and of which many in publishing tend to be blissfully unaware) is the competition for the bookstore's buying dollar and shelf space. Publishers in general fully understand the need to get books into the stores. What is not fully understood by many, however, is the effect one publisher's success has on another's prospects—and the effect success in the bookstore has on the competition for authors.

Back in the middle of the 1950s, at the height of the reorganization and expansion of the Doubleday sales effort, I attended a dinner meeting in Los Angeles of the booksellers of Southern California. During the cocktail period before dinner, I was taken aside by an author whose latest book, number seven on the best-seller list, had been published by an important New York publisher. He was obviously very upset.

"I've been touring California for the past two weeks at my own expense to promote my book," he said. "Everywhere I go, I see Doubleday books. In every little town and in every little bookstore. I have to plead to get a store to take my book because my publisher did not manage to get it in. My book is on the best-seller list only because I worked myself into a frazzle to get it into the stores. Yet Doubleday books of almost no importance and no public recognition are everywhere. I don't want to be published by Doubleday, but I want to be read. What is an author like me supposed to do?"

That author was unusual because of his intimate knowledge of the bookstore situation. Most authors may feel happy or unhappy with their publisher's performance, but very few really know what is happening in the field.

Space in bookstores is limited. The publisher who gets his books in is, to some degree at least, leaving less space for his competitors. Prime space—tabletops near the entrance, eye-level shelf space—is even more limited. The attention span of bookstore clerks is similarly finite. If they are conscious of some current titles and recommending them, there are other titles that are being ignored.

There is a definite limit to each store's budget, whether it is formal, as in department stores, or informal, as in a personal bookshop. In each case, whatever portion any one publisher takes of a store's available purchasing funds leaves less for those who follow.

This sales competition does not send up signals, like winning a rights auction or a contract-signing ceremony with a best-selling author who has just left another publisher. The only signals are subtle: getting fewer titles into a store through advance orders (which is not likely to be noticed by the publisher); getting a smaller advance sale on a lead book (if it is noticed, it will be explained by "they are not buying heavily this season"); returns coming back earlier than they might have (which will evoke a comforting generalization such as "stores are looking for turnover this year"); and slow payment of invoices ("all retailers are pressed for cash").

The point is that the publisher does not know whether *all* publishers are experiencing these subtle signals *to the same degree.* Are his books being returned early because the store needs cash to buy someone else's titles? Is his advance sale lower because others have gotten more of their titles in? Is payment to him slower because the store is more concerned about keeping its account current with another publisher?

Publishing *is* a very competitive business. It will become more so as publishers become more conscious of the many areas of largely unsuspected competition. This consciousness will be accelerated by the entrance of mass market publishers into trade publishing. All the elements of competition—which seem so subtle in trade publishing, like competition for space and for better display—are front and center in mass market publishing, so mass market publishers come into the trade sales arena with some "street" savvy that the more traditional publishers lack.

Distribution is not book publishing's only problem, but it is the most important, and the rewards for improving it are too great to be estimated. Fortunately, they are rewards not for the publisher alone, but for the author and the book buyer as well.

4

The Book Retailer

Little Help from the Publisher

RETAILING, the last step in the distribution chain, makes the product available to the ultimate consumer.

□ *One of the comforting things about the book business, financially speaking, is the large number of books bought but never read. I've heard estimates, and I believe them, that unread books may run as high as 50 percent of the books purchased. It's comforting to those whose livelihood depends on publishing, because it suggests that lack of leisure time or competition from TV may be less of a constraint on book buying than people imagine. Available shelf space in the home may be more of a factor than time or money.*

A retailer obviously buys his stock at lower prices than those at which he sells it, and the difference is supposed to cover his costs and yield a profit. He does more than simply bring the product conveniently closer to the consumer. He selects the styles, the shapes, the flavors, the price levels, that will appeal to the people who frequent (or whom he would like to have frequent) his store. He does not do this narrowly, because customers want to be free to choose, and he wants them to expect much to choose from in his store.

Although the retailer cannot dictate his customers' taste in clothes or furniture or food or books, he wants them to feel that his preliminary selection has made their final selection easier.

As his income is the difference between what he pays and what he charges, he must buy so that the difference is as large as possible. If he chooses well and his goods sell quickly, he has the money to use over and over again, acquiring for himself over and over again that difference between his cost and his price.

The chief concern of any retailer is to have the right merchandise available. Other things matter, of course. Sales will be better if his store is well known, if he makes shopping in it pleasant and attractive, and if he demonstrates a desire to be helpful. But the most important ingredient in his success will be his inventory, which will also be his largest financial investment. Success will depend on how well his merchandise attracts customers and creates sales and on how much it costs to maintain that inventory.

The bookseller's need in this respect depends on a number of things, including his clientele. An airport bookshop can survive very nicely with fewer titles, but it must have the currently popular and easily recognizable titles in ample supply. A neighborhood bookshop, with the same customers coming by regularly, needs many more titles to encourage them to return soon. In this case, depth of supply (the number of copies of each item) is much less important; because the rate of sale is lower and more predictable, there is usually sufficient time to reorder before running out.

The problem for the retailer is to have an inventory broad enough to generate sales, but not so broad that it costs too much to maintain. If another dollar invested in inventory will return that dollar plus an acceptable percentage of profit over the interest on the money invested, then inventory should be added.

Looking at the same problem from another direction, the retailer needs to decide which items to buy with his available working capital, and how many of each he should have in stock in order to extract the maximum benefit from that investment. In considering how many of a given item to keep on hand, he will consider not only how popular it will be with his customers, but how frequently he can practically and economically reorder it and how long it will take to receive a fresh supply.

The effective use of the dollars invested in merchandise is measured in at least two ways, markup and turnover.

Markup is a measure of the *value* of sales. If a $10 item is bought at 40 percent discount, costing the retailer $6, the markup is 67 percent—the percentage by which the inventory investment ($6) is increased to arrive at the retail price ($10). If the retailer can manage to buy at higher discounts and earn higher markups, he will be making his inventory investment more productive.

Turnover is the measure of the *speed* of sales, how often the retailer is able to reinvest his inventory dollars in the course of a year. If he buys and sells a $10 item and reinvests the $6 cost three times in a year, that inventory investment has a turnover (or "stock turn") of 3. The retailer has earned his $4 markup three times (for a total of $12) on the same $6 investment. The more "turns" the retailer can get from his investment by choosing merchandise his customers want, the more productive his inventory investment.

Neither markup nor turnover alone is a complete indicator of the retailer's buying success. He could be buying merchandise at a tremendous discount that sells very slowly so that the resulting margin does not even equal current interest rates. He could be buying merchandise that sells very quickly, but at such a low markup as to be hardly worth the trouble.

A much better indicator is his annual gross margin, the markup multiplied by the turnover. A markup of 67 percent (a discount of 40 percent) and a turnover of 3 means that the retailer is producing $2 of "gross margin" each year for every dollar he has invested in inventory. That is, every dollar he has invested in inventory will "produce" $2 above the cost of the merchandise itself, from which the retailer can pay his expenses (such as rent, salaries) and realize his profit, if any. Gross margin per dollar of inventory investment is the most important index of the effective use of the retailer's working capital.

The nature of book retailing does not really differ from the nature of retailing in general. However, because of the special complexities that apply to books to a greater degree than to other merchandise, bookselling is much more difficult. The most pertinent of the special complexities of book retailing are:

1. *The number of items the retail store is expected to keep in stock is much greater and the average life of each item far shorter for books than for most other products.*

Presumably there are approximately 40,000 different titles published each year, of which perhaps 20,000 are of sufficiently broad interest to be eligible for bookstore sale. The number of titles (including backlist) available in a bookstore for sale at any one time will vary, depending upon the store, from 4000 to 40,000 or more. (The B. Dalton store on Fifth Avenue in New York has *over 100,000 titles.*)

Obviously, the percentage of the approximately 20,000 new titles that will be purchased by any retail bookstore will vary accordingly. Of the titles purchased, it is safe to say that 90 percent will not survive a year; that is to say that within twelve months they will either have been cleared from the shelves or, if still on the shelves, will have no prospect of being sold. And among this 90 percent, probably half will not sell a single copy after the first six months.

This can result in the equivalent of a complete change in merchandise assortment as often as three times a year in a small bookstore or once every three years in a large bookstore. Outside of books, this might happen only in the most high fashion merchandise. It multiplies the number of stocking decisions and increases their complexity.

2. *The information available to the bookseller on which he can base his decision on whether to buy is less substantial than that available to the retailer of any other product.*

Customarily, the bookseller will only see the book jacket or paper cover and hear a sixty-second description from a publisher's representative that is certainly inadequate and frequently incorrect. A very few books may be presented to the bookseller in a more elaborate manner, but he is aware of many others only through a short catalogue description or an advertisement in *Publishers Weekly.*

3. *The average value of each title in the store's inventory is probably lower than the average value of each item in any other retailing situation.*

It is true that books are generally more expensive than, for example, candy bars or cans of soup. However, of the 4000 or 40,000 titles in a bookstore, probably 90 percent are in most stores in only one or two copies, so the total inventory value of each item (what retailers call a stock keeping unit, an SKU), for which the retailer must keep records, make decisions, etc., is extremely low.

4. *The bookseller must deal with a larger number of suppliers operating under a greater variety of rules and trade customs than any other retailer.*

A small bookstore may buy books from 100 to 150 publishers plus two or three wholesalers; a large bookstore will deal with as many as 400 publishers. Each publisher has (deliberately) different discount schedules, conditions for returning unsold books, terms of payment, etc. The service among publishers varies widely and erratically, as does the quality of their customer service departments.

5. *The booksellers' own suppliers create competition unknown in any other area of retailing.*

The two most important forms of this activity are the remainder, when a book in its original edition is suddenly made available at a price approximately one fifth the original price, and the paperback, when a paperbound edition of the original book is widely distributed at a much lower price. In neither case is the bookseller likely to be informed in advance, but he could not deal with this profusion of information on 20,000 titles annually if he were.

6. *The bookseller has less market information per dollar of sales than any other retailer.*

In the case of new titles, there is virtually no market information because the bookseller buys them weeks, and sometimes months, before any market reaction is possible. On a very few such titles (e.g., those by known authors), it is possible to draw (questionable) market inferences from the record of previous titles.

In the case of the backlist (already published titles), the rate of sale is usually too low (six copies a year is better than average, even for a large bookseller) to make a reliable judgment about the actual market.

7. *The clerical costs and burdens are higher in bookselling per dollar of sales than in any other branch of retailing.*

Because of the large number of suppliers, the number of orders to be placed, shipments to be received, invoices to be processed and paid, the confusion of terms, the large number of titles on which records must be kept, etc., the necessary clerical procedures are extraordinarily complex.

8. *The bookseller is the only retailer whose merchandise is available free of charge to anyone who wants to go to a little trouble.*

While it is true that the public library system is not convenient to everyone and limited budgets restrict the levels of service available, libraries do supply some of the public's need for books, particularly when the price is high or the book is obscure enough that the customer may assume he is unlikely to find it in a bookstore.

The bookseller does have one advantage not generally available to other retailers. Most publishers permit the return for credit, within one year, of any books that remain unsold. The bookseller pays the cost of shipping the books back to the publisher (as he has previously paid the cost of receiving them from the publisher); some publishers apply other restrictions and penalties. The return privilege reduces the risk of buying books before they are published, before they are reviewed, and sometimes before the writing has been completed. The return privilege plays an important part in distribution-by-negotiation, and we discuss it in detail in Chapter 5.

Retail bookselling has never had the glamour of high profits. It is supposed to attract people who "love books" rather than people who love money—a disturbing thought in itself. There have been a number of highly successful *and* profitable book retailers, but they have, until recently, been the exception. Today the growth of the bookstore chains, among other indications, suggests that bookselling *can* be profitable (see Appendix A).

Of all the difficulties confronting the bookseller, the most important one is inventory control. It is sadly true that the bookstore is a bottleneck, on one side of which many titles are produced by publishers, and on the other side of which many titles are wanted by readers. On both sides there is frustration, but opening the bottleneck is not a simple matter. Because of the sheer number of titles (even in smaller stores), the rapidly changing list of titles in stock, and the constantly shifting levels of stock, title by title, control of the inventory is not possible without some sort of system.

It is hard to keep all those thousands of titles in mind, and the bookseller does remarkably well with the subjective methods available to him. Yet there are frequent complaints that consumers cannot find the titles they want in the bookstore. The complaints are justified, but it is not the bookseller's fault. He spends more effort and thought on the stocking of his shelves than on any other single activity.

The answer is universally accepted to be "inventory control" in the retail store, but genuine attempts at inventory control are hard to find. Many people in bookselling talk about inventory control when they are really addressing only the informational needs of an inventory system. Control means much more: It means making the decisions to achieve the desired result. Gathering information is the first step, but only the first step: What is in stock? What is on order? Are the discounts on the publisher's invoice correct? Which books are close to return deadlines? What should the credit be for the return? And on and on.

The bookseller must keep track of the particular discount schedules, the restrictions on returns, and the other rules of each of the hundreds of publishers with whom he deals so that he is sure to order at least twelve assorted books from Publisher A, fifteen assorted from Publisher B, etc., to avoid buying books at unfavorable discounts. It may even be sensible strategy to *order only* twelve assorted from Publisher A, even if eighteen books seem to be needed at the moment, so that another economical order can be placed reasonably soon.

As each order is placed, the discount at which the publisher will bill each title must be calculated or it will be difficult to check the invoice when the books arrive. As books come in, they must be noted in some way according to the publisher's return policy to be sure they are not held beyond the deadline.

The books on any order rarely arrive together. If the order is for new titles, the publisher ships the books as they are ready. If it is from the backlist, it is virtually certain, except for the rare publisher with an adequate *publisher's* inventory control system, that some of the titles will be out of stock and will trickle in as they are reprinted.

As each shipment arrives, individual books must be checked against the invoice to be sure that they agree. If the invoice includes any books not in the package, the publisher must be charged back for the missing books and the charge-back explained. The shipment also has to be checked against the original order to be sure that the books received were actually ordered and that they were billed at the correct retail price and the correct discount. In the case of any discrepancy, a charge-back and further correspondence may be necessary. Since publishers frequently change retail prices and/or discounts without adequate notice (which would be, admittedly, hard to transmit to the entire trade), the charge-backs and correspondence may simply cause a futile and time-wasting exchange, but they are unavoidable in the present distribution system.

When it comes to returning books, the credit given often depends upon the discount at which they were purchased. In order to get full credit, the bookseller must find the original invoice and supply the publisher with the necessary details.

In addition to placing orders and making returns, the bookseller has other pressing clerical concerns. If he is a good businessman, using his cash resources to their limit, he needs to project all purchases into the month of their probable delivery so he can foresee the amount of money he will need, month by month, to meet his bills. (He wants to have enough cash, but only just enough, because excess cash is an expensive thing to have around.) These projections change as publishers postpone books or inform the bookseller that various titles he ordered are out of stock.

The bookseller also needs to know his stock at any given moment, without actually poring over the displays, so that he can, for instance, answer customers' queries and choose titles to flesh out an order to benefit from discounts. He should know what has been sold, how it relates to the stock level, and how close he is (if it can be calculated) to running out of any important title.

His records must also show the value of the books he has sold so that he can calculate the taxes on his profit to the satisfaction of the IRS. When booksellers try to adjust their inventory levels to the anticipated sales, month by month (chasing the almighty stock turn), or control levels of stock by subject category, inventory information must also be available for those purposes.

Above all, the bookseller must buy wisely. With the recent rise in interest rates, buying with an eye to how quickly each item will sell is becoming increasingly important for all retailing. More than ever, the bookseller must buy more accurately, more frequently, and in smaller quantities.

Permitting the attraction of high discounts to influence a buying decision unduly has always been tempting for booksellers. But with an interest rate of 20 percent or thereabouts, money costs very close to 2 percent per month. That translates into approximately one percentage point of discount per month. This means that a bookseller who buys at the very tempting discount of 45 percent, but fails to sell the book in five months, now has the book effectively at the not as attractive discount of 40 percent; if it continues to wait for an interested browser, it is rapidly becoming a costly buying mistake.

It is much more important, faced with the high cost of money, to turn merchandise over more quickly than to buy at an attractive discount. An essential condition to rapid stock turnover is the right to return books and to substitute other titles that will turn faster.

A publisher who restricts the right to return and offers high discounts to induce the retailer to buy more is throwing money away in the case of a thoughtful retailer; he will be buying according to his judgment of how quickly the copies will sell rather than (within limits) the attraction of the discount. The bookseller will find a publisher's guarantee of turnover (see the chapter on the merchandising plan) much more attractive than a discount as the implications of the high cost of money become more evident.

The proper mix and level of book inventory is the most important ingredient in increasing sales and improving store profits for two reasons:

1. Inventory is the store's biggest single cost; even slight variations have dramatic effects on profits.

2. A store's merchandise is the most important reason that customers walk into it; gaps in a store's merchandise are the most important reason some customers walk out empty-handed and others never walk in.

If someone walks into a store and fails to find the book he wants, the bookseller has lost a sale, which has cost him the markup on that sale *plus* some of the customer's confidence, which may result in his looking elsewhere in the future. Whether the lost sale is a title the browser specifically wanted or one that he was not even aware he would have bought had he seen it does not matter. It is a lost sale. If the bookseller does not have the title the customer wants, it does very little good to have twenty-five copies of a title he does not want. *At that moment,* the bookseller would be better off with twenty-four copies of that other title and one copy of the title this customer was unable to buy.

Obviously, a larger assortment of titles would result in more sales.

But if a larger assortment requires a larger investment, it may cancel out the advantage of more sales. The object is to offer more titles without increasing investment unduly. The customers served by each store are different—in number, income, taste, and in educational level. Therefore, the problem for the bookseller is how, within his limited investment, to make the best selection of titles for *his* store, for *his* potential customers. This is called *inventory control,* and the scorecard for performance is called *inventory productivity.*

The bookseller needs to know, not only what and when to add to inventory, but also which titles are dead and when to flush titles partially or completely out of the store. Unfortunately, publishers' customs and the bookseller's own constant battle against the encroaching jungle of confusion make it easier for the bookseller to deal with the cutting process than with the adding process.

The bookseller flushes books (frequently prematurely) almost entirely by exercising his right to return unsold books for credit, and more specifically, within twelve months, as required by most publishers. The bookseller cannot permit himself to lose track of what to return and when. No matter how careless his other business habits may be, he can survive; but failure to make returns accurately and carefully will surely put him out of business.

It is probably not an exaggeration to say that, for 90 percent of the stores (including, and perhaps above all, the chains), 90 percent of the inventory purging decisions are determined automatically by the publishers' returns policy. If the publishers were to reduce the deadline from twelve months to nine or ten months, the returns would be made earlier and stores (and publishers) would simply lose more sales; but the decisions on what to remove from retail inventory would still be dictated by the returns policy, not by any attempt (in the classic textbook manner) to balance, for each title, the cost of possible lost sales versus the cost of keeping it in stock.

Because the decisions to purge are made almost automatically, with little need for reflection or analysis, the initial book selections become the bookseller's most important deliberate management decisions in the operation.

In retailing generally, it is clear that precise control of the merchandise is essential to the success of the enterprise, and the methods for operating such controls are well developed and widely understood. Described broadly, these methods consist of determining the rate of sale of each item in the inventory (each SKU), how often reorders should be placed (based on delivery time and the cost of being out of stock), and the size of an order (based on the cost of ordering versus the cost of holding inventory). Once in place, such an inventory control system is continually adjusted according to changes in the rate of sale (or known seasonal aspect), altering the timing or size of orders to make the inventory investment as profitable as possible. For the retailer who hates arithmetic, IBM has the whole thing built into computer programs that keep the inventory system and the inventory automatically updated.

The only trouble with these systems and with the IBM computer program is that *they do not work for books.* Sad, because the need for inventory control is greater and the payoff from a working system would be much more dramatic for books than for most consumer merchandise. It is not just that these systems do not presently work for books, they will *never* work for books.

□ *That is why the discussion of inventory control among booksellers and in articles in* Publishers Weekly *all deal with "inventory record-keeping," not with control at all. The matters usually dealt with are whether records should be kept on index cards or in a computer, whether sales should be recorded at the cash register or by counting stock and subtracting, and so on. They all avoid the key question in inventory control: By what rules should the decisions be made to determine what titles should be in the store, how many copies should be there, when should each title be reordered, how should inventory levels be adjusted title by title, and when should a title be returned? (See Appendix B.)*

These inventory control systems cannot work in an individual bookstore quite simply because the sales in any one bookstore, title by title, cannot be usefully predicted by any statistical method. Mathematical methods depend on a sufficient frequency of sale of each SKU for the figures to detect the pattern of sale from which to make a prediction. This is possible, even theoretically, for no more than 5 or 10 percent, at most, of the titles in any bookstore.

Without the projection of future sales, the systems are no more reliable than the subjective gut feeling of the store manager; actually, they are less so, because the system removes the element of experienced "feel," the value of which every bookseller knows well.

□ *I have to hedge this statement just a little. Although inventory records cannot predict mathematically, booksellers who have installed precise record-keeping systems have usually improved the store's profitability and inventory control. This is because the records focused the bookseller's attention on important details and enabled him to be more aware of what was happening: how close Title A was to being out of stock, how long it had been since a copy of Title B was sold, etc. Though it is a tremendous step forward from simple chaos and usually results in improvement, it works because of the improved and more orderly information base, not because record-keeping provides the decision rules essential to real inventory control.*

Among the 4000 or 40,000 titles in any bookstore, most (possibly 75 percent) will sell fewer than twelve copies a year—one copy per month, on the average. It would take any mathematical system operated in a single store about four or five years to identify a title that is averaging a sale of one copy a month, and it could only do so if the title were kept in stock at all times *and* if the rate of sale remained constant for five years. If a book is selling very well, the inability of an individual bookstore to predict sales with any accuracy is less important. Sales may go from fifty a week down to twenty and up to sixty-five and then back to fifty, but these fluctuations will not seriously affect the theoretically correct stocking policy or inventory levels.

Most of the books that sell at respectable rates, unfortunately, have a short sales life. If mathematical systems were applied to these few best-sellers, they would supply answers long after the titles were dead and beyond help. The sad fact of the bookseller's inventory is that most of the titles that sell fast enough for statistical prediction to work don't sell long enough for it to do any good, and most of the ones that sell long enough don't sell fast enough.

An inventory control system would be frustrated by other factors. One of these is knowing precisely how long it will take to receive an order, since this is a key factor in determining reorder point and quantity. As any bookseller can tell you, wearily and fatalistically, when he sends an order to a publisher—any publisher—he has no idea when (or even whether) the books will arrive. It may be three weeks or three months; publishers' performances vary greatly and are unpredictable. Moreover, it may not be economically sound for the bookseller to place the order when his control system suggests because the publisher's discount schedule may require grouping several titles to avoid penalties.

The unhappy conclusion is inescapable: Title by title, store by store, inventory control by mathematical prediction is simply not a practical possibility for books.

As an alternative to or as a framework for title-by-title control, a budgeting method of controlling *dollar* inventory levels (not titles) is advocated by many, including the American Booksellers Association in

A Manual on Bookselling. What this method does, essentially, is to
force the dollar inventory level to conform to the annual turnover
target at all times. It does not tell the bookseller which *books* to have,
simply how many dollars of inventory he should have. To quote the
Manual: "Remember that if you want to get four turns a year, the
stock you have on hand at the beginning of the month should not
exceed the sales you plan to make during the next three months."

This approach assumes that turnover can be maintained at a steady
rate, which is almost certainly not possible and probably not even
desirable. A turnover of four is *not* the result of a steady rate of
turnover each hour, each day, each week, and each month, a precise
necessary fraction of four each time, totaling four at the end of the
year. Accountants recognize that sales vary throughout the year.
Turnover will also vary. If the bookseller follows an inventory plan
that requires steady turnover, he will lose sales in the slow periods (his
customers will have too little choice) and he will be wasting
investment in the fast periods (he will have more stock than he needs).

Budgeting and turnover are a great deal more complicated.
Actually, the turnover that is desirable, or even possible, will be
influenced by two main factors. One is *rate of sale.* A title or category
selling ten copies a week can be made to turn its inventory value
faster (with an equal risk of lost sales) than a title or category selling
one copy a week. The second factor is the *standard deviation of the
rate of sale.* If two titles each average ten copies a week, the one with
sales ranging between eight and twelve can be made to turn faster
than the one ranging between four and sixteen, even though the
average sale is the same.

Attempting to get each title or each category or each month to
conform to the *average* turnover—a simplistic application of the
concept of turning stock—will probably lead to less than optimal
results. Averages can be traps. It is said (with no basis in fact, I am
sure) that when the Brooklyn Bridge was built, it was set high enough
to clear the average height of the masts on the ships that had to pass
under it to get to the Brooklyn Navy Yard. As a result, half the ships
had their masts knocked off.

Although, as we have seen, the bookseller cannot hope to predict
the future rate of sale title by title, that does not mean it cannot be
done. By recording the sale of a single title in sixty reasonably similar
stores, it is possible to learn in one month almost the same information
an individual bookseller can learn by accumulating a five-year history.
But the bookseller is not in a position to gather that information. Only
the publisher (or a retail chain with enough outlets) is. The publisher's

reps are in and out of hundreds of stores every month.

Since an individual bookseller cannot get this statistical title-by-title guidance, he is forced to rely on general indicators, like rate of turnover of total inventory. High turnover does not necessarily mean higher total profit. Frequently the reverse is true. Narrowing the inventory to achieve higher turnover may cost more in sales than it gains in better use of investment. The reasons for high or low turnover are more important than the rate itself. And although watching the overall rate of turnover is useful, a valuable refinement is the rate of turnover by category or subjects. This tells the bookseller how well he is matching his inventory to the interests of his clientele.

Whatever the overall turnover rate, there will be different turnover rates for different categories of books. These rates will depend on a number of things in addition to the two mathematical factors already mentioned. One is certainly the nature of the community and the interests of a store's clientele, which may be biased toward particular subjects or types of books, resulting in higher sales in those categories and probably a faster turnover. A category may also do well simply because it is displayed better or because a knowledgeable clerk recommends books in that area.

The decision of the bookseller to make the assortment broad or narrow and his skill in choosing the titles will affect the turnover for each separate category. Failing to choose the most appropriate books on gardening or matching their quantities poorly to the probability of sale, or a combination of these factors, will result in a lower turnover rate for gardening books even in a community with an intense interest in gardens.

One general factor affecting turnover may be a store's policy on maintaining inventory levels or frequency of ordering. For example, if a store tends to have large stocks of the more popular titles, which seems logical enough, turnover will be reduced. A store that maintains fairly low stocks of the more popular titles and orders more frequently is likely to have a higher rate of turnover.

Turnover can be improved at the expense of sales volume by narrowing the breadth of the assortment, eliminating the titles that sell more slowly. Having only the few most popular gardening titles will result in a high turnover in that category, even though it also results, of course, in reduced sales volume and possibly reduced profit.

Clearly, it is the relative turnover among categories rather than absolute turnover that is significant. The turnover in all categories will not be identical, and it would be foolish to try to make it so. The bookseller should not sacrifice breadth of choice by eliminating categories simply because they have a slow turnover.

However, a low turnover rate can be the symptom of a problem: The range of titles in that category may be too broad or the ordering pattern should be changed to a more frequent one so that stocks can be kept at a lower level without narrowing the range. A high turnover rate for a category suggests that sales can be increased by broadening the assortment of titles since it is a reasonable assumption that a high turnover rate indicates that sales are being lost either by books being out of stock too often or by a failure to offer greater variety.

Without trying to bring all categories to the same level of turnover, management should examine the situation to see whether to accelerate the turnover rate where it is low and slow the turnover rate by adding titles (not by increasing quantities) where it is high.

Examining turnover by category is one of the best ways for a bookseller to check his subjective judgment about how well the store is using its money, about what should be in inventory. Obviously, when a store is first opened, the bookseller has to make completely subjective decisions on how to stock it. These decisions may be laboriously made title by title or (preferably) consciously by subject categories first and titles second; the result in either case is that the variety of titles in any store has a certain character, reflecting the conscious or unconscious judgment of the bookseller about the nature of the traffic he expects.

The actual traffic, as it differs from this a priori model, will influence future buying decisions and gradually change the balance among subject categories and their relative representation in the inventory. This will happen more surely and swiftly if the bookseller keeps track of sales by category rather than by title, for the interests of a store's clientele are much more difficult to discern in the profusion of individual titles than by subject categories.

One of the minor benefits of dealing with books by category is that it is easier for the bookseller to use *substitutability* to reduce the number of titles he may need—the degree to which a customer will readily accept one book in place of another.

Obviously, it is important to stock the specific titles that have a high particular demand and therefore very low substitutability. The penalty for being out of stock of a given title goes down as more customers are happy to accept something else, providing titles that can be substituted for it are in the store.

Although substitutability relieves, to some degree, the pressure on the bookseller to have a wide range of titles available, breadth of assortment remains a major goal of any well-run bookstore.

As we have pointed out, turnover is one dimension, and markup another, of the measure of good inventory policy. Breadth of assortment is an important third dimension. The greater the variety the bookseller can offer, the more likely it is that something will be bought. Breadth need not be exclusively in books. In some ways, adding other merchandise, such as greeting cards or gifts, seems to make it easier to avoid reducing turnover rates. But even if a retailer adds merchandise other than books to increase traffic and sales per square foot, there is always the question of how much the assortment of books itself can be broadened.

Breadth of assortment, desirable for any retailer, has an even greater importance for the bookseller. The purchase of a book (with some exceptions) eliminates that particular buyer from the potential market for that book (even though word of mouth *may* create other buyers). A title assortment, therefore, gradually loses sales potential within the more or less static circle of customers, however large, for that store, as they each choose the titles that interest them. The titles with the greatest potential sales are the ones sold earliest. Therefore, the rate of decay of sales, if the assortment is not rejuvenated with new stock, is probably logarithmic. The more frequently an assortment is restored with *new titles* as well as replenished with the more popular sellers, the greater the sales per dollar of inventory or per square foot of selling space.

Some years ago, Doubleday ran an experiment in the ten largest supermarkets in Washington, D.C., with about twenty of the best-selling titles of two leading trade publishers. The results could be (and were) predicted. There were good sales the first week, moderate sales the second, only a trickle the third, and virtually no sales thereafter.

The reason (like all good reasons) is fairly simple. The traffic in a supermarket is overwhelmingly *repeat* traffic. Some return more frequently than others, but almost all shop in a regular pattern. The supermarket is visited by a very large percentage of its customers each week and by almost all of them every two weeks. The person who has browsed the book rack one week—perhaps buying something, perhaps not—may glance over it the second week as well. If the rack looks essentially the same, he is less likely to give it any time the third week and even less thereafter because he thinks he knows what is there and he has already decided that he does not want what he has not bought, and he does not need additional copies of whatever he bought.

That experiment, back in the 1950s, cost Doubleday a few hundred dollars. A more recent failure, demonstrating the same principle, cost (according to *Publishers Weekly*) a much more spectacular $3 million to $3.5 million.

The Hanes Corporation, which had had overwhelming success selling L'eggs pantyhose, decided in 1977 or 1978 to explore applying the same techniques to the sale of paperback children's books in supermarkets. They made elaborate plans for test-marketing the idea. They hired experts in marketing, in children's literature, in book illustration, in book production, in the negotiation of reprint contracts —in just about every aspect of book selection, packaging, promotion, and sales imaginable. Publishers were eager to cooperate with Hanes. Success seemed inevitable, and many expected these "modern" merchandising methods to demonstrate the "backwardness" of the traditional booksellers.

A handsome format and a distinctive display were developed. The rights to 226 outstanding juvenile titles were acquired and 180 titles were manufactured. The program was tested in four cities—Rochester, Kansas City, Milwaukee, and Salt Lake City—sparked with prime-time television commercials and heavy space advertising. The test ran from March 1980 to 1981.

Why, after spending something like $3.5 million, did Hanes scrap the entire program? Hanes won't say, but I suspect they found that in each location, sales were great the first week, less spectacular the second, only so-so the third, and downright discouraging the fourth. Among the imposing array of experts Hanes assembled, they failed to include one who understood that books must be displayed and sold differently in a supermarket—differently from other supermarket merchandise and differently from the way books are sold in a bookstore.

Books *can* be sold successfully in supermarkets, but only if the distinctive nature of books is recognized and inventory methods adjusted accordingly. The mix of titles offered the browser must be changed often enough, approximately every two weeks, and extensively enough to maintain interest. Although the number of titles displayed at any one time may be small, frequent changes will offer the small number of book buyers among food shoppers a very large selection.

In general, if the traffic in potential customers (not just *any* human traffic) is constantly changing, the same level of sales per square foot can be achieved with fewer titles than are needed where the traffic represents multiple visits of fewer potential customers.

An airport bookstand would be foolish to strive for a broad title assortment even though the thousands of people streaming past certainly represent a broad range of interests and backgrounds. It is more important to use the limited and costly space to assure that the best-selling titles (which are *most* likely to be of interest to *most* people) are there in sufficient quantity to prevent running out rather than to catch the small percentage who would respond to a more obscure title. Besides, airport browsing time is limited.

The personal bookshop, on the other hand, could not exist on best-sellers alone. It has to have more space (which is fortunately less expensive than high-traffic space) to display a broader assortment of titles. With its fewer, more deliberate browsers, it must satisfy a greater variety of interests in a smaller number of buyers.

There is an analogy to Einstein's theory of relativity here. We are concerned with the relative movement of books and book buyers per unit of time. We can have many books passing before few buyers or few books passing before many buyers. The relative combination of the two expresses the relative likelihood of sales if the titles are reasonably well suited to the traffic. This is a *quantitative* aspect of the necessary judgment. It does not take into account the *qualitative* factors: how well the titles match the interests of the traffic, how well they are displayed, how buying is encouraged, and so on. Neither does it take into account the balance of costs against sales volume. The airport bookstand could sell more books by broadening its assortment (requiring more space), but would profits increase correspondingly? The personal bookshop can reduce its space and clerical costs by narrowing its assortment, but would profits increase?

In the long run, each retailer must discover for himself the optimal breadth of assortment that he can achieve with his sophistication in budgets, inventory control methods, etc. However, on the way to that point it may be useful to have guideposts. One such guidepost is the degree to which sales concentrate in few titles. According to the IBM study of wholesale operations generally, about 20 percent of the items account for 90 percent of the dollar sales, but in retail operations, as much as 45 percent of the items usually account for only 80 percent of the dollar sales.

□ *These IBM statistics apply, of course, to sales of consumer items in general. We do not have reliable figures specifically for the book industry. However, indications strongly suggest that the situation in the book industry is much more extreme. That is, book wholesalers do 90 percent of their dollar sales on considerably less than 20 percent of the items, and bookstores need more than 45 percent of the items to reach 80 percent of their sales.*

The number of items available in a bookstore is generally greater than the number of items in other retail stores. The spread of sale among items is also greater. The bookseller who tries to reduce his inventory problems by concentrating on a narrower range of better-selling titles is sacrificing business to convenience. The other direction is generally the right way to go. In this connection, the Book Industry Study Group revealed in its report, *Book Industry Trends—1980*, that only 5 percent of books distributed in this country are best-sellers.

Many booksellers, faced with the competition of price-cutters and remainder specialists, can testify that the attraction of a broader, fuller assortment of titles enables them to hold their own, even to gain patronage against the bargain shops. I certainly can.

Soon after I arrived at Crowell-Collier and Macmillan, the company acquired the Brentano chain of bookstores, which reported to me. That gave me an excellent chance to learn about retailing from a fine teacher, Leonard Schwartz, then president of Brentano's. Shortly after Brentano's was purchased, Korvettes opened a large store diagonally across the street and installed an impressive book department that sold at discount prices. We had to decide whether Brentano's would cut prices, perhaps only on best-sellers, to prevent Korvettes from drawing traffic away from us. We decided to stay with list prices and make Brentano's more attractive by increasing our emphasis on breadth of assortment. We were counting on Korvettes' stock being narrow, generally restricted to lower-priced titles, and it was. Brentano's sales went down for a few months after Korvettes opened and then increased to levels higher than before. It is probable that Korvettes actually attracted more book-buying traffic to the area; then many of their customers, finding the inventory thin, went across the street to Brentano's to have a better choice.

Although there is very little question of the power of a broad assortment of titles, increasing the number of titles in a store by 10 percent will not increase the store's business by 10 percent. Presumably, the titles already in the store are the more popular and salable ones, so those that have been omitted should not be expected to sell as well as those that have been included. But if we cannot expect an increase in sales proportional to the increase in the number of titles, we do know that people leave bookstores empty-handed, so we know that increased sales will result from offering the browser a wider selection.

Let us assume, for example, that a store has an average of 4000 titles and does $100,000 a year sales at retail, roughly $25 per title on the average. Let us further assume that these titles have been so carefully chosen that they represent the 4000 best of all possible titles for that store. If we add a title, we assume it will sell more slowly than the slowest of the 4000 titles presently in stock. If we expand the inventory from 4000 to 5000 titles, we should certainly not expect the additional titles to sell at the rate of $25 per year. Possibly their rate of sale would average something like $12 per title, and if we added still another 1000 titles to bring the total to 6000, the additional titles would perhaps average no more than $8 or $10 per year. As this store adds titles, one expects it to demonstrate the law of diminishing returns, in that the productivity of each title added is somewhat lower than the productivity of the titles already there.

It doesn't necessarily work that way. The addition of breadth may reach the point where it makes the store more attractive because it clearly offers the customer a much wider choice. Titles added in such a situation will actually improve the average sales rate for *all* the titles in the store. This is because the customers' perception of the availability of merchandise and the freedom of choice in the store has changed, and the store is actually drawing traffic away from competitors whose selections offer the browser fewer alternatives.

In New York, Barney's monster clothing store draws customer traffic from a wide area, attracting men who go to Barney's instead of a more accessible clothing store because they expect Barney's to offer every conceivable style, color, and size. And because Barney's has so much variety and so many items, the shoppers frequently walk out with more than they intended to buy. In books, the Brentano–Scribner–Barnes & Noble–Doubleday–B. Dalton concentration of stores on Fifth Avenue has developed a similar advantage.

Breadth of assortment may explain a now generally held belief in the book industry: The larger the bookstore, the more profitable it is. This was noted by Cheney back in 1931, though its significance was not generally appreciated at that time. If it had been, Carl K. Wilson and Lawrence Hoyt (Walden) would not have opened such tiny book operations in the 1940s. Even Brentano's and Doubleday were happy to open small branches years ago. Just a few years ago, Brentano's put the "large bookstore" theory to an interesting test in Short Hills, New Jersey, where its small branch store was doing badly. Instead of closing it, they expanded it—and put it into the black. The expectation now is that larger stores will not only bring in more sales but, surprisingly, more sales per square foot.

The key question is, of course: What is the cost of expanding the store's assortment? Is it good business to invest more money to increase the store's inventory if the additional sales will bring in a smaller return for each additional dollar invested? This is a calculation that the bookseller (or his outside accountant) can make, but I contend that an appreciable increase in the breadth of titles can be achieved in ninety-nine out of a hundred bookstores, as they are currently operated, *without adding a single dollar* to the inventory or to working capital.

In my own experience, we were able, in Gimbel's book department in Philadelphia, to double the number of Doubleday titles without increasing the store's investment a single penny. It happens that in this experiment the sales actually doubled as the number of titles doubled. One may consider these results exceptional, particularly since the Philadelphia Gimbel's was recognized at the time as having one of the best-run book departments in the United States. I will discuss the Gimbel's experiment further in Chapter 7, on the merchandising plan.

A sensitive inventory control system is necessary to double the number of titles with the same investment. But there is no question that better methods of inventory control will increase the number of titles that can be maintained within a given budget and that these additional titles will noticeably improve total sales.

Any broadening of the assortment without additional investment can have a dramatic effect upon profit because it does not increase a store's cost of money, space, personnel, insurance, etc. And most of the costs of the store's usual operation do not increase with these dollars of additional sales. For example, the figures in the Booz, Allen & Hamilton survey for the American Booksellers Association suggest that additional sales from inventory that is broadened without an increase in investment would result in an increase in profit of *54.32 cents for every dollar of additional sales;* the existing average profit is 2.5 cents per dollar of sales. Therefore, even if the addition of titles is far less spectacular than was achieved at Gimbel's and the additional sales considerably more modest, the result in increased profit is well worth the effort.

□ *Although I believe strongly in the importance of offering the customer more titles to choose from, and even more strongly in the use of statistical techniques to do this with minimum investment, breadth of inventory is not the only key to success. For example, on Eighteenth Street in New York City, Barnes & Noble has two stores facing each other across Fifth Avenue. The traffic in both stores is extremely heavy, particularly for this relatively uncrowded part of Fifth Avenue. One store has a very wide assortment, perhaps the largest in New York, and offers no bargains. It draws people who expect to find what they need, even if it is obscure. The other store has a much narrower assortment, all at bargain or discounted prices. It draws people who are looking for the most value for their money and who are confident that they will find something suitable. The store with the broad inventory would not increase its sales significantly if it offered bargains; the bargain store would benefit little from a broader inventory.*

Since the character and breadth of stock in a store are generally acknowledged to be the most important factors in its success, the key to bookselling is not *selling* but *buying*—choosing the titles that go into the store. That explains why the most talented executive, usually the owner in a small store, is assigned the task of buying. Consciously or subconsciously, the store buyer is recognized as having the major responsibility for the store's well-being.

In view of the difficulty, already described, of predicting sales by title for an individual store, buying is a slow, deliberate, careful process of deciding on extremely skimpy information. Quite aside from the quality of the decisions made under adverse conditions, the process is expensive simply because of the amount of time it takes. Though the quality of their decisions (judging from the volume of unsold books returned) appears to be no better, the bookstore chains have the advantage over independent stores in being able to spread the administrative cost of buying over many stores; even though a chain's buying staff may be larger, the cost per store is only a fraction of the cost of management's time in an independent store.

I recall that in the 1930s one of the popular topics for high school debating teams was whether chain stores in general were advantageous and should be encouraged. (The chain stores of those debates were the forerunners of our present supermarkets.) Today we seem to have a similar situation in the book business as the chains, particularly B. Dalton and Walden, continue to grow at a very rapid rate; they have already put small retailers out of business in some parts of the country.

The question of the desirability of bookstore chains is much more than a matter of simple economics or efficient distribution. Whatever the economics of retailing groceries, and whatever hardships the existence of supermarkets may create for small grocery stores, the existence of these chains does not represent a danger to the communication and dissemination of ideas. Although they certainly do not intend it, book chains (unless they change their inventory and buying policies) do represent such a danger, and their growth at the expense of the independent bookseller threatens to reduce very sharply the efficacy of books as a medium of communication. One need only imagine the extreme case of one chain controlling all the bookstores in America, at which time one man would be deciding what titles would be made available to every bookstore browser. Any title not included because he thought it would not sell or because it duplicated something else—or for whatever reason—would simply become a non–published book.

In this sense (unless they find a way to present many more titles), it can be said that the growth of bookstore chains represents an incipient threat to significant democratic rights. It is, therefore, important to buttress the economic strength of the independent bookseller or, at the very least, not permit his economic base to be further undermined.

The bookstore chain has essentially five clear advantages over the independent bookseller. The first of these is, in practical terms, unlimited financing. The second is the ability to buy at a better discount because of volume purchases. The third is the spreading of heavy administrative costs, particularly buying, over a larger number of stores and a larger volume of business. The fourth is their attractiveness as tenants, which enables the chains to preempt the most desirable new store locations. A fifth and potentially the most powerful advantage, more effective control of inventory, has not yet been exploited—or really even developed.

Unlimited financing makes it possible for the retail chain to open new locations almost at will and to do so at places where money and time must be invested patiently until the store reaches the break-even point. Such locations are not likely to attract independents, whose limited funds make it essential to break even fairly quickly. In fact, the chains have the resources to open a store near an existing independent one that is doing well; they divide the business so neither is profitable, but it is the independent who will have to close when his resources run out.

The high discounts given to the chains are frequently contrived. Being human, the publisher gets weak when he is offered such easy large orders, which are his for a little discount concession. Theoretically (and presumably legally), the high discount is justified by the order's size, which results in economies to the publisher in packing and shipping costs. However, it could be argued that since the publisher is required to ship individually to each store in the retail chain, each location should earn its own discount. If this were so, there would be no discount advantage for the retail chains, since many of the stores in the major chains are small.

Although no information is generally available on the profitability of the chains, judging from their mode of operation, one would not expect it to be very high, and it probably depends heavily on the discount advantage. The negotiators for the chains, who are constantly pressuring the publisher for improved discounts (and advertising allowances that translate into discount), virtually say—and it certainly seems to be true—that if the bookstore chain's discounts were no better than the small retailer's, the chains would have to curtail their operations sharply.

The simple fact that buying for the chain is done centrally reduces the need for management at the local level, since the principal activity of store management is buying. This in turn reduces the normal overhead ratios enough to permit small units to break even at sales volumes too small to support an independently managed store. Leaving aside the question of the *quality* of buying, the reduced *cost* of buying is in itself a significant advantage.

At this moment, the quality of chain buying is not visibly better than the quality of buying by independent booksellers; some could argue that the chains' high level of returns and the heavy use of wholesalers by the branch stores indicate rather poor buying. Perhaps so. But, *in principle,* because they truly have enough timely sales information, which could be analyzed statistically, chain buying could be very much better than any independent's performance—if the chains learned how to *use* the information. When and if that happens, the scales will tip very sharply in favor of the chains.

Two serious problems must be solved before that can happen, but the solution to both is very much in the hands of the chains themselves.

The first problem is getting rid of the "model stock" approach of controlling inventory. This approach was developed by B. Dalton, and Walden seems determined to copy it. Model stock works reasonably well for cereal or soap or haberdashery but very poorly for books. It works best for products that have a long and fairly steady sales life. Most books do not. Any inventory system for books must allow titles to move in and out of the store effortlessly and adjust its inventory levels as frequently as the demand levels themselves change.

The second problem is the present lack of control over delivering books to the branch stores. It is hard to know when or how many to reorder if you don't have a good idea of when books will arrive. The only practical way to take control is to operate a central depot and shipping station.

B. Dalton did have a central warehouse in its early days, but it was a disaster. The costs were high and the advantage hard to find. It was closed, and the memory of that experience makes it unlikely that B. Dalton will soon try again. The error, of course, was not in the warehouse itself but in the absence of an inventory control system, so the warehouse did not fit into any overall buying and inventory strategy.

Operated under tight control within the framework of an inventory system, a central depot should hold books no longer than an average of two weeks, which is equivalent to a stock turnover of twenty-six times a year. This means that, properly operated, a central depot should not lower the chain's overall turnover rate. Quite the contrary. And the saving on shipping costs and time by moving books in larger quantities would cover its costs even without the important advantage of the wholesale discount over the retail discount, which should accompany warehouse operation.

To justify the wholesale discount, the central depot would probably be forced to sell at wholesale to outside customers. This need could be a blessing, since it would provide the opportunity for creating a parallel chain of franchised, independently owned stores that would be supplied by the same mathematically controlled inventory system used for the original chain.

One important advantage to both the public and the publisher would be the increase in the number of titles represented in the branch stores—as well as the increase in the number of branches.

Will it happen? It's doubtful, though financial pressures on both major chains may increase as a result of the revision of publishers' discount schedules forced by the threats of suit for treble damages from independent stores. There is also growing competition from the Barnes & Noble and Crown discounting and remaindering operations, which is hard for the chains to meet with their restricted assortment of titles resulting from the model stock approach to control and the general unreliability of supply. It is hard to believe that even now, in what is considered their heyday, either chain is making a satisfactory profit, so their situation must be very sensitive to any negative trend.

We know that the key to higher profit in bookselling is better control of title assortment. Improving the control depends essentially, as I have said, on the ability to predict, using more accurate methods than those now available, how well a particular title will sell at each location and to stock the store accordingly. One would imagine that the chains, with information from many stores, would be in an excellent position to develop objective, statistical systems for controlling title assortments. Although they classify books roughly into sales categories such as "hot lists" and "warm lists," none of the chains has tried to quantify the meaning of these categories, much less the sales rate of the titles within them. None of the chains seems close to developing the kind of mathematical predictive system that would give it real control of inventory assortment in each store. The result is that, even in the chains, the inability to control assortment mathematically results in continual pressure to reduce the number of titles with which inventory managers must deal. Subjective systems work best with fewer titles. This narrowing of assortment is generally true among independent booksellers as well and for the same reasons. The few truly professional independent booksellers, like Krochs & Brentano's, Scribner's, Sam Weller's Zion Bookstore, and a few others, which strive to maintain very broad stocks even if many books are represented by only one or two copies, are the exceptions in retail bookselling.

However, even though the chains do not differ in this tendency from the smaller bookseller, their restriction of title assortments represents a much greater threat to the publishing industry than the same tendency does among independent booksellers. An independent bookseller who may decide not to carry Title A because he simply cannot deal with that many different books is balanced by another bookseller who decides not to carry Title B but does carry Title A. The result is that, inefficient though the distribution system is, virtually any book that deserves to be in a bookstore finds its way into *some* stores, even though many others overlook it. The two largest chains are presumed to account for a third of all retail book sales; on some titles the figure must reach half of all retail sales. So when a chain decides it will not take a particular book, the effect on the book's distribution is very damaging. This sales effect creates heavy pressure on the publisher to tailor his list to the preferences of at least one of the major chains, preferably to both of them.

We have not yet reached the point where the publisher regularly asks the chain store buyers for their opinion when he is considering book proposals, but it is easy to imagine such a situation developing. The subtle and essentially involuntary censorship that the chains exert would then become formal and deliberate.

The apparent indifference of publishers to the fate of the bookseller—independent or chain—is hard to understand. Most industries producing consumer goods become very involved in the channels by which their goods reach the individual buyer. In book publishing, the interest in distribution channels is usually expressed by complaints at the inadequacy of the bookselling network and lamentations that book publishing is cursed with such an inefficient distribution system. If books were sold through vending machines, the publisher's sales department would be right there to shine them up, repaint them, oil the mechanism, clean up the area around them, and generally to make each one attract as many browsers as possible. Every location that seemed eligible for a machine would be studied and all the ways of getting a machine there would be explored. The sales in each channel of each machine would be analyzed so that the weak titles could be removed promptly and stronger ones substituted. The channels would not be allowed to run out because the flow of books to the machines would be carefully matched to the rate of sales.

In short, if retail distribution were reduced to its simplest and starkest terms, the publisher would handle it straightforwardly and well. But because the distribution network appears to be, not a simple, well-engineered, planned program for reaching the consumer, but a hopelessly complicated, inefficient, uncoordinated confusion of individuals sometimes working at cross purposes, the publisher throws up his hands. It is a world he never made and believes he is not likely to change, so it seems easier to accept it as someone else's responsibility and make the best of it.

No doubt the failure of book publishing to devote that kind of care and attention to its distribution system is partly due to the highly fragmented nature of the industry. Each publisher commands such a small percentage of the total retail sales that a general increase in retailing effectiveness is likely to return him very little in absolute dollars. Since even a fairly substantial publisher is likely to get only 2 or 3 percent of the volume represented by a new store, he has very little reason to involve himself in either effort or money to help such a bookstore get started.

Yet, increasing the number of retail book outlets is certainly very much in the interest of the industry. Established bookstores may not welcome competitors, though it is not evident that additional stores are necessarily harmful. The short stretch of Fifth Avenue in New York that houses Brentano's, Scribner's, two elaborate Doubleday shops, Rizzoli's, and, more recently, Barnes & Noble and B. Dalton, cheek by jowl, has demonstrated that such proximate competition (including a notorious price-cutter) does not destroy business—it actually seems to generate it. At the present level of our book distribution system, it seems that an additional opportunity to buy books does more to create new interest than to divide existing buying, though some competing independents have discovered that limits exist.

Even if new bookstores are not likely to harm old ones, one can hardly expect the established bookseller to spearhead a drive to bring competitors into the business. If there is to be an expansion in independent retail bookselling in which the principal beneficiary would be the publisher, it is the publisher who had better do something about it.

How does one make bookselling more attractive financially? One might expect booksellers to reply in chorus: "Higher discounts!" Even in four-part harmony, that would be the wrong answer. Unattractive discounts are not why books have lost their powerful position in department stores and have failed to gain a position in other general retailing establishments. Book discounts, particularly in light of the right to return unsold books, are equal to or better than the discounts retailers enjoy from many other manufacturers. A drugstore, variety shop, stationer, gift shop, or department store is not likely to balk at adding books because the discount is unattractive. *They have much better reasons.* Assurance of profitability, which booksellers tend to translate mechanically (and wrongly) into higher discounts, is certainly one. But at least as important, to my mind, is the fantastic complication of operating a business under the procedures imposed by publishers' trade practices.

The fact is that entering bookselling requires going through a nightmarish obstacle course that contributes toward keeping the fraternity small, select, and dedicated. And although one cannot rationally accuse publishers of deliberately discouraging bookselling, it is they who created a confusing situation almost unique among American industries.

To a potential bookseller, no discount policy, no matter how generous, is adequate compensation for the burdens of dealing with publishing's confusions or, because of inadequate publisher service, with the need to become an expert in the tens of thousands of titles in print and the additional thousands coming each year.

Consider how many retailers (none of them booksellers, to be sure) cheerfully accepted discounts of 25 to 30 percent on paperback books from independent magazine distributors who made the retailer's life simple, asking him to contribute only the floor space and the operation of the cash register while the distributor did the rest. This arrangement broke down in some places for other reasons, notably because the distributor did a poor job of stock replenishment or because the publisher seduced the retailer with better discounts for direct purchases. The point is that retailers that were candidates to become regular book outlets were sufficiently attracted by the simplicity and routine quality of the arrangement to accept discounts that the bookseller would (rightly) consider ruinous.

What can the publisher do to make bookselling simpler? How can publishing offer a potential bookseller the assurance that he will not have to become a book expert for the privilege of adding books to whatever merchandise lines he currently carries? How can publishing change its image from an industry in petulant conflict with its marketing network to one that recognizes its dependence upon the retailer and is eager to be of service?

The key to such a change is, of course, for the publisher to adopt a cooperative attitude. This may result in a variety of changes in practice, the ultimate of which would be some version of a merchandising plan to make bookselling as painless and surefooted as possible. Anything that is done to reduce the complications and confusion in bookselling will, to some degree, encourage more people to enter the profession.

What is critical to the growth of book retailing, however, is improved profitability, for the profitability of bookselling directly determines the size of the retail distribution network and its effectiveness in reaching the American public. If classical laissez faire economics operates in retail bookselling (and if it operates anywhere, it operates in retail bookselling), as the business becomes more profitable, more people are tempted to enter it (and do), and as it becomes less profitable, more people are forced to leave it (and most certainly do). The key factor in these decisions is the break-even point. Move the break-even point up and bookstores decline in number; move the break-even point down and bookstores increase. Not a very profound concept, but it is only the beginning.

Profitability in bookselling is distributed like virtue—and a lot of other things (which surprises the virtuous, but not the mathematicians). "Twenty percent of the stores make 80 percent of the profits." The very profitable stores are few. The moderately profitable stores are more numerous, and the stores on the edge of profitability are the most numerous of all. That means that the bookstore population is very sensitive to this break-even point. Moving the point a little moves a lot of stores in or out of business.

Industry statistics are thin and unreliable, but we can draw some reasonable conclusions without the actual data. Assume that there are approximately 5000 bookstores in the country, and assume that the most profitable of these are returning 20 percent on inventory investment, with the least profitable returning 3 percent. If profitability follows something like a curve of normal distribution, there will be a large number of stores at the low profit end and a small number of stores at the high profit end. Because figures are not available, we do not know precisely how the 5000 stores are distributed, but we can make some reasonable assumptions. A likely possibility is that, among the 5000 stores, 500 to 600 stores earn 3 to 4 percent and 10 to 15 stores earn 19 to 20 percent, with the others strung out between them in a normal distribution curve.

Now suppose the economic results for all the stores can be improved by an additional five percentage points, so that the store now making 20 percent goes up to 25 percent and the store making 3 percent goes to 8 percent; what would happen to the store population if 3 percent were still the lowest acceptable return on investment? We expect that increased profitability will draw more people into bookselling, and that the distribution of profitability will regain its "normal" shape as the situation stabilizes under the new economic conditions. Assuming that new people can enter bookselling freely (obtain funding, find store locations, etc.), which is perhaps not completely likely, the calculations suggest that the number of stores would increase by approximately 50 to 60 percent—2500 to 3000 additional stores. It seems like an incredibly large increase. This calculation is influenced greatly by our assumption about the distribution of profitability among the present stores. If that distribution is flatter, or if there are an appreciable number above the 20 percent we have assumed to be at the top of the range, the expected increase from a five-percentage-point improvement in profitability would be somewhat lower. Without more information, the figure of 2500 to 3000 cannot, therefore, be assumed to be even an approximation of the correct figure.

But it can be taken as an indication of the sensitivity of the bookstore population to profit levels. The continuing expansion of the Walden and B. Dalton chains demonstrates that book retailing is far from the saturation point. The minor advantage these chains have over the small independent bookseller—in somewhat higher discounts, advertising rebates, and lower management (buying) costs—is enough to permit them to add hundreds of additional branch stores over the next few years.

How difficult is it to achieve an increase of five percentage points in return on investment? It is surprisingly easy. The average store in the Booz, Allen & Hamilton survey (described in Appendix A) earned an average profit of 12.8 percent on its inventory investment.

Increasing that theoretical store's profit by five percentage points, to 17.8 percent, sounds formidable, but it is not.

The store achieved the 12.8 percent profit on a markup of 54.32 cents per dollar of inventory (or an income on the sale of each dollar of inventory of $1.5432) and on an inventory turnover of 3.32 times per year. This resulted in a total annual sale per dollar of inventory of $5.1234 ($1.5432 multiplied by the 3.32 times it happened).

Of the $5.1234 sales per dollar, 12.8 pennies were profit, and we must raise that sale by five more pennies, to a total of 5.1734, to bring the profit to 17.8 cents per dollar. If we keep stock turnover right where it is (3.32 times annually) and manage to increase the markup from 54.32 to 55.83, it would do it.

That could be done by reducing the cost of books to the bookseller from 64.8 percent of retail to 64.1 percent of retail—only 0.7 of 1 percent. That could be done with no change in discount schedules. If the publisher helped the bookseller buy more carefully and if the publisher shipped more carefully to hold postage and freight costs down, it would certainly save 0.7 of 1 percent.

Or it could be accomplished, with no change in markup, by improving turnover from 3.32 to 3.35, an almost insignificant change. Reducing returns very slightly (which could certainly happen if the publisher wanted his sales force to do it) would be enough. It would even suffice, without changing the returns percentage at all, for the publisher to encourage those returns that he can identify as inevitable to be made a little earlier. That would improve the bookseller's turnover and give the publisher his returned books while they are still useful. The turnover can also be increased by spacing the orders for the more popular titles to keep the inventory on those titles lower. This would also tend to increase the average discount, since the more frequent orders for those titles would raise the discount on the books now ordered in small quantity combinations.

Even with no help from the publisher, an increase of five percentage points of profitability is not difficult. *With the publisher's help* it would be very much easier, and the publisher need make no financial sacrifices or offer subsidies of any kind. It would be enough to restrain overselling, handle returns promptly, combine shipments to reduce postage costs, and, in general, to keep in mind the basic goal—to increase the profitability of the store without any decrease in the profitability of the publisher.

I am well aware that anything that requires an industry to act in concert is doomed before it starts. It is difficult enough to get one company moving, let alone involving others. But even if a few of the large publishers, acting independently, did something to improve bookstore profitability at no cost to themselves, it would have a positive effect. Because "20 percent of the publishers account for 80 percent of the sales," a few large publishers can affect a bookseller's well-being profoundly. And, of course, because the large publishers are a large portion of a bookseller's business, they would gain proportionally.

5

Returns and Remainders

RETURNS ARE THE BOOKS that are returned to the publisher, with his permission, for credit, having rested in wholesalers' warehouses or on booksellers' shelves for a reasonable period of time without being sold. Remainders are the books that the publisher, finding their sales too slow to warrant retaining them, sells at a fraction of their retail price, usually below the bare cost of manufacture, to dealers who supply them to bookstores; called "publishers' overstock," they sell for one fifth or one tenth of their original retail price.

The return is, in books at least, a peculiarly American invention. Though it is decried by some and regarded with fear and horror by British and European publishers, I consider it one of the better examples of Yankee ingenuity. It has been so badly used by publishers that it has become an industry nightmare, but that does not detract from the essential brilliance of the device. Properly handled, the return is the most useful and least expensive selling tool for any publisher, and it should result in more titles being available for longer periods instead of fewer titles for shorter periods, as is presently the case.

The bookseller's right to return, which had been granted sparingly and selectively, began to be offered more broadly in the 1930s and 1940s, first on particular titles, to reduce the bookseller's risk of ordering quantities of such titles with little knowledge of how well they would sell. Booksellers had very limited capital to invest in inventory and were correspondingly conservative in placing orders: They preferred to see the book they were buying before committing themselves heavily, and they would have also preferred to wait until they had some indication of the book's market appeal. Since the publisher needed to have the book in the stores when the reviews appeared, he could not allow booksellers to delay their orders. So, to overcome the bookstores' reluctance, he presented them with elaborate mockups of each title—showing the typeface, binding, and a sample of the actual text—*and,* more important, agreed to take back any copies the bookseller could not sell.

As it became clear that those titles that were offered "fully protected"—that is, unsold copies to be returned for credit—were purchased more readily by booksellers, the privilege was gradually extended to cover all titles. Originally, there was no time limit on returns. The publisher wanted the book in the store as long as possible, both to improve its chance of being sold and to postpone issuing a credit. But later, when paperback reprints became more frequent, making the original editions almost worthless, publishers applied a time limit to be sure they received the returns before the reprint appeared.

The start of the broader returns privilege coincides roughly with the start of the mass market paperback revolution—and also, not coincidentally, with the beginning of a period of phenomenal growth in trade publishing. The contribution of the mass paperback industry to the healthy growth of trade publishing is obvious: hundreds of millions of dollars of reprint royalties. The contribution of the returns privilege is not so obvious—and many will dispute that it has made any contribution at all—but it certainly has made it easier for publishers to get more books into more stores before publication. The fact that returns have reached disastrous levels because publishers have overused the device is, paradoxically, evidence that it has been useful.

In the early years of the return, books came back at a modest rate, sometimes 3, 5, 7 percent of the copies taken by the booksellers. Publishers, conscious of their high investment in manufactured books, did not press for large advance sales. Gradually and steadily, the situation changed. As the publisher sold more new titles to reprint houses, he found that a large advance, even at the cost of higher returns, made the reprint rights more attractive. As more titles went into paperback and the deadline of one year for the acceptance of returns became more general, thereby limiting the life of the original edition, the publisher had another reason to push for a large advance: He wanted enough copies in each store to protect against running out of stock during the book's sales life. The short selling period and the overstocks caused by aggressive selling and uncertain demand led to an increase in remaindering, which simply emphasized for the bookseller the importance of timely return.

As these factors interacted, the level of returns climbed with increasing velocity. At the present time, returns represent, not 3 or 7 percent, but approximately 25 percent of trade book sales.

There is general agreement that the returns situation is out of control, though the reason is unclear. Although the right to return unsold books still serves to reduce the resistance of the bookseller, it is now a "trade custom" that has become extremely expensive, more to the publisher than the bookseller, but a serious burden for both.

The right to return is supposed to protect the bookseller against the cost of overstocks. Overstocks occur, of course, in all consumer items. In other lines of retailing, it is customary for the retailer to dispose of excess stock by holding a sale, offering the merchandise at perhaps 25 percent off the regular price. These periodic sales recover the retailer's investment in the goods, introduce new customers to the store, and reward the old customers.

Such sales cannot work for the bookseller. The book-buying public is not impressed by 25 percent off. For whatever reason, perhaps due to remaindering, unless the book is 80 percent off it's not really considered a bargain. Selling excess stock at such a great sacrifice makes no sense to the bookseller, and if that were his only recourse, he would certainly buy more cautiously. It is much smarter to return the books to the publisher for full credit, even with the cost of the postage and the nuisance routines the publisher requires before accepting them. There is nothing as dead for the bookseller as a dead book, and he wants to be sure it becomes the publisher's property again before it breathes its last.

The care with which the bookseller combs his stock for the titles eligible for return results in another important benefit. It purges inventory, an essential step in any useful inventory control system— and for many stores the only practical control over inventory they have. In fact, using the returns policies as a way of purging inventory is, for good or ill, virtually the universal practice of booksellers.

The use of the returns system also provides a renewal of working capital to enable the store to purchase new titles and established backlist. It also corrects some of the errors of overbuying. The mistakes of *underbuying*, which result in lost sales and in some decline in the store's attraction to potential customers, are *almost never corrected*. The cost of underbuying is simply absorbed by all the sectors of the industry, including the unfortunate authors, without any way of even measuring it effectively.

The conversion of returns into working capital is frequently more difficult for the bookseller than it need be, and it will be even more so under the growing (but certainly temporary) practice of penalizing the bookseller for returns. Many publishers, rather than facing squarely the question of whether they will stand behind the salability of their titles, circumscribe the returns privilege with nuisance conditions. One of the most common is that the bookseller must first "request permission to return." (Remember the street game we used to play, "May I?") For every book to be returned, the bookseller's request must cite, at the very least, the original invoice of approximately eleven months earlier and the discount at that time. After gathering the required data for his "request," the bookseller must quarantine the books, packing them away in a storeroom or in the basement or under somebody's desk. The "permission to return" comes from the publisher in due course—"due" meaning that no speed records have been broken—accompanied by a label that must be used on the box in order for it to be accepted at the publisher's warehouse. Only then can the bookseller return the books—and wait for the credit.

Understandably, the publisher's warehouse treats returns as filler work, to be handled when there is a lull in normal activity. So there is no rush to open the package, verify the contents, and inform the accounting department to issue the credit. It is usually a matter of weeks, frequently of months, before the process is complete. (Not all publishers are equally petty in the way they handle returns; some are fast and very fair. But the bookseller can be excused for wondering how seriously the publisher means "fully protected" when he assures the bookseller that overstock may be returned without question.)

Returns now stand at about 25 percent of sales, according to statistics compiled by the Association of American Publishers. That is, the books shipped to retailers and wholesalers equal 125 percent; returns equal 25 percent and net sales are 100 percent. These figures suggest that retailers and wholesalers return one out of every five books they purchase. While this statistic sounds bad enough, it drastically *understates* the magnitude of returns. Returns are measured against the sale of *all* books. Backlist titles are almost never returned; it is the new books, almost exclusively, that are returned.

New titles represent approximately 60 percent of publishers' sales (no reliable figures are available). The 25 percent returns must be measured, therefore, not against the 100 percent of total sales but the 60 percent of frontlist sales.

    □ *It is an interesting sidelight that, when I came into publishing in 1945, the ratio was probably the reverse. The backlist represented 60 percent of total sales; today it is down to 40 percent. In thirty-five years, the paperback and the publishers' pursuit of the big advance have shortened the life of most books dramatically.*

Of the new titles eligible for return, almost one out of every three copies purchased is returned unsold. But that is still an understatement. The return rate from libraries—whether new books or old—is virtually zero. Of the 100 percent of the books shipped by publishers that are not returned, approximately 32 percent go to libraries and institutions from wholesalers and another 15 percent directly from publishers. Probably these 47 percent are divided between frontlist and backlist in the same ratio as sales in general.

We can now put the AAP figures in better perspective. Of the 125 percent of books shipped by publishers, 47 percent go to libraries and institutions. Fifty-three percent find their way to consumers through the wholesale and retail networks. Of this 53 percent, only a little more than 31 percent (60 percent of 53 percent) are eligible for return. Since returns amount to 25 percent, the sad conclusion of all this arithmetic is that, of the new books shipped by publishers for sale to the general public, almost one copy of every two is returned unsold.

Returns therefore represent a waste so staggering that, although it is by no means the greatest of several staggering wastes in the distribution by negotiation system, it is hard to believe. But the numbers are certainly very close to the truth.

How much do these returns cost the industry?

Curtis G. Benjamin, former president of the McGraw-Hill Book Company, observed in the *Publishers Weekly* for April 24, 1981:

> The costs, direct and indirect, of handling returns of such magnitude are beyond accurate appraisal—which could partly explain why publishers and booksellers alike have not faced up to them more forthrightly. Working from operating cost ratios stated in the AAP statistical reports for 1979, I have come up with $80 million as a very rough estimate of the direct cost to publishers of handling out-and-in shipments in that year. Since booksellers and most other customers pay the carriage cost of shipments both ways, the total of their receiving and shipping costs must have been an equal amount. Thus, the combined costs of profitless shipments was at least $120 million by my rough reckoning.

To the handling cost of books that do not get sold, one must add the cost in returned copies too damaged in handling to be salable and of returns that may be salable only as remainders, at an outright loss to the publisher. And there is also the perhaps even greater though not measurable cost of the books that would have been sold if they had been in the stores in place of the books that weren't sold.

Ignoring, for the moment, the cost to wholesalers and booksellers, and considering only the cost to publishers, we should perhaps approximately double Curtis Benjamin's estimate of the cost for handling returns alone. This would give us an approximate cost *to the publishers* of about $150 million. For an industry doing about $1 billion in sales, making a profit of approximately zero before subsidiary rights income and approximately $100 million afterward, that is a very impressive and scary number. And publishers are becoming properly scared.

It is perhaps a good thing that publishers are concerned about the cost to *them* of high returns because there seems to be little realization of the *booksellers'* somewhat less dramatic but nevertheless difficult burden.

It is interesting to see what a reduction in returns by ten percentage points (from 25 to 15 percent), would mean to the average bookstore described by Booz, Allen & Hamilton in its survey for the American Booksellers Association. If it never bought the dead stock represented by books that are later returned, the bookstore's investment in inventory would be correspondingly lower. With a 10 percent reduction in purchases to arrive at the same level of sales, the rate of stock turnover would increase slightly, from the 3.32 in the Booz, Allen report to a little more than 3.42. The cost of shipping, handling, and returning goods would decline by 10 percent as well. Markup would increase slightly, from 54.32 to 55.28 cents per dollar of inventory investment. Multiplying the markup by the turnover of 3.42 gives us an annual gross margin of $1.89 per dollar of inventory investment. This is 8.66 cents higher than the survey's average gross margin per dollar of investment, which means 8.66 cents on top of the 12.80 cents of profit reported in the survey, or a new profit on investment of 21.46 percent, *an increase of 67 percent* over the profit at today's levels of returns. That indicates how damaging returns are to the bookseller's profit even when he gets *full credit,* with no penalties.

Despite the impressive out-of-pocket costs to the publishing industry of returns, the most serious negative effect of returns is more subtle: the gradual, persistent, and insidious transformation of the book from a communication medium with an indefinite, but rather long, life into one with a typical life of twelve months. The determination and thoroughness with which the bookseller goes through his stock to return every copy before the returns deadline effectively destroys the possibility for any but the most exceptional title to survive into a second year.

□ *I can almost hear some of my publisher and retailer colleagues protesting that they know of many titles that go on selling for years—look at the* Random House Dictionary—*and that generalizations don't apply in publishing because "every book is different." True. Some few titles survive each year because it is so very, very obvious that they are almost certain to have a long and solid sales life. If this exception rate of 2 or 3 percent of the titles still on hand after eleven months negates my generalization, I stand negated. It is interesting, by the way, that even among these few surviving titles, bookstores frequently return copies at eleven months just to be safe—and then reorder them shortly thereafter if public demand shows unusual strength.*

When faced with the enormous cost of returns, a sales manager may argue that low returns or the complete absence of returns may indicate an even more serious distribution maladjustment. Consider the extreme case of a publisher without a sales force to urge his titles on booksellers and wholesalers. The returns will be very low, even as a percentage of his very low sales, because many booksellers will not buy at all (denying the publisher 100 percent of their possible sale) and most of the others will buy overcautiously (denying the publisher something less than 100 percent).

This argument—that high returns may be better than low returns—has been used over and over again as a kind of rationalization for being less unhappy with high returns. The current level of returns is simply too costly for many publishers to continue to accept such a justification from their sales managers. Nevertheless, the foundation of that argument is perfectly valid. While high returns are clearly a symptom of bad distribution of one sort, low returns may simply mean that the bad distribution is of a different sort. We shall have more to say about that.

Today, the returns practice is universally bemoaned by the descendants of the publishers who created it. Most publishers concede that the bookseller needs some inducement to buy books, but they feel that returns have gotten out of hand. The publisher, of all people, knows that the bookseller has good reason to be cautious. But, publishers like to point out a little plaintively, booksellers in Germany and England, and in many other countries, get along fine without the benefit of the returns privilege.

□ *American publishers need to be reminded that (a) the German and British publishers have not subsidized the wholesalers' usurpation of the booksellers' library market; (b) the practice of accepting returns is gradually becoming more prevalent, particularly in England; (c) European publishers, though frightened of the "American" returns practice because they do not*

*understand it, would sell more books if they introduced the returns
"privilege" and used it wisely; and (d) the American publisher
should shift his attention from the cost of high returns when badly
and wastefully used by the publisher to the profitability of low
returns when the returns privilege is properly and skillfully used.*

In an attempt to reduce returns, some publishers are sharply
penalizing them or forbidding them altogether, offering the bookseller
additional discounts instead as an inducement to take buying risks.
This tradeoff is advocated by some booksellers as well as by some
publishers.

I discussed this idea recently with an important spokesman for the
booksellers, and he favors the proposal. Even with the higher discount,
I asked, won't the booksellers buy much more conservatively if they
cannot return unsold copies? He acknowledged that of course they
would.

What would happen, I asked, if a publisher felt that the booksellers'
orders for important titles were too conservative and undermined the
chances for the book's success?

"Well," he said, "the publisher could always offer to sell such a title
or titles protected, agreeing to take returns of unsold copies."

"In other words," I suggested, "we would soon come back to the
same returns situation we now have, except it would be at a 50
percent discount instead of a 40 percent discount."

"I guess that might very easily happen," he acknowledged.

This seems to me to be a losing proposition. Nevertheless, the idea
of trading an additional discount for lower returns seems to be
growing in favor, and we will undoubtedly live through a period of
costly experimentation before the fallacies in this approach become
obvious. Some booksellers, as I have suggested, say they are prepared,
for an adequate quid pro quo, to give up returns altogether. To date,
only one publisher of any consequence, Harcourt Brace Jovanovich
(HBJ), has gone so far as to institute such a policy. Its new retailer
discounts range up to 58 percent on a sliding scale to induce the store
to buy, but once bought, the books may not be returned. Wholesaler
discounts have moved up correspondingly, ranging up to 60 percent.

A story in the *New York Times* of November 18, 1980, which
announced this change in HBJ's policy and its reasoning, stated that
"returns were running between 35 and 50 percent." The story then
described the case, cited by the company, of a recent novel "in which
the first printing was 50,000 copies and reorders demanded a second
printing of 7500. Within eight months, 21,000 copies came back."

HBJ's perception of what happened was probably faulty. It is extremely doubtful that the "reorders" were, in fact, reorders. They were probably, for the most part, *first* orders from some stores, coming in enough later than the first orders from other stores that they completely misled sales management, which assumed they reflected the public response to the book. HBJ's press release suggests that their own sales department erred in distributing 50,000 copies of a book so badly that almost half came back, and it was so unaware of what it had done that it asked management for another 7500 copies. It is bad enough to put the wrong quantities in the wrong places (it certainly happens often enough), but not being aware of what is happening to the books you put out there compounds one serious error with another. To correct that situation, do you correct the returns policy or the sales management policy?

By jettisoning the returns privilege, HBJ has created a new set of economic realities for itself. Consider the economics of books selling in the range of 30,000 to 40,000 copies. At that level, HBJ's average discount will be in the neighborhood of 57 to 58 percent to retailers, and the wholesalers will get a whopping 60 percent! An author selling in those quantities will be getting a 15 percent royalty. Discount plus royalty, therefore, equals 72 percent of the retail price. This leaves a margin of 28 percent.

The cost of manufacturing, even under a frugal production manager, will be 20 percent of retail, on the average. This leaves 8 percent of retail to pay editorial costs, advertising and promotion, the sales force, warehousing and billing, and everything else. Profit comes out of whatever is left. It is a heavy price to pay for "no returns."

And, in fact, will we really have "no returns"?

Consider the following scenario. Bookstore A is behind in its payments to HBJ, and the credit manager is on the phone, threatening to cut it off unless it settles its account. He has to listen to the following answer: "Sorry. We are really strapped for cash right now. There are some of your newer titles we'd love to have because we know they would sell, so we don't want you to cut us off. We have a rather large representation of your slow-moving titles here in absolutely mint condition. If you let us return some of these for credit, I can send you some cash for the difference, and I'll be glad to take the new faster sellers. That is what I am doing with other publishers, and I have to save my cash to use that way. Let me know if that is OK."

Or consider the situation if the store is not clever enough to bargain the right to return into its offer to pay more promptly and to continue to buy. The store holds the books, waiting for slow attrition to reduce its stock. But back home, at the HBJ ranch, there are no more orders coming from bookstores for that title because our store is not the only one stuck with excess inventory. The stock sitting in the HBJ warehouse is, of course, remaindered. What does the store do? Does it wait for a customer to point out that he can buy the book for 80 percent off in a store down the street or does it accept HBJ's decision that the retail price of the book has just been changed *at the store's expense?*

Well, HBJ's way is one approach to the problem of high returns. (Such an approach would solve the problem of the high cost of automobile insurance by simply abolishing automobile insurance.)

□ *As type for this book is being set, HBJ announces that the "no returns" policy has been rescinded.*

A more popular tactic, promoted by a number of other publishers and copied from the mass market publisher New American Library (NAL), is to charge the bookseller a stiff penalty for any books returned. It is a carrot and stick treatment of the bookseller.

In this type of scheme, the highest discount step is raised (from 46 percent, say, to 48 or 50 percent), but, even more important, the steps in the discount schedule are drastically shortened to apply the higher discounts to smaller orders. A small bookseller is offered an opportunity to buy at 45 or 46 percent those quantities that previously earned only a 41 or 42 percent discount. That is the carrot.

The stick consists of the penalty imposed for returning unsold books. In most such plans, the returned books are credited as though they had been bought at some arbitrarily high discount (frequently 53 percent), so the bookseller gets back much less than he paid. For example, if the bookseller buys at an average of 45 percent (very attractive when compared to the present 41 or 42 percent), the returns at the theoretical 53 percent give him 15 percent less than he paid for the books, which is a penalty on top of the cost of postage both ways.

One of the assumptions underlying some of the new returns policies is that the bookseller can decide for himself how to deal with his overstock. He may decide to hold the books at retail price indefinitely, letting the stock dissolve slowly with no markdown. Or he may mark the books down, say 20 percent or even 40 percent, to dispose of them more quickly, forgoing his markup but suffering no out-of-pocket loss. Or he may decide that taking a loss makes sense to recover working capital, and he may remainder the books at drastic reductions.

Quite aside from the question of whether the publisher should, ethically or in his own self-interest, place the burden of these options on the bookseller, would the bookseller really have such wide freedom of choice? That assumption ignores the likelihood that the bookseller is not alone in having overstock. Other booksellers probably have overstock as well, and if one bookseller decides to remainder, is not another bookseller's hand forced? Much more serious is the probability that the *publisher* has overstock, lots of it. Will the publisher hold his stock in the warehouse until the booksellers have all freely exercised their options and no overstock remains at retail? That is not likely. If the publisher decides to remainder, how much freedom of choice has he left the overstocked bookseller?

But the logic of the returns penalty is questionable for other reasons. To have a sales force and promotion department touting the salability of your list while you threaten the buyers with a returns penalty is just a little bit like heating your home in winter by running the furnace full blast and opening all the windows to be sure the furnace doesn't overheat it.

It has the publisher saying to the bookseller: "I'm sending a salesman in to see you to tell you about my fantastic new list. He'll be fresh from our sales conference and a little overenthusiastic. Don't believe everything he tells you because he'll be repeating some exaggerations our editors fed him at the conference. Unfortunately, our company policy is to punish you rather than the sales rep if his mistaken enthusiasm misleads you into buying generously. So, please be properly suspicious of whatever he tells you. It would pain us terribly to hurt you for taking our sales rep seriously."

The short steps to high discount in these new schedules will tend to frustrate the sales rep's attempt to get a larger order even before the bookseller thinks about the penalty for returns. The bookseller is likely to be content with getting 45 percent on an order that would previously have earned 41 or 42 percent. His logic (and very sound it is) will be that he can now order more often in smaller quantities. In fact, he won't do so.

How quickly the threat of the penalty stick will scare the bookseller into even more cautious buying will vary with his personality. Those who feel that they know the market may change their buying habits only slightly until they are burned by their first big return. Others will sense the danger immediately. They will decide that losing an occasional sale because the store does not have the book is less painful than giving up 15 percent (when your profit is a magnificent 2½ percent on sales) for the privilege of returning books.

Sooner or later, all booksellers will learn to buy more cautiously. In one sense, that is precisely the purpose of the new discount schedules: to encourage stores not to buy those copies they will later return. It is very doubtful that the reduced purchasing will be so perfectly targeted. It is likely, for example, that titles that the bookseller might have bought in quantities of one or two with the right to return (which are very rarely actually returned) will be skipped altogether. The effect of this, ultimately, will be to narrow the spectrum of titles that the publisher can profitably publish.

Even the lead titles will be bought with greater caution. The old order for 150 will become an order for 100, or even 50, with a promise to reorder promptly as needed. But, as publishers who introduced some variation of this scheme earlier have learned to their surprise, it is precisely in the reorder that the bookseller becomes most cautious. Having sold his initial order, the bookseller is not inclined to tempt fate by taking more.

Selling costs will go up. Facing an added risk, the bookseller will need more convincing, requiring the sales rep to supply more information and spend more time. Also, because the wholesaler's discount to the retailer will be relatively less attractive, the bookseller will be less eager to place reorders with the wholesaler. The publisher will discover that he has sharply reduced the ability (and the eagerness) of the wholesaler to be helpful without having provided a practical substitute. The publisher will have to give the bookseller more sales attention to keep even the obvious titles in stock.

Publishers promoting this approach to controlling returns may find repercussions even among their authors. All things being equal, an author will prefer a publisher who encourages the bookseller to stock his books by permitting returns without penalty.

Will the discount penalties (the discount *concessions* will soon be accepted as normal; it is the *penalties* the bookseller will have constantly in mind) reduce returns? *They certainly will!*

It is perhaps a little exaggerated to point out that decapitation has never failed to cure a headache. The remedy being proposed here is not nearly so extreme, and its effect will not be so final. Its side effects will also be a lot more difficult to detect and, more important, to measure. Sales will go down, but the object of the policy is, first, to reduce gross sales by approximately the amount of the returns and, second, to keep net sales about where they are. (Actually, if the policy truly improved buying practices, net sales would go up, because money now uselessly invested in books that are later returned would be put into books that are more likely to be sold.) When sales go down, how is the publisher to judge (since every title, and each season's assortment of titles, is *truly* different) whether they have gone down just enough, so the publisher is better off, or have gone down too far, so the publisher is worse off? How can the publisher judge whether he has made a good tradeoff between lower sales and lower returns?

The cost of filling orders averages about 10 percent of sales, so we can assume that the marginal cost of filling any one order is about 5 percent. Shipping an unsold book costs 5 percent and receiving an unsold return costs 5 percent for a total of 10 percent of sales value. The manufacturing cost averages about 40 percent, but the "run-on" cost of extra copies is probably no more than about 20 percent of sales value. If we assume that between completely damaged returns and returns remaindered at less than manufacturing cost, half of this manufacturing investment is lost, we add 10 percent of sales value to the average cost to the publisher of a return, bringing the total to 20 percent.

The margin for the publisher on each copy sold, after he subtracts the production costs, the royalty, and the variable overheads, is approximately 48 to 50 percent of revenue (though the accounting department may mislead him into thinking it is much less by subtracting overheads that have nothing whatever to do with the case).

A comparison of these two numbers—20 percent of sales, the cost of a return, and 50 percent of sales, the cost of a lost sale—shows that the publisher can tolerate the loss of one copy sold for a reduction in returns of two and a half copies. If a publisher who finds that returns are running about 35 percent of sales manages to reduce returns to 25 percent—and, in the process, reduces gross sales by 14 percent (of which 10 percent represents those books that would have been returned and 4 percent represents books that would have been sold and not returned), he is as badly off as he was before the attempt to reduce returns.

But the author isn't. His royalty income is reduced by the full 4 percent.

We can safely assume that, in order to achieve a ten-percentage-point decrease in returns, publishers who penalize returns will suffer a drop in gross sales of considerably more than 14 percent, so their net income will go down with the author's. These losses will not correspondingly improve the bookseller's situation. On the contrary. His caution in buying will result in less to sell and less income to cover overhead. Returns will not be eliminated by his caution, simply reduced, and the cost of each return will be considerably higher for him. If he holds on to returnable books, hoping to avoid the penalty by selling them eventually, at list price or on sale, he will be seriously damaging his stock turnover rate as well as the attractiveness of his inventory in drawing customers.

If there is no improvement in selling or buying methods, then will scaring the bookseller into reducing returns by ten percentage points result in his reducing his purchases by 20 percent? Twenty-five percent? *Certainly* more than 10 percent! How is he to make up the income lost from the books he would have sold but did not buy? The loss from the penalty for returns would, in fact, be only the beginning of the decline in the bookseller's income.

If a bookseller goes out of business, how is one to judge whether this is a normal casualty or a symptom of the difficulties introduced by forcing him to know more about the forthcoming books than he can possibly know?

Some of these proposals for solving the problem of returns make one wonder if we aren't forgetting what a return is and why it was created.

It seems odd to find a number of booksellers openly arguing against the right to return. Of course, they don't really think the return is wrong. The Sears, Roebuck catalogue tells you much more about a Sears product than the publisher's rep does about his, and if you don't like it when it comes, you can return it, no questions asked. It is not giving up the right of return the booksellers are so eager for, it is the higher discount they consider absolutely essential. If the tradeoff must be made, they are eager to make it. With no returns, they'll buy *and sell* fewer books but, they hope, make more money on the higher margins. Unfortunately, they haven't stopped to figure *how much less* they will buy and sell when they have no returns protection to help them gamble on the publisher's new titles.

The publisher's position is much more peculiar. By imposing a penalty on returns, he is punishing the bookseller for believing the sales rep. Since the *publisher* devised returns in the first place, it is interesting that some publishers now are missing the point so completely.

Punishment has no place in business relationships. A much sounder concept is payment for services rendered.

The bookseller, by displaying the (demonstrably) excess copies of the publisher's books to give them the best opportunity of being sold, has clearly rendered the publisher a useful service. If the book is sold, the bookseller has his compensation; if it is not, the bookseller has rendered service without compensation. The longer he has displayed the book, the more valuable his service and the greater his cost. Whatever else may figure in the publisher's discount policy, the publisher's response to this service should be payment, not punishment.

If I were the publisher (and not yet ready to institute a merchandising plan), I would credit any returned copies at a discount one percentage point *in the bookseller's favor* if the books were on display a reasonable time. The policy might be, for example, that books sold at a 40 percent discount would be credited at 40 percent if returned before fifteen months and at 39 percent if returned any time thereafter.

The publisher who sees this approach as a truly productive use of the returns policy—and certainly a fair one—will leave his competitors wondering what hit them.

We know that the best cure for high returns is matching a bookseller's stock more closely to the likelihood of sale. Does penalizing the bookseller for returns offer any hope of improving the match of inventory to demand? None at all. These proposals assume a situation that does not exist. The apparent logic in penalizing the bookseller is to encourage him to buy more cautiously.

But the existing situation, even under the more generous returns policies, offers enough reason for the bookseller to be cautious. Excess inventory ties up valuable money and space, and returning books is expensive and a nuisance.

Examine the returns figures on any title, store by store. Are there any stores that did not return any copies at all? *There are.* Are some of these stores already so cautious that they bought no copies at all but could have sold some? *Some are.* And did other stores that made no returns buy some copies, so that no return suggests they sold what they bought? *Yes, indeed.* Do some stores return some titles and not others, indicating varying success with their efforts to buy cautiously? *Undoubtedly.* Now examine the stores that *did* return copies and compare the returned quantity with the purchased quantity. Is the percentage returned fairly consistent among these accounts? *It is not.*

So the publisher will do himself no favors by any strategy intended to produce a *uniform* increase in the bookseller's resistance to the line being fed him by the sales rep, e.g., by increases in returns penalties.

If any publisher analyzes sales to determine what uniform reduction he should aim for in the size of advance orders, he will discover that he does not want a uniform reduction at all. He will discover that he does not have a *consistent maldistribution* but rather an *inconsistent maldistribution.* And, of course, that is precisely his problem. The restriction on the returns privilege, or its outright elimination, would simply substitute one inconsistent maldistribution for another. The *cost of returns* might decrease or disappear altogether. *The cost of lost sales,* on top of the cost of higher discounts conceded to make a no-returns policy palatable, would never appear as numbers on a management report, so it would not embarrass anyone personally, but that cost would certainly be higher than the savings on returns.

Suppose, by some miracle, that a publisher existed who, on examining his returns, found that they were uniformly distributed by title among all his accounts, so a uniform reduction in orders would uniformly reduce returns. Is the best way to accomplish this to send an unclear signal to 2500 different booksellers in the form of a threat of punishment? Can one really expect that each one of the 2500 will react in exactly the same degree to each degree of severity in the threat, like robots to a change in the voltage? Is it not more reasonable to suppose that these stores will, for all sorts of subtle reasons, react differently to identical deterrents (as experience proves they *do*)?

Wouldn't it make more sense for the publisher, instead of sending an unclear signal to 2500 booksellers he does not control (or even really know), to send a very clear signal to the ten or fifteen or thirty sales reps *who work for him,* to whom he can speak in clear, unequivocal language, and who are obliged to follow his instructions? *It would.*

Dampening the sales reps' eagerness to load bookstores with copies they are not likely to need can only be done by a sales management that has itself seen the light. Management cannot be of two minds: devoted to the ideal of a high advance on the few lead titles at whatever cost, yet still bewailing the resulting high returns.

It is reasonable to expect that, as the rapidly declining interest among mass market publishers to purchase reprint rights is understood to be more than a temporary aberration, sales managers will no longer prod the sales force for higher advance orders to make reprint sales easier. Such a change in attitude should reduce overselling, reduce returns, and even reduce remaindering.

That would still leave trade sales reps with all the other reasons for overselling (lead titles only!), so it would certainly not solve the entire returns problem. Publishers would have to devise a way to bring their selling practices under control and manage them by rational rules. A rational distribution (along the lines discussed in Chapter 7, on the merchandising plan) would, in my opinion, reduce returns to a range of 3 to 5 percent at the most while providing other, more important benefits at the same time. Such a seemingly radical change may not be too much to hope for, though it is presently too much to postulate. But in the present grotesque situation, even a simple change in publishers' selling goals could work wonders. It is certainly reasonable that simply exercising self-restraint in selling out of consideration for the cost of returns, without any attempt to threaten the bookseller, could in itself easily cut returns by ten percentage points.

    □ *Because returns, for obvious reasons, are almost exclusively new titles, the returns percentage is very sensitive to the ratio of new books to backlist sales. Present publishing policy is steadily decreasing the percentage of backlist books in the sales mix, thereby contributing to the problem of returns. If publishers adapted their selling strategies to favor the backlist, that in itself would make a dent in the problem.*

The returns come from the bookseller, but they are *made* by the publisher. It is the publisher who decides (deliberately if he has a well-managed sales force, by default if he doesn't) how the book will be presented to each store. Since most sales forces are loosely managed and each rep has his own selling approach, the effect of selling policy is very easy to see when reps are shifted among territories. The returns percentage does not stay in the territory; *it moves with the rep.* Further, the same accounts show a different percentage of returns when they are sold by different reps.

Having done it, I know that strong sales management can sharply reduce returns *and increase sales at the same time.* If a publisher is unhappy with his percentage of returns, he should stop maligning the booksellers and look to his sales manager.

Logically, the reason books are returned is that the bookseller bought (or, more exactly, *was sold*) too many copies. Overselling, repeated in a number of stores and wholesalers, determines the *absolute* level of returns for any given title. The *relative* level of returns for a title (the percentage of books returned of those shipped) is increased because some stores were undersold (i.e., got *too few* copies) and did not reorder, or reordered late, or never had the book at all, though they might have sold modest quantities with few returns. Those copies that were never sold but could have been tend to increase the returns *percentage.*

    □ *This points up an additional advantage of wide distribution. If the book is in more stores it will improve its sale everywhere, because it will be more visible and will promote stronger word-of-mouth support.*

With good sales force training and an imaginative approach, returns can be sharply reduced even without a merchandising plan. The major element is better supervision of the orders written by the sales reps. But other special steps can also be taken. Consider the following example. Immediately after Christmas, returns are likely to be substantial. The retailer's inclination to bring inventories down sharply after the holiday rush is supported by all sorts of valid reasons. Among the less valid reasons is his desire, widely prevalent, to pay off his debts to publishers in merchandise instead of cash. This heavily pads the return of unsold Christmas merchandise with books that could in fact be retained. Many such books or their equivalents will be reordered within a short time. These returns cost the publisher unfairly and cost the bookseller either in lost sales or in additional freight charges on the reordered books.

Without a merchandising plan relationship between publisher and bookseller, these wasteful returns are very hard to discourage. Publishers are relentless in dunning for payment, and since a large return is virtually inevitable at the end of the year, the retailer is tempted to add enough to get the publisher off his back and to bring the dollar value of his inventory closer to the levels the experts recommend for the leaner months of January, February, and March.

One way to forestall these wasteful returns, a way we developed and found very effective at Two Continents, is to offer the bookstore credit for *not* returning the books. This saves the store the expense of shipping them back *and* keeps the books available. We called the plan "credit for overstock" and it worked as follows:

In January, our rep took an inventory of our books in the store. Our sales service department then determined which books were truly overstock and which were within sensible stock limits. The bookseller got two lists: the books we thought should be returned and the books we thought should be retained *on the selling floor.* If the store agreed to keep the books we recommended, we issued a credit equal to half their value. The credit expired on May 1, giving the store, in effect, extended terms until that date. We found, as we had hoped, that many of the books were sold by May 1, so the store was, in large part, paying us for the books after they were sold. This was a nice bonus for the store and ultimately for us as well, since we would have lost all those sales if the books had been returned.

The mark of all good schemes is that everybody benefits. We turned some returns into sales and protected the booksellers' credit ratings so they could continue to buy; the booksellers kept their stocks in better balance and saved the cost of shipping some books two ways.

Returns are one indicator of the character of distribution. Heavy returns on a few titles from a few accounts are an indication of very bad distribution. Light returns distributed among many titles and scattered among many accounts indicate better distribution. To improve the returns situation, the representation of titles in each store must be more closely matched to consumer demand. This requires minimizing overstocks *and understocks* on as many titles as possible, *not only* on the few titles that cause the publisher the anguish of heavy returns.

The return is created at the moment the bookseller places his order. The rest is gestation. And the bookseller usually places his order while sitting across the desk from the *publisher's sales rep.* Ironically, *most* publishers find it more difficult to control the pressure exerted by their own reps than to appeal generally to the stores to be realistic in resisting that pressure.

When the sales rep goes forth from the publisher's sales conference, his clue to the intensity with which he is expected to sell is usually the announcement of a first printing quantity and/or the total number of advance orders the publisher expects from his sales force. Sometimes that total advance is broken down by the percentage for each territory. So the sales rep whose territory is 10 percent of the whole is expected to sell 1000 copies if the total advance desired is 10,000 copies.

Although the publisher uses numbers as though they had a specific meaning, the fact is that an advance of 10,000 copies on each of three different titles can mean a very different distribution among bookstores and wholesalers for each one. This is not to say that *every* store will order a different quantity of each title, but many will. The stores represented in the advance for each book will probably differ, some ordering one but skipping another. There may also be variations in the ratio of quantities going to wholesalers and retailers or to different areas of the country. Of course, the ideal order for any store *should* probably be different for each book, even if the total turns out, quite accidentally, to be the same. The traffic and the ambience are different in each store.

But in today's distribution system, the special nature of each store is, unfortunately, not the principal reason for the difference in distribution of orders. The difference is largely accidental, for some of the following reasons:

1. The rep's misreading the editor's presentation of the substance of the book, leading one rep to oversell it and another to undersell it.
2. The happenstance of the stores visited with that list (most reps do not sell each successive list to precisely the same stores) or the order in which the stores were visited.
3. The accident of the sales rep's personal interests.
4. The accident of the response of a buyer for one of the large chains. His decision may shift the pressure elsewhere to reach the target totals.

As a defense against the inadequate information available on a given title, some buyers for the larger stores simply order a set percentage of the publisher's first printing. It's not a very clever way to make the decision, but something cleverer is rarely available.

The result of all this is that when the publisher says, "Get me an advance of 10,000 copies," he is saying something that may really be one of a thousand different things.

Moreover, the editor or sales manager will frequently fudge a little. He is, after all (as he well knows), using the advance quantity as an abbreviated way of expressing his enthusiasm for the book. If he wants an advance of 10,000, he may announce the goal as 12,000, which in his mind is another way of saying 10,000 with a double underlining. And, contrary to the unhappiness he will feel when the returns come in, he believes the industry folklore that if the returns are low, sales were lost, and that if you don't get large quantities out, you are undermining the book's chances.

Every rep knows that he will be praised for each *large* order he sends in. He may be criticized for small orders, but the publisher who will criticize the rep for taking too large an order is hard to find. (When we began to do exactly that at Doubleday in the 1950s, the veteran sales reps and some of the editors thought management had lost its mind.)

Because the publisher's present instructions to the reps are so vague, he has every reason to fear that any advice to sell less aggressively because returns are too high would lead not to a more discriminating placement of books but simply to an overall lowering of enthusiasm and a real loss of sales. If the publisher is going to use his sales force to hold down returns by putting a more accurate quantity in each store, he has to tell each rep what the appropriate quantity *is* for each title for each store. It may amaze sales executives outside the book business that the publisher's sales manager *cannot do it.* He has all the information in his files to arrive at the best quantity for each store, but he doesn't even think that way. "Every book is different." "Every buyer is different." "Every rep is different." "Every day is different."

Publishing management—which knows all there is to know about each new book, which knows precisely what is going to be done in advertising and promotion, and which has the record of previous sale of similar titles in each store—does not seem to know how to determine how many copies the store should have. It is entirely counterproductive to penalize the bookseller, who has none of these advantages, because he doesn't know either.

The waste that returned books represent in the work of the author, the editorial staff, and the manufacturing costs is bad enough. But the publisher has managed to compound it by creating the remainder, publishing's own ingenious contribution to the age of pollution.

Here is the publisher, stuck with growing piles of prematurely dead books, some in brand-new cartons never shipped because he printed too many, some in secondhand cartons returned from his retailers and wholesalers because he "sold" too many. It's not much good to say that a better printing policy and a better sales policy would have avoided this. It's true. They would have.

□ *As a demonstration, at Doubleday we went for two years in the late 1950s without any remaindering—a remarkable change for Doubleday. Overprintings during those two years were inconsequential and returns were very modest, though sales were dramatically higher.*

But at least for the moment, the publisher doesn't have a better printing policy or sales policy. What he has is a growing pile of books. Destroying the books is somehow anticultural and uncouth, whereas destroying or at least seriously damaging the *market* for books is not. So the pile of new and secondhand cartons goes to the remainder dealer at distress prices.

These books soon appear on the "publishers' overstock" tables at a fifth or a tenth of their retail price, which raises the question in the customer's mind as to how smart it was to buy that book at full price only, it seems, a few weeks ago.

It would be inaccurate to ascribe this practice of fouling one's own nest completely, or even principally, to the returns privilege, though returns must be drastically reduced if the remainder evil is to be corrected. At least two other causes play a substantial role. One is the twelve-month time limit on returns. Once a title is cleared out of all the retail stores, bookstore sales are over, finished. Even a publisher's small inventory at that point represents overstock except to the degree that there may be some latent demand from libraries or some special, nontrade markets. The time limit signals bookstores: "Return!"; the return signals the publisher: "Remainder!"

The other cause for remaindering is the haphazard, blindman's-buff methods by which most trade publishers decide how many copies to print. The determination of printing quantities is discussed in some detail in Chapter 14. In deciding on first printings—the books needed to cover the advance sale and the early weeks of the book's life—the scanty information available (consisting principally of the first few orders received) is usually so badly used that either far too many are produced or too few, precipitating a hurried second printing that produces the excessive quantities. Either way, publishers manage, on an amazingly large proportion of new titles, to accumulate substantial warehouse stocks that are never shipped to anyone, never removed from the containers in which they arrived from the bindery, pleading to be remaindered.

The determination of printing quantities can be improved in a number of ways. Even with no change in the publishers' selling methods, some elementary calculus applied to the scanty sales information available at printing time would result in a much more accurate prediction of the advance sale. With a merchandising plan, the advance would be brought under complete control; the publisher would know, even before a single order was written, precisely how many copies would be needed in the bookstores on publication date.

Without going to the extreme of a merchandising plan, the publisher can improve his selling, reduce returns, *and* improve the accuracy of first printing quantities by determining how many copies of each title he wants each store to order. A little practice will result in sales reps getting very nearly those orders. Although more accurate printings are not the principal aim of sales management—the aim is to increase sales and reduce returns—they would be a useful by-product.

Some idea of the dimension of the remainder phenomenon can be gathered from the survey conducted for the American Booksellers Association by Booz, Allen & Hamilton. It showed that in moderately large retail stores ($500,000 to $1,000,000 sales at retail), hardcover books accounted for 38 percent of sales and remainders for 10 percent. Since remainders sell, on the average, for considerably less than one fourth of the original price, we can be sure that these stores were selling *at least as many copies of remainders as they were of new books.* And since that 1977 survey, the sale of remainders has increased.

Most publishers see the economics of remaindering simplistically: Whatever they get from the remainder dealer reduces what would otherwise be complete loss. The damage that remainders do to the overall book market—partly as a substitute for a book at full price and, even more, in undermining the concept of retail price itself—almost never figures in the publisher's calculations of the "cost" of remaindering.

Remaindering is sometimes justified as a device that builds store traffic, which encourages the sale of other books as well. It is true that in the hands of creative retailers, remainders can be used to attract customers, but whether those customers will be conditioned to buy books at full price is, in my opinion, extremely doubtful. The opposite is much more likely.

Barnes & Noble, a chain of bookstores in New York and Boston, has shown promotional skill and merchandising know-how that clearly contradict the publisher's usual characterization of the bookseller, and it has used the remainder to help build stores that draw people in crowds and sell lots of books. With much of their basic stock in the form of remainders and "promotional books" (titles produced very cheaply for remainder tables only), Barnes & Noble is able to discount a wide range of current hardcover and paperback books as well. As a result, it can ask, in its advertising and on large display signs in its growing number of stores, "Why Pay Full Price?" A second chain, Crown Books, which started in Washington, D.C., and has expanded to Los Angeles, seems to be copying (and outdoing) the Barnes & Noble formula and is growing at a rapid rate.

There is no question that Barnes & Noble gives the book buyer the best value for his money by far, and the crowds in the stores prove that value builds business. According to Leonard Riggio, the head of Barnes & Noble, who transformed the company from a modest supplier of college textbooks into the merchandising dynamo it is today, the contribution of the remainder is not a major factor. Riggio is confident that in the unlikely event that remainders disappeared from the scene, the pattern of Barnes & Noble's growth and method of operation would not change appreciably because promotional books would continue to serve that function just as well. I am not as sure as he is.

The price-cutting on current books, which are being sold at full price almost everywhere else, attracts the public because it includes all the best-sellers and the other titles very visible at a given moment. Great care is taken by the price-cutting retailer to restrict the assortment of current books to these highly popular titles. It is important to balance the sale of these books, on which the store's markup has been reduced, with the sale of remainders and promotional books, on which the store may take a considerably higher markup than usual. The development of this merchandising mix and the sales techniques that have made it so successful are a tribute to the genius of Len Riggio. But, contrary to his opinion, I think that remainders are vital to that success.

If remainders disappeared because the publisher had better control over distribution and was able to prevent overprintings, the promotional book would be undermined in two ways. First, fewer titles would be available to promotional publishers, since some of the titles arise from those very remainders. Second, the steps that would eliminate the waste of remainders would also, inevitably, reduce retail prices for original publications, which would reduce the comparative bargain appeal of the promotional title.

As for the contention that buying remainders is followed by the customer's paying list price for other books, there is little evidence in its favor. Barnes & Noble does not display books at full price next to the remainders and discounted current titles, so one must assume that Len Riggio does not agree strongly with that contention. Logic argues the contrary. Remainder buyers are being *trained,* like Pavlov's dog, to avoid paying list price.

ARA Distributing Services, a powerful factor in the distribution of magazines and mass market paperbacks that reputedly accounts for 15 percent of the volume in this field, has been experimenting with putting large, comprehensive book assortments into the new generation of super supermarkets. These "bookstores within a store" range in size from 1000 to 2000 square feet, larger than the typical personal bookshop, and they may have 5000 or 6000 titles or more. Hardbound books, quality paperbacks, and mass market paperbacks (at full retail price) are all represented, but the centerpiece of each bookstore is the collection of remainders and "bargain books" dressed up to look like remainders.

Dwight deGolia, who is in charge of book distribution for ARA, expects books to be a growing segment of the company's activities and stresses that these new book departments are reaching large numbers of people who never saw the inside of a bookstore and would resist going into one. Yet, when presented with books in the friendly atmosphere of their supermarket, these new customers buy in large quantities the books that "offer value."

What Barnes & Noble, Crown, and ARA have proven (in a kind of inadvertent market research) is that there is a large untapped book market out there if books that offer value for the money are brought within reach of the potential customer. Clearly, the publisher cannot offer such "value" by selling all his books at remainder prices and still stay in business. (The author will starve.) But if the publisher will face up to the inefficiencies (instead of compensating for them by increasing prices), he will be able to offer the consumer more value in the original edition than he now does.

It is completely reasonable that the cost of manufacturing books can be reduced by a fourth without any loss in physical quality whatever. On the contrary, the average quality of design, materials, and fabrication should improve. The elimination of overstocks (and, therefore, of remaindering) would, in effect, further reduce manufacturing costs. Distribution costs can be reduced approximately in half: by placing more titles in more stores, by reducing returns, by making sales rep coverage more efficient, etc. These and other improvements could reduce retail prices to half their present average levels.

Reducing book prices (and, in the process, sharply reducing the availability of remainders or eliminating them altogether) will not bring them into the "value for money" range for every title and every browser, but it should expand the market for original hardcover and paperback books beyond their present levels. It's hard to say by how much. Twenty-five percent? If so, it would drop retail prices even further.

Remainders, like the day-old bargain bread and pies of our childhood (when baked goods were distributed as inefficiently as books are today), may seem a wonderful bonanza to the customer, one he would not like to see disappear. In fact, he pays heavily for each remainder bargain—in overpriced books, fewer bookstores, and more limited selection.

The author has no reason to kid himself. Remainders mark an unmistakable end to his sales, they imply (unfairly) that the title has failed, and they do not even give him the consolation of any of the remainder income.

"Of course," the publisher may say, "remaindering is unfortunate, and it does hurt the industry. But will the few books I remainder make any difference in a remainder market fueled by thousands of titles from hundreds of publishers? If I destroy these excess books and take a greater loss, it will only be a useless and empty gesture." True.

The industry's problem of remaindering cannot be solved by any one publisher, and a financial sacrifice by any publisher on behalf of the industry would, indeed, be an empty gesture. The solution for each publisher is to determine his own printing needs more rationally and to place his advance sales to get maximum exposure and minimum returns. Any publisher who does that will see an immediate improvement in his profit, which will prove it is worth the effort. If several large publishers do it, the remainder problem will essentially fade away.

6

Sales Management

A DISTRIBUTION SYSTEM that does not work, that cannot work by its very nature, would present a sufficiently formidable problem in itself. But this problem is compounded by the attitudes it often fosters in the person who is responsible for book distribution: the sales manager. The very confusions generated by the system, which should be a constant reminder of the need for organization and planning, tend instead to encourage despair, the feeling that real management is simply not possible. But even within the present distribution system, sales performance in almost every publishing house could be dramatically improved, with consequent dramatic financial improvement for the author, the bookseller, and the publisher himself.

Under any system of distribution, what should the goal of a publisher's sales department be? Obviously, it should be to attain the maximum net sales (gross sales minus returns) within the budget allowed by management. The budget includes the cost of the sales force in the field and its expenses; the in-house sales staff, advertising and promotion, catalogues, sales conferences, and the like; incentive discounts; returns; attendance at the American Booksellers Association, the American Library Association, and other conventions; and so on.

Stating the goal in these terms presents immediate difficulties, because, for example, the cost of returns is not considered a sales cost (and is *certainly* not budgeted as one) in any publishing house I know. Yet that is exactly what it is. Neither is the cost of incentive discounts, which exist *only* for the purpose of encouraging sales. Actually, although every publisher is aware of the *volume* of his returns (because the accounting department needs that number), though not the *cost*, probably none is aware specifically of what he is paying in the discount steps above the standard discount to make the sales reps' job easier. Consequently, the sales manager usually has no cost budget against which his results can be regularly compared. Management does not say to him (as you would say to your financial adviser), "Here is what you have to work with. Let's see what you can do."

But let's continue with the definition of the sales manager's goal. Achieving maximum sales within an established operating budget applies in any industry. The situation in trade book publishing is sufficiently special to require translating that general immediate objective into more specific terms. Since the greatest selling problem by far in distribution-by-negotiation is getting books into the stores, the maximum sales objective can be converted into two objectives for the sales manager, given the present distribution system: The primary objective is to get the maximum number of titles into stores in correct quantities, and to maintain as many of these as possible in the stores at all times. The secondary objective is to help the store sell those books, thereby increasing the publisher's share of the store's sales volume and the store's total as well.

Implied in all these definitions of goals is the understanding that *management* has the responsibility for deliberately using its budget efficiently. That is to say, if returns are to be increased by $100,000 (which may cost $30,000 in handling costs and destroyed books), what will be the net sales increase? Would the same money spent on higher discounts or more advertising accomplish more? Obviously, since sales costs are not budgeted in this manner, the sales manager is never asked to justify the results against the costs—and he would be a damned fool if he volunteered to do so.

Let us see what happens in most sales departments, and what might happen under a different concept of the role of management. What does happen varies somewhat with each publisher and is determined by the attitudes of sales management and, depending to a large degree on the size of the house, by the selling tools the publisher can afford (or thinks he can afford).

As we have said, returns and incentive discounts are rarely budgeted. They are seldom thought of as sales tools for which an accounting must be made. The most obvious tool is the sales force in the field. The smallest publishers have none except the sales manager himself, who covers the major accounts personally as well as he can, communicating with the rest by mail and through ads and announcements in *Publishers Weekly*.

The next level is the commission sales force. These reps are independent entrepreneurs (or small teams of independents), each covering some part of the country, usually several states, to sell a number of equally independent publishers' lists. Each publisher puts together his own jigsaw puzzle of twelve to eighteen commission reps to cover the country, so Rep A may carry the titles of Publishers X and Y while Rep B carries Publishers X and Z, and so on. Most serious trade book publishers, simply because they do not feel they can justify the high fixed cost of salaried sales reps, depend upon this independent sales force, the cost of which relates directly to sales. When they feel they can afford more, they usually hire their own reps to cover the more productive territories, or the bigger accounts generally, and leave the rest to the commission reps.

The best situation, of course, is a proprietary sales force, selling one publisher's books and only his books and being paid a salary (plus expenses) or a salary plus some sort of bonus.

In almost all sales forces, the territory assigned to each rep is defined geographically. Sometimes that rule is violated to have the sales manager cover key accounts (like B. Dalton or Walden). Sometimes the "major" accounts in an area will be assigned to a senior rep and the "minor" accounts to a junior.

How are territorial boundaries determined? Sometimes by the volume of business from that area—or, more exactly, the volume years ago, when the territory was created. Sometimes it is by number of accounts. Since periodically, as the financial fortune and the mood of the publishing house ebb and flow, territories are added (by dividing some to create new ones) or subtracted (by combining adjoining ones), most sales managers are not sure how their territories were ever created. However, very rarely is an analysis made to see whether, in the light of new information, the existing lines should be redrawn.

Except when a change in the budget dictates expansion or contraction, territorial lines are usually adjusted to suit some momentary convenience. A rep complains he has too many accounts or too much travel, or he moves to a different part of the territory, so the old configuration is no longer convenient. Sometimes a new wholesaler opens at the edge of a territory held by a weak rep and near a territory held by a strong one. This does not mean that the territories that result from this rule of thumb, gut feeling, or educated intuition are necessarily bad. They are probably pretty good, for the most part. But if one were to ask whether the available reps are deployed on the map for maximum effectiveness, the answer would have to be: "Approximately, but not very precisely."

In each territory, the sales rep is usually his own boss. He decides which accounts he will visit when and how much time he will devote to each one. In many sales forces, the rep will submit an itinerary in advance that outlines his expected travel pattern, but it is far from a uniform practice. In only a few houses are such itineraries examined by sales managers to see how much sense they make, either in the amount of time devoted to each area or to the economy of the travel pattern.

Submitting itineraries is standard procedure among the commission reps. Being paid strictly on results, they regard their time and travel expenses as valuable assets. They plan their time meticulously to get the most out of each working day and every traveled mile. Filing the itinerary also forestalls a call from one of their client's sales managers, asking them to cover an author tour or some other last-minute promotion miles out of their way.

In most sales forces, very little is done to supervise the work of the rep. The sales manager will almost certainly look at any order from an important account and perhaps a random sampling of other orders. In only a few houses will the orders be tabulated as they arrive, and in fewer houses still will the tabulations be looked at critically by someone in sales management. The figures will often show only the quantities ordered of the top five or six titles (out of a total of 100 or 200) so that management can see how the advance sale is building on the "titles that matter"; the tabulation is not even intended to be a supervisory tool. Only in a tiny minority of sales departments (perhaps five or six in the entire country) is the tabulation used to determine whether the accounts visited include all the ones that should be visited. In only some of these is the omission of an account called to the attention of the sales rep while there is still time to correct it.

Only a handful of sales forces require the sales reps to report where they have been. George Blagowidow and I introduced such a "call report" at Doubleday in 1955 so we could measure how sales levels changed with the sales time invested. It has since been introduced in a very few other sales forces. Where call reports are not used, the sales manager does not know which accounts or even which cities the rep visited except by laboriously (and inaccurately) tracing his travels from the paper trail of orders received.

If the publisher said to his sales manager, "We are paying for so many thousand hours of selling and sales rep travel time. Do you know how many hours are actually worked? How many are actually used in selling? How many of those hours are used for neither traveling nor selling?," in nineteen out of twenty publishing houses he would have no idea.

Obviously, if the sales manager does not know how the rep spends his time in general, he will not know how he spends it in particular. When the rep calls on a bookstore, what happens? How long does the call take? What is the sequence of events? To what extent is the visit controllable by the sales rep, and are some such patterns more productive than others?

Several sales managers have expressed to me the essence of their attitude somewhat as follows: "I don't need to supervise these guys in detail. They're professionals. They know their jobs and they know their territories. I judge by overall results. The rep who gets good sales is a good rep. The rep with poor sales is asking to be replaced." This attitude, with some minor variations, is typical of sales management in book publishing. Clearly, the word "manage" rarely applies.

When the sales manager calls his reps together for a sales conference at the beginning of each selling season, they are exposed to some pep talk, to a confusing capsule of information on each new title, and to a general idea of the total advance orders expected for each book. Then each rep is on his own, back in his territory and to a large degree unobserved. He knows he will be judged only by overall results. How close was the advance sale on the lead titles to the targeted advance? Did sales in any territory vary widely from the general trend of sales? Did any accounts complain about the sales rep?

The problem is that these gross indicators reveal nothing until there is a serious variation from the pattern of the rest of the sales force. If sales are down 3 percent in a territory, or 5 percent, what does that mean? Could population movement account for it, or regional unemployment, or the inroads of a wholesaler from another territory? How does one judge what the sales might have been? Or what the rep is doing right and what he is doing wrong?

The truth is, very, very few sales managers in book publishing are *managers.* What is frequently lacking is the determination to manage. The very notion that *management* is possible seems strange in the world of confusion and surprises that publishers believe they inhabit. The lack of order or predictability in publishing seems greatest in sales, the possibility of control most remote.

The same anarchic philosophy that constrains management in other aspects of publishing deters management in sales. "Every book is different, every sales rep is different, every store is different, every season is different"—on and on they go. These differences, which in other situations would be an argument for the *need* to manage (after all, uniformity manages itself), become in publishing an explanation of why management is not possible.

If the sales manager does not truly manage or even measure the effectiveness of his sales force, what does he do with his other selling tools? Perhaps the most important of these, and certainly the most expensive (unless returns are more so), is the discount schedule.

Books are somewhat unusual, compared to other consumer goods, in that the producer—the publisher—determines their retail prices. Actually, because setting the retail price is a violation of the law, the publisher determines a "suggested" retail price. Since that is the advertised price and the price printed on the book jacket or cover, it is *the* retail price even though it is not enforceable and every retailer is legally free to sell any book at any price he chooses.

Obviously, since the bookseller is expected to sell the book at the retail price, the publisher must sell the book to the bookseller at a discount and to the wholesaler at a somewhat higher discount (to enable the wholesaler to allow the bookseller a discount).

The discount has two purposes. The first one, which is clearly legitimate, is to provide the margin between cost and selling price that any reseller, wholesale or retail, needs to survive. This "basic" discount is generally in the range of 40 percent off the retail price for retailers and 46 percent off the retail price for wholesalers.

□ *It should be noted that many publishers allow booksellers only a discount of about 30 percent on so-called technical or professional books. These are not, strictly speaking, trade books, even though some move through bookstores. They are generally higher in price, which lessens the pain, somewhat, of the smaller discount. It is not a discount that wins friends among booksellers.*

The second purpose, which is by no means so clearly legitimate, is to influence the nature of the order placed by the wholesaler or retailer, usually its size. To discourage the bookseller from placing occasional small orders and to make it easier for the sales rep to write a larger order when he is in the store (or sometimes for the misguided purpose of driving the retailer to order from his wholesaler), the publisher applies penalty discounts to small orders. The bookseller may get no more than 25 or 33⅓ percent on orders for one to four copies, for example. On the other hand, the discount schedule is used to encourage the bookseller to increase the size of each order placed. To accomplish this, the publisher customarily grants a higher discount on a larger order, increasing the discount as the order gets bigger.

One difficulty with the discount schedule as a selling tool is that, while the publisher may have created each step and nuance in the schedule with a kind of customer in mind (and sometimes a *particular* customer in mind), the bookseller who is conscious of discounts sees the *entire* schedule before him and is influenced accordingly. So the publisher may increase the discount for 26 copies from 40 to 41

percent to encourage the smaller bookseller to take "just a few more."
But that bookseller (or a slightly larger one) is aware that if he reaches
101 copies he will get 42 or 43 percent, so he may be tempted to
postpone ordering until he can buy that many books. The publisher
may have intended that next discount step to tempt larger stores into
a larger order—and it may do that in some cases—yet in others it
results in no order at all.

Actually, most booksellers are not completely aware of the detailed
discount schedule for each publisher. The large chains know the
schedules well and know how to use them. So do the giant stores and
the wholesalers. Those booksellers with computers use them to store
the discount information and help control its use. But, given the
confusion resulting from each publisher's insistence on having different
discount terms and from the complications some publishers have built
into their schedules, the details are more than booksellers, without
active reminders from the sales rep, can keep in mind.

And, considering that the discount steps are primarily a selling tool,
it is surprising how many sales reps can't keep the schedule in mind
either, and most do not use the schedule effectively. More significant,
very few sales managers teach their reps how to use discounts
effectively, and fewer still check to see whether they do.

My contention—that most reps do not use their discount schedule
effectively—can be checked very easily by any publisher. He need only
tabulate the orders from each rep by size; that is, he need only total
the number of orders for one copy, for two copies, etc. If the discount
schedule is being used, he will find more orders for the quantity just
above each step than he will for the quantity just *below* each step.
The result of this little exercise will be an eye-opener for nine
publishers out of ten.

Sales management must be sure that every rep knows the discount
schedule (keeping it simple will help) and how to use it properly. On
the other hand, the discount, like other selling tools, may be traded or
adapted for greater cost-effectiveness. Because the discount is not the
only ingredient in the buying decision, the stronger the sales force, the
less the discount schedule is needed to mold the results. A well-directed
sales force, by anticipating the bookseller's needs, will, with or without
a discount penalty, reduce the frequency of the small nuisance orders.
The information, service, and personal attention that the rep supplies
make it less important to give discount rewards to bring an order
from 25 assorted books to 26 assorted.

All of this, of course, sidesteps completely the question of whether
encouraging the bookseller to place larger orders is, in itself,

necessarily desirable for the publisher. Getting the *right* quantity into the store may be worth a large discount, but is a *larger* quantity necessarily closer to the *right* quantity? The heavy returns of unsold books cast some doubt on that idea.

Special offers are another selling tool that is rarely used effectively and is, in fact, of doubtful value. A popular one is "one free with ten," by which the bookseller gets an eleventh copy free if he buys ten copies. The theory behind this device is that it will enable the rep to increase what might have been an order for five or six copies to ten copies by the offer of the free eleventh copy. Does it work? Possibly, depending greatly on how well the sales force knows how to use it. But usually by far the largest quantity of free books goes to the accounts that would have placed big orders anyway, where the increase in the size of the order is of doubtful practical value even if it could have been accomplished at no cost.

It is easy to see what the effect of the "one free in ten" offer is by tallying orders by size and comparing the total to tallies for other titles in a similar range of total advance. The difference will show where the offer has bumped up the order.

A similar device is the prepublication or pre–January 1 price, when the book may be marked: "$20 till January 1, $25 thereafter." The bookseller buys it at the lower price and is urged to buy enough copies to ensure that he will have some copies left to give him a higher profit when the price goes up. The difference between the two prices must be large enough to make the early price a real bargain, but not so great that the later price will inhibit sales. This offer tends to be most useful for the large expensive book—an art book, for instance. But here, too, the degree to which it works is very sensitive to how the sales force uses it.

How well does sales management use returns, which are frequently more costly than discounts? The whole question of returns was covered in depth in Chapter 5. Let us here consider returns only as a selling tool and how its proper use would be guided by a sales manager.

The obvious question has to be asked: Why offer the bookseller the privilege of returning unsold books? The purpose is to bring his order closer to what the sales rep (speaking for the publisher) thinks is the *right* order rather than the cautious point at which the bookseller starts. It is definitely not to get the bookseller to order larger quantities than the rep believes he needs. If there is an inclination to do that, the rep should get the order cut immediately. Holding out the "safety net" of returns should encourage the bookseller to order a few more copies of the title he is buying too conservatively and to include one or two copies of some of the titles he is inclined to skip altogether.

Suppose a bookstore sells 250 copies of Blockbuster A. The rep who has done a perfect job will have sold it 251 copies, so one copy will be returned. (A perfect selling job would *not* have been 250 copies. Unless a copy is returned, we would not know whether the store could have sold 251 or 275.) Selling that store 300 or 500 copies and getting a heavy return would have been misusing the returns device. Any return above one copy is waste—perhaps, realistically, unavoidable waste, but certainly waste.

We then have a two-dimensional measure of the sales reps' use of returns. One is the percentage of returns, which should be as low as possible. The other is the number of titles and number of stores represented in the returns, which should be as high as possible. The rep who does best has a low percentage of returns that includes many stores and many titles.

Returns, as we have said and will say again, are made by the sales force and not by the bookseller. The level of returns (as a percentage of sales) is completely under the control of the sales force, if anyone is bothering to exercise control. Being a selling tool, returns should be measured and evaluated as such. Actually, the tool is the offer to take returns of unsold books; the actual returns are the evidence of how it was used.

If returns are high, the selling tool has probably been poorly used. If returns are low and widely distributed among the reps, the accounts, and the titles, it has been well used. But one cannot characterize returns as satisfactory or not on the basis of percentage alone. Low returns do not necessarily mean proper selling. The total percentage of returns may be low, but returns may have been too high in some territories and too low in others, or the range may vary widely by title, according to how different books were presented by the reps. An overall rate that management considers acceptable could easily mask overselling in some aspect and underselling in another. In order to *manage* returns, it is essential to know how they are distributed, by sales rep as well as by account and title, so that the sales manager can know what specific selling errors he must correct with which reps.

There is another aspect to returns—as there is to the incentive discount, the size of the sales force, or any of the publisher's selling tools. That is the degree to which trading off the cost of one tool for the cost of another (assuming each is used reasonably well) may result in lower sales cost or more effective selling. Let us construct a hypothetical example.

In Chapter 12, on the economics of trade publishing, we present the figures for an actual publisher breaking even on a sales volume of $8 million a year. Suppose that this publisher has returns running 35 percent of sales—$2.8 million—as many publishers do. What do these returns cost?

If the publisher's cost of shipping and handling outgoing books (not including freight) is 2 percent and the cost of receiving, handling, and accounting returns is 2 percent of returns, the "in and out" cost of returns is 4 percent, which is $112,000. If the run-on manufacturing cost of books is 16 percent of sales, and if a third of that is lost on returns because of damage or the low sales value of remainders, that would represent an additional cost of $149,000. The combined cost of returns is, therefore, *not less than* (there are other cost factors) $261,000 a year.

Let us make the reasonable assumption that this publisher has a sales force of ten reps, which costs $275,000 a year in salaries and expenses. Covering the United States with ten reps is not easy. Even with good sales management (which the 35 percent returns rate denies), infrequent visits to accounts may encourage selling errors because the store must buy each time to cover a longer period. Selling errors create returns.

The sales manager could argue that half the cost of returns ($130,000) might be invested in enlarging the sales force. Since, with smaller territories, each rep's travel expenses would be reduced, the $130,000 would buy at least a 50 percent increase—to fifteen reps or, more likely to sixteen or seventeen. Since the reduced territories would also reduce the time spent traveling and increase the time spent selling, the 50 percent increase in personnel would be almost equivalent to a 100 percent increase in actual visits to accounts. If the sales manager believes (and the evidence would not be too hard to assemble) that doubling the number of visits to accounts will cut returns in half, he should recommend the tradeoff, because there is absolutely no question that doubling the number of visits will also dramatically increase sales.

But the use of these selling tools, or their cost, is rarely presented by the publisher to the sales manager as his responsibility. And the sales manager does not usually see his job as one of measuring and comparing how the selling tools are used to get the most value for the publisher's money.

Consider advertising, which must not only be managed but also coordinated with the overall sales effort. Coordinating advertising and sales management would imply, for example, putting the ads where the books are. But rarely does the publisher's "information system" make that possible.

Advertising is not always the instrument of the sales department and not always primarily intended to sell books. Sometimes the main purpose is to cement relations with an author or to build the image of promotional savvy that will attract other authors. One function of advertising that has grown in recent years is influencing the buyers of subsidiary rights, particularly paperback reprint houses. So the decision of what to advertise and where will often be made by the subsidiary rights manager. If such advertising sells books, so much the better, but it is not the central concern.

Regardless of the immediate purpose, one would hope that every scrap of advertising would be used by the sales department to maximum advantage in selling books. The key is much less the effect on the public (except for the rare, truly massive advertising campaign) than its effect on the bookseller. Publishers resent any analogies made between selling books and selling soap, but certainly in this area there is a great deal to be learned from those who sell soap. Long before the large sums are spent on the impressive advertising campaigns the soap industry can well afford, the sales reps are in the stores with proofs of the ads, stills from the television programs, tallies of the millions of people who will see or hear the message, pictures of the posters, aisle displays, and other store paraphernalia that the soap company will provide just as the campaign breaks. The rep gets the store's commitment to give his products more display space than usual, to use the promotional material, and, in general, to make as big an effort as possible. The consumer may not be moved by the cleverness or the ubiquity of the advertising, but when he walks into the store, he certainly cannot miss the presence of the soap company's products.

Advertising campaigns in publishing are never on a comparable scale, but the impact of the dollars spent is usually much weaker than it should be because "selling" the advertising campaign to the retail stores is not done properly, if at all. Except for the likelihood that the salesmen will carry photostats of the ads (if they are ready on time) or, more likely, photostats of sketches of the ads, there is usually little coordination between the advertising department and the sales force in the field.

□ *The editorial department, which must be more low key, cannot use the company's advertising as blatantly to present its case to prospective authors. However, because the company that advertises heavily should be attractive to many authors, the editorial department of such a company should find dignified ways to inform authors. Perhaps a monthly packet of reproductions of advertisements supplied to each author's agent just "for your information" would help make the point.*

Perhaps just as important, very rarely does the sales manager attempt to measure the effectiveness of the money spent on advertising (the techniques to do this are well established) to determine whether he should ask for more or whether he would prefer to trade some advertising money for more sales reps. The idea that advertising too must be managed, that it must justify its costs, and that it is the sales manager's responsibility to determine how to use it best is not widely held.

But, of course, the sales manager's responsibility extends to all the resources that the publisher puts at his disposal to get the job done. It is not only his responsibility to use these resources well but also to recommend when those resources should be increased or decreased or when money should be moved from one area to another to make the selling effort more cost-effective.

To a sales manager who is so handicapped that his resources consist essentially of his own efforts, I can only advise: Work hard, try to get the publishing program expanded to justify a larger sales budget, and be alert for the moment that hard evidence supports expanding your resources. The initial expansion would be a collection of independent commission reps, an easy transition because the cost of representation is directly proportional to the sales the reps produce.

Since these reps are their own bosses, a sales manager tends to feel that they cannot be "managed," and in that respect, a sales manager with a commission force is greatly handicapped compared to a sales manager with a proprietary sales force. But that's not altogether true.

The authority the manager has over reps who are on the payroll *simply because* they are on the payroll is more apparent than real. The salaried reps, being human, do not do things just because the sales manager tells them to. Like anyone else, they perform better when they are led (and inspired) rather than driven. The sales manager coping with independent and independent-minded commission reps is not very much different from the architect or general contractor who has one independent do the foundation, another the plumbing, etc., all against a fixed plan and schedule. The sales manager (as soon as he becomes a manager-planner-strategist) must be a salesman. The rule is: When you know what you want done, first you sell your management, then the people who work for you, after which you can effectively sell the market. Whether the sales force is on commission or on salary, the best rule for management is: "Don't tell 'em, sell 'em."

With that in mind, the goal of a sales manager working with commission reps is to have the reps perform as though they were salaried reps, working exclusively for him. It is not dissimilar to his goal when he approaches the bookstores: to have them sell his books as though he owned the stores, but to leave the ownership headaches just where they are.

It should not be overlooked, however, that although the sales manager can strive to exercise greater direction over the commission reps, he will not, in fact, exercise as much control or achieve the level of result that is possible with a house force. For one thing, he cannot nullify the obligations each commission rep owes to his other clients, even if he gets more than his share of the rep's time and energy. For another, the commission rep is appropriately conscious of his own interests, one of which is receiving value for time invested. As a result, it is hard to convince commission reps to sell the full list (rather than just the leading titles) and to pay attention to the backlist, which, as we shall consider in detail in Chapter 14, tends to yield less value for time invested by presently accepted selling methods.

As a result, it is a good rule of thumb (though only that) that a house sales rep will sell two to three times what a commission rep will sell in the same territory. I do not claim that a house rep will triple sales from an account like B. Dalton or Baker & Taylor, where more complete coverage of the list can only yield marginal advantages. However, in any geographical area, the additional time available to the house rep, the superior communication with the home office, the greater attention to the backlist and to the lesser forthcoming titles, and the greater willingness to cover more accounts will improve sales results very quickly. It is also worth mentioning that the sales to B. Dalton or any chain, the branches of which are usually ignored by commission reps because they do not get commissions on the sale, can be *dramatically* improved by calling on the individual stores to inform managers, get display space, assure reorders, etc.

Obviously, the greatest opportunities to manage exist when the sales force is on salary or at least proprietary, working exclusively for one publisher. In many such cases, the compensation is a salary plus some sort of incentive commission. A well-managed house sales force should *not* be on commission or some kind of mixture of commission and salary. Commission, like piecework, is a substitute for management. It is based on the thoroughly discredited notion that the worker can effectively manage himself given enough incentive.

Motivation, or incentive, is of great concern, but there are better ways to inspire it than cash carrots. A sales force that is well trained, well directed, and well supervised will produce well; for such a sales force, incentive pay only creates confusion.

One of the very first obligations of the sales manager (to himself and to the publisher) is to resist accepting uncritically the advance sales targets presented (usually by editors) for the lead titles; such targets may hurt all the other books on the list and frequently damage the longer-term prospects for the lead titles as well. It is all very fine for each editor to be concerned with his most important title and to think of the total sale in round numbers. The sales manager must be concerned with the total effect of the sale of the entire list on the company's welfare. He must think in a very detailed way of how to extract the maximum sale for that list from each retail location. And he must consider how to accomplish this in relation to the costs of covering that retail location—in sales time, in discounts, in returns.

Orders should be, *not* the direct, but the *indirect* objective of the sales force. To the degree that the sales force attains control in the retail store, orders will result automatically.

What is control? Essentially, it is mastery over the fate of that publisher's books in the store. The first and most important ingredient of control is winning the freedom to put into the store whatever titles in whatever quantities (and, ideally, at whatever time) the publisher wishes. Such a privilege, even if subject to severe restrictions, is worth every effort by the publisher; the only way to achieve it is by a long history of dealing fairly with the bookseller and of putting in books clearly in his best interest.

This freedom, obviously, is by no means "free." It is constrained more by the publisher's own restraint in the bookseller's interest than it would be by the arbitrariness of an authoritative buyer. The payoff will be, by eliminating or reducing the effect of negotiation, to sharply reduce the element of chance, which should increase the publisher's total sales and decrease returns in that store.

The second ingredient of control is influencing how the books are handled when they arrive in the store. Getting better display space will increase the likelihood of sale, no matter what the intrinsic merit of the title. The window is the best display point, but *only* if additional copies are easily accessible inside. A good goal for the rep is to have as many titles inside the store face out, eye level, and as close to the front door as possible.

Cultivating and informing bookstore clerks should be a sales force responsibility. They should be friendly to the publisher—they are very much aware of imprints, even if the public is not—and they should know enough about as many of the titles as possible so they can convincingly recommend appropriate ones to browsers.

The third ingredient is developing and making available special selling tools for the bookseller or helping him develop them himself. If he has an active mailing list, it should promote the publisher's books. If he sells by phone, if he sponsors a reading circle, if he encourages local businesses to give books as gifts, if he manages book fairs at schools, if he solicits libraries—in any of these activities, in which only a few titles can be promoted, the influence of the publisher's rep can make a big difference in which titles are chosen and how effectively they are promoted.

These do not exhaust the possibilities for enhancing control, but they are enough to suggest that "getting the order" is only one detail in a complex program to create a position of strength at the point where books and book buyers meet.

In the long run, there can be no question that a house sales force that is tightly organized, well trained, and closely directed is ideal. But the long run may start quite a way down the road for a small publisher who does not have the money to field his own sales force or the flow of books to sustain it when it is in position. Obviously, the smallest publisher would be foolish to saddle himself with the cost of a house sales force and the largest would be foolish if he did not. For those in between, this decision depends on the particular circumstances.

The key question, once it is established that the publisher has a suitable sales force, is: How effective will the management of that sales force be? A commission sales force that is well managed will outperform a house sales force with flaccid management. The distinction lies in the extent to which the publisher's sales manager influences where the reps go and what they do when they get there. Good management, based on this definition, which may require no more than one manager with a small support staff, can multiply the results achieved by fifteen or twenty reps, whether house or commission.

Publishers who believe that the sales force is an "expense" consciously encourage booksellers, particularly the smaller ones, to place their orders with wholesalers; by reducing the number of accounts his sales force must cover, the publisher also reduces his expenses. But the publisher who thinks this way has overlooked three elements.

1. If you do not actively try to *get some copies of new titles into the retail stores,* there will be virtually no orders from the stores to the wholesaler.
2. The wholesaler's breadth of inventory is deliberately *always* narrow. Any order for a title the wholesaler does not have, or an order forestalled by discovering from the wholesaler's microfiche that the book is not in stock, is a sale lost forever. This is happening to *every* publisher at *every* wholesaler *every day.*
3. The cost to the publisher in discount differential is significant. If the average retail discount is 42 percent and the average wholesale discount is 48 percent, the difference of six percentage points of discount means he is getting 12½ percent less from the wholesaler (6 divided by 48) than he does from the retailer for the same book.

In the confusion of the publishing world, the *value* of a strong sales force is not readily apparent, though its *cost* is clear. Now and again, best-sellers suddenly appear on the lists of small publishers with no sales force or a very weak one. This is frequently taken to demonstrate that the sales force doesn't do much after all. The fact is that best-sellers bless publishing houses with weak sales forces less frequently than they do publishers with strong sales forces. More important than the occasional best-seller, of course, is the success of a *list,* the list of the publisher with a strong sales force compared with the list of the publisher with a weak one.

Although the sales force's contribution to actually creating a best-seller is not immediately evident, it is very evident, even without sophisticated analysis, in squeezing more sales out of each best-seller. With a strong sales force, even the best-seller will be available in more stores and will be out of stock less frequently. So the effect of a strong sales force on the sales and profit of a best-seller is considerable. Its effect on the more run-of-the-mill books can be a doubling or tripling of sales even in the initial few months of sale.

The strong sales force, because of its efforts in getting store display, clerk support, and prompt reordering, can also maintain a continuing rate of sale, add to the active sales life of the title, rescue it from the eleven-month death sentence, and slow the rate at which backlist sales decay.

The sales force is, without question, the most important and productive (as well as, in larger publishing houses, the most expensive) selling tool available, and it is usually the sales force that determines

how well discounts, returns, and the other tools will be used.
Therefore, it is essential that *management* determine the way the sales
force is used.

The tasks of sales management, with respect to the sales force,
would appear to be:

1. Determining how to set up the sales territories.
2. Determining, within each territory, how the available time is
   to be allocated.
3. Determining, to the degree possible, what each rep is to do in
   each territory and with each account, making that clearly
   understood through instruction and training.
4. Monitoring each rep's performance to see that the desired
   work is in fact done, to correct errors or misunderstandings
   early, and to identify and make generally available
   improvements in methods devised in the field.
5. Measuring the cost-effectiveness of the sales force as a guide to
   better management and as a means of knowing when to
   recommend its expansion (or contraction).

Let us start at the beginning: how to determine what portion of the
United States to assign to each rep. If the sales force is composed
entirely of commission reps, the sales manager's options are sharply
circumscribed. The reps cannot be asked to change their territorial
boundaries. What the sales manager can do is try to bring together the
largest number of selling hours for his books by selecting the
commission reps carefully.

The manager with a proprietary sales force of ten or twenty or fifty
reps obviously has much more freedom. The most logical way to divide
their time is according to the potential market to be covered. The
potential is of two sorts. There are the large, identifiable customers—
such as B. Dalton, Walden, Baker & Taylor, Ingram—the sales to
which are not directly proportional to the time invested but for which
some maximum level of attention (twenty-four visits a year?) is likely
to be as productive as any sales force attention can be. The amount of
attention each of these accounts should get, in view of the list to be
sold and the time available, can be decided arbitrarily, and relatively
simply, by sales management (it may depend somewhat on that
account's susceptibility to additional attention).

The other potential is the much less structured possible sale to the
smaller and medium-sized accounts (and to accounts that are not yet
accounts). This potential depends on how population, income,
educational level, and other factors that may identify book buyers are

distributed over the country. After subtracting the time required for the major accounts, management should allocate the remaining sales time to this potential market as nearly proportionally as possible, making later adjustments based on experience.

To begin even to think about this, sales management needs to estimate potential so it has some idea of how to distribute its sales effort. A number of yardsticks of potential are available and are regularly used for planning sales coverage in other consumer industries. Many of these measures have been developed by the U.S. Census Bureau and the U.S. Department of Commerce. Probably the most convenient ones are a series of measures developed by the magazine *Sales and Marketing Management,* a number of which (like population, income level, and general retail sales) relate well to book sales generally; but each publisher will have to find the particular indicator or combination that correlates best for his sales.

□ *Attempting to measure in detail the relative potential market for books makes sense only if the publisher is large enough and has a list broad enough for "potential" to have some influence. There is no hard and fast rule, but I would judge that a sales volume in the $3 million to $4 million range is a minimum.*

Demographic (social statistical) information that suggests sales potential, and a great deal more, for geographical and economic units called SMSAs (Standard Metropolitan Statistical Areas) is available from a variety of sources, including the U.S. Government. An SMSA is, essentially, an urbanized area, the limits of which are usually defined (for convenience) by county lines but which ignore city and state boundaries if they do not actually define the market area. The top three hundred SMSAs include about 80 percent of the U.S. population, but because the retail sale of books (at least, through the "trade") is very sensitive to urbanization, they probably include about 95 percent of the trade book market. (See Appendix C.)

The available time of the sales force can be allocated to SMSAs proportional to the potential each has for the sale of books. The time allotted to each one can, in turn, be further divided among the localities and the specific accounts to encourage greater productivity.

□ *The SMSA also provides a convenient yardstick for adjusting sales coverage as conditions change. For example, in the ten years between 1970 and 1980, the population of metropolitan Houston increased by 45 percent, Tampa by 53 percent, and Phoenix by 55 percent, while the population in and around Cleveland declined by 8 percent. How many sales managers reallocated their sales effort accordingly?*

The result is a daily plan for each sales rep that balances the available time against the relative sales potential of each part of the territory. This is what we mean by "territory management." It is presently neither practiced nor contemplated by any sales manager I know about, but I expect it will become commonplace soon after the first manager experiments with it.

At the beginning, it will be difficult to judge how much time to assign to each bit of geography. It will be hard to translate number of days into number of sales calls. Planning is certain to increase the number of visits per day that the sales rep can make. And some places may appear to have too few accounts because many of the areas, particularly those farther from the rep's home, have been neglected because of the lack of prior management and, therefore, fewer accounts have been developed.

□ *If you study where the sales rep* now *spends his time, you will find that in the usual laissez faire sales force, time is* not *spent in proportion to potential sales. The rep spends a disproportionate amount of time close to his home. When he does give a distant area some attention, look for a special reason, usually a personal one. If the sales manager is convinced that the sales force does not need help in planning coverage because each rep "knows the territory and knows the accounts," he should at least be sure that each rep lives in the part of his territory with the most sales potential.*

In cases of apparent account shortage—where calculated potential is markedly greater than the proportion of existing bookstores—it may be necessary to do some prospecting to find and develop accounts. You may be sure they are there.

The detailed coverage plan that results from relating management's analysis of potential to the available resources in selling time and manpower, which is the *beginning* of the process of supervision, must be discussed thoroughly and agreed to by each rep. This is to ensure that his very particular knowledge of the territory is taken into account, which is certain to improve management's first cut at a plan. And as a result, the rep will understand better what is expected and will be more likely to be more productive.

After the coverage plan is defined, the rep would be responsible for making appointments with store buyers, wherever that is desirable, and planning each day based on the accounts listed by the plan. The plan can be completed for the entire selling season, with the understanding that the daily listing of accounts is subject to adjustment based on the availability of appointments, the result of the previous visit to that area, or unforeseen selling demands (like the eruption of a best-seller). To protect this flexibility, the rep might be sent a final version of each week's daily assignments two weeks before the actual work week. The daily plan can provide space for the rep to use it as a call and an expense report, returning it each day with the day's orders attached.

□ *Our technology has certainly reached a level that would easily permit a relatively inexpensive planning and communications system to be built around a microcomputer in each sales rep's home, communicating by telephone to a large central computer in the publisher's office. The rep's computer would maintain "files" on his accounts, with the pertinent portions going to the central computer, and the central computer would communicate the visiting plan and receive the results. Communication would be at nighttime telephone rates.*

The final version of the daily plans should be closely coordinated with the publicity and promotion. For example, if an author promotion is planned for a particular city, the daily plans for that city should remind the rep several weeks ahead to get orders for that title so that books reach the stores in time to benefit from the attention and to protect the publisher's relations with the author.

The guidance and supervision of the sales force have several objectives. One is simply to see that as many accounts as possible are covered, that the attention they get is related to their importance, that each rep's production is in the acceptable range and climbing, and so on. Another goal is to sell advance orders, which is of particular importance to the success of the frontlist. Still another is improving the *quality* of account coverage, which is completely separate from number of visits or even number of orders and which includes selling the backlist.

The advance sale has a mysterious, almost cabalistic fascination for the publisher. The purpose of the advance is to have copies as close as possible, and as readily available as possible, to as many customers as possible at the moment the publicity and reviews announce the book's publication. The advance represents an investment for the publisher in the cost of books as well as in the cost of the sales force to get the advance orders. Achieving the equivalent distribution with fewer copies means a lower investment and a lower risk.

In our present distribution environment, the advance sale is truly the key to the title's immediate and long-term success. The key to the value of the advance, in turn, is *where* the books go rather than *how many*. It is true that a very high advance is not likely to be reached without a wide, even if badly balanced, distribution. But very few books reach advance sales of that magnitude, and below that level the total number says very little about the quality of the advance.

Management needs to know, and needs to tell the rep, how many copies should ideally go into the Personal Bookshop in Northampton or the Dartmouth College store—in short, into each of the rep's accounts. If management told him that, it would not have to saddle the rep with the need to translate the national figures into the numbers for his territory and his accounts. Actually, that is how management should arrive at the total national forecast, by adding up all the individual orders it wants.

It is not surprising to find a sales manager who declines to state an optimal order for any particular store. But I have actually met a sales manager who sincerely believes that the result of each negotiation between rep and bookseller somehow distills the "right order." Most managers accept negotiation *because no alternative seems possible,* but it is strange to find someone who has actually watched the process, and seen the results, who believes that it has special virtues.

The idea of negotiation is based partly on the seemingly reasonable notion that each bookseller "knows" his customers and that each rep "knows" his books. That idea is badly flawed on both counts. Chance and accidental factors so dominate the negotiation that the resulting order will rarely be carefully considered even if both parties approached it with better information.

We are dealing with *probabilities.* There is no absolutely correct prediction of how many copies each store will sell of each book. Within the range of copies we believe are likely to be sold, we must weigh the cost of the danger of losing a sale (by not having a copy) against the cost of the danger of making a return (by having too many). Those costs are different for the books of a publisher who penalizes for returns and for those of one who does not. They are also different when the discount to the bookseller is 50 percent and when it is 40 percent. Since the danger of being out of stock depends on how quickly additional copies can be available, we must consider whether the bookseller is three days or three weeks from the publisher's warehouse. From all these factors, the object is to arrive at the order that, on balance, offers the highest probability of maximum profit or minimum cost to the store.

Almost every publisher has the information from previous titles in its files to project the range of probable sale and to calculate an optimal advance order for each title for each account. Though some elements in the calculation (such as the time required for a package to reach the account) must be estimated somewhat crudely, this approach to determining the optimal quantity will nevertheless enable the publisher to give the bookseller a much more profitable balance between the cost of returns and the cost of lost sales than can possibly result from hasty, underinformed negotiation between rep and bookseller. Those calculations, for every new title and every account, should be in the hands of every rep as the sales conference adjourns and the advance sale begins.

At the very least, these optimal orders should give each rep a clear understanding of what management wants him to accomplish. The way in which the optimal order is used may vary with the rep and with the account, but the rep will know that management has set the criterion by which to judge the success of his negotiation.

If the rep is going to make a bad buying recommendation, it should be *management's* bad recommendation, not his own. Management should know what it wants its people to do. And the rep has a right to ask, "If you don't know what you want, why are you sending me?"

The rep should be encouraged, wherever possible, to show the optimal order to the account as calculated and to explain that it has been carefully prepared to give the store maximum sales and minimum returns. Even if the bookseller rejects the order the first time, and perhaps a second and third time, he will ultimately realize that it is really not a trick to oversell (and it better not be).

There are many reasons for sales management to pay closer attention to selling the backlist, and there are also many reasons why both sales reps and booksellers would rather deal with other problems, as we noted in Chapter 3.

The plant costs of the backlist have long since been absorbed, so the accounting department explains (completely falsely, of course) that the margin of profit on these books is higher. Almost all backlist books are titles that are in stock, consuming valuable space and tying up valuable funds. Translating existing stock into current dollars is certainly a worthy activity. Selling the backlist increases the size of the average shipment to the bookstore, reducing both the bookstore's average freight costs and the publisher's average shipping and warehousing costs. Keeping backlist books in print makes authors happy and gives the publisher a good reputation to help attract other authors with long-lived books.

However, as we saw (in Chapter 3, "Getting Books to the Public"), it is not possible for sales management to write backlist orders for the reps before each sales visit, title by title, in the same way they can for the frontlist. The rep must laboriously create each backlist order in the bookstore itself.

The role of sales management in the present situation is clear. It is precisely because selling the backlist *is* so uninteresting that the reps should not have to decide whether to do it. Management must guide the sales force to see to it that inventories *are* taken and the backlist *is* sold.

Management has to consider all the aspects of the salesman's job, particularly the places where performance can be sharpened through training. It has to consider all the ways in which a salesman can perform each aspect of the job and decide which ones are the most effective. This is not to denigrate the skill of the sales rep. Even the professional ballplayer is told when to bunt and when to take the pitch.

Training should never stop. The performance of each rep can always be improved, because an active management learns new things (usually from the reps) all the time, and because constantly changing conditions require frequent adjustments in the sales force's role.

Alas, in many publishing sales forces, training never starts. Many sales managers avoid the need to train, though in fact they compound it, by hiring experienced reps who have either been trained by someone else or have learned by doing. Even when neophytes are hired, "training" usually consists of several days in the office, meeting people and learning the essential paperwork, and several days with one or two experienced reps, watching them work and getting their practical advice. Rarely does this "training" include discussion of such basic issues as how the territory is to be covered, how time is to be allocated, how travel can be made most efficient, and how to set performance goals. Even more rarely does management discuss the nature of the sales call itself: what is to be accomplished, useful strategies in different situations, the most efficient sequence of selling steps, how to handle the variety of reasons the bookseller will have for not buying, etc.

The low interest in sales training stems in part, no doubt, from the feeling that sales training is not really useful or even possible. The training methods and goals used in other industries are not expected to apply to publishing because "books are different," as we have often heard. Further, the idea of training jars the usual relation between sales manager and reps—that of a senior among equals. Most managers avoid any implication that they can do the job better than the man in the field; it would be embarrassing to play the teacher to the colleagues with whom they were, until a short time before, learning by trial and error.

The reps "train" each other in an informal way. At evening bull sessions during sales conference, over drinks at poker games, there is enough shop talk to touch on many of the subjects that would normally be part of any formal training. However, the points of view developed are not necessarily as useful in implementing management's objectives.

Training involves both what to do and how to do it most effectively, with sureness and a minimum of effort. Sales management itself learns about selling by developing the training program. There are many ways to take inventory in a bookstore. How can it be done quickly and with the least danger that titles will be missed?

Defining the sales territories properly, specifying clearly the job to be done by each rep, and training each rep do not add up to the whole job of sales management. There remains, at least, the need to monitor what is actually done so that results can be judged and the activity of the reps corrected where necessary. This follow-up activity will pay off for the sales manager whether the sales force is on commission or proprietary.

A savvy sales manager can learn a great deal by visiting a cross section of booksellers and wholesalers, cutting through the polite chitchat that always marks the visit by the boss. How many of the publisher's titles are in the window? How much do the clerks know about this month's titles? How well is the backlist represented? What are other publishers doing that the bookseller finds of interest?

A great deal of very effective monitoring can be accomplished simply by analyzing the orders sent in from the field. In many publishing houses, the appearance of such monitoring is maintained by passing all the orders over the sales manager's desk as they arrive in a random fashion. Depending on each publisher's internal systems, that looking may delay the shipment of books by a day or two, but it accomplishes little else. The sales manager may believe it gives him a "feel" for the market; in fact, all he gets is a misleading notion that he has an overview of the sales situation and some assurance that, if there is anything shocking or unpleasant in those orders, he will not be surprised by someone else in the company knowing it first.

The orders are packed with information, but to be useful it must be extracted in an organized manner. The computer departments of publishing houses are not always very helpful. A proper analysis of even the first scattered orders can tell the manager what the total advance sale will be, which salesmen are following their travel plan, how each salesman *really* feels about each of the new books, which salesmen are "high-spotting" the list and which are selling the entire line, which titles are worth an extra promotional effort and where it should be put, and which salesmen are selling the backlist along with the new books. When the rep has been given the optimal new book order for each account, the analysis will show how closely the actual order resembles the desirable one. Without such analysis, the management of the sales effort cannot be very effective.

I have looked at enough sales departments to know that where central planning of territorial coverage is not practiced and/or sales reps are not analyzed in this manner—in other words, in nine out of ten publishing houses—something as simple and essential as visiting all the eligible accounts does not happen. Some accounts sold one list are not sold another. The loss in sales can easily run 5 to 10 percent, depending on the season.

We discovered the uneven coverage of accounts at Doubleday in a very roundabout way. We (principally George Blagowidow) developed, in about 1954, a method for predicting the total advance sale on a book by analyzing the first orders sent in by the reps. The method, regression analysis, results in nineteen out of twenty predictions falling within the "control" range unless conditions have been somehow changed.

George Blagowidow noticed that the accuracy of the predictions of the advance sale—the degree to which we were "in control"—varied with the season of the year. It soon became clear that this had nothing to do with the weather. Each rep was simply not visiting the same bookstores each season, and this affected sales sufficiently to throw the predictions off noticeably.

□ *This illustrates one of the great values of objective measurement as opposed to "feel," "experience," "judgment," or whatever was being used to set printing quantities before. The salesmen had been failing to cover all the accounts with each list for years. Why hadn't the predictions by the committee deciding printing quantities ever revealed that inconsistency?*

This variation in accuracy of prediction showed us what should have been obvious: What the sales force does or does not do will affect sales. It was a revelation!

This led us to analyze Doubleday's sales city by city, comparing sales volume to the size of the cities and the amount of sales effort we put into each. Sure enough, more effort equaled more sales! This insight enabled us to calculate how much the Doubleday sales force should be expanded—and emphasized the importance of monitoring the sales force to ensure we got the coverage we had planned.

Reorganizing and expanding the sales force required winning the cooperation, not just of skeptics, but of outright opponents of the idea. Sales management, which did not monitor sales rep activity and therefore knew very little about it, did not believe a sales increase was possible. "We get 80 percent of our business from 20 percent of the accounts. We're covering all the accounts worth covering now. There's nothing more out there." The sales reps' annual commission at Doubleday was very high. Despite our assurance of increased sales, the reps were certain their income would be cut drastically because of the reduction in the size of each territory. We guaranteed each rep no reduction in income for the first two years, to give each one a chance to see the sales increase. (Before the two years were up, almost everyone was earning substantially more than before.)

Our original analysis had been hampered by lack of precise information. Like most publishing sales forces at that time, Doubleday's had been run without very much direct supervision. Each salesman organized and covered his territory as he saw fit. In our study, we deduced approximately where the salesman had been by laboriously going back over the trail of orders he had sent.

That was far from being a precise measure of the degree of sales attention Doubleday was giving each account and each area. Having proven to ourselves how sensitive sales are to the level of sales effort, we wanted to measure that effort precisely. We asked each sales rep to submit a weekly call report that listed the accounts visited each day.

These call reports were very useful, and the information they provided resulted in further expansion of the sales force. For example, before the reorganization, Florida was part of a larger territory, including Georgia and Alabama. In the enlarged sales force, against loud protests from the sales experts, we made Florida a territory by itself. Within two years, we had divided Florida into three separate territories, each of which was producing more sales than we had had from the entire state before. Stores that had been buying $25 or $50 worth of books a year without sales coverage blossomed into $500 and $700 accounts when they were cultivated. We found accounts we never knew existed. This did not surprise the newly hired sales reps, who did not know any better, but it amazed the veterans. All talk about loss of income faded as the sharp increase in sales proved that the mathematical analysis reflected the situation better than the opinions of experienced reps.

And we continued to expand our sales analyses. The call report was resisted because the men saw it as a management tool for checking on their work—and it was. Our analyses, which fed back pertinent information from the reports, to which no one objected, were actually even more effective checks.

For example, we had an excellent line of Catholic paperbacks, called Image Books. We tabulated the Catholic population by sales territory and compared it to the sales of Image Books. The irony of that analysis was heightened because it showed that the Jewish salesmen, generally, were doing better with Image than the Catholic salesmen were. It was very easy for a salesman to see that if his territory had 5 percent of the Catholic population and he was getting 2 percent of the Image sales, there was room for improvement. And we got it. Similar analyses for other subgroups—juveniles, books for college students, for example—showed us and the salesmen where improvement should be easy, and the results confirmed it.

Anchor Books, the new paperback line directed principally at the college market, was an interesting case. Because Doubleday did not effectively reach the professors directly, we were going through the slow process of waiting for them to learn about the books through advertising and through their own browsing. A problem arose, however, because a vice-president of Doubleday very aggressively resented the investment the company was making in a line of books that had not yet reached the break-even point. At the sales conference inaugurating the expanded sales force, this vice-president got into a violent shouting match with Jason Epstein, who had "invented" Anchor Books and was running it, threatening to have the board of directors close down Anchor and throw out Jason as well.

We turned that threat into a challenge to the new sales force. The reps who had high ratios of Anchor sales explained to the other reps how they did it. We analyzed the sales against the college population to identify the places with the best potential. We encouraged reps to enlist the help of college bookstore managers in reaching professors. Anchor's sales climbed steeply, and within a few months it was safely and securely in the black.

In the first year of the expanded sales force, the sale of a representative group of backlist titles, which had been declining almost on schedule 10 percent per year, went *up* 35 percent. Within five years, Doubleday's trade book sales increased almost fourfold, even though editorial production did not increase in quantity and remained essentially the same in quality during that period.

The improvement was not due only to the increase in number of reps. We also learned how to use the reps. We learned about pushing for a larger number of titles on each order instead of number of copies; the importance of the store's clerks; the value of store display and how to control it; how to reduce the length of a sales call without sacrificing effectiveness; and so on. We continued to get more sales by applying more effort and by applying it more skillfully. In the large accounts that had been considered well covered before the expansion, sales went up because the rep now had additional time to check and replace stock more often, get more titles into the store, get better display of Doubleday books, make friends with more clerks, etc.

In outlying areas, like South Dakota and Brooklyn, New York, Doubleday reps found accounts that were visited by few, if any, other publishers. We soon discovered that, although we estimated our national sales to be about 7 percent of the total, in areas and individual stores overlooked by our competitors, we were getting 25 to 35 percent of the sales, sometimes more. No doubt our presence in these areas broadened the assortment of books the store or book department could offer, and that in itself led to an increase in sales from which we were the principal beneficiary.

The accounts the rep covers and the orders he writes are only part of the picture. In view of how crucial the retail store is to the very existence of the trade book publisher, it is amazing how little interest the publisher, and specifically, the publisher's sales manager, shows in what goes on inside the store.

Other producers of consumer goods consider it a natural obligation to monitor the situation in the stores. Indeed, it is hard to see how a sales organization can function without knowing what happens where the products meet the consumers. How do the clerks feel about the company and its products? How are its products displayed? Are display space and location improving vis-à-vis the competition? How are new products selling? Are reorders placed promptly? What is the consumer response to an advertising campaign or promotion and how quickly is it felt? For companies (in other industries) who do not wish to divert their own sales staffs for this work, commercial monitoring services have hundreds of part-time employees around the country available to patrol the supermarket aisles or sections of department stores and report back in minute detail. In publishing, there is no interest.

I recall that back in 1955, when I was involved in restructuring the Doubleday sales force, we found a sales rep in Los Angeles, Jack O'Leary, who recognized the importance of display and made it a part of his responsibility. At that time, we estimated that Doubleday represented about 7 percent of trade book sales (which Jack had no way of knowing); he had set for himself a display goal of 20 percent. That is, if a window or the most active selling area in a store he covered had one Doubleday title out of every five books displayed, Jack felt he had met his goal. If display was poorer, he went to work on whatever influenced display in that store to raise the percentage.

We named this measure of store display the "O'Leary" and gave the one-in-five ratio a rating of one. Regional managers and the "experts" from the home office began to count books on display whenever they visited bookstores; sales reps soon became very conscious of how their "O'Leary" compared with others. We soon had a lot of stores with an O'Leary rating of two (two Doubleday titles in every five). And there is no doubt that better display paid off in higher sales.

But display is more than measuring O'Learys, though that would be a big step forward for those publishers who have not even thought about it. The object of display is, at least, getting the books "face out, at eye level, and as close to the front door as possible," leaving the other space to competitors. A book is more effectively displayed if it can be seen in more than one section of the store; this is clearly part of the sales rep's obligation.

In addition to getting these display advantages, winning the cooperation of sales clerks should be part of the rep's regular duties.

Monitoring the retail stores can supply all sorts of useful information. As we suggest in Chapter 14, on determining printing quantities, the publisher should know at what rate his titles are selling *out* of the stores, so he knows the rate at which they should be going *into* the stores. The publisher can determine how quickly books are selling by having his rep take an inventory. If the publisher is operating a merchandising plan (for which periodic bookstore inventories are essential), this information will be flowing in automatically, and frequently, from many stores. If not, a few representative stores can be polled regularly.

Management should choose these representative stores according to two criteria: They should be large enough to be expected to sell *some* copies of a moderate best-seller each week and be broad enough to indicate general, rather than specific, consumer interest. They should also be near the reps' homes so that inventories can be taken frequently (once every two weeks or so, during critical periods) without affecting the territory's coverage on the whole. Twenty or thirty such stores, scattered across the country, should give sales management a very good continuous reading of the market situation.

In addition to telling the publisher something about his own titles—

to help decide whether a reprint is really necessary or to gauge the effectiveness of an advertising campaign or a national TV appearance —these stores can reveal something about selected competitors' titles, how they are faring in relation to chance events or to the competitors' special efforts on their behalf.

The publisher should know which wholesaler each bookseller customarily uses and how much he relies on the wholesaler for his books. He should know how many titles are customarily in the store— divided at least into the broad categories of adult hardcover, juvenile, quality paperback, and mass paperback, if not more precisely—so he can assess his own success in getting titles included in that mix.

Finally, if sales management includes control, the need to *measure* is inescapable. Control of anything requires measurement as a principal ingredient, and sales is no exception. In particular, if there is to be any intelligent supervision of the sales force, it is important to measure results rep by rep.

The first item to measure is sales itself. All sales managements look at the figures in each territory and compare them with the previous year's to get an immediate rough measure of each rep's accomplishments. Since each rep was in part dependent on that year's publications as created by the editorial department, the measure must be relative, not absolute.

But this simple measure must be refined. Did any of this year's titles have a strong regional interest? How do the actual sales compare to the potential sales for each territory as measured by retail sales or population? How is the potential in each territory shifting? Potential in an SMSA can sometimes change 5 to 10 percent in one year, which can make a rep look like a hero or a bum.

The measurement of the final result in dollars is in some ways less useful to management than an analysis of the activities that contribute to that result. Such an analysis, which may explain why some reps are more successful, can help in training others. It is useful to compare number of bookstore visits ("handicapped" for the territory's travel burden), ratio of orders written to store visits, success with selling predetermined advance orders, distribution of accounts by volume of purchases (in a thoroughly covered territory, this will show a "normal" curve), performance on the backlist, and so on.

Setting absolute standards of performance in trade book publishing is virtually impossible and can be very demoralizing. I have seen it done in the sales department of a large publishing house with devastating results. Too many things change—the list, the economy, other publishers' lists—to permit such arbitrariness. However, comparing performance among reps is completely valid and much more useful. Management is not asking the reps to reach some standard but only that the reps doing less well improve their performance to achieve the level of others.

Measurement is also essential to making a judgment about the company's overall investment in the sales force as an effective selling tool. Most sales forces are their present size through happenstance. Rarely is it determined by any objective evaluation of the market to be covered and a calculation of number of reps needed to return the maximum profit. Even if such a study has been made, it would obviously soon be out of date because of changes in population, bookstore distribution, the general economy, or the publisher's own list.

An increase in sales force—or, for that matter, having a sales force at all—is not a matter of what the company can "afford" to spend. This decision is not the same thing as deciding whether to buy a living room sofa. The sales force is a vital tool of the business. It either produces more than it costs, clearly and without any question, or it is not affordable, no matter how large the bank balance.

The question of how many sales reps to have is not different in principle from the same question applied to the editorial department: Will the margin on the additional sales volume resulting from the addition of a sales rep be sufficient to cover all the additional costs?

When the size of the sales force is up for discussion in most publishing houses (usually with the hope of reducing it), it is most frequently considered against sales volume. It may be arbitrarily assumed that 5 percent of revenue should be budgeted for the sales force—or 3 or 7½ percent. Or it is suggested that annual sales of $300,000—or $450,000 or some other number—are needed to support a sales rep. Whatever the yardstick, it is usually not very much to the point. Additional net income for additional cost is the *only* pertinent criterion.

The way most publishing houses operate, this criterion is difficult to apply because it involves measuring subtle variables. They become easier to measure to the degree that sales management exercises control over the reps' activity. If the performance among the reps is wildly different, it is difficult to project how much one more rep will add to the current level of sales.

Once there is relative consistency in sales activity—similar working days per season, similar activity per day, consistent visiting of accounts, number of advance orders consistent with territory size, reasonable success with predetermined orders, etc.—measuring the effect of possible changes in field sales force is fairly straightforward. (See Appendix D.)

No matter how large the sales force is, management everywhere is concerned with productivity. Whether it is an automobile assembly line or an airlines reservation desk, management must constantly find ways to increase production without compromising quality, and a publisher's sales department is no exception. The only sensible way to beat rising costs is to increase the rate of production.

The sales rep produces sales. Part of the goal of sales management is to help the rep produce more sales per unit of time and per unit of cost. Much of what we have discussed here is, of course, directed toward that very goal: better design of territories, planning more thorough coverage, predetermining advance orders, measuring results, etc. There are other ways that productivity can be increased.

How can the number of miles traveled be reduced? How can the sales visits be shortened? Can the telephone be used to better advantage? Are all the days that can be worked being used? Can the reps' paperwork be simplified?

Management must constantly look for ways to make each rep more productive and for ways to measure its own performance in doing so.

It should be clear that, even though distribution-by-negotiation makes it very difficult for the publisher to reach respectable levels of distribution across the major portion of his list, a great deal can be accomplished by resourceful sales management. The sales manager must use his selling tools as imaginatively and productively as possible, measuring the effectiveness of each tool and his own effectiveness in using it. Since his most important sales tool is the sales force, the sales manager must learn how to shape it, direct it, and control it rather than let it run itself. The successful sales manager must *manage* because, in a laissez faire situation, all the evils of distribution-by-negotiation are free to do their worst.

7

The Alternative

Distribution Through a Merchandising Plan

WE HAVE CONSIDERED the shortcomings inherent in distribution-by-negotiation. The costs are high: an army of publishers' sales reps supported by headquarters staffs, briefed at expensive sales conferences prepared by important editorial and promotion executives, provided with elaborate sales catalogues, jacket proofs, and other material, and supported by advertising in *Publishers Weekly* and mailings to booksellers. To negotiate with these reps, the booksellers must commit a major portion of management time. And significant indirect costs include the absolutely useless delays, probably averaging a full year, that this method of distribution imposes between the finished manuscript and publication. In addition, the lack of precision that characterizes the publisher's management of printing quantities is largely due to the vagueness of his connection to the market because of distribution-by-negotiation.

The eleven-month life of the typical book, whether it is taken by the bookseller in the negotiation or skipped—a short life due in large part to the time limit on the return, which is an essential feature of this distribution system—is certainly another substantial cost levied on the entire industry.

So, too, is the weakness of the bookstore network itself. Individuals hesitate to open bookshops because of the prospect of unattractive profits and the dull clerical and bookkeeping burden imposed by the system. General merchandise chains also face the uncertainty and unpredictability of results and their apparent dependence on some mysterious buying expertise that no one knows how to measure or test.

Because, like the tango, it takes two to negotiate, the commitment by the retailer to the negotiation process is not a matter of choice. He must be willing to face the publisher's rep or his catalogue, try to visualize the book from its description, estimate how many are likely to be sold and how quickly, and commit money to the validity of the decision on each title. The degree to which this process reduces the number "willing to play" was dramatized by the paperback "revolution" after World War II. The number of retail locations quickly grew from less than 5000 to about 100,000 when magazine distributors freed the retailer from the need to make detailed buying decisions. And that growth took place even though the magazine distributor cut the retailer's margin *approximately in half.*

The restraints on the spread of retail outlets can certainly be counted as a considerable cost of distribution-by-negotiation.

If the costs are bad, the results are worse. The buying decisions that emerge from these negotiations are, as we have seen, disastrous. The most visible disaster and the one that agitates publishers the most— massive returns—is not the most serious (though the millions it costs disqualify it from being considered minor). The largely invisible result of the negative decisions, the skips, and the cautious insufficient buys that put books out of stock too early are much more damaging. We cannot measure the direct result in lost sales to the publisher, author and bookseller, but we know it is huge.

In most parts of the country, where bookstores are modest in size and are not constantly pushed by the competition to offer customers a greater choice, the negotiation system quietly produces one of its natural results: a range of titles far narrower than it needs to be for an equivalent investment by the bookseller. The restricted choice does, of course, result in a larger number of disappointed browsers; more serious, perhaps, it also reduces the number of browsers. It does not take too many disappointments to convince a reasonable person that going down to the bookstore in the hope of finding something useful or diverting is just not worth the trouble.

With neither low cost nor high performance to recommend it, distribution-by-negotiation survives out of a natural conservative human tendency to assume that what has survived for so long must correspond to nature's laws and an equally human tendency to avoid the risks that come with making changes. However, for all the reasons we have discussed, the mounting pressures within publishing are suggesting even to the most conservative observer that the risk of change may be smaller than the risk of standing still. If so, what should the changes be?

It is easy to cite the characteristics of a desirable distribution

method, particularly after our experience with the present one. To list
a few:

1. It should enable bookstores to serve their clientele more
   efficiently by a combination of reduced costs and increased
   sales, thus reducing the size of the population base needed to
   support each store, making more bookstores possible and
   increasing the profitability of existing stores.
2. It should relieve the bookseller of the need to make buying
   decisions title by title and of the drudgery of controlling
   inventory title by title and provide him with the means to
   control inventory more effectively.
3. The titles in the store, in breadth and depth, should be
   matched better to the probable demands of customers.
4. The risk of poor matches of supply to demand should be
   minimized by avoiding the need for buying for a long period,
   particularly of strong titles, by permitting smaller increments
   to arrive more frequently and adjusting those increments as
   actual demand varies inevitably from predicted demand.
5. It should increase the number of titles (and therefore the sales)
   per dollar of bookstore inventory investment.
6. It should improve the profitability of bookselling and, just as
   important, the predictability—and with it the control over
   retailing results.

The most likely distribution method to produce such results is some
variation of the "merchandising plan." Its essential element shifts the
responsibility for the inventory of books in the store from the
bookseller to the publisher. Once the publisher is responsible for the
results of the inventory decisions as well as the decisions themselves,
some improvements become immediately apparent.

One of these is the application of the superior market information
available to the publisher. Presumably he knows what audience he had
in mind when he decided to publish the book. Before publication, he
knows which previously published titles are comparable to each
forthcoming book and how each of these titles sold *in each store* that
carries his books. He therefore knows the limits within which the sales
in each store are likely to fall. But, since he will have the authority to
put copies in at will, he can reduce the inventory risk on titles
expected to sell strongly by initially putting in a fraction of the
expected sale and adjusting future shipments to actual experience.

After publication, the publisher can monitor sales in as many stores
in as many different kinds of neighborhoods and parts of the country

as necessary to grasp sales trends and overall public demand much more quickly and more precisely than any bookseller trying to interpret his own spotty experience.

When this shift of responsibility becomes a fact of the publisher's life, as it is in the lives of suppliers in some other consumer industries, and the rewards become clearer to him, it seems inevitable that the publisher will develop and refine methods for improving the inventory decisions, objective methods using the information he has and can obtain.

It might be interesting to consider why a bookseller or a publisher might want to change from distribution-by-negotiation to a merchandising plan. In my opinion, each should not only want it, each should be actively pressing the other to agree to it.

Consider an average bookstore, which may have 6000 to 8000 titles in stock at any one time, mostly one or two copies of each. According to a number of book retailing executives, the stock position on each title should be reviewed monthly, but we know that is almost impossible even in well-run establishments. Every two months is more like it. Once every two months is six times a year. Examining 6000 to 8000 titles six times a year requires about 40,000 buying decisions: to buy or not to buy, to keep or to return. The buyer also has to consider each forthcoming title. Whether done from catalogues or with the publisher's rep, this certainly adds the equivalent of 10,000 decisions each year.

The buyer must, therefore, make something like 50,000 buying decisions a year, probably many more. These range from a $1 decision to get one copy (or *not* to get one copy) of a $1.95 book to a several-hundred-dollar decision on a large quantity of a potential best-seller. Since most of the titles in the store are represented in very small quantities, the typical decision is probably worth no more than $10. Actually, if the store with 6000 to 8000 titles is doing $300,000 a year in sales, on which the bookseller's margin is $100,000, the 50,000 decisions are worth exactly $2 each.

The number of titles is not decreasing, and the average size of the retail bookstore is definitely increasing, so the number of $10 decisions is going up for the average buyer each year.

Some 50,000 decisions over 250 working days a year comes to 200 decisions a day, but since publishing is a very seasonal business, some days are 500-decision days. How much research can the bookseller afford to do on each decision? How much thought can he give each of 500 independent decisions in a day? How much time and thought is a $10 decision worth? How good can such decisions be?

One could argue that the bookstores' survival proves that they are "good enough." But could they be better? Could more bookstores survive and prosper? Is the rest of the business world crazy for trying to save top executive time and thought for the fewer, larger management decisions? If the business world is not crazy, how can the bookseller be freed to make the fewer, larger management decisions? Who is going to make the $10 decisions that must be made?

If the routine buying decisions on individual titles could be assigned to others, with the bookseller remaining in control, the buying function would come a lot closer to the executive job it should be.

Who can do the actual buying, making all the title-by-title decisions that average between $2 and $10 each in value? It should be someone who:

1. Knows each title intimately.
2. Knows how much and what kind of promotion will actually take place.
3. Knows how well each title is selling in other stores.
4. Knows whether the sales trend for each title is generally upward or downward.
5. Is highly motivated to do a good job and make the bookseller happy.
6. Is paid as little as possible by the bookseller to do the work, preferably nothing.
7. Can be put under the complete supervision of the bookseller.

The bookseller may feel that there is no such person, but there certainly is—the bookseller's friendly enemy, the *publisher.*

The bookseller finds it hard to imagine any alternative to the present situation. Having the publisher make the buying decisions, he will say, is like putting the fox in with the chickens. The bookseller can also say:

1. Nobody knows his customers as he knows them, so how could anyone else (even if he could be trusted) possibly know which titles belong in the store?
2. The quality of publishers' sales reps is very spotty. Some of them know less about their own titles, or even their own company, than the bookseller does (he finds he is constantly educating them), so how can they be very helpful?
3. Available cash is the bookseller's greatest need, and the only way to husband it is to supervise personally the expenditure of every penny, both in choosing titles and quantities and in taking maximum advantage of publishers' discount schedules.

4. Having made thousands of decisions, he can recall with satisfaction the specific cases of his buying acumen (different examples for each bookseller): the time the publisher recommended a large quantity but he knew the book was a "dog" and bought conservatively, saving the cost of heavy returns; or the more popular example of the best-seller that the publisher sold very gingerly, not realizing what a gold mine he had, but the bookseller could see the avalanche of sales coming and bought heavily so he was never out of stock even though the publisher was himself out of stock.

If other responses don't seem convincing enough, there is always: "This is my store and *nobody* is going to tell me what to have in *my* store." These defenses are contradicted only by the results.

The dangers in handing the buying function over to the publisher seem very real until one considers how easy it would be for the bookseller to control the publisher's performance. That changes the risks altogether, because it makes the publisher the instrument for achieving the bookseller's goals. Control would be difficult if the bookseller allowed each of the hundreds of publishers with whom he does business to do his own buying. Fortunately, ten or twelve of the largest publishers are likely to account for 70 percent of the store's business. If the burden of 70 percent of the buying were lifted from his shoulders, the bookseller could handle the rest easily under the present methods, particularly if, in the process, that 70 percent became much more profitable.

In the early period of such controls over the publisher, it may be desirable to specify minimum standards of performance.

The first step is to determine the present rate of inventory turnover. Because the publisher has better information about what is selling and because he would no longer have any incentive to "load" the store, the publisher should be able to improve turnover by at least 25 percent. (Taking some inevitable returns a little earlier is almost enough to do that.) So, if the store's turnover is 3.0, the standard should be set at 3.75. If the store is on the Booz, Allen & Hamilton average of 3.22, the stock turn standard should be 4.0.

The second step is to establish the discount. The publisher will be writing the orders and deciding how often they should be written. The size of each order will depend on the publisher's own success in making buying decisions, so relating discounts to the size of large orders makes no sense. And since the publisher will be deciding when to ship and when to consolidate shipments, neither does a separate charge for freight. The discount might be fixed at 40 percent, with freight paid by the publisher both for delivery and returns—and, of course, no penalty on returns.

The third step is the amount of inventory to be permitted each publisher. The easiest way to arrive at that is to determine the approximate present inventory in the store for each of the top ten or twelve publishers.

With that information in hand, a letter might go to each of these publishers, somewhat as follows:

Dear valued publisher-supplier:

We are prepared to move away from our present practices of negotiating with your sales rep over new titles, and frequently over the backlist, and of keeping detailed inventory and sales records to make reorder decisions. In effect, we are prepared to remove ourselves altogether, in your case and with a small number of other publishers, from the title-by-title buying and returns decisions.

We are going to hand you our order forms and our checkbook and let you do the buying of your own titles for our store. You may place any orders you wish as often as you wish. You pick the titles and you decide the quantities. We will continue to control display and will concentrate our attention on *selling* books rather than buying them.

This arrangement is subject to the following conditions:

1. The inventory value of your books must average no more than your present inventory in our store, which is XX dollars, at cost, until further notice. You will control how this average inventory is divided among your titles month by month. You are under no obligation to use the full amount of this allowance, but we expect you will not exceed it.

2. Your discount to us, if you accept this plan, must be 40 percent *delivered,* and you must pay the freight on all returns. Since you are in control of the inventory, you will decide what books will be returned and when.

3. The stock turnover on your books for the twelve months must be at least 3.75. That means that the minimum annual gross margin we must realize on your books is $2.47 (the markup of 67 percent multiplied by the turnover of 3.75) for each average inventory dollar. In the future, the number of dollars of average inventory allocated to you will be adjusted upward or downward depending on how the annual gross margin on your books compares with the annual gross margin on other publishers' books. Beginning two years from the date we begin this new arrangement, and after you have had an opportunity to develop some familiarity with

sales through our store, if your annual gross margin should fall below the minimum standard of $2.47, we will expect to bill you for the shortfall.

4. Your sales representative may visit the store as often as you like and you may write orders as often as you like. You may instruct us to return books as often as you like. Once every three months, at least, your sales representative must take a complete inventory of your books in our store and submit it to us for our control and for us to review your inventory dollar limits.

Please understand that we are giving you this freedom to control your own books in our store in the expectation that as a result of your efforts, we will sell more of your books so that both you and we will make more money from your titles. The guidelines on discount and turnover we are asking you to meet are realistic, based on experience, not arbitrary whim. In the future, we expect to adjust those guidelines according to further experience. Publishers who give us higher gross margins and higher profits will be rewarded and encouraged by being given more of our buying money. Publishers whose books produce a low gross margin, either because of poor titles or bad buying policy, will have their average inventories reduced accordingly.

You can count on our complete cooperation in helping you get better results. We are all in this for the same goal: higher bookstore profits.

We are looking forward to your favorable response so that we may set up a meeting with the proper member of your organization to get the new plan started.

Sincerely,
Your Bookseller

Not every publisher will be eager to be responsible for the profitability of his own books in the bookstore. Not every publisher will see that this change will be as valuable to him as it is to the bookstore. But all it takes to start the change is a few determined booksellers, preferably larger stores, whose business is important enough that the publisher cannot ignore them. Once the change starts and the results begin to show higher profits for the bookstore and higher sales for the publisher, we can expect the new approach to spread quickly through the industry.

If some of the large publishers were asked to manage their own inventory in the bookstore, they would probably not know what to do. But they would learn. They would discover the meaning of such things as stock turnover, gross margin, and the simple rules of retailing.

Putting the publisher to work for the store creates more time for store management to manage the store. Every bookseller is aware of the merchandising, the special promotions, improvements in service—

the hundreds of useful things he *could* do—if he had the time.

Imagine, each morning, the manager of each supermarket discussing with each driver for each bakery his estimate of the day's needs for soft rolls, hard rolls, the various styles of bread, crullers, English muffins, etc. And he would tell you that nobody else knows his customers' preference for cracked wheat over whole wheat. He also will remember when a driver left too many bagels, so he had a heavy return, and another time when the bakery made the buying decision and the store ran out of frankfurter buns at three o'clock on a Friday. Ridiculous? Of course.

But I can remember when that is exactly how baked goods were sold. The bakery truck drove up; the driver went to the manager or owner and was told what was wanted that day; he went back to the truck and got it. The grocery store owner was not going to let someone else tell *him* what bread to display in *his* store. The idea that some clerk in a bakery miles away could make better buying decisions seemed as ridiculous to the grocery owner as the corresponding idea seems today to the bookseller. (And it probably seemed just as ridiculous to the baker that he should assume the grocer's responsibility, as it does now to the publisher.)

"But," the bookseller will say, "books are not bread. There are only a few varieties of bread, but there are at least 100,000 titles to choose from. Books are different."

Books certainly are different! Controlling retail book stocks is clearly much more complicated than controlling bread stocks. Yet the grocer used to insist on making his own bread decisions precisely because they seemed very complicated. Nevertheless, as it has turned out, the statistical methods the baker is forced to use yield better decisions than the subjective methods of the grocer. The much greater complexity in controlling book stocks suggests that statistical buying methods will yield even more spectacular advantages for books than they do for bread.

One would imagine, in view of his success, that the baker must have an involved, sensitive system for making these decisions. Not at all. Different bakeries use different methods, but the several systems I have examined are amazing in their simplicity, usually based on some version of averaging previous sales. But can the baker be trusted to make honest decisions? The food retailer has a very simple instrument for keeping the baker honest and on his toes. The baker's portion of the store's buying budget, as I have suggested the publisher's should be, is awarded strictly on results. The baker who makes better choices gets more money and more freedom; the one who makes poorer choices finds more of his competitors' breads in the store and less of his own. There is no need for an honor system.

The miracle of improved distribution in bread is due, for the most part, to a single factor: the simple transfer of responsibility from the retailer to the supplier. The supplier's strategic position makes it possible for him to make immensely better decisions without superior ability or intelligence or even the use of sophisticated computers (books will be different in this respect). The supplier has information the retailer does not have: He can see patterns in the forest of sales while the retailer is still puzzling over the tree; changes in popular taste or regional preference are evident quickly; even without statistical methods, the masses of information and experience suggest operational rules. Today, publishers don't bother gathering or studying such information in relation to books, but it is available to *them, not* to the bookseller.

Perhaps just as important is a subtle change in motive and point of view. When the retailer is making the buying decisions, being resistant at every step, the supplier's natural inclination is to sell his products as forcefully as possible—and probably to sell too much. As we know, the cost to the publisher of putting too many copies into the store is the return of unsold books—a cost he is accustomed to accepting. When the responsibility for buying is shifted to the publisher, however, the cost of putting too many copies into the store becomes much more serious. In addition to accepting the returns, the publisher will also have to accept a reduction in the buying budget available to him, based on his poor "buying" performance.

Among the many ways in which book publishing differs from baking is the variation in each publisher's volume of sales from one year to another, or even one season to another, because of the difference in that season's list. The actual yearly variation in sales is considerably less than is generally supposed, but it may be enough to strain the agreed formula for inventory level or monthly deliveries for that period. If it appears that it will be, it is a simple matter for the publisher to lay the facts before the booksellers and negotiate an increase in the formula of 10 or 25 percent for the period of the expected surge.

Of course, in our example of baked goods, the prediction is much easier and less critical than it is for books. The number of items to be controlled in a retail outlet is usually much smaller, frequently only a tiny fraction of the number of titles in any bookstore, and the number of units sold in a given time is almost always much greater than the number of any one title sold in a typical bookstore. But it is exactly because inventory control in retail bookselling is very complicated that the bookseller needs more help and is entitled to get it from his supplier.

Years ago, when statistical prediction was in its infancy and computers were unsophisticated and hard to come by, the publisher was perhaps in no position to help or even to understand that he could. Today, he no longer has an excuse for shirking his responsibility; he can easily allocate some of his computer time to figuring out the most economical inventory levels for his customers.

There is no question in my mind that any publisher can guarantee a stock turnover of 4 and that he can profitably sell to the bookseller at 40 percent, freight paid on deliveries and returns. This can be done while *expanding* the number of titles in the store and *increasing* the sales. Since there is no way to guess how broad the assortment would be in any given store, we cannot calculate the absolute profit advantage that would result. But we can see what a stock turn of 4 and a cost of 60 percent would do to the rate of profit for the average bookstore in the Booz, Allen & Hamilton survey.

A cost of goods of 60 percent means that for every 60 cents of cost, the bookseller marks up the item 40 cents to arrive at the retail dollar. This amounts to a markup of 67 cents per dollar of cost, which, multiplied by the turn of 4, gives an annual margin per dollar of inventory of $2.68.

The Booz, Allen survey showed the average store earning 12.8 cents on an annual margin of $1.80. An increase in margin to $2.68 with costs unchanged increases earnings to $.88 per dollar of inventory, or *seven times the present rate of profit*. Actually, the bookseller's costs would *not* remain unchanged: They would go *down*. Returns would be reduced, as would the overhead associated with buying, record-keeping, and the like.

As it happens, as this book is being prepared for publication, a small bookstore chain, Under Cover Books in Cleveland, Ohio, is instituting the transfer of inventory responsibility to the publishers recommended here. The move is being "coached" by my son, Mike Shatzkin. All the indications are, not only that the shift in control will work, but that Under Cover Books will very quickly become one of the most profitable book retailers in the United States, creating a bandwagon for other retailers to jump on.

□ *The initial reaction of publishers to Under Cover Books' suggestion is predictable and interesting. Sales managers are very suspicious and wary; they wish it wouldn't happen. On the other hand, the sales reps almost unanimously love the idea. They know the orders they write are, through no fault of their own, frequently wrong and can be improved to benefit both parties.*

One should have expected the initiative for publisher control of store inventory to have come from a publisher rather than a retailer, for publishers should be much more aware of the advantages of having a greater voice in what books are in the store. Actually, publishers have made such moves before. Years ago, Grosset & Dunlap sales reps controlled the inventory of children's books in many stores, using a simplified model stock system that overstocked the store and gave many advantages to the publisher and few to the retailer. Random House currently has a plan under which its rep has a stronger influence on the store's advance order in exchange for a more favorable discount. And here and there can be found "agency" plans, which reward the store for greater representation of titles, and isolated situations where a trusted rep will be informally in control of his titles for some of his accounts.

The most ambitious and sophisticated publisher's effort to date was the Doubleday Merchandising Plan of the late 1950s and early 1960s. The mathematical basis was rudimentary; it was handicapped by the model stock approach; and, most serious of all, it suffered because we did not have the courage to push it far enough. Nevertheless, the results were spectacular. Here's how it happened.

Doubleday had a salesman in Los Angeles in the mid-fifties who had cultivated a very close and amicable relationship with the area's most important wholesaler at that time, Vromans. The salesman argued, very sensibly, that because of the long travel time for books, particularly small parcels, a local source of books was needed that could reach booksellers quickly while the source itself was replenished with truck shipments that moved faster. He developed the idea beautifully, and Doubleday was soon moving mountains of books through Vromans. The difference to Doubleday between the wholesale and retail discounts was a small price to pay for this advantage.

But, because the salesman was properly concerned about being fair and not overloading Vromans with books and equally concerned about running out of stock, he was spending almost all his time controlling Vromans' inventory levels instead of calling on the retail accounts. He would phone in orders to New York for Vromans almost daily, and despite his close attention, he frequently had to ask for shipment by air freight. We were also experiencing heavy returns from Vromans. A very sound idea had created some very unsatisfactory side effects.

Not only did the salesman resist the demands from New York that he cover the many retail stores in the territory properly, so did Vromans. They didn't know the books and therefore didn't trust themselves to pick titles and quantities, and it was important to them to have good stock turnover. Our rep had brought the stock turnover to almost four times annually, and they were concerned that with less attention it might slip.

How we convinced Vromans I do not know, but George Blagowidow and I proposed a plan and they agreed to test it for three months. Our salesman would come into Vromans only *one day* each month to take a complete inventory of Doubleday titles, which he would send airmail special delivery to New York. George Blagowidow would study the previous sales on all the titles and integrate that information with the rep's monthly inventory to determine the quantities for a *single* monthly shipment (except for new books, which would be shipped at normal times in the normal way). Since they had been taking inventory almost every day and receiving fifteen or eighteen shipments each month, there was great skepticism that *one* inventory and *one* shipment could possibly do as well. The salesman himself expected that the experiment would fail and he would soon be permitted to resume his daily stock checks.

From our records, we totaled previous sales to Vromans by title and set up some formulas (which now seem childishly simple) for predicting future sales by title and calculating shipments. Everything worked as planned, with one inventory and one shipment each month.

By the end of the fifth month, it was clear that stock turnover was up to 7, the out-of-stock situations were trivial, returns were down sharply, and, of course, shipping (paid by Vromans) was a fraction of its previous costs. And we recaptured the full-time services of one salesman, which served further to increase our sales in Southern California.

Since the method had worked so well for a wholesaler, we asked ourselves, Why not bookstores? And the Doubleday Merchandising Plan was born.

Under pressure from a nervous sales management, which had opposed the Vromans experiment, we made the mistake of letting caution prevail. Instead of asking stores to let us control *all* Doubleday titles at *all* times, from delivery to returns, we restricted the operation of the plan to the backlist. Doubleday's sales management worried that booksellers would strongly resist any attempt "to tell them what titles they should have," but felt they would be more amenable to ceding the largely housekeeping chore of tending to the ones they had already chosen. This greatly restricted our freedom to maneuver. Furthermore, it is on the new titles that a merchandising plan can deliver the most spectacular stock turnover increases and greatly reduce returns. Restricting ourselves to the backlist also meant that we were essentially locked into a model stock concept, controlling inventory according to each title's sales in that store.

We mitigated that restriction to some degree by persuading our own reps that an advance order from a store on the plan should have as many titles as possible to give the plan more books to work with, and that we preferred too few copies of any title rather than too many because small quantities would automatically be corrected by the plan.

We can see now how much we sacrificed by agreeing to be less radical. Our restriction to the backlist imposed on us many of the same handicaps that make the job virtually impossible for the individual bookseller. The Doubleday plan made better decisions only because it introduced order and objectivity and because our sales reps (reluctantly) took inventory every month. But it could have been operated just as effectively by the bookseller himself if he had taken monthly inventories and followed simple ordering rules.

In fact, Doubleday never used the tremendous advantages that the publisher inevitably has over the bookseller in predicting sales. The publisher can do it better *before* the book is published because he has complete information (slightly distorted by the copies supplied through wholesalers) on the *actual* sale (*after* returns) of earlier, similar titles in every bookstore. He can do it better *after* the book is published because, knowing how well the book is selling at that moment in many stores, he can discern national, and even regional, trends long before any single bookseller can. He knows if any advertising and promotion are truly imminent and where their effect will be felt. And he can easily collect more information if it seems pertinent. Moreover, he has ample computer capacity to use all these figures to advantage.

□ *Since future successful merchandising plans will be using statistical methods of prediction, the more stores that participate and the more titles per store, the more accurate the predictions will be—and the more successful the plan. This gives a very significant advantage to the large publisher.*

In spite of the self-imposed restrictions, which made the plan far less effective in improving turnover and increasing sales, the results demonstrated the validity of publisher's control of inventory. Stores were invited, in effect, to give their backlist order pad and checkbook to Doubleday. The sales rep took an inventory each month of the Doubleday books in the store and sent it to the Merchandising Plan office, where the record of each store's inventories and shipments was maintained and the sale of each title was calculated. The sales history of each title was used to predict its future sale and the inventory was adjusted to have between six and twelve weeks' stock on hand for any title.

The plan approximately doubled sales and brought returns down to a third or a fourth of previous levels. *Women's Wear Daily* described the results of the Merchandising Plan in the book department of Gimbel's in Philadelphia. Sales doubled and, because one order was placed each month instead of many, Gimbel's also benefited from very much higher discounts. Because inventory investment was not increased and other costs were not affected, *Women's Wear Daily*'s figures suggested that Gimbel's profit on Doubleday books had actually increased thirteenfold (1300 percent).

For all its crudeness, the plan did work. It had the great advantage of being thorough in every detail, and operating by *objective, arithmetical rules*. It increased the sale of Doubleday books in every store in which it was used. When it was operating in 650 stores, we calculated that it was creating $1 million of *extra* sales in those stores and reducing returns by two thirds. Figures were not available to calculate changes in the stores' rate of inventory turnover, but there is no doubt that it was substantially increased.

The principal reason the merchandising plan worked so well was that it systematically reduced the inventory levels of the important books, replenishing their stock in each monthly shipment if necessary. The investment thus released was put into additional, less important titles, which led to increased sales. The result was higher total sales and a more efficient use of the store's investment.

But the inevitable result of the store-by-store, book-by-book system, restricted to backlist titles only, was the *contraction* of the number of titles in each store instead of the intended expansion. Perhaps it was the realization that this was happening, plus the resistance of the sales reps to the monthly inventory (which is unnecessary in an unrestricted, more sophisticated system), that caused Doubleday to let the plan wind down from its high point of about 850 stores, reached about two years after the plan was inaugurated.

The Doubleday Merchandising Plan, the Grosset approach, the Random House advance selling strategy—these are all steps in the right direction, though they are all far from what I am suggesting here. I would like to see the publisher assume responsibility for *all* his titles in the store—deciding which titles should be there and how many of each, when books should be returned, and when titles should be allowed to sell out and not be reordered. This responsibility should start before each title is published and extend for its entire sales life.

One ingredient of such an arrangement on which the publisher should insist, even if the bookseller seems to have little interest, is the measuring and reporting of results. If they are good, the figures are the most convincing reason for the bookseller to give the publisher more of his buying budget. If they are bad, it is critical for the publisher to know that he, as well as the bookseller, is losing sales.

To prove the value of his service to the store, each publisher (whether using a mathematical system or his reps' ingenuity) should supply each store with a "report card" of his own performance, perhaps every six months. Such a report card would show:

1. The average inventory value of the publisher's books at cost and at retail.
2. The sale of the publisher's books in that store for that period and for the previous twelve months.
3. The annual return to the store on each dollar invested in the publisher's inventory.

And the publisher must take great pains to insulate whoever is responsible for the plan's operation from any inside attempt to influence the placement of books or the quantities. The ego or parochial strategy of an editor or advertising director or subsidiary rights manager must not be allowed to interfere with placing books as nearly as humanly possible to the advantage of the bookseller. It should not be permissible, for example, to increase the size of advance orders to provide an impressive figure for subsidiary rights negotiations. If the system is operated completely objectively, by strict mathematical rules, so much the better, but it must not attempt to serve two masters.

But neither the objectivity of the system nor the degree of refinement of its mathematics is very important at the start. The simple fact that the publisher is free to put in whatever books he wishes and that the results of his decisions will be evaluated is sufficient to work wonders.

If books can be put into the store *without negotiation* and without the need for prior authorization from the store, much of the reason for the large advance disappears. On the contrary, it is in the publisher's interest to get the largest exposure (number of retail locations) with the smallest investment in manufactured books and the smallest risk of returns. He will want to have enough copies in any store to serve until additional stock can arrive, but since the publisher can dispatch additional copies at will, a relatively small inventory will assure that protection, even for a runaway best-seller.

This change dramatically improves the store's use of working capital. For example, under the present system, a store buyer who senses a best-seller might buy 500 copies. If he sold all of them within six months, he would, by any criteria, have done very well. His average inventory during that period would have been half the total inventory, or 250 copies. Selling 500 copies from an average inventory of 250 is a stock turn of 2, which translates to a stock turn of 4 for the entire year. Not bad. With the freedom to ship in books at will, the publisher might start the store with 200 copies and ship in more stock at the rate of 100 copies a month, or whatever made sense *in relation to the actual rate of sale in the store.* The average inventory in such a situation might be 100 copies or 125 copies, so the annual stock turnover would be on the order of 8 or 10 instead of 4. But that's only part of the story.

Among the titles that the store buyer decides to purchase in quantities of 500 copies are some on which he makes an honest error. They may sell no more than 350 copies, perhaps fewer. (Remember that *one out of every three* new books bought by the stores is returned unsold.) Those errors would virtually disappear if the initial quantity shipped to the store represented 20 or 40 percent of the order the buyer would now normally make. On titles that did not come up to the original expectations, the replenishment shipments would be correspondingly smaller or would simply never happen.

Even though the publisher would use the bookseller's working capital, made available by sharply reducing the advances on lead titles, for putting in titles currently skipped, the turnover of the store's inventory investment would still be dramatically better than it is today. And the small quantities of the additional titles would increase the sales and the margins per square foot of store area.

The improvement in the use of working capital would be just as dramatic for the publisher as for the bookseller. First and most obvious, since the publisher would decide how many copies to put into each store and each wholesaler, he would know, before any books were printed, how many copies would be needed. The guesswork that is now the largest ingredient in the first printing decision would disappear completely; the only decision would be on how many copies of tactical reserve stock would be best for that title. When reprint quantities needed to be decided, the publisher would know which retail (or wholesale) locations needed copies and at what rate those locations were selling books. It would be a simple matter to decide how many to print because the publisher would already know where to put the books when the bindery delivered them.

The publisher fails to realize, perhaps, how much he is currently the victim of buying decisions made by others (usually with the connivance of his own rep, of course), which force him to print or reprint books because other people are making buying errors. In other words, *other people,* with judgment ranging from the most careful to the most haphazard, are deciding how the *publisher* should spend his money producing books. He can only hope that they are not making too many mistakes.

Under a merchandising plan, the publisher would reduce his own overstock to an insignificant level and would control returns (because he would control the shipments to his customers) at whatever level he thought most advantageous. And because he would print the quantities he needed *when* he needed them, his stock levels during the entire life of the book would be minimal, depending upon the current cost of money. The effect on the use of working capital, quite aside from the other obvious reductions in cost and improvements in sales, would be dramatic.

A merchandising plan is simply an organized, "programmed" way to accomplish the purpose of merchandising: adjusting the retail stock in each store, in its variety of suitable titles and quantities, to get the highest possible profit with the lowest possible investment. Every bookstore is truly different from every other one, so each should have its own, unique merchandising assortment. No two assortments will be truly identical. Merchandising is aimed at a stock assortment balanced so that the three operating factors—volume, markup, and turnover— will yield the highest possible profit.

If not pushed into this obligation by the stores, why should the publisher do it? He can say that inventory control is the retailer's problem. Why shouldn't the publisher stick to making books less expensive and making jackets prettier?

The first and perhaps most important reason is that such a plan sells more books. My experience at Doubleday and Two Continents indicates that it is safe to count on a doubling of sales from even a crude merchandising plan if the sales rep and the store buyer have previously been doing a good job, and a bigger increase if they haven't. This increase usually comes with a substantial improvement in stock turnover, with the result that, while the operating publisher gains great advantages, it also makes more money available for the store to buy books from other publishers.

□ *One of the most dramatic results of a well-operated merchandising plan, and one that confounds the bookseller skeptics, is the precipitous drop in returns. This happens despite the increase in sales. A merchandising plan can operate comfortably with returns at about 5 percent, but the publisher can reduce returns below even that level (with some decrease in sales) by simply adjusting the inventory control rules.*

This improvement is particularly important in department stores and other retail outlets that operate with "open to buy" systems, which determine the buyer's budget by his success in getting stock turnover. The tragic decline of book sections in department stores, which have gone from being the leading segment of book retailing to a few scattered relics of minor importance, is directly due, it seems to me, to the failure of book department managers to meet the stores' criteria for acceptable stock turns. Other departments in the store manage to produce satisfactory margins and stock turns. Book department managers are the victims of the complexity of inventory control. They always seemed to be (and the remaining ones still are) struggling without sufficient open-to-buy to keep inventory current, and all because the books they had bought previously were selling too slowly.

A merchandising plan approach by publishers would have saved those book departments, and might still bring them back.

Second, publishers must recognize that they have a "resource responsibility" to the retailer. The bookseller buys on faith. Even if the publisher's rep spends ten minutes explaining a particular book, the bookseller is still buying on faith. This responsibility is not just a moral matter, though it is that as well. It is a very practical matter in the success of the bookstore—and therefore, ultimately, of the publisher.

Third, to the degree that the merchandising plan replaces distribution-by-negotiation, it will free the publisher from the lockstep list-building sequence of catalogue to sales conference to territory coverage. There will be no need to collect orders to know the advance sale or to determine printings. The initial number of copies of each title going into each store will be determined by the merchandising plan.

When the plan is operating in most stores, there will be no need for seasonal lists and the related wasteful and time-consuming procedures. Publishing will be a continuous process, without the need for months of lead time to precede the publication date of a title.

Titles that would benefit from months of lead time can have them, but if the production department can have finished books ready to ship in six weeks, it will be possible to publish any book routinely three months from the release of the manuscript. And the book issued on that schedule, under a merchandising plan, will be in more stores three months after the manuscript's release than it can reach under distribution-by-negotiation on a twelve-month schedule. It takes but little quiet contemplation to see the ramifications of such a change through all the aspects of publishing and writing. They are enormous.

The fourth reason is that improving the productivity of the bookseller's investment is the most important single contribution the publisher can make to rejuvenate independent bookselling. The independent bookseller has increasingly been losing ground to the chains, relatively and absolutely. The dominance of the chains is already having a restrictive effect on the range of publishing and is likely to have a further restrictive effect on the growth of smaller publishing houses. A merchandising plan tends to reduce the disadvantages under which the independent bookseller faces the competition from the chains.

But the chain would also benefit from the use of a merchandising plan. The significant change would be the industry-wide decline in the relative importance of the discount as a factor in store profitability and the enhancement of the importance of inventory selection.

Fifth, the publisher, as we have pointed out, is in a unique position to be helpful. He starts with the best information about his own books, and he can easily and quickly accumulate a great deal more. Most publishers have ample computer capacity to use this information to guide inventory decisions; if they don't, outside computer services do.

Sixth, there is a tremendous reduction in the cost of distribution for the publisher as well as the bookseller. The most obvious saving is in the endless hours of rep-bookseller negotiation. The booksellers' and the sales reps' time can be devoted to moving books *out* of the stores instead of into them. The publisher will also save the cost of the sales conference and all the effort that goes into it.

But even more important will be reducing the many millions of dollars of waste inherent in distribution-by-negotiation: the heavy returns, books being out of stock, books not getting deserved representation in the stores.

The seventh reason is that anything that simplifies operating a bookstore and that contributes to making the profit more attractive and more predictable encourages the growth of book retailing. And though the publisher may (mistakenly) express exasperation with the bookseller's supposed shortcomings, he cannot avoid seeing the very simple relationship: little bookselling, little publishing; no bookselling, no publishing; much bookselling, much publishing. Of course, the very increase in sales and profitability in existing stores will encourage newcomers to enter the book retailing field. But that is still not all.

The three principal obstacles to the growth of retail bookselling are:
1. The expensive, unpleasant drudgery of present clerical procedures.
2. The need to have an expert to do the buying.
3. The uncertainty of the results.

As we have already pointed out, the clerical cost per dollar of sales is probably higher for booksellers than for any other retailers. Not only must the bookseller write thousands of orders, process thousands of deliveries, write hundreds of checks, correspond endlessly over questions of discount, unfilled orders, and returns. He must also keep track of the inventory and sale of thousands of titles so that he can write the orders to process the deliveries, etc., etc.

The merchandising plan simplifies most of this nonsense instantly. There is one delivery a month, occasionally two, from the publisher. The publisher keeps the inventory and writes the orders. He also keeps track of sales and analyzes the results. The bookseller's mountain of paperwork has evaporated.

The publisher does the "buying," so there is no need for someone completely current on forthcoming books who can do battle with the publisher's rep. Obviously, knowing the titles is helpful in selling to the retailer's customers, but that is much easier to absorb (and the jacket copy certainly helps) than the more esoteric knowledge today's buyer needs.

The results, in terms of both sales and profits, are remarkably consistent and predictable as well as controllable under a merchandising plan. After a little experience, it is a routine matter to predict dollars and margin per square foot and to adjust those figures within limits to suit a particular situation.

The reduction of these three obstacles to attracting new book retailers will be helpful not only in encouraging individuals to enter bookselling. Perhaps more important, it will be able to speak about bookselling in a language that mammoth retail chains like Sears and J. C. Penney can understand. Such chains sell a great variety of goods, but books presently represent a special, difficult, low-profit product of great mystery with greater risks than rewards. These highly professional merchants know very well how many dollars per square foot any department must bring in to justify its existence. They are not eager to make such a department the prisoner of some self-styled book "expert," but *if* it can be run by any competent manager, and *if* it does not need a larger clerical staff, and *if* the results are predictable and within acceptable limits, *then* . . . With statistical matching of stock to potential demand putting inventory turns of 4 and more within easy reach, and discounts of 40 percent delivered, the income from a book department is very likely to be comfortably above the acceptable limit for any retailer.

The operation of the plan would have to distinguish, as do all inventory systems, between "fashion merchandise"—best-sellers and potential best-sellers, whose sales are volatile and highly concentrated in time—and "staple merchandise"—backlist titles and those new titles with a potential for the backlist, and, in fact, the spectrum of titles in between.

For new publications, the predicted *range* of sale in a particular store can be projected from the history of other titles in that store. The projection for any new title would not be based on the sale of any *one* previous title; that would be much too uncertain and risky. But the means exist to combine previous histories in highly reliable ways. The error in the prediction (there is *always* error in prediction) would be mitigated, as we have already suggested, by the fact that the publisher would not put the predicted sale quantity into the store all at once. That is unnecessary as long as the publisher can send in additional copies before the store runs out of stock.

The prediction of backlist titles would be based upon the sale *of those titles,* with no need to extrapolate from any other figures. That prediction would be based, however, not on the experience of one store alone (as in the Doubleday plan), but on the combined experience of many *similar* stores. "Similar" refers to the store's similarity specifically only for that title or type of book. For example, one store may be similar to another in the sale of Italian cookbooks, or cookbooks in general, yet be very different in gardening books, fiction, or juveniles.

At the beginning, the publisher would have to make a tentative judgment about the similarity or difference among stores for each book or type of book, but as sales history accumulated, the computer would spot those similarities based on actual sales patterns rather than subjective judgments. As with new publications, the prediction of backlist sales would be used to place quantities of the appropriate titles in each store to get the maximum return on the store's investment. Here, too, without the present pressure of trying to pile as much into one order as possible, backlist could be fed into the store's inventory more nearly *when it is actually needed.*

For both new books and the backlist, the information would come from title-by-title inventories taken in the stores by the publisher's reps. Time for taking inventory would be made available from the time saved by eliminating negotiation.

The object would be, in principle (except for the happy emergency of an erupting best-seller), to have a single monthly shipment to each store with the new and backlist books for that month. The frequency of the shipments might vary in peak and slow periods (depending in part, for example, on the current cost of money), striving for the most advantageous use of the store's working capital.

Whatever system of control the publisher developed, the store would retain the right to override the merchandising plan at will, to introduce titles, or to change the quantities based on the store's own information or expectations. The store might sponsor a Hemingway Circle, a Sherlock Holmes Club, or some book gift-giving scheme that would confound any statistical system and that no merchandising plan could anticipate. Obviously, the bookseller's eagerness to interfere with the operation of the plan would go down as the plan's results went up, but the store would retain that option in any case.

It is senseless to claim that a merchandising plan or any system could provide a store with a perfect inventory assortment. For practical purposes, such an assortment does not exist; if it is perfect one moment, it will be imperfect the next. The object is to provide a *better* assortment than is currently provided, or can ever be provided, by the negotiation between sales rep and bookseller.

The principal goal of the publisher's present selling effort—and budget—is to get books into the stores. The cost is not only in the sales force itself but in the catalogues, the mailings to booksellers, the advertising in *Publishers Weekly,* the sales conference, the gimmicks (one free for ten, extra discounts to stock up for fall, etc.), and in attending national conventions and regional meetings.

A merchandising plan suddenly changes everything. There is no longer an obstacle to getting a book into a store except its salability. Now all the apparatus, all the money, all the management brains once devoted to getting books into the store can be marshaled to work with the bookseller to get books *out* of the store. And the publisher will benefit directly. Whereas, previously, the publisher could not depend upon profiting fully from building popular demand—the bookstore might be out of stock or might fail to reorder when the last copy was sold—when he controls the bookstore inventory, he can be confident that wherever he has created demand, the customer will find books.

In redirecting his selling effort from the bookseller to the customer, the publisher serves both of them as well as himself. The customer and bookseller benefit if the consumer is better informed about what is available, and both benefit, of course, if the bookstore has the books that the consumer wants.

The publisher's advertising would also change somewhat in tone and content. Much of it fulfills an obligation to the author and is not seriously intended to sell books. Very little is done to direct the public to bookstores, where they would see all the competitors' titles. With the assurance that the publisher's line will be well represented, there is every reason, no matter what title is being advertised, to encourage the public to visit the bookstore.

The sales rep will also be able to redefine his job. His responsibility will be to help move books *through* the store by giving the sales clerks useful information (just before books arrive, not months in advance), providing display material and encouraging effective store displays, helping the bookseller develop mail and telephone selling techniques, providing local publicity media with information and promoting its use —the possibilities are endless.

The realization that the world of distribution has really changed will take a while to sink in. When it does, the changes in publishers' selling activity will be profound.

Once the efficiency at the retail end becomes a matter of real interest for the publisher, it is not out of the question that one of the larger publishers would organize traveling seminars, going from city to city, helping store management and sales clerks learn how to be more effective.

Years ago, it was common practice for publishers to supply stores with "statement stuffers," lightweight circulars to be included in the bookseller's monthly mailings to charge customers. Sometimes the pieces were used; sometimes the store threw them away. Charge accounts are much less common today and publishers much more frugal, so this practice has more or less died. With the sales rep on the scene to help the bookstore develop its lists, perhaps with the publisher maintaining them, the use of the mail (and the phone) to sell books before they arrive in the store could be revived.

The benefit to both the bookstore and the publisher could be considerable, aside from the very obvious one of the number of copies sold. For the publisher, having a large number of copies in the hands of customers before or at the same time as the reviews would give a very strong boost to word of mouth. For the bookseller, selling so many copies immediately, before payment is due to the publisher, would work wonders on stock turnover rates and on the bookseller's need for cash.

It might be helpful to summarize what the *publisher's* goals should be in replacing the present practice of distribution-by-negotiation with a merchandising plan:

1. To shift the responsibility, and the cost, for ordering and returning books and for stock control of the publisher's books from the store management to the publisher.

2. To serve the customer better by maintaining the broadest possible assortment of titles in the store consistent with delivering a better gross margin per dollar of inventory investment than the store management achieves on the average—or at least a gross margin the store management is willing to accept.

3. To take better advantage, for both the store and the publisher, of any surge in public interest in a particular title by unilaterally distributing additional copies of it to participating stores, anticipating the store's needs for books.

4. To ensure the representation of more titles, in more stores, before publication, increasing overall sales, and decreasing the percentage of overall returns.

5. To "meter" copies of new titles to stores in monthly shipments guided by the rate of sale in order to reduce the rate of returns and the risk of overprinting potential best-sellers (which now occurs because of the need to press for large advance orders).

6. To hold bookstore inventories low by ensuring regular, calculated stock replenishment.

7. To reduce both selling costs and buying costs.

8. To shift the goal of the sales rep from getting books into the store to helping the store move books out.

9. To provide the publisher with continuing information on the rate of sale of each title at the point of consumer purchase.

10. To encourage better performance from publishers by tying their success in each store to results.

11. To increase the number and range of backlist titles that can be sold.

12. To stabilize bookstore buying budgets to permit better financial planning by both the bookseller and the publisher and to enable the bookseller to control cash flow more precisely.
13. To reduce shipping costs by reducing the number of shipments per store while increasing the total business with each customer on the plan.

Book distribution in its present form has developed so many obstacles to smooth and fruitful performance, so many varieties of irritating disappointment, that it teeters in a state of dynamic disequilibrium. It should not require an impetus of great force to displace it with some form of merchandising distribution. Certainly no industry-wide effort is necessary.

It could happen by the success of Under Cover Books' experiment in Cleveland. If the store goes through with its plan, profits should multiply. It will not take other booksellers very long to install the same system, and publishers will find themselves pushed into a good thing whether they like it or not.

Without the spread of a bookseller initiative, it would take only one major publisher to create the revolution all by himself. A merchandising plan introduced by a publisher of respectable size, with the resources to finance the sales growth that would quickly develop, would take business away from competitors so quickly, they would have no alternative except to scramble after him as fast as their dignity would allow.

8

Wholesaling

ANY DISCUSSION of wholesaling in trade books must begin by
clearing up some confusion in terminology. In most industries the
wholesaler is the middleman, specifically between the producer and
the retailer. Sales to institutions (giant cans of soup to hospitals or
restaurants) or to other consumers not usually served by retailers are
considered a different category of business, usually handled directly by
manufacturers or through a different, "institutional" distributor.

In book publishing, the wholesaler sells to both bookstores and
institutions, such as libraries. Wholesalers tend to specialize more in
one side of this business than the other. There is not much question
that the sale of trade books to libraries through wholesalers is four to
five times as great as that to bookstores, and the sale to libraries and
institutions is, in general, the more stable and profitable part of book
wholesaling.

In addition to supplying trade books to libraries, the wholesalers
also supply them with professional and technical books, university
press books, and other more specialized titles that never go near a
retail bookstore. In connection with these specialized books, which go
in large part to university or research libraries rather than public
libraries, wholesalers frequently offer the libraries additional valuable
services, principally assistance in selection. This may take the form of
actually sending copies of any new titles on subjects chosen by a
library, or sending detailed descriptions of the books as soon as they
are available. A close monitoring of the new books and matching titles
to libraries' wants, frequently using fast computer-sorting techniques, is
of great value to library staffs.

Some wholesalers, for an additional fee, supply the appropriate
catalogue cards, a card pocket for the book, a protective plastic jacket,

and other material to make processing the book easier and faster. However, the two principal reasons that libraries buy trade books from wholesalers are, not this service but rather the discount on small orders and the convenience of placing one order for the books of many publishers. These services rarely apply to trade books.

In many countries, such as England, Holland, and Germany, which have a much stronger book retailing network than the United States, public libraries buy their books from the neighborhood bookseller. Library sales in those countries are an important part of the bookseller's total business, and they justify carrying larger and more varied stocks.

Since it is common for American publishers to point with envy at the superior European retail networks, it is interesting to review how the present U.S. situation came to be. John P. Dessauer, a respected student of the publishing industry, commented in the *Publishers Weekly* of November 27, 1972:

> Prior to the War and the Depression, many booksellers served their local public and educational libraries, thus enlarging their income and increasing their value to their communities. When the wholesalers absorbed this function, they in fact competed with these retailers and, we might add, in a most remarkable way. *They persuaded the publishers to continue to extend, or even to increase, the discount they had received when they were still purchasing books for resale to retailers, and in turn offered to libraries (on a contract basis) an up-to-then unprecedented discount roughly equivalent to that which they might have given to the retailers they were abandoning.* [Emphasis added.]

If this shift of a substantial part of the institutional business from retailers had strengthened wholesaling (in its true sense of supplying retailers), the damage to retailers and to book distribution might not have been very great. Unfortunately, not only did it weaken the retailer by removing a stable and reliable portion of his business, thereby reducing his incentive for carrying a broad assortment of books, but it also weakened the potential wholesaling service to retailers. Making the library market easy and lucrative while substantially reducing the size of the retail market proved to many wholesalers that they could prosper very nicely by concentrating on libraries and virtually ignoring retailers.

For example, Baker & Taylor, which probably controls more than half the book wholesaling in the country, until recently did less than 10 percent of their volume with bookstores—over 90 percent with libraries and institutions. Recently, largely for internal and very likely temporary reasons, bookstore sales have increased to about 15 percent of its total.

Baker & Taylor and the other wholesalers that have managed to secure a strong foothold in the library field have very little interest in booksellers, and any potential interest they might have is not strengthened by the ease and profit of the library business. Actually, over the years, by supplying most libraries under a contract that put incipient competition under a tremendous disadvantage, a few large wholesalers have consolidated their position in the library field. They have a minimal interest in the less profitable, more competitive business of supplying bookstores, and they seem happy to leave it to those who find it very hard to crack the library market and who are prepared to struggle hard for every dollar of sales.

It is perhaps unfortunate that the library business moved from the retailer to the wholesaler; nevertheless, it is very unlikely to change. In the meantime, the title selection, cataloguing paraphernalia, and wholesaler services would be difficult for a bookseller to provide. From the publishers' point of view, although it does cost more in discount, distribution through wholesalers passes the crucial test: It works. No doubt some of the larger publishers could multiply their business with libraries by being more aggressive in selling directly, but this makes no sense for the vast majority of publishers and cannot ever be the industry pattern.

But if institutional selling works, book wholesaling—supplying books to retailers—certainly does not. No one—not the publishers, booksellers, nor the wholesalers themselves—seems to be satisfied with the operation of the system and with the results.

The book wholesaler enjoys no franchises or exclusive territories. Although he may have an advantage with nearby retailers, each wholesaler competes with every other wholesaler, regardless of location. And he competes each day for each day's orders; there are no contracts with retailers as there are with libraries. In addition to the competition from other wholesalers (the number of which is understandably small), the wholesaler faces the infinitely more aggressive competition from the publisher himself. Each sales rep who sells to the wholesaler then rushes out to sell to each of the wholesaler's customers, usually offering them discounts to persuade them to buy at least the initial order directly from the publisher.

The book wholesaler also has a very thin market; there are few bookstores per square mile. This obvious economic handicap makes delivery to his customers, usually via common carrier, expensive and slow.

Discount margins, the difference between what the wholesaler gets from the publisher and what he must give the bookseller, are very much narrower than in any other industry of which I am aware. The pressure of these margins is very real, since, if he wants the retailer's trade, the wholesaler cannot deviate very far from the discount the publisher offers directly to the retailer. Yet the complications in maintaining inventory, in filling orders, and in handling returns are much more difficult (and therefore much more expensive) in books than in other products.

The wholesaler must offer to take returns from booksellers because the publisher does. This complication adds to his own returns, which tend to be high because of the great uncertainties in bookselling.

One cost in book wholesaling that used to be extremely high has been brought under control by a very clever innovation. Because of the large number of new titles, their short and uncertain life, the extensive backlist, and the irresistible pressure on wholesalers to concentrate their investment on the new titles, orders from retailers frequently contained many titles not in stock. This forced the wholesaler to check his inventory for these titles and tell the retailer that it was out of stock. The clerical costs for the titles not shipped was not much less than for the titles shipped; the loss of goodwill from the bookseller probably made those not shipped actually more costly.

Ingram, then an aggressive newcomer to trade book wholesaling and now the largest by far (about $100 million), introduced the practice of supplying retailers, for a fee, a weekly, updated microfiche showing every title currently on hand. It represented an imaginative application to books of a very successful practice in other fields (drugs, for instance) and immediately changed the bookseller's perception of his relation to the wholesaler. A bookseller could quickly see which titles were certainly not available and should not be ordered. While a title showing on the microfiche might no longer be in stock, the bookseller could gauge the risk by the number of copies reported on hand and by his own judgment of the probable rate of sale. As a result, a typical order from the bookseller to Ingram contained more titles and almost none that was out of stock. The wholesaler's cost of handling the orders went down sharply and the average size of the orders went up.

Ingram's spectacular growth, sparked by the microfiche innovation (now copied or adapted by others) and sustained by imaginative management, has undoubtedly increased the volume of books going through wholesalers. (It has also, by the way, put some sleepier wholesalers out of business.) Nevertheless, the margins under which Ingram and other wholesalers must operate remain very narrow. The momentum of wholesaler expansion seems to have slowed and is likely to decline without another equally dramatic innovation.

□ *It will undoubtedly occur to the reader who has covered Chapter 7, on the merchandising plan, that this could be precisely that innovation. By anticipating the bookseller's need and putting into the store the books that should be there without waiting for an order, the wholesaler would multiply his sales, reduce his processing costs, and virtually eliminate returns. If large publishers institute their own merchandising plans, a wholesaler's plan might be the small publishers' greatest insurance against being frozen out of bookstores altogether.*

The large bookstore chains contributed somewhat to the health of wholesaling: first, by simply increasing the number of retailers, and second, by permitting their branches to use wholesalers to correct some of the inadequacies of their central buying systems. However, that seems to be changing, for the cost of buying through wholesalers is high and an inadequate central buying system cannot be indefinitely tolerated.

A new handicap that all wholesalers, including Ingram, must overcome (see Chapter 5, on returns and remainders) is the new, higher discount publishers are offering to retailers in exchange for penalties on returns or the outright elimination of returns. This attempt to reduce the catastrophic level of returns is badly conceived and unlikely to last very long, but while it does, it will direct retailers' orders away from the wholesaler and to the publisher.

In spite of Ingram's impressive growth, in spite of the clearly expressed desire of many publishers to force booksellers to place more business with wholesalers, book wholesaling remains pathetically weak. Probably no more than 15 or 20 percent of trade books reach bookstores through wholesalers, and that volume of business is not very securely held.

Many in publishing argue that wholesaling should be strengthened, believing that it could cure such problems as:

1. The high cost of sales coverage by publishers.
2. The confusion caused among retailers by the great variety of discounts and selling terms.
3. The high cost to the bookseller of placing many small orders, processing many invoices, and handling many shipments.
4. The cost of publishers' warehousing and billing facilities.

5. The discouragement of special ordering by booksellers because of the delays and uncertainties.

6. The need for booksellers to carry a heavy investment in inventory.

7. The cost to publishers of excessive printings to cover inflated advance orders and heavy returns when sales slow down.

These difficulties tend not to exist in industries that have strong wholesaling. Ergo, it is argued, if book wholesaling is made strong, these difficulties will tend to disappear. Perhaps, but we shall probably never know, because the *nature of book publishing itself* makes it just about impossible for wholesalers (short of using a merchandising plan with their customers) ever to become the retailer's principal source of books.

Not that the retailer would mind. Buying from the wholesaler has many attractions. Buying from the publisher has only two—higher discount and advertising allowances—but they are compelling.

The bookseller likes the idea of placing one order to cover the titles of many publishers and receiving the books in one shipment covered by one invoice. He would rather get his books from one source than from four hundred different sources. He knows that, by and large, the wholesaler's shipment will be on its way days or weeks before the average publisher is ready to ship, and it will probably take less time to get there. With ample copies in the wholesaler's inventory, the bookseller can more easily resist the pressures to buy large quantities of the likely best-sellers. The wholesaler can keep him in stock with regular monthly or even weekly shipments. That would all be fine, but there is the publisher, sending his sales rep in, pleading for an order, offering attractive discounts and advertising allowances, and using all the persuasion possible.

If the publisher did not make this effort, much more volume would move through the wholesaler—though not all, because the range of inventory wholesalers' stock is considerably narrower than booksellers need. And, what may not be quite so obvious, the number of titles published would decline, the total number of books sold would go down, and the odious best-seller emphasis that already plagues the industry would be even more exaggerated.

Some publishers may be momentarily (and mistakenly) annoyed by the cost of handling small orders from bookstores and attempt to change things, not by correcting their selling or order fulfillment methods, but by imposing penalties that drive the bookseller to the wholesaler. Some publishers may skimp in their service departments and shipping staffs to the point of frustrating the bookseller into buying more from the wholesaler. Publishers may make concessions to wholesalers, even self-defeating concessions such as those that lost the booksellers the library business. Nevertheless, most publishers recognize that the publisher-bookseller link is a vital one, much more so than the link between producer and retailer in other industries. And they recognize that this link cannot be maintained through the wholesaler. It must be direct, and it must almost certainly include taking orders. What publishers seem to want is the impossible combination of selling to retailers themselves *and* a strong wholesaling network to provide support if it is needed.

The publisher needs to deal intimately with the bookseller because he must be sure that the information on his titles is brought to the attention of each bookseller in good time to ensure that books are in the store by publication day. And only by sending his own representative to the store can the publisher be sure to achieve this goal.

It is a truism in every industry that while a wholesaler sells in the sense of filling orders, the wholesaler cannot sell in the sense of informing retailers about each product. He cannot solicit specific orders or create retailer demand. If the retailer places orders, the wholesaler may be able to fill them, but he does not inspire them.

In trade book publishing, with hundreds of thousands of old titles and tens of thousands of new ones, each new one fighting for immediate attention, the publisher cannot gamble that each title will find its proper place. He has to intervene energetically by informing the bookseller about the book and, if he is successful, getting an initial order. Thereafter, depending on the relative enterprise of the publisher and the wholesaler, reorders may go to either one.

Just as the publisher cannot depend on the wholesaler for selling, neither can he completely depend on him to fill the orders he receives. The wholesaler will simply not have many of the titles the retailer would like to order. And the result is more serious for books than for other products. In other industries, the wholesaler can special-order from the producer a particular item and ship it to the retailer later, but that is not acceptable in books. An order that cannot be immediately filled by the wholesaler is automatically canceled; the sale has thus been lost to wholesaler, publisher, and author. The use of microfiche, which may forestall the retailer's order, may save paperwork, but it does not retrieve a lost sale. And microfiche, for all its positive features, has reduced the span of titles the wholesaler will carry.

The wholesaler wants to work with the *minimum* number of titles that will bring in profitable volume. IBM reports that in wholesaling generally, 90 percent of the business is done in 20 percent of the items. The ratio must be more extreme in bookselling: Of perhaps 220,000 titles that should be available to retailers, a wholesaler is not likely to have even 10 percent of them. Every additional title costs money in space, inventory investment, inclusion in microfiches or catalogues, etc. Each title must sell, and continue to sell, enough copies to cover those costs.

A wholesaler serving booksellers is straining when he reaches 10,000 or, in some truly exceptional cases, if his inventory controls are very good, 15,000 titles. That means he has only some of the new titles and very little of the backlist. What kind of bookstore assortments can be supported by 15,000 titles? What publishers can consider themselves fairly represented?

The smaller publishers suffer most dramatically, but the larger ones lose as well. A smaller publisher probably has only a few of his outstanding titles, if any, represented. But the larger publisher, though he has many more titles there, does not by any means have them all. When the wholesaler gets an order for thirty assorted titles published by Doubleday or Houghton Mifflin or Simon & Schuster, does he have them all? Can he fill that order completely? Almost certainly not.

But that is not the end of the wholesaler paradox.

Which titles will the bookseller order from the wholesaler? Interestingly, they are the very titles the bookseller has been sold, or at least told about, by the publisher's sales rep. He has to know that a title exists to order it; more likely, he has to have the positive experience of selling a copy or two that the publisher sold him directly.

How often has a publisher (usually a small one) purred with satisfaction because a wholesaler was persuaded to take 200 copies of that season's big title, allowing the publisher to assume he had repaired the damage of his failure to cover the retail accounts? Then, at returns time, how often has the same publisher moaned because he got the same 200 copies back, minus the few copies lost to pilferage?

If the publisher diligently covers the wholesaler's customer, and he also bludgeons or cajoles the wholesaler into having a broad (though, unfortunately, never complete) backup stock, the wholesaler *can* perform a useful function, particularly in distant parts of the country. In such rare cases, the publisher can avoid seeking excessive advance orders from the retailer because he is sure that backup copies are readily and quickly available. This can help the publisher hold down his investment in books and can definitely contribute to reducing returns.

But only if the publisher is certain that his books *are* well represented by the wholesaler is it sensible for him to refer the bookseller to the wholesaler for replenishment. That condition applies to very few publishers at very few wholesalers. Even where it does apply, the publisher must consider the cost. He saves nothing on sales coverage of bookstores and loses something in discount.

The more the publisher directs sales through the wholesaler, the more he pays in discount differential and the more he needs the wholesaler's cooperation in holding inventory levels, reordering promptly, postponing returns, etc. To develop such an arrangement, the publisher must find a cooperative wholesaler and he must make the necessary investment. His sales reps must cover the wholesaler's customers thoroughly, making them aware of the titles, checking stock, and creating orders for the wholesaler. He must pay attention to the wholesaler as well, being sure that as many titles as possible arc in stock. The result, if the publisher does his work well, is much higher sales and much lower returns. If the publisher shirks his responsibilities, he will find the wholesaler to be a much weaker distribution link in practice than in theory.

Like every other aspect of the book industry, wholesaling is itself dynamic, as Ingram demonstrated by introducing microfiche. There is no reason to assume that innovation and dynamism have ended with the microfiche system, at Ingram or anywhere else. A great deal of experimentation is now going on with computer inventory systems in retail stores and at the wholesalers. Out of this, or out of inventory control schemes such as the one promoted by Chas. Levy, an independent distributor in Chicago, or the "bookstore within a store" innovation by ARA, a tighter connection could develop between wholesaler and retailer that would make the wholesaler more valuable to the publisher and to the entire book distribution system.

There is some question whether a wholesaler like Levy can operate a trade book rack-jobbing operation; the subtleties of dealing in ones and twos among thousands of titles are far greater than dealing, as the mass market wholesaler does, in dozens and half-dozens among hundreds of titles.

Perhaps the wholesaler can "rack-job" a partial, sharply defined section of the store's inventory, leaving the more subtle inventory needs for store management to handle. Perhaps the wholesaler's automatic distribution can be confined to introducing the title into the store initially, leaving it to store management to reorder as sales allow. This might take the form of a weekly or biweekly package of new titles delivered to subscriber bookstores, each title represented according to the wholesaler's estimate of the book's potential in relation to the store's size and personality.

The use of the wholesaler's central position and impartial judgment in stocking the retailer was a central feature of the Little Professor chain of franchised bookstores. The plan was a dismal failure, but not because it was faulty in conception. Little Professor never developed a system for making the buying decisions, so the idea did not have a fair test. If it had, it probably would have worked.

Probably the most exciting development in wholesaling, though it threatens to cut the publisher off completely from the retailer, is the "bookstore within a store" concept pioneered by ARA Services, the largest distributor of magazines and mass market paperbacks in the United States. With distribution companies in many cities across the country, it accounts for perhaps 15 percent of all such distribution.

ARA set up a complete bookstore within a giant supermarket in Norfolk, Virginia. It occupied 2000 square feet, which is probably more space than most bookstores enjoy, and displayed hardcover books, trade paperbacks, and mass market paperbacks—approximately 7000 titles in all—as well as magazines. Featured among the hardcover books, otherwise a narrow range of "sure-fire" titles, was a generous display of remainders and bargain books. The speed with which these books sold astonished ARA and the supermarket chain. The overall sales volume certainly justified the space, and ARA has now repeated the experiment successfully in a number of other cities and plans to expand it still further.

Dwight deGolia, who is in charge of book sales at ARA and who is guiding this program, fully understands the particular problems presented by the static (albeit large) clientele represented by supermarket shoppers. He is determined, he says, to "keep the display fresh." Titles are systematically rotated, and some are deliberately kept out of the stores for weeks at a time before being put back in the inventory. The concept is miles ahead of the model stock approach (practiced by Chas. Levy and B. Dalton), which is restrictive and would show its inherent defects quickly in a supermarket situation.

One of the most hopeful indications in the ARA experiment is that growing numbers of shoppers are not simply normal supermarket traffic but come deliberately to the bookshop. Some saw in this development the hope that mass market paperbacks would experience a revival, but their sales performance in the supermarkets is only so-so, far less impressive than the performance of the remainders and bargain books. Those books do well, deGolia says, because they offer real value for the money. Mass market books, it seems, no longer do.

Despite the immediate success of these ARA book departments and the intelligent leadership offered by Dwight deGolia, the test will be whether they depend too heavily on the appeal of remainders. Selling remainders may be fine for the retailer, but they have less than zero value for the author and publisher. And remainders, even at the ridiculously high rate at which publishers produce them, can supply only a limited number of outlets. When remaindering disappears, as it should, what will happen to the ARA bookstores?

One significant difference between the ARA relationship to these bookstores and the usual wholesaler-retailer relationship is the full control that ARA exercises over the outlet. The publisher cannot sell directly to the retailer, and ARA assumes the responsibility for retail stocking decisions that the usual trade wholesaler never faces. The difference is critical.

In the traditional publisher-wholesaler relationship, the size of the publisher (assuming corresponding sales muscle) is an important factor. The large publisher can use the wholesaler to greater advantage because he can more effectively get his titles represented in the bookstores before publication, patrol stores after publication to take full advantage of the additional copies at the wholesaler's, and make sure that the wholesaler has the books he should. The alternative for the large publisher is to strengthen his own direct ties to the retailer.

The question arises: Might there be a level in the size of the publisher and the nature of the list at which it would be advantageous for the publisher to give up supplying booksellers through wholesalers altogether? While it is a perfectly reasonable question, the answer is not at all obvious, but it can certainly be obtained through a dispassionate, factual study of the situation of a particular publisher. It is a study I would enjoy doing.

It supposes that the publisher is now giving wholesalers enough in discount differential to cover the cost of operating perhaps two local depots to supply bookstores quickly in remote areas. It also supposes that the publisher can operate those depots on a tight inventory control so that he uses fewer books to operate this system than is required in dealing through wholesalers.

The publisher would have to decide what stance to take toward libraries: whether to solicit orders directly at modest discounts or to let the wholesaler buy from the publisher at retailer discounts to supply libraries. Obviously, this possibility is open only to the largest publishers—if, indeed, it makes any sense at all. And, as one can see from the description of the merchandising plan in Chapter 7, such a plan may be a kind of painless first step toward exactly this kind of distribution.

9

Mass Market Publishing
An Industry in Trouble

MASS MARKET PAPERBACKS are still relative newcomers to book publishing. Pocket Books, the American pioneer of this revolution in publishing for the popular market, was founded as recently as 1939. It was inspired by Penguin Books, which had been started by Allen Lane a few years earlier in England and was just then beginning to be sold widely in this country.

Robert de Graff was at Doubleday when he got the idea that a line of 25-cent paperback reprints could be established in a large country like the United States even better than in England, where Penguin was already a solid success. But he was unable to sell his idea to Nelson Doubleday, perhaps because Doubleday was strongly committed to hardcover reprints, which would be competitive with the paperbacks. (The paperbacks were indeed knocking out the hardcover reprint business within a few years.) De Graff left Doubleday and managed to convince Simon & Schuster to finance his effort to launch Pocket Books.

This American version of Penguin was designed with colorful promotional covers more suited to the brash American audience, but otherwise Pocket Books was a reasonable facsimile of Penguin. The books were to be sold in bookstores, as Penguin books were. Nelson Doubleday was partially right, because bookstores were very cool to the idea of 25-cent books. But one of those rare historical convergences proved that even moderately well laid plans sometimes produce results a thousand times more wonderful than ever imagined. Pocket Books appeared at a time when magazine distributors had room for additional items and wanted something other than magazines. They took on Pocket Books as a long shot, and to everyone's surprise, the books melted off the racks. A new and spectacular publishing industry had been born, marketing its product without booksellers and reaching markets the bookstores were never able to reach.

Mass market paperbacks have changed the nature of publishing. When they were introduced just before World War II, the trade book industry saw them as providing a secondary market for the more popular hardcover titles and as expanding the opportunities to reach people who did not venture into bookstores. The trade publishers who sold rights to the paperback publishers were glad to have the extra income (marginal though it might be), but they did not envision the new format changing the industry in any significant way.

In fact, the changes wrought by the mass market publishers have been profound, and they have not all been salutary. There have been not only the changes evident to the public—the general availability of a wide variety of books at reasonable (once actually low) prices—but also those evident only inside trade book publishing. To some degree even when it began expanding immediately after World War II, and to a very marked degree in the past fifteen or twenty years, mass market paperback reprint publishing has subsidized trade publishing. It has pumped hundreds of millions of dollars of royalties into trade publishing, which has financed the remarkable expansion of trade publishing since the war. These changes have resulted in the dependence of many trade publishers on the sale of paperback rights in order to make any profit at all and a growing fixation on publishing the "big" book to get the "big" paperback sale.

The key ingredient in the spectacular rise of this new publishing industry was the ability of the paperback publisher, through the good offices of the magazine distributors, to place books in retail outlets without negotiating each title with each store's proprietor. But times are clearly changing.

Mass market distribution of paperback books through regional magazine wholesalers—"independent distributors"—is a sick business and likely to get sicker. It seems only a question of time before either the wholesalers give up trying to serve book publishers for lack of margin or the book publishers give up selling to magazine wholesalers because of poor sales and high returns. And when that happens the result may be catastrophic, because lost along with the magazine wholesalers will be the tens of thousands of small outlets that make mass market publishing possible.

The new industry was not created by editorial genius. Most of the early titles were easily identifiable solid backlist titles and classics in the public domain. There was no breakthrough in manufacturing methods. A friend of mine made a fortune setting up a *hand bindery* for the 25-cent books in those early days to keep up with the demand. It was purely the explosion in distribution.

The significant difference between the traditional bookseller and the new retail outlet presented to the paperback publisher by the magazine wholesaler was that the paperback retailer did not choose the books. He had to be consulted about the amount of space he would give to books or the number of racks he would accept, but he wanted someone else to decide what titles went in, when unsold copies were returned, when they were replaced. His concern, if any, was that the sales per square foot justify the space given to them.

This new outlet changed distribution in powerful ways. It reduced the publisher's selling and distribution cost to a fraction of that of negotiating books into a store, and it made bookselling profitable for the retailer at lower volumes and in limited retail space.

The fact that the retailer did not want his time wasted by a learned exposition of the author's talents or the plot of the book or a preview of the advertising campaign meant that accounts could be covered in an entirely different fashion. Instead of the few stops per week by a highly paid expert, the magazine distributor provided many stops per day by a truck driver clever enough not to pick up too many parking tickets. So the cost of covering an account was dramatically lower.

Removing the need for a book buyer opened book retailing to tens of thousands of smaller locations, whether a few square feet in a large department store or a section of the magazine display in a drugstore. The need for a buyer burdens the sales margins per square foot not only with the cost of the space but also with the cost of the buyer. A retail paperback installation even as large as a few hundred display pockets, though very profitable, cannot cover the cost of such an expert. With the wholesaler making the buying decisions, putting in a rack of paperbacks was as easy as putting in a rack of magazines or greeting cards.

The response of the public to the first tentative distribution of these paperback books surprised everyone. Manufacturing facilities—old letterpress clunkers printing in sheets, 96 pages on a side, 1400 sheets an hour—were not able to produce books fast enough. It was some years before high-speed web presses could produce books twenty-five times faster to make the later distribution gluts possible. For a long time the magazine distributors took the books as quickly as publishers could supply them, and they disappeared from the racks almost as quickly.

In the earliest stages, there was no need for "buying" decisions because the "distribution" decisions were made, essentially, by the publishers themselves, who allocated copies among the magazine distributors in a manner similar to the allocation of magazines. "Returns" of unsold copies were expected in the same way that unsold magazines are returned. During the period that production facilities were being expanded to satisfy this suddenly discovered public appetite, returns were modest and scattered, posing no great problem for publisher or distributor.

As the need for books in the retail outlets and the production of titles approached an equilibrium, more books had to be returned unsold to make room for the new titles, and a very important difference between magazines and books began to make itself felt.

A magazine is identifiable to both the distributor and the consumer. The number of copies of *Cosmopolitan* sold in one month in a particular neighborhood, and even a particular newsstand, will have some relation to the number sold in previous months, and the people who want *Cosmopolitan* are not likely to take *Playboy* as a substitute. The probable sales range for any magazine in any area is reasonably predictable. Sending in more copies will not displace sales of another magazine; it will simply result in heavier returns.

Book sales are not nearly as simple. The variety is great, and while some stand out, many titles on one publisher's list are very similar to those on other lists—even to others on his own list. For the book publisher, getting more of his *Cosmopolitan*s into the display at the expense of another publisher's *Cosmopolitan*s will result in a positive gain in sales. As a matter of fact, within pretty broad limits, the mix of titles from one publisher is so nearly the same in popular appeal as that of another that the sales level of two publishers one to the other will vary according to the relative number of titles each one has in the paperback display.

This characteristic of books (not yet recognized—amazingly, after all these years—in the sister industry, trade book publishing) caused the mass market publishers, as the rate of increase in sales slowed and the rate of returns accelerated, to allocate larger quantities to the magazine distributor in an attempt to gain more of his display space for their titles. This, of course, increased returns, but manufacturing costs, on the new rubber-plate web presses with high-speed adhesive binding machines, were then very low, so publishers were willing to endure high returns if they could increase their share of total sales.

The distributors reestablished some order in this situation by the most straightforward means available: They assigned quotas to each publisher. At first, this quota was usually the number of display pockets each publisher had physically supplied or paid for. Gradually, the more common formula developed of allocating a percentage of display space equal to the percentage of that publisher's sales in the distributor's total sales for some recent period. These adaptations to the increased crowding of the distribution channels had the advantage for the magazine distributor (and for the publisher, if he had only realized) that the publisher continued to allocate books to the distributor, essentially deciding what should be in the retail locations and in what quantities.

Throughout this period, there was a steady increase in the number of paperback publishers, an even more rapid increase in the number of new titles and surviving backlist titles, and a slowing in the expansion of display space. All of these factors contributed to increasing confusion in the distribution, which markedly slowed the rate of growth in sales and very sharply increased the rate of returns.

Publishers' costs were rising substantially at the same time, eating sharply into the very large profit margins with which the industry had started and which had been renewed, in the face of generally increasing costs, by the introduction of the high-speed presses. The battle over display space created additional costs by causing publishers to field sales forces to protect their interests at the distributors' and even at the retail locations. When the distributors established quotas, these sales forces patrolled the distribution system to see that the publisher actually got the space assigned to him (or more) and that it was used to best advantage.

The cost of acquiring titles went up. Competition for rights forced paperback houses, even in the days before the blockbuster, to pay higher advances and higher royalties.

The cost of manufacturing went up steadily. This happened partly because of general cost increases, particularly for paper, a significant item in the mass market book. Costs also went up because, as the number of titles increased, quantities went down, increasing the cost per copy of all the elements in the book—even the typesetting. And costs went up, surprisingly, because with the increase in titles, small physical differences among the books undermined the mass production methods introduced with web presses.

For example, in 1960, when I was negotiating contracts for Collier Books, a paperback line just being launched, I was surprised to learn from the printer that Pocket Books, whose books were all exactly the same size, was using approximately thirty different papers, distinguished by width of web, thickness, weight, color, texture, etc. By restricting Collier to two papers, a thin one for long books and a thick one for short books, and by making some very advantageous scheduling arrangements, we were able to arrange for Collier Books, in 10,000-copy quantities, to cost exactly the same per copy as Pocket Books in 100,000-copy quantities.

The increase in manufacturing costs made returns (since the "returned" books are physically destroyed) a much more serious burden. As books moved more sluggishly through the magazine distribution system and the cost of returns became more and more significant, publishers reacted to protect dwindling profits. One fairly early reaction was to reach for markets directly rather than through the distributor. The other, which came much later, was to involve the distributor in the increasingly catastrophic "buying" decisions.

When Pocket Books was launched, booksellers were initially cool to the line because they did not want to bring low-priced competition right into their stores; the fact that magazine distributors showed the interest that caused the market to explode was one of those historical accidents that make a good idea great.

As magazine distribution became the clear key to the paperbacks' success, Pocket Books, Bantam, and the other publishers adapted themselves to the trade customs of the world of the independent distributor. The magazine distributor almost invariably has an exclusive franchise for his territory, and after the paperbacks had proved their value, he insisted that this exclusivity apply to them as well. Since booksellers, with only isolated exceptions, had shown no enthusiasm, granting exclusivity to the suppliers of this avalanche of sales was no great strain.

But even before the sluggishness in sales through magazine distribution and the growth of returns became evident, some of the shortcomings of the independent distributors were clear enough to cause publishers to look for supplementary distribution. Among the first of these shortcomings was the general failure of the distributors to cover the educational market, principally high schools and colleges. Though some of the larger ones tried, most distributors could not supply the special knowledge of curricula as well as of the books available, nor could they economically supply the special service and attention that this market required. Jurisdiction in school distribution was unclear, even where magazine distributors claimed exclusivity, and the need was obvious, so publishers stepped in to serve the educational market directly, sometimes using the distributors as auxiliaries.

As it became clear that paperbacks were here to stay and that forcing people to go elsewhere to buy them was simply driving traffic away from the bookstore, booksellers began to take a greater interest in mass market books. In a few cases, booksellers actually permitted magazine wholesalers to set up the displays in the bookstore, but the distributor simply did not fit into the bookstore situation. The distributor was used to just that—distributing—putting in new titles and taking out old ones as it suited his adaptation to his allocation of the publisher's books. The bookseller, who wouldn't let the publisher himself select the inventory, was not about to let some untutored magazine dealer or his truck driver make those decisions. The bookseller wanted to pick and choose the titles and determine the quantities. The distributor could not afford to maintain the broad inventories this required, nor could he afford the heavy clerical cost of handling and filling such orders.

Besides, even if the distributor would accommodate all this, the bookseller could not accept the discounts of 20 and 25 percent that the distributor normally gave his customers. The bookseller wanted his usual 40 percent and up.

Somewhat reluctantly, here and there, paperback publishers began to fill booksellers' orders directly. They were afraid of angering the independent distributors, and they were also concerned about the higher clerical costs of handling bookstore orders after enjoying the easy bulk shipments that went to distributors' warehouses. But they were tempted by the discount advantage as much as by the prospect of expanding the paperback market. Selling to magazine distributors at 50 and 55 percent discounts made the 40 percent discount to bookstores very attractive. Moreover, the returns from bookstores were a tiny fraction of the returns from distributors.

And so, gradually and naturally, one thing led inevitably to another. The "direct sales" departments of the paperback houses grew, some more rapidly, some less. They moved into chain stores, such as Woolworth's, K-Mart, and others that also insisted on 40 percent discounts. They began to service the bookstore market through trade book wholesalers, who, no respecters of franchises, moved into the better parts of the magazine distributors' territory when they could. The growth of the bookstore chains B. Dalton and Walden provided more direct business denied the distributor.

Industry spokesmen conservatively estimate that the volume of "direct sales" has reached 50 percent of total paperback sales, and the direct sales percentage continues to grow. The distributor is left with large numbers of low-volume locations that the publisher cannot possibly handle and a scattering of higher-volume locations that the wholesaler manages to retain only by granting ruinous (to him) discount concessions to match what the retailers could get by buying directly from the publisher.

The distributor has one additional outlet, which becomes increasingly more important—his own retail store. Over the years, distributors here and there have opened paperback bookstores, enjoying the advantage of their larger discounts to help make them profitable. There are now probably several hundred such stores across the country; their volume is not insignificant. For example, David Turitz of the Portland News Company reported in *Publishers Weekly* that 15 percent of his paperback sales are through his own small chain of bookstores.

Nevertheless, the distributor's own retail stores cannot compensate for the large share of the market (50 percent or more) that the publisher has appropriated over years of steady reaction to what he has considered the magazine distributor's shortcomings. Direct selling has now reached levels that, in the eyes of many distributors, seriously undermine the economic base for the distributors' continued handling of mass market books.

Reaching some markets around, rather than through, the distributor and poaching on some of his other markets has been one reaction of the frustrated publishers. Another has been involving the wholesaler in the selection of titles and determination of quantities in a misguided effort to bring returns under control.

By piling more books into the distributor's warehouse than he can possibly use, publishers have forced him to choose what will go out to the retail outlets and what will remain until it is time for the overstock to be destroyed as returns. That kind of weighing, considering, and peering into the contents is unnecessary with magazines. But the days of easy book selection with high sales per title are gone. The distributor must now make for his customers the same kind of selection that the buyer in a traditional bookstore makes, faced with an avalanche of titles and severe limits on space and budget.

The increased complexity of the stocking decisions, the shorter time that the wholesaler can display each title, and the unrelenting output from each publisher have resulted in a steady increase in the rate of return (actually, destruction) of unsold books. Return rates from wholesalers of 50 percent and more have become commonplace. This situation has been particularly costly and troublesome to the publisher, especially as many of the returned books never got as far as the retail store. The distributor's judgment about which titles will sell, as well as about which titles are removed from the displays to make room for new arrivals, is vitally important to the publisher. It shows immediately in the returns—particularly in the return of unopened cartons.

Since growth has forced these shifts in the nature of the distributor's task, it seems only natural to involve him in the choices before the books arrive in his warehouse. In an effort to get more books into the display racks, the paperback publishers have tried to make the wholesaler more aware of the upcoming titles and more committed to their success. As a result, they have made the very serious but understandable error of involving the wholesaler in determining what titles and what quantities are shipped to him; in other words, they have introduced distribution-by-negotiation at the wholesale level.

High returns certainly indicated the need (among other things) for better decisions on the titles and quantities being put into the wholesalers' warehouses. Instead of retaining the right to make those decisions—and improving their quality—the publishers chose to give up that critical right and to negotiate with each wholesaler instead.

Increasing the distributor's problems by saddling him with buying decisions might have been justified if it resulted in better distribution or in any improvement in profit for him or the publisher. However, there is no sign of that nor even of a reduction in returns. Distribution-by-negotiation has already demonstrated, in trade books, its talent for narrowing title assortments and wasting potential markets. It is likely to be just as destructive in the relation between publisher and magazine distributor and will, no doubt, cause more distributors to question whether their rewards are worth the effort in paperback distribution.

As the rate of sale per display pocket drops, the magazine distributor's customer, the retailer, also finds the mass market paperback less exciting. It no longer builds traffic the way it used to when the pockets were more magnetic. With the lower volume per square foot, there is a growing temptation to put something else in that good traffic area. The retailer is perfectly willing to have the distributor switch some of the book space to magazines or give up books altogether.

It becomes increasingly difficult to get the distributor to represent the publisher's entire list aggressively. One way to do it in the past seemed to be to have at least one strong, "lead" title on each list to encourage the wholesaler to look favorably on the whole list. With disappointing overall sales, the lead title seems more important, with the result that paperback publishers are bidding increasingly ridiculous advances—into the millions—to get outstanding lead titles. But it isn't really working and it won't work; it simply runs up the publisher's editorial costs.

The publicity resulting from the payment of $3 million for paperback rights and the knowledge that a $1 million advance no longer merits publicity may give the impression that things are getting better and better. Not at all. The insider knows that these spectacular purchases are acts of desperation rather than calculated business decisions.

The crowding of the secondary titles out of the increasingly tight rack space has driven the paperback publishers to fight harder for titles that can command space easily. This has simply pushed up the price of "lead" titles and depressed interest in lesser titles. The original publisher is finding it harder and harder to get decent paperback offers for books that were sure candidates only a short while ago. The consolation that the big books have gotten bigger is helpful only to the few original publishers who have such books, and it is likely, even there, to be short-lived.

People in mass market publishing feel that part of the problem is a lack of space in the display racks. After the Harlequin titles and their competitors and imitators and the current best-sellers on each list have been allocated their space, there is no room for secondary titles. Even the "lesser" books that make their way through the crush into the racks aren't allowed to stay long, for new titles are stepping on their heels.

Further, the mass market publishers think that the lack of space is the result of overcrowding titles. It is certainly true that every distribution system has a limit. However, space is not simply the number of pockets but the pockets multiplied by the rate at which books move out of them. As the rate of sales per pocket has decreased, the industry has been effectively losing "space" no matter how many physical pockets there are. The limits are established by the speed of passage through the system as well as the crowding of the product trying to pass through. If the sales per pocket could be doubled (an easily achieved goal), the pressure on space in the racks would be very much relieved: The same sales level would be reached in half the time, in effect doubling the available rack space; and if each pocket were twice as effective, there would be more pockets because the sales and profits per square foot would be more attractive to retailers.

There is another perhaps more serious fallacy: the fatalistic expectation of so many in mass market publishing that events must proceed along the lines they clearly seem to be following. It seems reasonable that the number of titles will be reduced because the distribution system simply cannot cope with the present number. It seems reasonable that retail prices will go up because they must absorb the inefficiencies of the distribution system and because of fewer sales and smaller printings. The combination of these developments will have a synergistic, negative effect. It will further slow the movement of books out of the racks, making wholesalers' costs higher and margins lower, and further reduce the attraction of these books for the retailer. Any drying up of the wholesalers' market will accelerate their departure from the field, which, in turn, will reduce sales and raise prices further.

The rack situation is a dynamic one, and the forces now in motion have no reason to shift direction. Inevitably, there will be less and less room for "lead" titles as well. The high advance payments will be harder to recover from sales (if that has not already happened), and fewer paperback publishers will want to participate in the publisher's rights auction. The inevitable incidence of disasters will increase— rights purchased for millions of dollars for books that turn out to be duds, imposing the additional costs of large printings and large returns on top of the cost of the rights.

Two important elements that made handling mass market books practical and attractive for magazine distributors have been steadily leaching away as paperback publishing has grown: simplicity and the large spread between the publisher's and the retailer's discount.

Simplicity is very important. Magazine distribution is highly structured. Each magazine has its assigned position, and when the October issue arrives, you remove any September issues that remain. The number of copies of the previous three issues sold is a pretty good indication of how many new copies should be put out.

In the beginning, paperbacks were very much like that. No book carried a date. But the movement out of the racks and the steady expansion of rack space made it easy for the distributor simply to provide enough assorted titles in each delivery to fill the empty pockets. Titles that did not sell well were obvious because of the increase in their relative population among the books displayed. The drivers would be asked to return such nonproductive titles to make room for the newer ones. Or if the distributor complained that books were not selling fast enough, the publisher would suggest which titles should probably be returned. By restricting each publisher to a percentage of the available space, the distributor assured his cooperation in recalling slow-moving titles. The distributor had no need to know—or have any opinions about—the particulars of each title.

The system was not perfect, but it was simple. With today's profusion of new titles, the need to know about each book to make buying decisions as well as to control its short life in the racks, the competition from publishers and trade wholesalers, and the high rate of returns, that simplicity is hardly even a memory. And it is not just a difference in ambience. These complications have steadily pushed up the distributors' costs. Quite simply, complications cost money.

The discount situation has also changed radically. The magazine distributor used to buy books at a discount of 50 and 55 percent and sell to stationers, drugstores, and others at discounts of 20 and 25 percent. These discount spreads are far more attractive than those for magazines and are probably about the most attractive spreads available to any wholesaler of any consumer product. Though the discounts he gets have not changed much, the distributor has lost the advantage of the spread because he can no longer sell at the favorable discounts. Partly because the publisher has offered such generous discounts to retailers for buying directly, the distributor now finds himself forced to give discounts of 30 percent, 35 percent, and occasionally even 40 percent.

It is true that over these years the cover price of the 25-cent paperback has soared to $2.95 or more. But while that has increased the value in pennies of each percentage point in the wholesaler's shrinking discount spread, costs have soared even faster. This more complicated, more expensive business does not have the profit attraction it once had.

The intense competition among paperback publishers at the moment (it won't last long) for the blockbuster—the payment of $3.5 million for *Princess Daisy* was only the most outstanding example—is on the one hand a costly attempt to capture display space and on the other hand, and perhaps more important, an attempt to bring simplicity back to paperback distribution.

An important element in the appeal of *Princess Daisy*—or that of any book likely to be in great demand—is that everyone instantly knows what it is. The publisher, the distributor, the truck driver, the retailer, and the customer recognize it and are likely to react favorably with little hesitation.

The blockbuster does simplify handling in the distribution chain, but it is too small a factor in paperback publishing to solve the growing complexity and confusion that engulf the distributor. Besides, the blockbuster is a temporary phenomenon. Two elements tend to undermine its effectiveness. One is its cost. The possibility of recouping the outlandish author advances of from $1 million to $3 million and more is very unlikely, even with today's distribution. It cannot be done from bookstore sales; the almost universal availability made possible by magazine distribution is essential even to come close. As magazine distributors here and there give up paperbacks or simply curtail their space, the decreased earning potential of the blockbuster will become clear even to the most optimistic mass market publisher. This recognition will cool the auction fervor that drives up prices, but lower royalty advances will not be enough to correct the economic contradictions of the blockbuster concept.

The other difficulty with blockbusters is that the distribution system can only handle such titles in limited numbers. If the magazine distributor has one blockbuster for the month, he can give it the extra display pockets essential to the "star" treatment. If two or three publishers' blockbusters come out at the same time, the distributor cannot possibly give each one the space and attention it requires. The industry is obviously not going to be rescued from steadily deteriorating distribution by a dozen or a dozen and a half outstanding titles each year.

Parallel with the infatuation with blockbusters, there was an attempt to find titles that were universal, appealing to the least-common-denominator market, resulting in the brief flurry of interest in the "movie tie-in." This idea was hailed only a short time ago as the salvation of paperback publishing. After all, what could have broader appeal than the story of the movie currently playing in all the theaters and featured in millions of dollars of advertising and publicity hype?

Paperback publishers poured a lot of money down the drain before accepting reality. Dell paid $400,000 for a novelization of *F.I.S.T.* and $250,000 for *Ode to Billie Joe*; Warner Books paid $246,000 for *The Rose*. These reprints, and many others, returned to the publishers lots of unsold books but very little on their investment.

A move toward simplification that is likely to be much more successful and that may become the core of tomorrow's mass market paperback publishing (if this type of publishing survives at all) is the category book. The best, clearest, and most successful category book is the Harlequin series of romances. No doubt its spectacular success is partly due to the recognition that a considerable market for these books exists in the large numbers of women eager to consume larger numbers of romantic novels, all simple variations of four or five wholesome and predictable plot lines. But there are many other titles with a story line and writing style indistinguishable from Harlequins that don't sell nearly as well. The simple and effective twist that assured Harlequin's success was identifying these books clearly. Everyone knows what a Harlequin book is better than they know what *Princess Daisy* is. Those who want to read a sugary romance with a happy ending know exactly what the book looks like and exactly where to find it. And the titles are numbered to help the browser and, even more important, the magazine distributor. What could be simpler, except a dated *Romances Magazine* itself? And the magazine's racklife would be restricted to one month.

Harlequin's formula is now being copied by potential competitors for the very same market. Harlequin is demonstrating that the market is only part of the secret. It is now applying the same simplicity and identification to a new line, called Raven Books, to do for mystery story readers exactly what Harlequin did for readers of romances. They, or others, will then do the same thing with Westerns, for science fiction, and so on.

Rob Bartles, a successful and creative magazine wholesaler in Vermont and New Hampshire, insists that the only way he can operate on narrow margins is to handle paperbacks like magazines. That means absolutely minimum inventories, a short stay in the racks for each title, and prompt returns of slower sellers. He would like the paperback publishers to adopt the physical format of magazines to simplify his handling of them, and some new publications are doing just that.

It is not surprising that putting books in uniform and lining them up in ranks creates order out of expensive confusion. It is more surprising that it has taken publishers so long to recognize it.

What category publishing does for the distributor and the paperback book display is to introduce the simplicity of the magazine, with just a little more flexibility. The distributor's driver can bring back, say, romances numbered below 400, mysteries numbered below 200, and Westerns numbered below 100. How many of the more recent titles in each category are allowed to remain (and be replenished) will depend on how well that category is selling. It is even easier, if that is possible, than handling magazines. The browsers are preselected for each clearly labeled display just as the buyers of magazines are preselected. Publishers know how many copies to print because the sales record is consistent by category and the wholesaler knows how many he needs and exactly where he will put them.

Category publishing will soon demonstrate that titles outside the established subjects—and the easily recognized line of books the publisher establishes for each one—are too marginal and uncertain to be worth the effort. The "independent title" will rapidly decline as this simple truth becomes evident to both publisher and distributor.

Category books already account for perhaps 25 or 30 percent of the mass market publishers' lists, and their number and their percentage of the total is steadily increasing. The problem as it affects distribution is fairly simple: Will publishers shift their production to such easily distributed books rapidly enough to keep the magazine distributor interested? If they can, they will have saved the "mass market" aspect of paperback publishing by substituting a new, inexpensive, easily handled, totally different product for the kind of paperback with which Pocket Books started the revolution. Further, can category books support a publishing industry worthy of the name? Present developments suggest that today's mass market publishers may simply follow two completely separate paths: one, publishing "quality" paperbacks aimed at an enlarged bookstore audience; the other, grinding out today's cornball equivalents of yesterday's pulp magazines and dime novels.

At what level category books can support a publishing industry is unknown. There will undoubtedly be a shift of some kind in the reading audience, moving downward on the intellectual and literary scale, perhaps opening up a much larger reading public to the paperback book. But even if many more people are drawn to the category paperbacks than are lost by the demise of the more individual type, mass market publishing will shrink for the very simple reason that variety will no longer be supportable. Neither the public nor the distributor needs ten different suppliers of mystery stories; two or three can serve the market very nicely and with a good deal less confusion.

Trade publishers may hope that the paperback readers abandoned by the shift to category books will look to bookstores to satisfy their wants. Some certainly will, but the lack of choice in the stores and the high retail prices will not help.

One effect on trade publishing is, unfortunately, much more certain: The current sale of reprint rights and the millions of dollars of royalties from paperbacks will dry up. Buying rights to someone else's original edition is neither efficient nor economical for the category publisher. We are moving back into the days of pulp magazine writing: books commissioned by publishers, at so much per word, and produced to standard formulas.

The odds are very good that, in time, the lesson of a few spectacular lead book catastrophes, the reduced market for lead books in general, the reduced interest in the less outstanding titles, and the increasing reliance on category books will remove the pot of gold, and perhaps even the rainbow, from the image the trade publisher has of his paperback benefactor.

Some magazine distributors, unwilling to give up paperback distribution without a struggle and unable to wait for publishers to find some magic way—blockbusters, movie tie-ins, category publishing—to reverse the trend, are trying to develop their own systems to reduce costs and increase sales.

Chas. Levy, the mammoth magazine distributor in Chicago that has become the nation's single most important wholesaler of mass market paperbacks, has tried very hard to develop effective systems for stocking racks according to probable demand. These are the systems that one would have expected the publishers themselves to be scrambling to develop. Levy's effort has been valiant and, considering the many handicaps under which any wholesaler must operate, imaginative and intelligent.

Levy's system is far superior to the chance bumblings that usually determine distribution, and on the strength of the system, it has installed book departments in a number of J. C. Penney and Sears stores, among other locations. It is hard for an outsider to know the precise results, but the indications are that, though Levy may be happy with the added volume, sales have not been exciting from the retailers' point of view. The conclusion seems inescapable that Levy simply cannot overcome the disadvantages inherent in wholesaling. If a workable system is to be developed and applied, it will probably be by a publisher. If not, the mass market paperback industry (except, possibly, for category fiction) will probably be of principal interest to historians.

In an odd way, the early solid success of mass market publishers may now insidiously be compounding their difficulties. Success created fully paid assets that may now be being liquidated slowly, imperceptibly to the publishers, delaying the impact of the deteriorating situation on the financial statement. Some of these assets are subtle and intangible, such as the cost of training large numbers of employees in a variety of complicated jobs or the friendly relationships with wholesalers, which result in their continuing to distribute under badly eroded profit margins. Some of the assets are more palpable, like printing plates carried at zero value or undervalued inventories of finished books.

Some of the losses arising out of the changes now taking place may be painlessly covered by a decrease in these unacknowledged assets for a time—until the depletion of the assets becomes obvious. For example, the publisher does not compensate the wholesaler for the shrinking of his margins, so this shrinkage does not show as an expense to the publisher. Then, when the margins have gotten so low that the wholesaler no longer wants the books, even "for old time's sake," the loss in volume hits the publisher with all its financial impact.

The strength resulting from the assets built in the heyday of the paperbacks tends to understate the seriousness of the present malaise. When the industry becomes fully aware of its problem, it may seem like a sudden bolt from the blue rather than the slow cancer that it is.

The paperback publisher is caught in a difficult dilemma, which becomes more serious as he struggles with it. Magazine distribution does not work well because sales are low and returns high. That, in itself, makes it costly to both the publisher and the distributor. The inefficiencies of the system impel the publisher to sell more of the market directly while they also impel the distributor to ask the publisher for economic concessions.

The publisher cannot, indefinitely, refuse to give the magazine distributor higher margins and, at the same time, further worsen his position by taking more of the better accounts away from him. More and more distributors are saying the book business isn't worth it.

Publishers continue to look for hopeful signs that the wholesaler remains committed to mass market paperbacks. One publishing executive suggested to me that no wholesaler would give up paperbacks because he would then run the risk of a newcomer using paperback distribution as a base from which to invade the magazine field. It is very unlikely, of course, that paperback distribution, abandoned as unprofitable by a wholesaler who already had the magazine business to help pay for the trucks and the warehouse, would miraculously become profitable for a newcomer without these advantages.

One much more visible and somewhat hopeful sign for continued wholesaler loyalty is the interest in book distribution generated by the apparently highly successful "bookstore within a store" pioneered by ARA Service, the most important magazine distributor in the United States. This innovation, which was cited to me by a top executive in paperback publishing to prove that my pessimism is unwarranted, is described in Chapter 8, on wholesaling, and its importance cannot be denied. Unfortunately, the books that sell well in this situation are remainders and bargain books, not mass market paperbacks. Besides, the number of supermarket locations in which these book departments can be placed is strictly limited. Something much more substantial is needed to keep magazine wholesalers in the mass market picture.

Though he sees himself doing only what he is forced to do by circumstance, the paperback publisher, in weakening the economic viability of the magazine distributor, is assiduously sawing off the very limb on which mass market publishing sits. The danger is certainly evident to many in paperback publishing management. Along with the frustrations fed by lack of industry growth, the increasing financial demands from hardcover publishers and authors' agents, and the seeming absence of any "answer" to the growing industry crisis, the shakiness of the mass market business foundation has pushed mass market publishers toward establishing a second business foundation— trade publishing.

As Oscar Dystel, without question the outstanding thinker in the mass market industry, and the man with the greatest record of accomplishment, said in the Bowker Memorial Lecture on November 25, 1980, in New York, "Today, mass market paperback publishing has invaded the domain of hardcover publishing."

This trend began with the publication of "trade" paperbacks, intended to have a large portion of their sale through bookstores as well as through the selective use of magazine wholesalers, and it has now moved to include original hardcover titles as well, titles for whose sale the publisher can expect no help from the magazine wholesaler.

This movement into original trade publishing is painted as an "expansion" rather than the search for a haven against the time that abandonment by magazine distributors takes the "mass market" out of mass market publishing. The move is supposedly a reaction to the selfishness of trade publishers, who insist on unreasonably high royalty advances and unreasonably short reprint licenses. They have brought this expansion of paperback publishers into the trade field on themselves.

In his Bowker lecture, Oscar Dystel pointed out some of the unhappy implications that this change has for the present trade publishers. The pressure of the high advance costs, he said, and the insistence of original publishers on giving reprint licenses for only short periods will now be relieved because paperback houses will sign contracts directly with the authors for reasonable advance payments and for the duration of the copyright. The resulting implications "may be grim for hardcover trade publishers without paperback affiliations," he goes on, which means, of course, for 95 percent of all hardcover publishers.

The implications are a good deal grimmer than Oscar Dystel bothered to explain. There will be competition for authors, with the richly bankrolled paperback publishers at a distinct advantage, generally getting first choice of the obviously valuable names. There will be competition for the bookseller's space and buying budget, with the strong existing sales forces in the field giving the paperback publisher a distinct advantage. Furthermore, books that have been "farmed" to hardcover publishers by the paperback houses—books for which the paperback house holds the original contract and permits an established hardcover publisher to publish the first edition and enjoy that sales volume—will henceforth be published in hardcover by the paperback house itself, resulting in a substantial net decrease in sales to the publisher who has enjoyed these benefits in the past.

Dystel confirmed the deteriorating status of paperbacks among the magazine distributors, who were finding, he said, that "profits were better and easier in magazines. Where only five years ago paperbooks accounted for 30 to 35 percent of the magazine wholesaler's total volume, these days volume can be down to 15 percent. The figures say it all. Wholesalers seem to have lost interest in paperbacks."

Wholesalers are already getting out. A few years ago the number of wholesalers dealing in mass market books was estimated at about 550. Today many publishers are dealing through fewer than 400 wholesalers. Some of the decrease is the result of wholesaler consolidations or territorial expansions, but some represents the tiny beginnings of the wholesaler exodus. Some publishers already find it necessary to "sell" wholesalers on the advantages of continuing as book distributors. The pitch consists of the usual approach, first described by Aristotle, of exaggerating the cost to the wholesaler of giving up book distribution and understating the cost of retaining it.

There are other disturbing signs. Stripped copies of paperbacks (from which the wholesaler has removed the covers to get his returns credit) are turning up in junk stores more frequently. "Swap shops," to which the customer can take his old paperbacks and exchange them for someone else's old ones, are spreading rapidly. Higher retail prices and returns penalties are certain to promote this kind of activity.

The moves into trade publishing by the mass market publishers, in spite of the bravado with which they are announced, do not give the impression of a successful industry conquering new markets but rather of acts of desperation, of an industry finding that all those easy formulas don't seem to work anymore.

Once the mass market publisher has transformed himself into a trade publisher, whether of paperbacks or hardcovers or both, he will discover that more than one thing has changed. The cost ratios in trade book publishing are not accidental. They reflect the realities of an industry very different from mass market publishing.

The success of mass market paperback publishing, notwithstanding its recent nagging problems, has encouraged the illusion that paperback publishers are smarter than their trade publishing colleagues. It is easy for them to imagine that they will sell more books, at lower prices and higher margins, than the trade publisher has been able to. And, indeed, they do start with the advantage of impressive Hollywood-style art and promotion departments and oversized sales staffs, all of which have been bought and paid for by the publishing of the past but which may turn out to be much too expensive for the publishing these companies will find in their future.

The key ingredient in the success of mass market publishing was the availability of tens of thousands of outlets in high-traffic locations that gave space generously and wanted no voice in selecting the titles. Unless the mass market publishers can retain and service these outlets economically, they will find themselves battling the old trade distribution frustrations and wearing the same rags they wore before the old giant of magazine distribution, the American News Company, rubbed the magic lamp.

The end of the world is prophesied often and happens seldom. It may very well be that a little adaptation here and there will enable mass market publishing to survive in some other form, perhaps even in an improved one. For example, a new paperback industry may deal only in category fiction: women's romances, science fiction, mysteries, etc., while the present industry merges into trade publishing.

In this scenario, once category publishing is firmly established, the blockbuster or lead title will lose much of its charm as a leader of the list and be simply handled as a category of its own. Prices for rights to lead titles are likely to go down because their importance to the paperback publisher will have gone down. The lesser titles, which do not identify themselves recognizably to the public and do not carry the identification with a popular category, are likely to suffer greatly. If this is the way paperbacks survive, there is likely to be a regrettable decline in literary standards and of quality in general.

The trade publisher may lose more than simply the bonanza of the wild auction prices paid for blockbusters and the sharp decline in the paperback publishers' interest in the secondary titles. If the situation develops in this direction at all, paperback houses, as they restrict their reprint buying more and more exclusively to the lead titles, will also more and more tend to buy rights directly from the author, from whom they are sure to get more favorable terms.

That is one direction in which paperback publishing may go to solve its present problems. There are, perhaps, other directions. For example, it is possible (if unlikely) that the public will accept high enough retail prices to subsidize the growing inefficiencies of the paperback distribution system.

It may not be the end of the world at all. But if it should be, it may also be the opportunity to create a new and even more wonderful paperback world. Such a birth—or rebirth—depends on whether any paperback publisher is able to translate the essential basis for paperback success into a new, more practical form.

If paperback publishing is to be reincarnated as a supplier of inexpensive books in great variety, catering to a great multiplicity of tastes, it will have to find a way to reintroduce into its distribution the key factor that made possible the paperback revolution after World War II—the placement of books in retail outlets without prior negotiation and authorization.

It was the *distribution* of books to the retail network rather than the laborious *sale* to each retailer, title by title, copy by copy, that was the magazine wholesaler's contribution to popular paperback publishing. Unfortunately, neither the publisher nor the wholesaler supplied a second essential ingredient. Unless the privilege to put books into retail outlets without question results in putting in the right numbers of the right titles, adjusted according to the subtle variations and changes in demand from place to place and time to time, the privilege will become a trap instead of an opportunity. The strength of the magazine distributor has been his ability to get the retail space; his weakness is that he doesn't know with sufficient discrimination what to put there.

And, for a number of reasons, the wholesaler is not the one to learn what to put where. The subtleties of differences and changes in demand are much easier to see across wholesalers' territory lines than within them. The computer capacity required exceeds what most wholesalers can afford, and some moderately expensive programming is almost certainly necessary. Maintaining a wide range of titles means many will be in retail locations in ones, twos, and threes. The wholesaler's profit margin is fixed, and on small quantities it is too small to support even modest attention or to encourage him with the prospect of additional sales.

If the distribution of individual mass market titles of wide-ranging interest through retailers without negotiation is going to survive in a new incarnation, it will be a publisher incarnation rather than a magazine distributor one. And if it does happen, it will be a highly sophisticated translation of the methods that produced wonders in the greeting card field—taking greeting cards from the shabby displays in corner candy stores doing business in pennies to the glamourous displays of a multimillion-dollar industry, selling and servicing its product everywhere.

The key to greeting card success was the card manufacturers' direct operation of inventory control of cards in retail stores. It is true that inventory control of cards is child's play compared to books. The principles are the same; there is simply a considerable difference in degree of complication. But the methods for control of mass paperback books *do* exist now and would be relatively simple to install.

It is obviously uneconomical for each paperback publisher to control his own books in each retail outlet. Most retailers would not tolerate the confusion, and it would multiply the total cost of serving each retail store.

The system, copied from the greeting card industry, could operate something like this: Each retail outlet would get *all* its mass market books from *one* publisher who would offer to supply books from *all* publishers and to handle all stocking and returns, either supplying the necessary racks or taking over the existing ones. In consideration for taking on this responsibility, the publisher would reserve for himself, say, 60 percent of the space and volume of sales, dividing the other 40 percent among the other publishers. The publisher (or publishers, because the leader will be quickly copied) would not attempt to cover all 100,000 paperback outlets. The top 20,000 would be completely adequate. (Remember? You get 80 percent of the business from 20 percent . . .)

The publisher's own books would come from his own warehouse and be billed by him. The other publishers would ship their books directly to the store on the instructions of the "operating" publisher, and they would be included in his invoice. Thus the retail outlet would deal with one supplier and one invoice.

Books might be sent by book post, UPS, the publisher's own trucks, or under a contract with the local magazine distributor. Except for surprise best-sellers or for locations with exceptionally heavy traffic (such as airline terminals), the typical retailer would get one shipment every two weeks or every month from each source and one invoice every two weeks or every month. Sections of the racks would be clearly identified by category, like greeting card racks, and each package would be clearly marked to show where the books should be placed.

The books would be sold to the retailer at a reasonable discount, perhaps 30 percent, to ensure him an attractive profit. The profitability of the space would depend much more, however, on high turnover resulting from a good matching of titles to demand.

It should not be difficult for the operating publisher to buy books from the "cooperating" publishers at discounts approaching 55 or 60 percent (returns guaranteed to be kept below 10 percent). The alternative for the cooperating publisher is, after all, no business at all in that outlet.

The operating publisher would supply each cooperating publisher with a monthly order for each outlet. Books would be shipped with a packing slip, and the invoice would go to the operating publisher, who would include those books in his overall invoice to the store at the standard 30 percent discount.

Frequent inventories of new lead titles in the stores would be taken by part-time workers, perhaps as often as every two weeks in the better locations. Complete inventories by the publisher's reps would be needed, but probably not more often than once every three months.

The heart of this publisher's operation would be a fairly simple statistical department, supervised by an employee with a B.A. in mathematics, which would determine the title mixes going into the stores based on the inventories. The cost of operating such a system would be almost embarrassingly low. Sales per pocket should be at least twice what they are now; they would probably be higher. Returns should average 5 to 10 percent.

Why should the retailer accept such a scheme? Because it will work. His sales and margin per square foot will be at least twice what they are with magazine distributor servicing. The retailer's own role will be simple and painless.

Why should a publisher do it? Because it will give him a share of the market he can control. He will know before he sends the order to his printer exactly how many copies will be on display within reach of the public, not, as he knows today, how many copies are going to distributors' warehouses. He will be able to match his publishing program much more closely to the market. If his editors stay friendly with the young mathematics graduate, they will become very smart editors indeed.

Why should we care? Because it is probably the only way that paperbacks at low prices can be available to a broad reading community. Such paperback distribution could economically handle titles in quantities of 15,000 and 20,000, much lower even than today's paperback threshold. And its displays would benefit from variety. Most of all, it could save paperbacks from becoming pulp magazines.

10

Editorial

FOR MANY PEOPLE, the editorial function *is* publishing. Those who dream of careers in publishing are dreaming of being editors, not accountants, production men, or sales reps. Particularly for the outsider, everything else that happens in publishing supports the editorial activity, which is taken to be the reason for the existence of the publishing house in the first place.

Indeed, editing has long been at the heart of publishing because, until recent shifts to a more "business" orientation, it has been the focus of most heads of publishing houses. This is the most varied trade publishing function and the most difficult one about which to generalize. Although there are differences among publishers in the way they handle accounting, production, sales, sub rights, etc., there is a sameness in the essentials, and the few who differ in any considerable degree stand out sharply. The editorial department, more than any other, often reflects the personality of the head of the house, though the differences among publishers may only obscure their basic similarities.

The editorial department selects the manuscripts or projects to be published. In smaller houses, the editor's word may be final; indeed, he and the head of the house are frequently the same person. In larger houses, the editor's selection is likely to be a *recommendation,* with final approval residing in a business manager or a business committee. It is interesting (and, to me, comforting) that the efforts of the superimposed business intelligence, intended to curb the editors' impractical intellectual notions, is so often counterproductive.

Though many business heads mistakenly see the need to reduce editorial production, the fact is that one of the problems that faces big publishers is how to maintain, even to promote, editorial productivity and to keep it economically sound. Most large publishers go about "controlling" the editorial department the wrong way. It is well worth management's attention to find better ways.

In days gone by, those who set up publishing businesses were interested in what was to be published. They were moved by a very strong commitment to literary, political, or social ideals or because they saw potentially lucrative subject areas being overlooked by others. These motives are still behind the many new small publishing ventures launched each year.

In the larger, older, more prosperous houses, impartial business judgments are supposed to temper any editor's personal inclinations. The importance of editorial judgment is not belittled; it is simply not altogether trusted. The business minds believe the industry wisdom that "you are what you publish." If you publish books that sell, you will prosper; if you publish books that do not sell, you will fail. Although they recognize the importance of editorial judgment (frequently to the point of trying to stifle it), they feel the need to hobble the independence, elan, inclination to experiment and to take risks in the editorial activity that built the house. This new business orientation among large houses (and some copycatting among smaller ones) has created more similarity among editorial departments than was ever intended by the editors.

The image that "editor" projects to the outsider, aside from the tweed jacket with leather elbow patches and a thoughtfully puffed pipe, is one of great intellectual activity and power. The editorial department is, in truth, a center of intellectual energy. In many cases, the brains are working not so much to guide the writing skill of today's Dostoyevsky or to challenge his plot or character development but rather to figure out how to get his manuscript approved for publication by the business committee and how to get the sales department to take it seriously.

As for the power, it is another matter entirely. There still are a few editors whose word is law in their publishing houses. There are some, like Richard Marek, David Lawrence, and Eleanor Friede, who have achieved a level of personal prestige and recognition and have the loyalty of a sufficiently large following of best-selling authors to enable them to become independent editorial entrepreneurs. Publishers are happy to put their production, sales, accounting, and other essential functions at the service of such reliable and steady producers of salable books in exchange for a fee or a share of the profits.

These editors are the exception. They, and the few who have achieved almost that status but still operate as employees, are the "stars." Allowing for the difference in the breadth of the arena, they carry the authority analogous to that of the stars in movies and sports.

But the prestige of the stars is little help to the other toilers in the editorial vineyard. Except for these few, the power of the editor has steadily declined in recent years, particularly, perhaps, with the advent of the conglomerates. In a publishing house where management believes that "we publish too many books," the editor's responsibility is always in question. This point of view automatically casts suspicion on the editor's activity. It is one of the real tragedies of modern publishing, and a serious obstacle to its growth, that too often today's editors have all the frustration and none of the power.

For some books, the editorial department (and frequently the design and production departments) exists outside the publishing house. These are the so-called packaged books, created by independent organizations that conceive the idea for the book, get it written, edit it, and frequently have it completely manufactured, delivering finished books to the publisher's warehouse. These books run the gamut from expensive, meticulously printed art books to quite ordinary cookbooks, biographies of celebrities, or formula fiction for the mass market audience. They even include college textbooks on virtually every subject.

In the case of the expensive art books, manufacturing control by the packager is essential. It ensures the targeted level of quality and the manufacturing economies essential to the project. The packager sells publishers in several countries an edition to be manufactured in one large run. Though the text may be in a different language for each publisher, printing all the color illustrations together provides the economies that make the entire project attractive. Subjects of reasonably universal interest—French impressionism, art treasures of the Vatican, mammals of the world, the history of ships—are not in unlimited supply, so this type of packaging, which produced many titles in the two or three decades following World War II, has used and reused much of the eligible material and is now of minor importance. Contributing to its diminution, in addition to the public's weariness with insufficiently different treatments of similar material, was the gradual disappearance of low-cost quality color printers, who were once available for just this kind of work in Italy, Japan, and Hong Kong, among other places.

□ *Among the places where the price was low but the quality was lower were some of the Iron Curtain countries. I recall that in the 1950s, printers from Romania and Czechoslovakia were offering color printing by the pound; that is, the price did not depend on the number of illustrations, the complexity, the size, etc., or even, in some cases, the length of the run beyond a stated minimum. The charge was so much per pound for the printed paper, carrying whatever illustrations (and text) the publisher wished. This was part of a drive to get American dollars, and these printers, being subsidized by their governments, could sell printing to Western countries at a loss.*

For books with no illustrations, the packager may deliver to the publisher a copyedited manuscript, marked for the compositor. If there are some illustrations or if control of the layout is desirable, the packager may have the type set and deliver to the publisher complete "boards," with type and line illustrations in position and half-tone illustrations indicated, ready for printing plates to be made.

Although the impressive growth of the illustrated packaged book in the postwar period tended to equate the term "packaging" with this special type of book, packaging in the broader sense has been ubiquitous in publishing for a long time. The children's series that were the foundation, sixty years ago, of Grosset & Dunlap's initial success—the Bobbsey Twins, the Hardy Boys, Bomba the Jungle Boy, Tom Swift—were all created by writing syndicates, an early word for "book packager." Western Printing and Litho, a printer with large color presses, created and produced the Golden Books for children, which made Simon & Schuster supreme in the field.

The reasons a publisher uses a book packager will differ. It may be to get a high-priced and high-quality title in the modest quantity within the publisher's sales capability. It may be to include subjects on his list—travel guides, home maintenance—in which his own editors have neither the expertise nor the connections to outside advice. It may be, as it was with Golden Books, to have someone else assume the financial risk even at the expense of an unusually large share of the profits. It may be to start a fiction series, or a series of such series— Hardy Boys for children or more sophisticated tales for the adult market—which can capture a repeat audience, providing an assured level of sale into the indefinite future. (A number of successful series of this type—a recent one is the Kent Family Chronicles, by John Jakes— have kindled a new [and vain] hope among the mass market publishers that packaged series will reverse the trend toward lower sales and greater disillusionment among magazine wholesalers.)

The book packager certainly performs a useful function and has recorded some spectacular successes. It is a great temptation for the innovative editor who is fed up with corporate inertia to set up shop as an independent packager (very little capital is required) and develop his own projects. Being a packager and being independent allow him to offer his ideas to a number of publishers with a variety of personalities and internal systems. What has no appeal to the first, second, or third may be enthusiastically accepted by the fourth.

But packaging has its limitations. From the publisher's point of view, though his risks are minimal, his profit is very much smaller than it would be if the project were all his own. So, except for the occasional "sleeper" best-seller, it is not the most attractive investment for the publisher. To protect himself, the publisher frequently overprices the packaged book, which discourages sales and confirms the drabness of the enterprise.

From the packager's point of view, there is the danger that a good editorial idea, even well executed, will collapse ingloriously like a badly leaking balloon. This may be because the publisher overprices the book or skimps on the advertising and promotion budget. Or the publisher may have an inept sales force or none at all. The packager, too, is in a marketplace. He may not be able to sell his project, at a profitable price, to the publisher who can handle it best. The publisher who does buy it may not have the capacity or the ambition to do more than an absolute minimum with it.

Probably the most successful packaged book was Alex Comfort's *The Joy of Sex,* created by Mitchell Beazley of London, and there have been others. But the profusion of packaged books on the remainder tables tells the other side of the story. Though packaging in its various forms may at times contribute a significant or at least a very visible portion of trade production, the use of packaged books can only supplement the work of the publisher's own editorial department.

The term "editor" has at least three different meanings that apply to three distinctly different functions. An "acquiring" or "sponsoring" editor is responsible for finding new manuscripts or ideas, evaluating them, and proposing for publication the ones that in his judgment meet the publisher's stated or tacit criteria. Such an editor is normally on the publisher's payroll, though that is also the function performed by the stars I mentioned who act as independents while associated with a publisher.

An "editing" editor, who is sometimes the same person as the acquiring editor, has the skills to develop or improve the author's manuscript or to advise on matters of content, organization, or literary style. Such editors are frequently free-lancers, working for hire, project by project, for either the publisher or the author himself. In recent years, this function has frequently been bypassed or left to the author's agent, the book going to the copyeditor essentially as the publisher receives it.

The "copy" editor goes over the manuscript in detail to check facts, correct errors in grammar or punctuation, ensure consistency, watch for possible libel or plagiarism, note typographical problems the book designer will have to solve, and, generally, to perform all the editorial housekeeping chores the manuscript requires before it goes to the typesetter. The demand for copyeditors may vary greatly in any publishing house with the concern for quality, the season of the year, and the overall publishing program, and they are frequently free-lancers. It is not unusual in larger houses to have a staff of copyeditors, supplemented by free-lancers during the busier periods.

Here we are concerned with the acquiring editors. The "editorial department" or "editorial function" as used here refers to the evaluating and acquiring of new book projects.

Asking what the editorial department is doing in a publishing house does seem foolish. It's there to get the books, of course. Well, not exactly to get lots of books. After all, everyone knows there are too many books published. One of the chief functions of the editorial department is to slow the publishing process down and to keep too many books from getting on the publisher's list. But that isn't right either, because the editors *do* try to get books, and the publisher has others (publishing committees, business managers, etc.) whose job is to impede and discourage the editors from following their normal inclinations too enthusiastically.

Actually, in many large publishing houses, if one tried to deduce the function of the editorial department from the actions of the publisher rather than from job descriptions or the idealizations in the literature, it would be very difficult indeed. In some extreme situations, management places so many obstacles in the way of every publishing project that it does not seem at all silly to ask why they hired all those people in the first place.

The purpose of a publishing house, after all, is to publish books. All the difficulties invented to slow down and discourage each proposal are management's ineffective way of weeding out the poor ones. They are intended to improve the list. Alas, these methods fail, as the results demonstrate year after year. Nor is it true that all publishers use the make-it-tough-on-the-editor technique for improving editorial judgment (though most do) or regard the editorial department as an unavoidable nuisance to be curbed. One outstanding example of where a creative and aggressive editorial approach worked is St. Martin's

Press, where the editorial genius of Tom McCormack has transformed a comatose company into a leading best-seller-conscious publisher. How many such publishers are there? Simon & Schuster? Yes. Morrow? Yes. Random House? Yes. Workman? Yes. Not many more.

The usual attitude of publishing management toward its editors is that they should be slowed down and forced to prove each enthusiasm. Management does not usually inspire editors with strategic plans or supervise or measure them by tactical plans. Editors are rarely encouraged to do more, though they are frequently warned to do better. There are no rubdowns in the editorial locker room and certainly no pep talks. And the players may find themselves tripped by their own coach on their way to the field.

Authors, except the few very top names in publishing, know how painfully slowly editorial departments consider each project, how long it takes to get an opinion, how many hurdles must be cleared even after an initial favorable report.

Even in houses where editors feel welcome, it is rare that management sets, or invites the editors to set, clear editorial goals and policies designed to meet them. Editorial activity, even when successful, has an amazingly high component of aimlessness.

A sales rep knows his territory. And he knows that his results may be compared with the results of other reps in comparable territories and, almost certainly, one year's results will be compared with those of the previous year.

It is rare for a publisher to assign editorial "territories" (except occasionally for specialization by subject, such as cookbooks or mysteries), and almost never does he study comparative editorial productivity.

The editorial department should have a positive mandate as well as the usual caution to avoid publishing books that lose money. It must locate or develop enough manuscripts that meet the publisher's criteria to ensure sufficient sales at least to cover the annual fixed costs. Presumably, if it can produce more than this, in number or quality or both, that is all to the good.

How can this positive mandate be expressed and, if possible, performance under it be measured and controlled? The most obvious management tool is the budget.

The spending that results directly from the editorial decision to publish is the author's advance against royalties and the plant costs of the editorial preparation of the manuscript, the typesetting, the printing plates, and so on. The editorial decision does not determine spending for manufacturing. The editorial department does not, or certainly should not, decide how many copies to print. That decision belongs elsewhere, perhaps with the publisher, the business manager, or with the sales manager. Moreover, it should be made in relation to the prospect for immediate sale, so the printing decision cannot safely be predicted when the project is in the form of an outline or an unedited manuscript.

The editorial procurement budget should be made available with the object of achieving minimum stated goals. One of those goals might be the number of dollars of sales per dollar of editorial budget to be reached in the first year by the combination of all the books published under this budget. Or the goal might be stated in terms of dollars of margin over direct costs (paper, printing, and binding) rather than dollars of sales. Another goal might be the sales levels to be achieved in succeeding years from the titles that survive to become, at least to some degree, part of the backlist. A third goal, particularly for publishers with a strong subsidiary rights department, might be the number of dollars of subsidiary rights sales to be generated in the first year from the books published on this budget.

The editorial goals must be related to past performance, which means they must be realistic as shown by experience and realistic in the context of the ability of the other departments in the company to support the editorial product. The results of the books the editors select are not determined by their intrinsic merits alone. The results depend on the nature of the sales and promotional skills in the company as well as on conditions in general. You can't ask editors to find books with strong subsidiary rights potential if the company has an inept subsidiary rights manager (or doesn't have one at all). Sales will depend in part upon the strength and skill of the sales force, which can be gauged somewhat from its previous accomplishment. That does not mean that this year's goal must equal last year's performance. The new goal should certainly anticipate some improvement, but it cannot, if it is to be taken seriously by the editors, arbitrarily exceed anything that has proved possible in the past.

The goals apply to the entire budgeted effort, not to each book. Results will vary from book to book. The .300 batter does not, by definition, hit .300 in each game. A variation above and below the average performance is unavoidable. This aspect of the nature of the goals should be clearly understood by editorial management so it is not paralyzed by the supposed need to choose only those books that will meet the average goals as a minimum.

On the other hand, it is sensible to have some minimum criteria that apply to every project. Such gauges, set well below the target averages, will ensure that projects too trivial, either in percentage or in absolute return on time and investment, are avoided.

How the budget is applied depends on how the editorial function is organized (which is part of a later discussion). But it should be clear to all that the money is there to be used, not to be saved, and that if performance is satisfactory, the budget may be increased.

The goals have quality as well as financial dimensions. The publisher wants the editorial department to choose certain *kinds* of books, which must be defined as part of the department's goals and which must be part of the monitoring of editorial performance.

"Kinds" of books can be expressed in various ways. The first is the channel of distribution. A publisher who sells primarily by direct mail wants books that are appropriate to mailing lists that have proven to be consistently productive. If he sells primarily through bookstores, he may still want to distinguish among books for college stores, personal bookstores, and chains, since he may have a better entree or stronger distribution in some of these.

"Kinds" can also mean transient or long-lived. How much emphasis should the editors put on the backlist potential of the books it is seeking? Very little if the sales force is all commission reps; a great deal if it is a tightly managed house sales force. A publishing house that depends on a commission sales force does not want a title that cannot make an initial promotional splash, even though it could sell over a long period of time if stock were checked regularly and replenished in small increments. A publishing house with a workmanlike coverage of bookstores and a serious nonfiction list that sells steadily in low to medium quantities would approach a book requiring a high advance and expensive promotion very cautiously.

A publisher seeking to add long-lived titles will also be concerned with "shaping the list," the desirable "shape" varying with the publisher. For a large general publisher who needs to support a strong sales force and to provide each rep with sufficient merchandise to call on smaller towns or smaller stores, shaping the list means adding all the titles that would be bread-and-butter necessities for most bookstores. The nonfiction needs are obvious: cookbooks, gardening books, self-help manuals, decorating, travel, language study, and so on. A visit to a good bookstore like Scribner's or Kroch's & Brentano's with paper and pencil should enable a good editor in chief to put together a list of 250 or 300 desirable subjects in very short order. An analysis of the competitive product in each case would suggest, for each proposed title, the scope, editorial quality, format, and retail price that would be most desirable to match or overcome the strongest competition. The result can be a plan of development and acquisition that will keep any good editorial department busy for some time.

For smaller or more specialized houses, the approach could be similar, though limited. For example, a publisher with some successful gardening titles might decide to fill in the blank spaces in his gardening list systematically in order to establish himself as an important supplier of books on this subject to general bookstores, to enable his sales force to justify calling on more specialized stores and garden shops, and perhaps to justify an investment in building a mail order capability as well.

"Kinds" can mean titles that meet some minimum economic criteria, which are likely to be different for each publishing house. For example, a highly structured publishing house (of which there are many), burdened with heavy layers of middle and higher management, will have procedures that inevitably impose high publication costs on each book (such as heavy distribution of free copies, expensive cataloguing and announcement mailings, automatic allocation of advertising or publicity budgets in accordance with sales projections). It should either change its ways or require that any title to be published meet a financial threshold substantially higher than what it would need to reach for a house operating in a simpler manner.

For some houses, it may be important to acquire books that can be published just about the way they come in and to pass up those that require a lot of editorial time. A publisher with a small editorial department who wishes to keep that department small, will want to limit sharply the number of titles he publishes each year. He may set a high level of minimum requirements simply to avoid giving a place on his list to a title that might better be occupied by a more profitable one.

"Kinds" can also relate to subject matter. Editorial departments should have minimum and maximum guidelines for the rate at which new titles are to be added in gardening books, self-help, bilingual children's books, or whatever subject areas are being developed. It is probably wise to control the amount of fiction on each year's list and, within that group, the number of first novels, of mysteries, Westerns, etc.

Whatever the criteria, they should be determined by management and expressed clearly so that the editors can judge readily whether a title is suitable. The clearer the understanding of what kinds of titles are wanted, the more likely that the desired mix will be found. And it would probably be wise to let friends of the house—agents, authors, foreign publishers—know these goals since they are sources of manuscripts and referrals.

Most editorial departments do not reach out as aggressively as they should to encourage the submission of manuscripts and publishing projects. The publisher may not want to increase the rate of production, but the editorial department should nevertheless operate under an aggressive, planned policy of reaching and being attractive to as many likely sources of worthwhile projects as possible. Even if this policy simply provides the editors with more candidates from which to choose, the effort will be worthwhile.

Such an editorial mandate, which includes the elaboration of an editorial strategy, is very rare. Publishers are so conditioned to thinking about each project (usually a single title considered in isolation) as the focus of attention that a forest of editorial strategy does not seem possible amid the confusion of all the trees.

It is true that from time to time a publisher, exasperated by a high incidence of failures among his titles, will resolve to reduce his list. But even that "strategy" frequently does not last because making decisions a book at a time tends to frustrate the aim of having any specific total for the year. It is curious how often general management tries to cut back the list when involved with editorial policy on something other than a title-by-title level.

Since the almost universal shibboleth among publishing (and bookselling) management is: "There are too many books published," one would imagine that editorial departments are eagerly gobbling up every publishing project within reach. As any aspiring author can confirm, far, far from it. Most editors in most houses would probably agree. Early in their careers, editors discover that their job involves more selling than the salesman's because they have to sell their colleagues and their superiors on a proposition for which truly objective evidence will be available only after the book is published— when it is too late. Editors learn early to be lobbyists and politicians, skills they never considered when "editor" was only a career ambition.

The ambience of the editor is not the same in all publishing houses, to be sure, so any generalization must be made cautiously. Yet it is fair to say that in most medium-sized to large houses, the editor considers it essential to sell any important project "in the house," usually before he presents it to the editorial committee or the business committee or whatever person or group will have to approve it for publication. It is always helpful if he can say that others have considered the idea (which may only be a plot outline) and are enthusiastic and if he has a commitment from the sales or promotion department that something special will be done.

Except for the sure-fire titles, books compete with each other in the publishing house even before they get to the marketplace. The editor is more successful if he prepares the way carefully for each of his projects; first, to get acceptance, and second, to get a greater allocation of the company's selling resources. Conversely, management is inclined to look less suspiciously at the projects of the editor with the reputation for success than on those of the editor who is considered (rightly or wrongly) to have a mixed record.

Publishers are extremely sensitive to the danger of editorial mistakes. They remember the book that didn't sell as many copies as the editor projected, the one that cost much more to produce than the estimated cost, the one that did not earn its royalty advance, the one with such great promise betrayed by heavy returns. Most publishers protect themselves from future mistakes by requiring that each editorial proposal pass a series of tests in order to qualify for publication. There are generally two kinds of tests.

The first is some sort of budgetary high jump. Although each publisher has his own financial criteria that the project must satisfy, they all demand a prediction of very high profitability and low risk. In many houses, the financial goals of each project have actually been achieved by only a small percentage of previously published projects.

These procedures require the editor to get cost estimates (not an unreasonable requirement) from the production department for manufacturing the book in the expected range of sales quantities. These figures are then used to project retail price and the editor predicts the number of copies of the book that will be sold, sometimes with comical detail (e.g., X advance sale, Y copies the first year, Z copies the second year). These data are put into the company's profitability expectation formula. Some of the more affluent companies even put all this on a computer, which makes it easy to include discounted cash flow in the calculation.

These requirements are frequently met by projecting unrealistic expectations for the book or at least stretching expectations to meet the needs of the formula. These usually involve overestimating the potential sales (after all, no one really *knows* how many copies will be sold), which has the double advantage of exaggerating the anticipated income and reducing the production cost per copy. It frequently has the disadvantage of committing the sales department to trying to force this exaggerated quantity into the stores, which results in heavy returns and an early demise of that title, making its losses much greater than they might have been with a more conservative projection.

Sometimes the profit prediction can be achieved by making the book shorter, by using smaller type, by printing on cheaper paper, by eliminating the color illustrations, by some other form of lowering the quality that, it is hoped, will reduce costs more than it reduces sales. In fact, such measures may reduce the appeal of the book to the point of being self-defeating. Another way to meet profit criteria may be to get the author to accept a low royalty.

The second test, which is usually applied only if the project successfully passes the first one, is approval by some sort of board or committee. In some publishing houses this may be a very formal group that decides unanimously or by majority vote; in others, the committee may be an informal advisory body assisting a business manager or publishing director who actually puts his signature to the authorization. Frequently it is one person, representing the business judgment of the company rather than its editorial judgment.

The business committee approach appeals most strongly to the managements that accept the notion that too many books are published and that this confuses the retailers and the public, diluting the buying strength of the "hard core" of book buyers. What is needed, according to this philosophy, is a device to keep the bad books from getting through. The task of the editorial committee is to identify the failures before the contract is signed or, in rarer cases, to provide the key twist that will turn a run-of-the-mill idea into a best-seller.

There is a deceptively appealing logic to the idea of a committee applying its collective wisdom to editorial proposals. But the wag who said that the camel was the product of a committee was speaking of a very exceptional committee indeed if it was able to produce anything with the breath of life. The publisher using a committee might be analogous to an organization with ten football teams. Instead of having a coach for each team, it would have a committee of ten coaching each team, thereby giving each play in each game the collective wisdom that would be denied it if the team had only one coach. Aside from the time it would take to arrive at each decision, responsibility for coaching would disappear because no one would be sure, after the game, who was responsible for what decision—or, indeed, exactly why the game was lost.

I once had the opportunity to study the difference between having an editor responsible for his own decisions and a committee applying

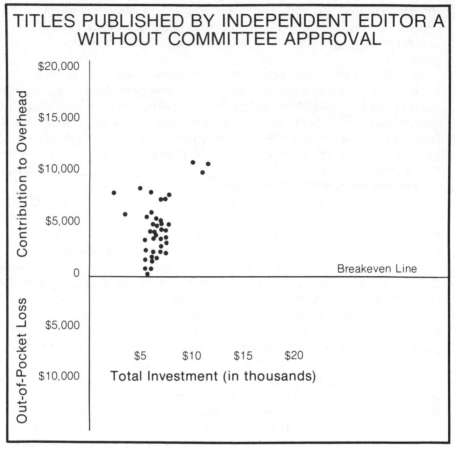

TITLES PUBLISHED BY INDEPENDENT EDITOR A WITHOUT COMMITTEE APPROVAL

FIGURE 1

its collective wisdom. The setting was a large publishing house that operated a kind of mixed economy. Most of the editors submitted their projects to a publication board, or business committee, which included people knowledgeable in sales, subsidiary rights, production, etc. After the business committee said yes, the editor was free to complete the contract. There were also a few editors who, for no particular formal reason, worked independently. Their projects were not submitted to the business committee, which was informed of each project and its probable financial requirements and which simply entered that information in its minutes.

We studied one complete year's list and analyzed each title to compare the costs against the income. In some cases, the costs were

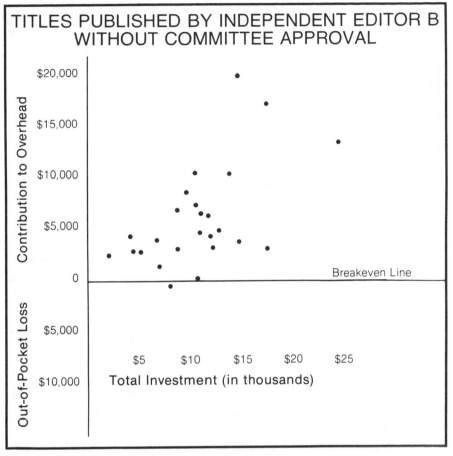

TITLES PUBLISHED BY INDEPENDENT EDITOR B
WITHOUT COMMITTEE APPROVAL

Contribution to Overhead

Out-of-Pocket Loss

Breakeven Line

Total Investment (in thousands)

FIGURE 2

higher than the income. Then we divided the books according to those
that went through the business committee and those that were
sponsored by each of the two independent editors. This gave us three
groups of books. For each book in each group, we had the costs
(investment) and the amount by which the income from that book
exceeded the costs (contribution) or failed to reach the costs
(out-of-pocket loss).

To make the comparison clearer, I have prepared three graphs that
show the results in each situation. On each graph, each dot is a book.
The dots *above* the break-even line recovered their costs and made a
contribution; the ones below lost money.

The size of the investment required (total costs) is indicated by the

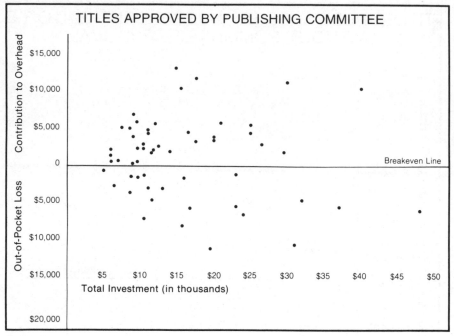

FIGURE 3

distance to the dot from the left edge of the graph; the distance above or below the break-even line indicates the size of the contribution to overhead or the loss.

Figure 1 shows one of the independent editors (Editor A); Figure 2 shows the other (Editor B). These editors, who were very different in personality and temperament, were doing completely different types of books, which is reflected in the difference in the shapes created by the distribution of dots on the two graphs. Figure 3 shows the results of the business committee.

The first difference one notices is the incidence of failure. Editor A had no failures; Editor B had only one. The committee decisions showed almost as many failures as successes.

The second is the *pattern* of decisions. It is clear that Editor A's record will be very much the same year after year. The pattern of dots for Editor B is less distinct and suggests that he is more likely to vary somewhat from year to year. The committee decisions have no pattern at all. The dots are scattered like grains of sand thrown over the paper. If the committee was created to give direction, there is clearly none in its decisions. Obviously, the committee does not represent the sum of the wisdom and experience of each of its members in making its decisions. It seems to neutralize them.

The editors who worked independently did not work in isolation. No one person is likely to see the whole book market in all its complexity or all the possibilities for promoting a book in any part of that market. Each successful editor looks for advice and opinions and knows how to contact the probable market and how to gauge it. Communication and research are central to the editor's job.

The business committee was formed chiefly to guard against errors of editorial commission. (It was obviously powerless against errors of *omission*—the worthwhile projects the editors never propose—which are not uncommon in large companies.) It required the editor to test his enthusiasm (theoretically) against the combined experience and sober judgment of his colleagues. At the very least, he had to investigate the project more thoroughly to organize his presentation and to answer questions.

As we see, the theory does not work in practice. But even in theory, a committee or similar review group would have a much smaller role and would do less damage in a publishing house with a planned, directed editorial effort. The committee does not seem, even in theory, to be useful in planning, directing, and supervising an editorial procurement campaign. Its strength appears (mistakenly, as we see) to be in selecting the better possibilities from a steady stream of unrelated proposals.

It cannot be said that committee decisions are always bad. They don't have that much consistency. They are largely random decisions with no clear point of view or policy. As one studies the decisions made by committees, it becomes clear that the same set of facts presented at two different times (or perhaps at the same time by two different committee members) would result in two different decisions. *Any* one of the committee members, acting alone, would probably obtain better results, on balance, than the judgment of the committee as a whole.

Some years after my study, as this publishing house became more businesslike and formal and "modern" business methods were introduced, the independent editors lost their independence. *All* editorial projects now run the committee gauntlet and must be approved by a business manager.

In many publishing houses, the paradoxical reluctance to publish, the constant demand for assurances that the project is financially sound, and the implication that the editorial department must be controlled to protect it from its own (bad) natural instincts all tend to discourage editorial ingenuity and to reduce productivity. It must be demoralizing to an editor to be asked over and over again to put himself "on the line" for some proposed title and to know that he will be blamed if it fails to deliver the anticipated sales and profit.

Whereas production, sales, billing and shipping, and probably some other publishing functions benefit from increased size, it is a serious handicap to the editorial function. Being large may make a publisher attractive to authors and their agents, but it simply makes the editorial department more unwieldy and, at least in my experience, reduces each editor's productivity and lowers the average quality of editorial judgment.

Editorial judgments, by their very nature, cannot be made by committees. The way to cope with editorial growth is by creating as many small groups as necessary to ensure that the desired level of production is reached without compromising individual editorial judgment, no matter how large the department becomes.

How should the editorial department be organized and the available budget allocated? In a publishing house with one editor, the problem does not exist, but it arises the moment there are two. If they share the editorial budget, some way must be found to weigh their judgments in making selections or to provide an objective arbiter. However, if the budget is divided between them, each can function as a separate editorial department, setting priorities independently.

There is no limit, even in the largest publishing houses, to the number of independent "departments" into which the editorial staff can be divided, each with its own budget. The budget serves, of course, as a resource, giving each editor the wherewithal to publish the books he selects, as well as a control, forcing the editor to choose from the possible projects so that he gets the best results from his resources.

The object, of course, is to protect the independence of an individual editor's judgment from the deadening stewardship of either a committee or a business manager. The object is to stimulate the creativity that can be seen dramatically where some editors operate independently, as in the publishing house described by the three graphs or where an independent editorial "star" has a profit-sharing arrangement with a large publisher. The independent editor's books on a given list are almost always more interesting and on the average more successful than the books contributed by the publisher's own editors. And the independent editor tends also to be more productive

—in number of books and/or in number of dollars of sales—than even the more senior members of the editorial staff.

The difference is no doubt due in part to the genius of the independent editor. But it is also due to his freedom from the need to find titles of broad enough interest to be lobbied successfully through a number of authorities. Perhaps it is due even more to the independent editor's good judgment (the independent editors with poor judgment were discarded long ago or never got there).

The independent editor attached to a large publishing house illustrates the advantages of small size in the editorial function combined with those of large size in production, promotion, sales, order fulfillment, and the like, where smallness is a disadvantage.

There is no reason why the trade publisher cannot organize his own editorial department to realize exactly the same advantageous relationships. It is simply a matter of creating the equivalent of independent editors, giving limited freedom to a few individual editors. The best limitation on this freedom, far more effective than any committee or business manager, is the budget.

The editor who will have freedom of action should, of course, have sufficient experience so that some idea of his performance can be projected. New editors should be responsible to one of the senior editors, as apprentices, until their performance earns them their own freedom of action. Care must be taken that editors are not, in this process, turned into "managers" of apprentices. It is important that each editor devote himself as much as possible to the job of editing.

The editor-in-chief should apportion, each year, the available editorial budget for advances and plant among the senior editors according to their demonstrated level of productivity. The editor with a record of choosing books that produce more revenue per dollar of budget should get a larger share of the available budget; the editor who chooses less productive titles, a smaller share. Each year, the scope of each editor's freedom should be adjusted by how well he demonstrated (within the context of the publisher's sales, promotion, and other pertinent efforts) his skill as an editor.

This seems to me to be the most practical way to break what appears to be a limitation on the growth of trade book houses. They tend to lose their vitality as they grow larger, and editors become less innovative and productive as they become more submerged in the mass. Decisions on publishing take longer to reach, and their quality becomes more erratic.

With this kind of editorial organization, growth presents few problems. The editorial manager would not want editors unknowingly competing with each other for some project or developing books that will undercut each other in sales. He would, therefore, want a good internal communication system so each editor knows and is guided by what the others are doing or contemplating.

Every publishing house should have a kind of editorial schedule board that lists, in relation to probable publication date, every project (identified by initiating editor) from the moment the idea arises to the time it becomes a signed contract and an approved final manuscript. By noting the present status of each project, the schedule shows management at a glance what the probabilities are for meeting its editorial goals in the next year, and the year after that, and how the overall list is changing or maintaining its character.

Under such an arrangement, editors would conform, of course, to guidelines on the size of advances, royalty rates, etc.; any unusual contract terms would be approved by the editorial manager. For the final step of negotiating the contract, the publisher could use a "contract officer" rather than leaving it with the individual editor. The publisher would be balancing the improved negotiating skill that the author's side of the contract relationship has gained, with the increased participation of agents and attorneys. And it would recognize the value of a *business consistency* while protecting an *editorial inconsistency.*

If the publisher puts no constraints on the editor except the limitations of budget, the editor will develop his own, selecting books of a type or in an area with which he is familiar and has been successful. In some publishing houses, subject areas are assigned to certain editors, so one is a cookbook editor, another handles mysteries, and so on. As long as this division is not interpreted too strictly, it is probably helpful, and follows the editor's own natural tendency to specialize and to want to be able to judge each manuscript against his own experience.

Some of this specialized experience can be gained more efficiently through the use of consulting editors who are specialists in one field or another. They frequently have the additional advantage of knowing where to find or develop quality manuscripts in their special field.

The editorial department, as we have said, also is responsible for mining all the worthwhile sources of manuscripts, the most important of which are the author's agents. Even if the ore is then redivided among the editors, the responsibility for each agent should be assigned to a particular editor. Just as the sales manager evaluates the share of a bookstore's business the rep assigned to it gets, the editorial manager should be concerned with the share of an important agent's manuscripts the editor assigned to him gets. Is the house getting its fair share? Is it getting that agent's better manuscripts? The editor in chief should have a running tally on the contribution made by each agent, similar to the tally he keeps on each editor. He should expect the contribution from each agent to grow each year if the editor assigned to him is doing a proper job.

There are other sources, such as schools of creative writing, that should be similarly assigned.

The appropriate sources—agents, for instance—should understand how the budgeting system works and how they can open the publisher's door wider for the acceptance of their manuscripts. And if each source is the responsibility of a particular editor—as each store is the responsibility of a particular sales rep—who sees to it that a flow of information is maintained in both directions, productivity is certain to improve in quality and, if the publisher wishes, in quantity as well.

Yet, whatever is done to cultivate resources for books and to allow individual editors maximum freedom to make publication decisions, no editorial department can escape the realization that a large part of its success is determined in other parts of the publishing house. The most important place is sales and promotion, which successful editors acknowledge by cultivating the sales and promotion managers and letting them know how much their efforts mean to the success of each book. The same editor, with the same innate talent and the same valuable contacts in the writing community, can have a very different record of success in different publishing houses.

The relationship is certainly one of mutual dependence. The success of sales depends as much on a desirable product as it does on assiduous coverage of the market, and the product, no matter how worthwhile, will reach only a fraction of its potential without such coverage.

The mutual dependence extends even further. An editor who pays close attention to what is happening in the bookstores, which he learns a great deal about by listening to his own sales reps, is likely to have a better success record than the editor who imagines his office is an ivory tower or believes he can create reading fashion.

In a publishing house that gives each editor maximum freedom (and hence maximum recognition) and where the editor can feel that his decision to publish—and, for that matter, the thrust of the book itself—has not been distorted by a committee or an unsympathetic business manager, the editor is most likely to try to get the cooperation of those other departments that contribute so much to the success of any book. And he is likely to listen more sensitively to what they can tell him simply because he knows he can *act* on what he learns.

Although it is wrong to expect a publishing house to succeed on its editorial genius, it is by no means wrong for the publishing house to let each editor believe that *he* will succeed on his editorial genius— and to create the situation that makes it most likely.

11

Don't Forget the Author

"I CALCULATE THAT WRITERS today pay, out of their own pockets, about one third of the true cost of producing most books. The stark truth is that, as presently constituted, the publishing industry exists only by the grace of subsidies provided by writers. In the United States, all publishing is vanity publishing."

That indictment of the way publishers treat their authors is from James Lincoln Collier, a prize-winning professional writer, commenting in *Publishers Weekly* on a national survey of writers' incomes. The survey revealed that income from writing is distressingly low and, without additional personal income, would put "most authors below the poverty line."

How valid is the accusation that authors "subsidize" the publishers? It is certainly not the *intention,* though it is a distressing fact, that the author, who makes the principal contribution to the publication of any book, is very shabbily rewarded on the average.

The author is, from many viewpoints, the principal reason that the trade book publishing industry exists at all. For even though he creates the work, he has no way of bringing it to potential readers or even to let them know it exists. Publishers were "invented" to do that for him.

□ *This is not altogether universally true, and it becomes less so as publishers become more "market oriented." The creative publisher, who searches actively for the needs of potential readers and finds and guides the writers to supply those needs, is providing more than a distribution service. Yet, even in such cases, the author's income depends largely on the publisher's ability to reach the market he thinks he sees out there.*

The overriding importance of distribution among the various functions performed by the publisher is obscured somewhat by another role: bankrolling the project. Because the publisher finances the publication of the book, it is the publisher who hires the author, whereas *functionally* it is the other way round. It is also because he provides the initial financing that the publisher is usually in a position to dictate how much he will take for his services and how much he will leave for the author.

It is probably for the same reason—it is the publisher's money that is at risk—that the publisher's capacity to get the publishing done is so rarely questioned, and least of all (before publication, anyway) by the author.

This is simply another handicap for the author in selecting the publisher and in negotiating the working arrangement. The author's contribution—the manuscript—is right out there in the open, whereas the publisher's contribution—the ability and determination to publish effectively—is only vaguely understood and difficult to examine.

Although it may be an exaggeration to say that authors subsidize publishers, there is certainly sufficient ground to suggest that authors should not blindly accept as a given the publisher's ability to publish the book in the fullest and most active sense of the word. Though it will not win me new friends in the publishing community, I would counsel the author to look very closely at the publisher's ability to publish—at his tools, his competence in using them, and at his motivation to market aggressively—and that close look had better precede signing the contract to reduce the anguish that so many authors suffer after the first joy of seeing the printed and bound book.

The choice of publisher or editor is academic, of course, for the writer who is collecting only rejection slips with each submission. For such an author, any publisher, any editor, and any contract is welcome. He will gratefully accept publication by any bona fide publisher on any terms, though he may ungratefully criticize his publisher later for failing to advertise or get the book into stores or keep it in print, etc.

The not-yet-published author, and sometimes one who has been published, faces the question of whether to go directly to publishers himself or to let an agent represent him.

Author's agents were not nearly so ubiquitous when I entered publishing thirty-five years ago as they are today. In those days, they were generally resented for "butting in" on a cozy relationship between the publisher and the author. Today, the publisher is likely to prefer dealing through the agent and may suggest to an aspiring writer that he would benefit from association with an agent. The change in the publisher's attitude comes from the fact that, though the agent may drive a harder bargain for the author, he also introduces order and spares the publisher the problems of negotiating with someone whose naiveté and lack of business experience can create even more difficulties.

Agenting has benefited from changes in the economic conditions of publishing, changes that may now have run their course. The explosive growth of mass paperback publishing, beginning shortly after World War II and ending as you read these lines, pumped large amounts of royalty income into the trade book economy. This provided, in large part, the margins necessary to support the influx of agents and provide the advances so vital to them.

The end of an era can already be detected, though it is not yet part of the general awareness. Several agents have reported to me that the retrenchments in mass market publishing and the shift toward more category fiction and less middle-range and intellectual fiction have resulted in publishers rejecting titles that would easily have had offers of $10,000 advances only a year or two ago. There are going to be fewer advance dollars for agents to scramble for, and the agent will have to work much harder for every dollar.

Many agents feel, and I certainly agree, that their life is not likely to be as happy a one over the next few years, and a shrinkage in numbers would not be surprising.

Though it may be harder to find one, there is no question in my mind that the first thing an aspiring author should do is to get an agent.

A skilled agent will probably give the author a more useful appraisal of the book project and the author's own skills than he will get from the typical form rejection letters of publishers.

The agent is much more likely to get the publisher to evaluate the book project than the author could himself, even with persistent pressure. If the agent wishes to draw upon his reservoir of goodwill, he can often get a marginal book accepted for publication in recognition of his past contributions to the list or as part of a current attractive "package" of several titles.

The agent can negotiate contract terms much more effectively than the author can on his own behalf. Of course, the principal issues will be the royalty rate and the size of the advance, and the agent can ask for levels and justify them in terms that would be embarrassing coming from the author. The agent can also back down more gracefully if it is clear that he is aiming too high. But there are also many other contract provisions—some, like subsidiary rights, that are by no means minor—that the agent can haggle over more gracefully and with more good humor and objectivity than the author can. The agent is certainly more likely to be familiar with nasty little contract details, which can be costly to the author if not identified and deleted, as well as with provisions missing from the standard contract that should be included if at all possible. Even after publication, the agent can pressure the publisher on matters of publicity or advertising more effectively than the author can.

Unless the author is unusual and can do all these things well for himself, he will find that even a moderately good agent will earn his fee several times over.

Whether the agent or the author chooses the publisher, that choice should be made with great care. There are at least three concerns that the author must have in relation to the publisher. The first, in order of chronology and importance, is the publisher's competence to perform the variety of tasks that are his special province and how that competence relates to the author's own book. The publishing needs of all books are not the same, and, in any case, the author is likely to have only a limited choice of publisher. Second are the conditions— many, but not all, spelled out in the book contract—under which the publisher will do his work. The royalty advance and the royalty rate, though probably the most important, are only the beginning of the understanding that must be reached. Finally, there is the degree to which the author can participate in the publishing process, if he wishes, particularly in promotion and distribution.

At a cocktail party, you can recognize the publisher because he is saying that royalty rates are too high and that booksellers don't know how to sell books; the bookseller because he is saying that the publisher must give higher discounts or at least pay the postage; and the author because he says he can't find his book in the stores. There is some justice in the author's complaint, and it goes to the heart of the publisher's obligation to the book and to the author.

The publisher's function is not simply to get the book into the stores, even the ones likely to be visited by the author and his immediate friends, nor, in addition, to finance publication until sales revenue makes further investment unnecessary. It is more than that and, in its various aspects, will have varying importance for different authors—even, perhaps, for different books by the same author. What is important is that the author find out, before he negotiates a contract, before he even submits a manuscript or an outline, the strengths and weaknesses of the publisher. The author (of all people) knows that all books are different. He should also know that all publishers are—thank goodness—also different.

There is not, and never will be, a perfect publisher (though all publishers are not, therefore, equally imperfect) or a perfectly published book. And if there were a perfect publisher, he would be operating in a very imperfect real world. Choosing a publisher carefully will not protect the author against all possibility of disappointment. (There is, after all, even that remote possibility that the book is not as good as he thinks it is.) Publishers are only fallible people, presiding over organizations made up of people just as fallible. And the fate of every book also rests on people not the least bit under the publisher's control: booksellers and their clerks, wholesalers, and book reviewers, not to mention all the people in other publishing houses or with producers of other types of products fighting for the customer's attention.

Yet, while admitting that a better publisher—or one more suited to that book—can only reduce the factors of chance, not control them, there is still much to be said for the author starting, in a small way, to reduce those factors by being more deliberate in choosing his publisher. It will not avoid future disappointment; it may only help prepare the author to live with it.

And, while admitting even further that whatever the abilities of the publisher in sales, promotion, design, etc., the most valuable "ability" may turn out to be the publisher's enthusiasm for that manuscript and his commitment to it, the author, to the degree that he has that freedom, should examine each publisher's strengths and weaknesses critically. There is simply too much at stake.

Whatever the written provisions of the contract (and it must be admitted that some publishers' basic contracts take unfair advantage of the author), the intended moral and ethical relation between author and publisher is pretty clear. The author's fate is, in a very real sense, completely in the hands of the publisher. The author gives control over the book to the publisher, essentially for the life of the copyright if the publisher wishes to keep it that long. He usually also gives the publisher control over subsidiary rights for the life of the copyright; but even if he retains control of some of the minor rights through his agent, their value depends very much on the publisher's success with the original edition.

What help can the publisher supply? Editorial, perhaps. Great editors of the type of Maxwell Perkins, Ed Aswell, Pat Covici, or Ken McCormick are not to be found readily. They still exist here and there, though the growth of agenting and of the blockbuster syndrome has transferred much of that kind of creative editing to agents and to the entrepreneurial independent editors who live symbiotically with large publishers. For many authors, a top-notch, understanding editor, with the skill to help polish a manuscript or to restructure it and the stature within the house to get what he wants from other departments, is the quintessence of all publishing has to offer. Everything else is secondary.

There are many creative editors with a sensitive appreciation for the public's taste and current interest and an ability to get the very best out of an author by being sympathetically and constructively critical. Such editors have the touch that can multiply the author's chance to achieve best-sellerdom or, perhaps more important, a product worthy of his talent.

Most publishing houses have no such editors, or only one or two. In many houses the manuscript goes to the compositor only slightly changed from the form in which it was submitted. Even the copyediting may be of the most cursory kind. For authors with very strong opinions about their work, an editor's help may represent only interference. They disdain such meddling and may prefer a publisher who has no such inclinations.

Even if the author is not looking for an editor to be a "manuscript doctor" or even to be a coach, trainer, and cheering section, the nature of the publishing organization assigns, or relegates, functions to editors that profoundly affect the success of any book. The editor is a lobbyist, not only to get the manuscript accepted, but also to get the active interest of the production department, the advertising and promotion department, and, most critical, of the sales force. It is the editor who presents the book at the sales conference, an unfairly crucial moment in the life of the book.

Whether the author seeks out an editor or has the editor thrust upon him, he would be wise to try to make the editor an enthusiastic promoter of the book if he wants to get the most from his publisher.

The editor is the author's principal, and frequently only, contact with the internal structure of the publishing house. This is most clear in the early stages. It is the editor who argues for the book's acceptance. He negotiates with management on behalf of the author on such matters as the royalty advance, the royalty rate, and the advertising appropriation. He will prepare the catalogue copy, set advance sale targets, and approve the jacket design. He will also watch the sale of the book and report it periodically to the author, commiserating or congratulating as appropriate. He will be urging the subsidiary rights manager to do more. And he will probably be consulted when the time comes to remainder the book.

The physical and aesthetic quality of the book is not equally important to all authors. Each publisher has a fairly consistent performance in this respect, and the range runs from very bad to very good. The size or wealth of the firm is not necessarily related to its commitment to physical quality. The publishers who have opted for poor quality have decided that better materials and workmanship are not worth the cost (trivial, by the way), because the discrimination of the public is not sufficiently developed to affect sales and the more highly developed appreciation of the author is not felt strongly enough to affect the choice of publisher.

They are wrong on both counts, of course. While not all book buyers or all authors are affected, it is certain that enough browsers are put off at the bookstore display table to cost the publisher much more than the pennies he saved by debasing the product. It is also certain that among the authors who would rather not apologize to friends for badly printed and bound books are some strong enough to choose their publishers.

The key publishing function, the one for which publishers would have to be invented if they did not already exist, is distribution. Morton L. Levin, a vice president of Avon Books, said in *A Manual on Bookselling*:

> A publisher who selects, edits, and produces a book fulfills his obligation to the author only after he has made his best effort to get the book into the hands of interested readers. The publisher's success or failure with any book is the measure of how well he has been able to sell it to its *potential* readership. Considering that the potential sale may range from a few hundred copies of a book of poetry to a hundred thousand or more copies of a bestselling novel, success can have many faces.

I agree with that statement, but I would go further. Although no one can deliver more than "his best effort," is no further warranty required? Is not the publisher saying to the author when he agrees to publish the book that he has the ability, the wherewithal, the know-how, to get the book into the "hands of interested readers"? The author who gives his manuscript to the publisher expects that the publisher has the special knowledge, skills, and facilities to get the book into the hands of interested readers.

I have in mind honest commercial publishers, not the calculating types who aggressively solicit manuscripts that have been rejected as unsalable by commercial publishers. These people charge the author handsomely to turn the manuscript into a finished, acceptable-looking book that sits unsold in a warehouse while the author dispenses a few copies among his friends. These "publishers" have no interest in selling any books; their profits come from the payments extracted from the authors themselves. Because they are sustained by the vanity of these frustrated authors, they are justly called vanity publishers.

Still, there are, among the honest publishers, some who have inadequate facilities for getting the book into the "hands of interested readers." These houses do not expect the author to underwrite the cost of publishing the book. But because they are terribly weak in distribution, which is the first, second, and third obligation of the publisher to the author, they cost the author money and readership to which he would be rightfully entitled by the merit of his work.

Obviously, the publisher's obligation does have limits. Ours is a capitalist economy, and the publisher, no matter how generous, must make a profit to survive. He cannot afford to lose 20 cents to sell an additional copy, even if it earns the author a dollar.

Unfortunately, distribution is an activity about which trade publishers frequently know less than they should and in which they depend very much on gut feeling. The author may be the victim of the publisher's notions about kind and size of sales force, the value of publicity and advertising, etc. He may also be the victim of sheer incompetence.

Many authors do not have sufficient information to look critically at the publisher's distribution facility, and many are not aware that publishers may differ significantly in this respect. They *are* aware of a difference in the volume and the tone of different publishers' advertising and may equate advertising with distribution without understanding that distribution is much more.

A talented novelist and very good friend of mine recently went through the agony of a book that got excellent reviews but sold very poorly—about 400 copies. He is bitter at the publisher because, despite all his pleading and reciting of excerpts from the reviews, he could not get the publisher to invest in any advertising.

"Not one lousy ad," he complains whenever the subject comes up. "All those reviews, and not one ad to let the public know."

He misses the point, of course. The reviews did a better job than advertising of "letting the public know." Public knowledge was of no value in this case because the publisher's sales force had failed to get the book into enough stores so the public could find the book after the reviews appeared. Such a failure cannot be corrected with advertising.

A successful author, widely known to the reading public, may imagine that his book sells on the strength of the association with his name and that the distribution of the publisher is not a significant factor. That is very misleading.

Hitting the best-seller lists tends to reinforce the comfortable feeling that all is well. And all may, in fact, be well, but being on the best-seller list does not prove it. A book reaches the best-seller lists because it is selling well, or is reported as selling well, in those few stores that are polled by the compilers of these lists. That book may not be selling well, or at all, in many other stores. Best-seller lists are not precise measures and do not pretend to be. The stores that are polled are generally important enough to be visited regularly, even by weak sales forces. Many books have a more or less equal chance to make the list without having the same equal chance for the wide distribution that is essential for really coming close to the title's potential for sales.

Although all books are different and all publishers are different, the laws under which they operate tend to be very much the same. One of them is that a book, poorly launched, has very little chance to recover.

Clearly the first, if not the most important, selling function of a trade book publisher is to get the book into the stores. This can only be done by informing the store that the book is to be published, persuading the bookseller that it is in his interest to have that book, and getting an order from the store. The most effective way to do this (so far) is to have a salesman call on the bookseller, sell him on the merits of the book, take an order on the spot, and send it back to the publisher.

The author owes it to himself to find out just how strong, resourceful, and well deployed the publisher's sales force is. How many reps are on the sales force? How many are commissioned, selling many lines, and how many sell his books exclusively? How many accounts are visited regularly? How is the sales force supervised? To what degree is its effort concentrated on new titles? Is the author's book a good backlist candidate? How well is the backlist resold to the stores?

Though it cannot be taken as conclusive, there is a strong presumption that the publisher without his own sales force is *not* selling the backlist effectively, while one with a proprietary sales force may or may not be. In the case of new titles, the presumption is not so clear. Larger commission forces, well directed, may do better than smaller house sales forces.

To some extent, the degree to which a publisher is relatively successful with new titles as opposed to the backlist depends on how his publishing program is perceived by the bookseller. For example, the bookseller may pay close attention to each new timely title on the list of a publisher known as a heavy promoter of timely books while brushing aside the less spectacular candidates for the backlist from the same publisher. Although the public tends not to be aware of publisher imprints, booksellers have strong opinions about each publisher and ascribe a distinct personality to each one. And the booksellers' perception is, at least partly, based on fact.

It may seem far from matters that should concern an author, but the publisher's "conditions of sale" and his relations with the booksellers are very much to the point. Does the publisher penalize the bookseller for returning unsold books or forbid their return altogether? You may be sure that the booksellers buy with great caution any titles he offers, no matter how appealing, and they are more likely to skip the less outstanding ones. Is the service from the publisher's warehouse erratic? The bookseller will be reluctant to reorder and will avoid any special orders for customers who are searching for a specific title.

Getting the book well represented in the stores and persistence in keeping it there are not the only ingredients (though by far the most important) in successful sales. Once that hurdle is past, promotion, publicity, and advertising can help sales tremendously. Their effectiveness depends greatly on how well the book has been placed in the stores. A title in 2000 stores will show a different sales response to a full-page national ad or a plug on a TV program than will a book placed in 200 stores.

(The effect is much more than proportional. The sale of each copy generates interest and conversation leading to other sales, in somewhat the way neutron fission occurs in uranium. If it happens often enough, there is the enhancement from a multiplier effect that may create a best-seller. Sporadic sales here and there lead to a dampening and petering out of the chain reaction.)

Some publishers, apart from their skill at getting books into stores, are good at getting publicity or are liberal in their advertising; others are not. This particular ability is something the author must always consider.

The sales of the original edition through the bookstores is not the only potential source of the author's income. For some titles, a significant potential sale exists in the library market. Because librarians frequently buy later than bookstores (after the book appears and has generated some public and critical reaction) and because they tend to know more about books, the sale to libraries is less dependent on the publisher's selling efforts than the sale to bookstores. But only to a degree. The publisher who makes a greater effort to get library sales will get more of them.

Most publishers reach libraries through the mail, but the resources, skill, and budgets allocated to this market vary immensely. Only a few publishers use their sales force to reach the libraries, and these publishers (at greater expense, of course) attain very much higher levels of library sales.

Then there is the whole area of subsidiary rights: book club sales, paperback reprints, movie sales, translations. The responsibility for representing the author in the sale of subsidiary rights is frequently divided between the agent and the publisher. This division may take any form, though it is common for the publisher to handle book club and mass market paperback rights and the agent to handle all the others. The author needs to weigh the relative skills (and size of staff) and the nature of each party's contacts in deciding how to divide this responsibility. All things being equal (they rarely are), it costs the author less if the agent handles the rights, and the income is available promptly, whereas the publisher usually holds it until the next semi-annual royalty payment. On the other hand, the effect of incentive cannot be ignored. Where, for example, a more impressive sale in bookstores will enhance the value of paperback reprint rights, the author would be foolish to exclude the publisher from participating in the strategy of selling those rights and in the financial return.

In fact, few authors are so desirable that they can freely choose their publishers. On the other hand, many authors do have some choice, and it is surprising how few are able to judge the publishers among whom they can choose.

Mistakenly, the most obvious and mouthwatering criterion is not any of the publisher's attributes we have discussed but the size of the author's advance payment. This criterion has grown in importance as the influence of author's agents has grown. For many of them, it offers a twofold advantage: 10 percent of the advance promptly goes directly into the agent's pocket, and since it is a convenient (if misleading) yardstick of accomplishment, the agent can point to it with pride.

However, unless it is felt that the advance payment will never be earned under the terms of the contract and represents a device for getting the publisher to pay a higher royalty, the advance payment is simply the payment, in advance, of *some* of the money that the author will earn from the sale of his book and related rights. Getting the money up front may have some value, especially in times of high

interest rates or for the author with overdue bills, but the value of
early payment should be weighed against the possibility that another
publisher who is offering a lower advance may earn the author more
money in the long run or offer other advantages.

One would imagine that every author has two motives, which
operate in varying degrees. The first is to earn money; the second is to
reach an audience. Fortunately, these two objectives are very
compatible, and the author usually achieves one in the same measure
as the other—but not necessarily. Competition may impel one
publisher to pay a higher royalty (openly or concealed in an unrealistic
advance), so that even though he sells fewer copies, the author will
earn more. Or the publisher may compensate for a weak or
nonexistent sales force by giving the author a more favorable split of
the income from subsidiary rights. In either case, fewer readers may
equal more dollars.

What about the agreement under which the book is published?
Does the author accept the publisher's standard contract with the
blanks filled in by the editor's secretary, or does he try to negotiate his
own arrangement?

Many authors, perhaps the majority, are happy to be published at
all and are not inclined to jeopardize publication by questioning some
minor, or apparently minor, provision in the contract. For authors who
are negotiating from a somewhat stronger position, there are many
conditions, some spelled out in the basic contract and some never
mentioned, that deserve serious thought and are proper matters for
negotiation.

The first and most obvious one is the royalty itself. Although the
royalty is the usual basis for compensating the author, the publisher
may occasionally propose, and in some situations insist on, a lump sum
payment for all rights. I do not agree with some of my friends who
feel that there is something immoral about anything except a royalty
contract. The degree to which the author's work is his own
"invention" rather than the rendition of an idea suggested to him by
the publisher may be a factor to consider. Or, in the case of a series,
the degree to which the book has been presold as well as conceived by
the publisher may be pertinent. And the fixed fee may earn more
money for the author than a royalty would.

Most royalty contracts provide for steps in the royalty rate, starting
at a lower percentage for the first 5000 or 10,000 copies sold and
proceeding up to some higher plateau that applies to all additional
copies sold. This step arrangement is virtually universal, and it is a
measure of the relative bargaining position of author and publisher.

(For "big" authors there are no steps; royalties start at the highest percentage, which is generally 15 percent of the retail price.) The steps are justified to the author by the need for the publisher to make an initial investment in the production and advertising of the book, which is gradually recovered as more copies are sold. This justification may be spurious or real, but it certainly saves the publisher some out-of-pocket royalty costs, so it will be hard to revise this arrangement.

On July 15, 1981, the Authors' Guild reported that 55 percent of its members were getting standard contracts: 10 percent on 5000 copies, 12 percent on the next 5000, and 15 percent thereafter. Twenty-four percent were actually doing better than that. We can assume that other occasional authors, not members of the Guild, were not doing as well, on the average.

Back in the mid-fifties, those of us who helped to reorganize and expand the Doubleday sales force learned something very obvious (but which is still not accepted beyond lip service by many publishers today): the more sales effort, the more sales. We joked among ourselves that a reverse stepping in the royalty scale might be to the author's advantage because it would encourage the publisher to make an extra effort to get extra sales, but we knew better than to suggest it seriously.

□ *But in 1981 it is being suggested seriously. In his* Publishers Weekly *article about the economic plight of the author, James Lincoln Collier suggests stepping down, instead of up, not, as we had considered in the 1950s, to reward the publisher for trying harder, but to have the successful author subsidize the unsuccessful one. Subsidy of financially unsuccessful authors is no more the obligation, moral or otherwise, of financially successful authors than it is of grocers, lawyers, or any other citizens, and certainly no more than the obligation of the publisher himself.*

Royalty steps in either direction do not make too much sense. It is not logical to ask the author to subsidize the publisher's initial investment by steps up or to spur the publisher into a more vigorous selling effort by steps down. The financial reward to the publisher from sales over and above what he may save in reduced royalty payments should be enough to cover either or both.

There is today an increasing tendency among publishers to try to drive down the royalty rate. This is frequently accomplished by stretching out the steps between rate increases. It is a perfectly understandable, if misguided, response to the current economic difficulties in publishing. The bookseller hopes he can solve his business problems by getting more money from the publisher in higher discounts, which the publisher is sure he can't afford; but some publishers, faced with corresponding financial pressures, see reducing payments to authors as their salvation.

Some publishers speak bravely about facing their more important authors head-on in this matter. In the 1980 Bowker Memorial Lecture, Oscar Dystel said: "Today some authors are getting 15 percent of cover price and I believe this royalty rate has to come down once the advance is earned out. Our costs have gone up—*all* our costs. That's why we're hiking cover prices the way we are. But the author's costs haven't gone up beyond the increase in his cost of living—and that fact affects us all. As a matter of fact, a lower royalty would give us the needed cash to promote an author's titles more effectively, and a hundred other books as well."

I quote Oscar Dystel, not because he has been the foremost proponent of this idea, but because he has said it so clearly and so publicly. It is a widely voiced hope among publishers, more among the hardcover publishers than the mass market ones.

Whether authors should charge according to their costs is not the point, nor is whether the money the publisher wins back from the authors will really be used to increase promotion. It is whistling in the dark to believe that the 15 percent royalty author will allow such tampering with his livelihood. He is the author the publisher *needs,* and if one publisher finds the royalty rate onerous, another is standing ready to pay it. It is the 5 percent royalty author, who is grateful to be published at all, who will find his royalty cut and will be able to do nothing about it.

In short, the publisher who is determined to cut his royalty costs will get nothing from the big earners on his list, where it might be of some help; he will get it all from the lesser earners who have little to give and can't afford to give it. More important, squeezing the authors too weak to defend themselves will not solve the publishers' economic problems. The way to solve the business pressures now besetting publishing is to reduce the horrendous waste and, more important, *sell more books.*

Some standard contracts slyly provide that when the publisher sells the book at discounts greater than usual, the royalty paid to the author will be reduced, sometimes by as much as 50 percent. In many such contracts, the publisher's saving on the author's royalty is greater than the revenue he loses by giving his customer a higher discount. In that case, the author certainly is subsidizing the publisher. Such a clause is ethically equivalent to a surgeon charging more for unsuccessful operations than successful ones.

The standard contract also provides for semi-annual payments to the author. This is fair and reasonable when the payments are small, when it would be unfair to burden the publisher with the clerical costs of more frequent payment. However, during the period of the book's life (or the combined life of several of the author's titles) when earnings are high, there is no practical reason why payment cannot be made more frequently: monthly, for example. After all, the publisher gets *his* income from the book *daily*. Particularly during times of high interest rates, it is a contract provision the author should question. High interest rates are, of course, the very reason the publisher would like to hold the author's earnings a little longer before giving them up. Actually, for accounting reasons, many publishers routinely calculate their royalty obligations monthly. With computerized accounting systems, this is easy and adds virtually nothing to clerical costs.

There are niggling ways in which the author "subsidizes" the publisher to some degree—or at least makes contributions of which he is usually not aware. For example, the widely used (and in my opinion misguided) selling inducement of "one free for ten," which gives the bookseller one free copy with every ten copies he orders, is popular with publishers at least in part because the free copy carries no royalty cost. The author is similarly helping the publisher when books are offered to booksellers at lower "prepublication" prices.

A recent development is the newly christened "freight pass through," already solidified with the acronym FPT, which is becoming the publishers' general response to the booksellers' complaint about the sudden and precipitous rise in postage and freight rates.

As long as anyone can remember, publishers have sold their books FOB their warehouse, with the bookseller paying the shipping costs. This practice seemed tolerable so long as books were favored with low postage rates. When the post office was transformed from a service to a business required to pay its own way and the shipping cost for books rose sharply, booksellers complained that they could not afford to absorb the increases.

After a good deal of inconclusive consultations and some embarrassing silences, the idea evolved of billing the bookseller at a theoretical price with the understanding that the actual retail price the bookseller would charge would be higher by approximately the cost of the freight—hence "freight pass through." Since almost all royalties are based on the retail price, this maneuver has the effect of depriving the author of the royalty on the difference between the retail price on the invoice and the actual price charged the customer.

Publishers granting booksellers the FPT are, presumably, amending their standard contracts to legitimate the practice, but in many cases, and for books under existing contracts, publishers have appealed to their authors to show understanding and to accept the royalty reductions. Authors have, apparently, been much more understanding than I think they should be.

The traditional paperback split (something becomes traditional very quickly if you want to make it hard to change) was 50 percent to the author, 50 percent to the publisher. That was part of the contract way back when "reprint" meant hardcover reprint and it didn't happen very often or pay very much. Aggressive agents began to break that division down some years ago, when they represented a strong author, to 60–40, 70–30, and sometimes even more lopsided splits. In some rare cases, the agent signed directly with the paperback house, taking 100 percent of the paperback income for the author, sometimes leaving it to the paperback house to arrange hardcover publication, sometimes doing it himself. The newest development (discussed in Chapter 9, on mass market publishing) is for the paperback house to buy all the rights and to publish both editions, with all royalties, of course, going to the author.

The similar traditional split of bookclub royalties—50–50—has occasionally been successfully challenged by authors. But the chances are good that it too will become less "traditional" under the pressure of successful authors represented by strong-willed agents.

The contract usually provides that the book will be published within a specific period, generally one year from the date of the contract or from the date on which a satisfactory manuscript is delivered. This provision is rarely enforced and rarely taken as seriously by the author as it should be. A manuscript is perishable in varying degrees. At the very least, it is not likely to improve with age. If the publisher delays long enough and then fails to publish, the manuscript may have lost its appeal to an alternate publisher. The author can better protect his interest by insisting that work (text composition, for instance) must be started by some specific deadline (six months from signing or delivery of manuscript, for example) to ensure that publication will happen on schedule. If publication is delayed and the book stays with the original publisher, there is some justification for additional payment to the author.

Two contract provisions, so widely used that they were virtually considered standard, have recently become matters of debate and some bitterness between publishers and agents.

The first of these is a fairly standard provision that the author will supply a completed manuscript "satisfactory to the publisher in form and content." This provision seems to give the publisher the right to decide, unilaterally, what is "satisfactory," and, until recently, that seemed an unassailable interpretation. If the publisher judged the manuscript unsatisfactory, he could cancel the contract and recover the royalty advanced to the author.

This interpretation went unchallenged for years. If the publisher paid good money, should he not receive a product that he could use? And who else can judge what that publisher can successfully publish? Little weight was given to the investment made by the author in completing the manuscript—the commitment of time and creative energy as well as the relinquishment of any right to sell it to someone else.

There has been occasional abuse of the publisher's arbitrary power under this clause. Because it frequently takes so long between signing the contract (sometimes on no more than an outline of the project) and the final manuscript, many changes independent of the project may have taken place. The political climate may be different; the subject matter may be less appropriate, no matter how well presented; the management in the publishing house may have changed. No doubt authors have occasionally suffered the rejection of a manuscript as "unsatisfactory," even though it represented exactly what both parties had in mind when the contract was signed.

Such rejections have been occurring more frequently, and authors have become more aggressive in their protests. As publishers have responded to mounting economic problems by cutting back on their lists, they have found more occasion to invoke the "satisfactory" clause to get out of an obligation incurred at a more optimistic time. Authors have complained that "unsatisfactory" simply came to mean: "I have changed my mind."

There is a growing demand by authors that the clause be changed to specify that the manuscript be of "professional" quality, a determination that could, if necessary, go to impartial arbitration. Yet, even that is too timid a position for the author to take.

When a publisher signs an author to do a book, preempting the author from other useful activity and committing him to that specific project, the publisher does it on the basis of his judgment that the product will justify his investment and the author's efforts. It is on the basis of this supposedly expert judgment that the author stops trying to sell this idea or work on others. If the publisher is unsure, he can ask the author to submit more samples, or he may even avoid signing a contract, taking the risk that some other publisher will step in with a better offer. Once the contract is signed, the publisher is not entitled to the privilege of second thoughts.

The author's position under the "satisfactory" clause, even in its present unsatisfactory state, was considerably strengthened by a recent court decision. Senator Barry Goldwater delivered a manuscript of political memoirs to Harcourt Brace Jovanovich under a contract for which he had received a $65,000 advance. Harcourt rejected the manuscript as "unsatisfactory" and sued for the return of the advance. Unfortunately for Harcourt, the suit reached the court after the book had been very successfully published by William Morrow under the title *With No Apologies.* The judge ruled against Harcourt, holding that the publisher did not have "unfettered license" to reject a manuscript for which it had signed a contract. This decision is very helpful, but it is not a substitute for a more equitable contract provision.

The other hitherto "standard" that has been challenged recently is the so-called warranty clause, in which the author guarantees the publisher against any danger from plagiarism or libel. It is usual for the publishers, in spite of the assignment of responsibility to the author, to search the manuscript for any questionable material and to insist that it be altered or removed. But such searches, even by lawyers skilled in this area, are not infallible, so items vulnerable to a lawsuit sometimes get through. Recently, juries have been persuaded to see connections with litigating plaintiffs in references that would never have been identified as dangerous by any editor or lawyer. Some of these unexpected jury awards have been substantial. In one recent case decided against a Doubleday title, the amount involved was large enough to impel Doubleday to sue its author to recover the award, a most unusual, though perfectly legal, move.

Doubleday's action triggered complaints from many authors against the whole concept of author liability where there is neither plagiarism nor libel by any reasonable standard. They argued that the publisher was better equipped to absorb the financial losses from completely unexpected and unreasonable legal judgments. Viking Press seems to have cut through the problem, and to have won a warm spot in the hearts of all authors, by announcing that it is paying for a blanket insurance policy to cover these dangers for any Viking authors.

A matter the author will rarely find discussed in the printed contract is the possibility that the publisher may encounter financial problems, including bankruptcy. An alert agent will insist on a clause reverting the rights to the author in the actual event of bankruptcy. The absence of such a clause can create serious problems for the author, but its inclusion is not really enough protection. The author should negotiate the freedom to move his books whenever the publisher begins to throw ballast overboard to try to avoid bankruptcy. If the sales force is reduced, the advertising budget slashed, the promotional staff cut, or if other obvious emergency financial steps are taken that impair the publisher's ability to distribute the book, the author should be able to do something besides helplessly watch his book go down the drain. Similarly, if the publisher fails to pay royalties on time, the author should have a clear right to take action spelled out in the contract.

The author who chooses his publisher deliberately and for reasons that would not apply or would be seriously weakened under a different ownership should want his contract to permit him to move elsewhere if the publisher decided to be absorbed into a larger company with different policies.

P.E.N., the Authors' Guild, and other organizations concerned with the growth of conglomeration might find this tendency weakened if the acquiring company could not be assured that it would automatically get the entire list of published and not-yet-published titles.

The author needs to be very much aware as he considers the proposed contract that he is putting the fate of his book completely in the publisher's hands. The copyright, theoretically, was created to protect the author, but the contract can negate that intention very effectively. It is the contract that governs, and the contract usually puts the copyright under the control of the publisher and denies the author the right to take his own book elsewhere, no matter how poorly the publisher does his job. The contract, in effect, shifts to the publisher the monopoly that the copyright law intends for the author. The only protection the author has is the protection he writes into the contract.

□ *Many publishers seem to believe that the copyright gives them a stronger position in relation to the potential market than it actually does. Because the copyright gives the publisher an airtight monopoly on that title, anyone who wants that book can get it nowhere else. That may tend to justify a less aggressive (and less expensive) selling stance on the part of the publisher. However, copyright may provide less protection than the theory implies. It protects the idea only* in the wording of the original, *so it is of much greater value for fiction than for nonfiction. It is easy for a work of nonfiction to be imitated, and even improved, by a competitor. And whether a title has direct competition or not, it is amazing how many people can get along without that book or find some other title that serves their purpose.*

As we have seen, many titles are remaindered approximately one year after publication, a procedure from which the author usually gets no money and the publisher gets enough to tempt him, but which undermines the author's prestige and casts doubt on the original retail price. Since overstock due to overprinting or returns (or both) is largely the publisher's doing, the author is on solid ground for demanding half the remainder income or, still better, a ban against remaindering at all. Either way, this would encourage the publisher to learn his craft a little more thoroughly and, perhaps, to keep the book in print somewhat longer.

The usual contract also permits the publisher to collect his full share of the income from subsidiary rights even though he has remaindered the book and effectively washed his hands of it. There is some question, in my mind at least, whether the publisher is entitled to enjoy the full share of subsidiary rights income if he has let the original edition die prematurely. The author's position would be strengthened, and publishing practice in general improved, if the contract provided that the publisher's share of the subsidiary rights income decreased whenever the sale of the original edition went below some agreed percentage of the first year's sales. Even if that percentage were low (10 percent, say), the publisher would be encouraged to put some effort into keeping that title alive.

There are other matters, not so clearly financial or even contractual, that deserve at least a discussion between author and publisher. For example, the publisher is obligated to place the book in retail stores. How many stores will the publisher's staff visit, and in how many stores does he expect to place the book? Does the publisher have a promotion and advertising campaign in mind? How much detail can be spelled out in advance?

Then there is the question of how much the author should involve himself or let the publisher involve him in the promotion and sale of the book. There is no shortage of examples of authors who have by hard work, and by spending their own money, steadily plugged their own books until the public finally noticed they were there and accorded them respectable sales. In fact, a very few books have reached best-seller levels strictly as a result of the author's efforts, with almost no help and sometimes even no interest from the publisher.

Whether the author goes on tour to promote his book depends on the author and his appetite for exposure, on the book, and on the ease with which it can be tied into author appearances. For an author for whom this activity is distasteful or whose public presence will drive readers away, advice to hit the promotional hustings is not very helpful.

Actually, an author's involvement can and should start long before publication date. As soon as the book is accepted for publication, the author should start developing ideas for promotion and publicity. Suggestions for advertising expenditures, particularly for a book of moderate interest, will not be greeted warmly by the publisher, but press releases and background stories for the media are easy and inexpensive to get out. This may be particularly useful in getting some attention in *Publishers Weekly* so that the bookseller will find the title familiar when the sales rep arrives. It is the lack of ideas, not budget restrictions, that keep the publisher's production of publicity low. Feeding the publicity department "handles" for releases is likely to get action, particularly if most of the work, down to the actual wording of the release, is already done.

The author or his friends may have connections with review media or influential public figures. Building such connections into promotion plans at an early stage can be very helpful.

The author, because he is so personally and emotionally involved in what happens to his book, can become a pest to the publisher. To the extent that he insists on his "rights" or interferes with the normal functioning of the publisher's staff, he may find he is much less welcome than his manuscript was. To avoid that danger or out of a natural reluctance to appear pushy, many authors let the editor act as their surrogate in all dealings with the sales, promotion, and publicity staffs. On the other hand, the fate of the book will to a considerable degree be decided by those staffs. Acting judiciously, tactfully, and within the limits established specifically or tacitly by the publisher, the author can make his hours with the publisher's staff more productive of sales (and readers) than the equivalent hours he has already invested in his manuscript.

At the very least, the author is likely to have a much clearer idea of the market—the potential readers who have been in his mind's eye as he developed the idea and the manuscript itself—than is the sales or promotion person, who has probably read no more than snippets of the text. Although identification of the market is likely to be more important for nonfiction than for fiction, it is the first step in successfully selling any product.

Whatever the author can tell the publisher's staff about the market as he sees it—how to identify it, how to reach it, what will influence it —can only help develop a more effective sales approach. Sometimes this information leads to organizations that want to help, to mailing lists for selling the book directly or simply promoting it, to opportunities for publicity, to ensuring better attention from reviewers.

The author is a vital source of selling information. He should not assume that everyone on the publisher's staff recognizes that fact. It is much more prudent, though less modest, to put the information where it can be used most effectively without waiting to be asked.

There are some obvious ways in which the author can be useful. There is, for instance, the sales conference. If the author has a good stage presence and a good delivery, he may be included in the presentation of his book with a double objective: to create a friendly relationship between himself and the reps, and to provide two or three effective key phrases directed at convincing the bookseller that the public will be eager to buy this particular title.

The author can help his book immensely by establishing closer contact with the sales manager and with each sales rep than is possible in the few minutes available at the sales conference, perhaps by correspondence, perhaps by having drinks or dinner with each rep individually in his territory as soon after the sales conference as possible.

It is important that the author not make unrealistic demands of the rep—or, really, any demands at all. It is quite enough that the rep feels that he understands the book better, that he knows the author, that they are friends, and that the author will be grateful for whatever the rep can do in getting the book into the stores.

We have already commented on the author's participation in promoting the book after it is in the stores. Some authors resent the suggestion that their assistance should be needed, feeling that that's the publisher's job. In a sense, it certainly is, and if the author doesn't care about the results, he can leave it to the publisher. The fact is that with the confusion of hundreds, even thousands, of titles fighting for recognition among the book-buying public, it is very difficult for the publisher, short of a prohibitively expensive advertising campaign, to draw attention to any one title. The author provides a useful lever to accomplish that.

The usual arrangement is for the author to contribute the time and energy and for the publisher to pay the author's travel expenses and for the outside (usually) publicity service that arranges the bookings. Autographings at bookstores do not draw as much traffic as they used to, except for "star" authors. On the other hand, stopping in a store to talk to the clerks and to autograph the books in stock is useful. It makes friends of the clerks and assures the author that the publisher did indeed get books into that store.

And, as we have already seen, the publisher's failure to get books into sufficient stores in sufficient quantity in cities the author will tour is by no means rare. If the author wants to prod the publisher to make books available, he must act weeks before the scheduled appearance. Time must be allowed for the rep to get to the store, for the order to reach the warehouse, and for the books to arrive, be unpacked, and reach the selling floor. That is a requirement of distribution-by-negotiation.

Any failure to have books on hand, aside from the effect on the author's gastrointestinal tract and the lost sales themselves, loses the momentum of word-of-mouth advertising. Particularly after an author's appearance, the value of having people talking about the book because they have just started to read it is as important as the sales themselves.

The author who feels that he cannot participate in the book's promotion certainly owes it to himself (and to the public if his stuff is worth reading) to choose his publisher carefully so that all those steps are performed as well as possible. On the other hand, it is interesting to recall that the early authors, who told their tales or sang their ballads at the tribal campfires or wandered among the urban centers to find their audiences, were their own publishers as well and understood the value of promotion and distribution.

"Self-publication" today is an act of desperation, not the avenue of choice. But recognizing that the services of a publisher are, to all practical purposes, indispensable, the author should not contract for those services blindly and unquestioningly. He has the right to see that his interests are protected—and, more than that, advanced. And he should improve the effectiveness of the publisher by contributing his own judgment and energy to see that the job of publishing—of bringing the book to the public—is the very best possible.

12

The Economics
of Publishing

ALTHOUGH THE FAILURE of trade book publishing to deliver better service to the American reading public and to authors is primarily the result of a chaotic distribution system, a substantial part of the blame can be shared by archaic accounting systems that, in most publishing houses, confuse management instead of enlightening it. It is an amazing truth that most accounting departments supply management with figures that are frequently meaningless and almost as frequently misleading.

The influence of accounting-inspired thinking has been responsible for more errors in publishing management than any other single factor. The wreckage of publishing houses subjected to the "guidance" of conglomerate accounting departments and financial vice presidents is only the most dramatic example of a widespread disservice. Accounting thinking, as it is generally practiced, fails in two major ways.

First, it fails to provide a useful financial model of the whole publishing enterprise, which would give management a grasp of the cost, function, and contribution of the departments that make up the company. Such a model, commonplace in many other industries, would allow management to estimate in advance the probable effect on profit from expansion or contraction of the sales or editorial departments, for example, or the business consequences of changes in policy on author advances or royalty rates, or of changes up or down in discounts.

In place of an overall financial model, the accountants provide elaborate analyses of each individual title, the clear implication being the completely misleading notion that the whole, the total publishing business, is equal to the sum of the individual titles that are published.

The effect, in addition to assigning greatly exaggerated importance to the decision whether to publish each projected book, denies management virtually indispensable tools for strategic planning.

Second, having failed to produce strategic information that might help management control the activities of the operating departments and generally direct the progress of the company, and having, instead, overemphasized the importance of each tactical book-by-book decision, most accounting departments supply information on individual titles that is worse than useless. The guidance usually supplied as an aid to deciding whether or not to publish a particular book, how many copies to print, what retail price to charge, can only lead intelligent managers into making wrong decisions.

Such extreme criticism may seem intemperate exaggeration. The evidence, however, fully supports it.

Let us see, first, the economic model management needs, one that considers the publishing enterprise as an overall economic organism. The publisher starts, as do all businesses in our capitalistic society, with money. He converts the money into books (and sub rights), and he sells the books (and sub rights), converting them back into money. The process requires additional money along the way—to cover rent, interest on borrowed money, sales reps, editors, and many other expenses. The sale of books must, therefore, not only bring in what the books cost directly, but all these associated expenses. If the sale brings in more than that, there will be a profit; if less, a loss.

Publishers' costs are of two broad kinds. One kind is largely independent of which books are published, how many, or even of their relative success or failure. These are called fixed costs. The second are variable costs and are roughly proportional to sales revenue. Fixed costs include, for example, executive salaries and those of the editorial, production, design, marketing, and salaried sales staffs, order processing and fulfillment, rent, depreciation, interest on indebtedness, catalogues, office supplies, and the data processing department.

Of course, these so-called fixed costs or overheads are not altogether immutable. If sales increase sufficiently, more help will be needed in order processing and the warehouse. If sales go down sufficiently, some space may be given up, editorial and marketing staffs cut, and perhaps executive salaries moderately pared. But within fairly broad limits of sales volume, fixed costs do not change.

Certain elements within the fixed costs (variable overheads) *do* change with changes in sales levels. For example, although the order processing staff may not change in size, increased sales may result in the need for more overtime, invoice forms, statements, phone calls for order information or to accelerate collections, etc. It may also result in bonuses to sales reps and, perhaps, increased cost for processing returns.

Then there are costs that vary directly with sales. The most obvious is the author's royalty. The cost of advertising also varies with sales. In fact, in some publishing houses, the advertising budget is automatically fixed as a predetermined percentage of sales. Up go the sales, up go the advertising expenditures; down go the sales, down go the advertising expenditures.

□ *This mechanical control of advertising budgets gave us a little trouble at Doubleday in 1955. We were expanding the sales force, justified by the increased income that would (and did) result from increased field sales activity. The advertising manager wanted "his" 5 percent of the increase in sales, just as he had been historically allocated 5 percent of all sales. It took a little convincing to get management to agree that advertising was not sales tax, and that the 5 percent on* additional *sales should go to pay for the increased sales force or to profit.*

Where advertising money is spent more thoughtfully, the bulk of the expenditure may be for only a few "advertisable" titles on the list —primarily, of course, the important new publications—and the total for each year will be influenced by how many such titles are published. We can consider advertising to be variable, assuming that the number of such advertisable titles will vary fairly directly with the total number of titles published and the total sales.

There are two distinct components of manufacturing cost, and they relate to sales somewhat differently. The first is the amalgam of one-time expenditures independent of the number of copies to be produced. These are plant costs, and they include the setting of type, the design and artwork for the jacket or cover, and similar expenses. Some publishers include the editorial costs, particularly copyediting and proofreading, in plant costs; others do not. The plant cost is clearly, and by definition, a fixed cost for any individual title. Yet we treat the total annual plant cost as a variable cost against the sale of *all* the titles.

The *total* plant cost in any given year will depend upon the number of titles published and their complexity. The *percentage* of plant cost in any given year will, in turn, depend upon the success of the mix of titles produced by that year's plant investment *plus* the sale of previously published titles. Clearly then, the relation of plant cost to total company sales can be somewhat erratic; one is not functionally related to the other. It is generally true, however, that for any particular publishing house, other things (like sales force) being equal, sales will tend to relate somewhat to number of titles published. We will put plant down as a variable, but one should note that some ambiguity exists.

The other component of manufacturing cost—all the costs associated with producing books after the plant cost has been paid, which we simply call manufacturing cost—relates to sales volume in a much less ambiguous way. Books with a higher retail price generally cost more to manufacture—as we shall see, most publishers try to make cost and price a firm ratio. It is true that books that are *not* sold incur the same manufacturing cost as books that *are* sold. For any given publishing house, however, the waste of unsold books relates fairly closely to sales from year to year, so the "manufacturing" component of manufacturing cost is more truly a variable cost related to sales than is the plant cost component.

If sales are made through a commission sales force—paid, for example, 10 percent on sales to retailers and 5 percent on sales to wholesalers—sales cost will be very closely related to total sales. Sometimes the situation is mixed; the sales manager may cover the larger accounts to save commission costs, leaving the lesser accounts to the sales force. Where the proprietary sales force is essentially on salary, perhaps with some sort of bonus plan for exceptional performance, sales cost can be considered fixed, like rent and executive salaries.

An example shows how publishing management can use an economic model to evaluate the probable effects of alternative strategies.

A particular medium-sized publisher is doing $8 million in sales, just breaking even on trade sales and making its profit from the sale of subsidiary rights. Our interest is in the publishing and trade sales activity, leaving aside the sub rights income.

The company has a fixed overhead of $2,480,000 annually. This includes all its staff and facilities and financing costs, including administration, sales, editorial, and warehousing. Sales reps are on salary plus incentives. The variable overheads, such as invoice forms, overtime due to heavy workloads, sales incentive payments, etc., amount to $720,000 annually, which is 9 percent of sales. The so-called plant costs for the books being published are 8 percent of sales. The cost of manufacturing books, after plant costs are covered, is 27 percent of sales, and the cost of royalty, 16 percent of sales. The cost of advertising runs about $720,000 for the year, which is 9 percent of sales.

The total of all costs in this publishing house is covered when the sale of books (excluding any income from the sale of rights) reaches the level of $8 million annually.

The easiest way to understand these cost relationships, and perhaps to discuss them, is to visualize them (see Figure 4, page 267).

The graph shows the costs going from bottom to top (the vertical axis) and the sales going from left to right (the horizontal axis). Total fixed costs are represented by a horizontal line $2,480,000 above the base line. The fixed costs remain the same no matter how sales vary.

The variable cost lines, each of which rises in proportion to sales, start, not at zero, but at the level of fixed costs and go up from there. Because the variable costs are "on top of" fixed costs in real life, they are on top of them in the graph.

□ *Among the fallacies in "title accounting" and "unit cost accounting," which are widely used in publishing, is the tacit assumption that variable costs* do *start at zero rather than on top of fixed costs. Those accounting techniques assume that if no books are published, that publisher will have no costs. I will say more about that later.*

The total costs, at any level of sales, are the fixed costs, which remain constant, plus each of the variable costs, which increase as sales increase. The topmost variable cost line (which happens to be advertising on this graph) is also the line of total cost.

Sales, unlike variable costs, *do* start at zero. They are shown by the heavy line labeled Sales, which starts at zero and moves diagonally upward.

The use of straight lines is, of course, an oversimplification.

The relationship of costs and income, which are shown on the graph from zero to $14 million in sales, would not really hold across that broad range of sales. Clearly, as the company's sales approached the lower limits, staff would be reduced, so fixed costs would not remain constant and the relationship of some of the variable costs (advertising? plant?) would change with respect to sales. Similarly, at the higher sales ranges, there would certainly be staff additions to handle the heavier load, so fixed costs would rise. But within say, $6 million to $10 million, a range sufficient to cover catastrophic failure and fantastic success, the relationships shown on the graph would hold well enough to support the arguments we would like to make.

As we move along the graph toward the right, sales and total costs go up. The sales line is steeper—it goes up faster—than the top variable cost line. That is essential if the business is ever to make a profit. Subtracting all the variable costs from sales income determines

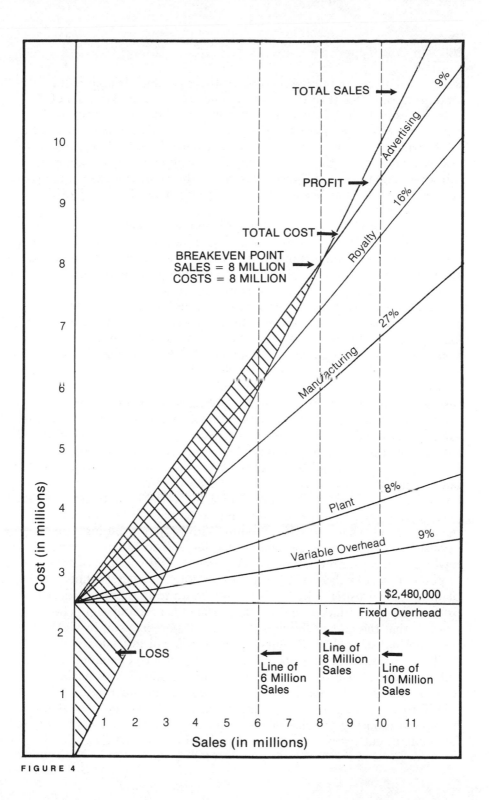

FIGURE 4

what is left to cover the fixed costs. In this case the variable costs amount to 69 percent of the sales income. That leaves 31 cents of every sales dollar to cover the $2,480,000 of fixed costs. Some quick arithmetic will show that 31 cents per dollar equals the fixed costs at a sales level of $8 million in sales. That is where the sales line and the line of total costs on the graph cross: the break-even point. Ignoring subsidiary rights income, below this point, the company loses money; above this point, it makes a profit. The graph shows how that profit, or loss, varies with sales.

The company's sales are running $8 million annually, so, except for subsidiary rights income, which does not show on the graph and which puts the company comfortably in the black, the publisher's operations are breaking even. This is clearly not satisfactory, so management should be looking for ways to improve this situation.

The most obvious way to improve it and the one favored by publishers nine times out of ten is by reducing costs. Any reduction in fixed costs (which would lower all the cost lines on the graph correspondingly) will go right into profit, dollar for dollar, except to the degree that these economies result in decreased sales.

Costs can be reduced readily by reducing staff: letting some sales reps go, reducing the promotion or publicity staff or the crew processing incoming orders or packing books for shipment, or (for this example) any reduction that does not reduce the output of titles. But if the people holding these jobs have been the least bit effective, eliminating them should be expected to reduce sales somewhat. As sales go down, every dollar in reduced sales does not represent an equivalent loss in profit because some of the variable costs are reduced correspondingly. Royalty does not have to be paid to the author for books not sold. That saves 16 percent. With proper planning, the publisher will anticipate the sales reduction and will manufacture fewer books, saving an additional 27 percent. The variable overheads (9 percent) should also be expected to go down as sales decline. But plant and advertising (which are related more to number of titles) are presumably not reduced, and fixed overhead is certainly not. The result is that the cost reductions (totaling 52 percent) still leave the publisher out of pocket 48 cents for each dollar of lost sales.

The conclusion is, therefore, that our hypothetical economizing publisher can afford to lose sales amounting to $20,850 for each $10,000 of cost reduction not affecting title output—or roughly $2 of sales for each dollar of cost saving. This may look like an attractive gamble in reducing the size of the order department, but not nearly so favorable in cutting out sales reps. It is hard to imagine a sales department so ineffective that sales would go down less than twice the cost of the sales rep for each sales rep subtracted. In any case, the publisher can make an intelligent judgment about how each possible economy will affect sales.

The nature of the gamble changes somewhat if the editorial department is reduced or other steps are taken to reduce the rate at which titles are published.

A reduction in the number of titles published would certainly reduce plant expenditures and almost certainly reduce advertising. The company's expenditures would, therefore, decrease with lost sales approximately as follows: advertising (9 percent), plant (8 percent), royalty (16 percent), manufacturing (27 percent), and variable overhead (9 percent)—a total of 69 percent. This would leave the publisher out of pocket 31 cents for each dollar of lost sales.

A reduction in editorial staff, if it resulted in a reduction in number of titles published, would allow this publisher to lose sales amounting to $32,250 (or roughly three to one) for each $10,000 of cost reduction.

As we have already said, any reduction in cost that does *not* result in a decrease in sales goes directly into profit. That might be accomplished by the elimination of duplication and overstaffing, savings in book manufacturing that do not degrade quality, more careful and deliberate policies of inventory control, and so on. There are certainly ways in every organization to reduce costs *without* reducing effectiveness, frequently even increasing it, and such ways are worth a careful search.

Whether or not costs are reduced, another way to increase profit is to increase revenue (sales) without increasing costs correspondingly.

One way to bring sales above the $8 million break-even point with one brilliant stroke of the pen is to raise the retail prices of all the books, which is how many companies in many industries have solved their financial problems. And it is a policy that has no shortage of advocates in publishing. Suppose retail prices were raised by 10 percent. If the sales level held, revenues would increase by 10 percent, reaching $8.8 million.

Profit would not be the full $800,000 increase, however, because raising the retail price would automatically increase royalties, which are generally tied to the retail price. Royalties of 16 percent, amounting to $128,000, would, therefore, be paid on the additional $800,000 of sales. The hoped-for profit would therefore be $672,000, which is 7.6 percent of the new sales figure of $8.8 million.

But an increase in price is certain to result in a decrease in sales, which, if large enough, could wipe out the gains of the price increase. How much will each dollar of sales lost actually cost the publisher?

As sales go down, the publisher saves the royalty, which is 16 percent on the new, higher price as it was on the old, lower price. He also saves the cost of manufacturing and variable overheads, which were 27 percent and 9 percent respectively of the old price, a total for the two of 36 percent. On the new price, 10 percent higher than the old, that 36 percent becomes 32.72 percent. As sales go down, therefore, the publisher's expenses go down by 48.72 cents per dollar (32.72 percent plus the royalty of 16 percent), and he actually loses 51.28 cents for every dollar of declining sales.

If the overall price increase results in a loss in sales of $1,310,452, or 14.89 percent, the gain from the increase in retail price will be wiped out. If sales go down any more than that, the price increase will have been counterproductive.

No publisher would, or should, contemplate an overall, across-the-list price increase. (Considerations that determine retail price are discussed in detail later in this chapter.) It is clear that a price increase will affect the sale of different books differently, depending on how much the typical prospective buyer wants a particular title. The margin above cost is different for every title, which makes each book vulnerable to damage from lost sales to a different degree. Obviously, any publisher who is tempted to improve his position by raising retail prices would do so by studying the situation on each title individually.

Increasing revenue by reducing discounts to retailers and wholesalers is another possibility. Although the publisher has limited maneuverability in adjusting discounts, he might increase his revenue from the sale of the same number of units by decreasing the average discount. Discount is, understandably, a very touchy subject with retailers, and a publisher who deals with it undiplomatically could experience a strong reaction out of proportion to the actual reduction.

If our publisher is selling at an average discount of 43 percent (not unusual), his revenue of $8 million represents 57 percent of the retail price. If he can manage to reduce the average discount to 42 percent without losing sales, his revenue will increase to $8,140,350, and instead of breaking even, he will have a profit of $140,350. In this case, the increased revenue is not shared with the author. The retail price is unchanged, so the royalty remains the same.

For each dollar of sales lost as a result of the 1 percent discount change, the publisher is out of pocket 48 cents. Hence, if his sales decrease by $292,395 (which is only 3.7 percent of the $8 million in sales), it will wipe out this theoretical possible profit and put him back at breaking even. If sales go down more than that, he will be operating in the red.

Price increases or adjustments in discount may improve profit, but they do not represent any real growth of the company, which can occur in a variety of ways. For example, if editors choose more popular books, more copies will be sold. Fixed overheads will remain unchanged, and the cost of variable overheads, manufacturing, and royalty will rise in proportion to increased sales. But there should not be any rise in plant costs (since the improved sale is from the same number of titles) or in advertising.

Therefore, if the increase in sales is due to better selection of titles, the only additional cost to the company for each additional dollar of sales is in variable overhead (9 cents), manufacturing (27 cents) and royalty (16 cents)—a total of 52 cents. On each additional dollar of sales, the profit is, therefore, 48 cents.

It is naive, however, to think that the editors are selecting inferior books simply because no one has suggested that they choose better ones. Periodically, someone suggests that publishing solve its problems by publishing better books, whatever *they* are. Obviously, the editors are selecting as well as they know how.

□ *Savants who suggest that editors should choose books that sell better overlook (among many other things) a rather subtle fact of life in trade book publishing: the distribution system. Built into the chaos and complexity of the publisher-bookseller and bookseller-customer relationships are numerous chance factors controlled by no one. These elements are present in each of the hundreds of thousands of salesman-bookseller negotiations, in whether the wholesaler has the book in stock when the retailer asks for it, in whether the book is well enough displayed to catch the attention of browsers, etc. The effect of these chance factors (we used to call them luck) is such that the same book has the possibility of selling over a wide range above or below its theoretical sales potential in a completely unpredictable way. These factors are, by their very nature, outside the control of the editor, and even of the publisher. As a result, it may be that the editors are already following the advice that they choose better-selling books that are simply not selling better.*

Management can, however, provide editors a better mix from which to select by making publication by their house more attractive. This can be done by offering higher advance payments or higher royalties or by agreeing to spend larger amounts on advertising important titles. Management may, as a general policy or by considering each publishing project on its merits, decide that the prospect of a margin of 48 cents on every additional sales dollar justifies one or another expenditure to get it.

But if "publish better books" is not as simple as it sounds, "publish more titles" (though it may be exactly the wrong thing to do) certainly is. This can be accomplished by adding more editors; if they are of the same general caliber as the present editors and have similar connections with sources of manuscripts, the additional books will be of the same average level of salability as the present list. If more titles are published, all the variable costs (advertising, royalty, plant, manufacturing, variable overhead) will go up in proportion. The margin on the increased sale will be the equivalent of the fixed overheads already paid for: 31 cents on every dollar of additional sales. (Actually, the margin will probably be somewhat less than that, because the enlarged publishing program may require more personnel in sales or promotion or order processing.)

Whatever is done with editorial production—improving it, enlarging it, shrinking it—the level of sales should be responsive to any increased selling effort. This could be the result of increased advertising or of enlarging the promotion and publicity staff. The simplest and most direct way to increase selling strength is to increase the number of sales reps to ensure that more stores are called on and that they are covered more methodically. The additional cost of the reps and any support facility would have to be covered by the increase in sales. These sales would not involve additional advertising or plant cost, so the publisher could afford to spend up to 48 cents for each dollar of sales added by a stronger sales effort of some kind. As we have already calculated, increased sales effort would pay its own way if it generated $2 of sales for each dollar of cost.

The logic also applies to advertising. As Figure 4 shows, each dollar of additional sales could make available 40 cents toward more advertising (31 cents of fixed cost and 9 cents of advertising ratio). Therefore, a dollar of advertising money is well spent if it increases sales by more than $2.50.

A matter of immediate concern among publishers and booksellers is the financial hardship caused by the recent series of sharp increases in postal rates. Since traditionally the bookseller pays the delivery charges, the entire burden of this increase is falling on him. The bookseller is protesting loudly that he does not have the resources to absorb the cost and that the publisher is in a much stronger financial position. Publishers are, of course, resisting the suggestion.

Figure 4 helps us see how the publisher can determine whether he should absorb the postage costs. These charges, which vary with the size of the shipment, may average about 4 percent of sales, so adding that cost would push the publisher in our example from breaking even to a 4 percent loss if sales remained unchanged. Presumably the first publishers to pay postage would be giving the booksellers an economic incentive to buy from them, which would improve those publishers' sales, and publishers who stand pat should expect to suffer some reduction of sales. It would be interesting to see, therefore, how the 4 percent in additional costs can be recovered by increased sales.

As we have seen, manufacturing (27 percent), royalty (16 percent), and variable overhead (9 percent) will vary directly with sales; they will be reduced if sales decline and will increase if sales increase. The other costs (fixed overhead, plant, and advertising), amounting to 48 percent, stay relatively constant with changes in sales level.

If paying the postage reduces revenue for the same titles by 4 percent, the revenue remaining to cover these costs will be correspondingly reduced from 48 to 44 percent. To bring the publisher back to the original level would require an increase in sales of about 9.1 percent (48 divided by 44 = 1.0909).

This puts the publisher's dilemma into focus: "If I give the bookseller the additional 4 percent, I will lose money to the degree that I fall short of improving sales by 9.1 percent. If I don't give the 4 percent, I will lose money to the degree that my sales fall by more than 9.1 percent."

Figure 4 also reminds us that the company has a fixed annual cost of $2,480,000. At the level of variable costs assumed in the example, each dollar of sales contributes 31 cents toward that impressive sum. Assuming no change in the variable costs, the publisher must sell enough dollars each year to accumulate enough 31-cent contributions to cover that fixed cost. That does not tell him which or how many titles to publish, but it does tell him the sales levels he must reach before there will be any profit at all. Put another way, no matter what the projection for any book says about its profitability, there will be *no* profitability for the company until the $2,480,000 is covered. Put still another way, a book that will be profitable in a year that the $2,480,000 has been covered will not be profitable in a year that it is not covered.

One cannot sensibly talk about the profitability of a single title. A title can clearly be *unprofitable.* If it fails to recover its out-of-pocket costs, it is unprofitable. But if it sells well enough to cover its costs with something left over, one cannot say if it is profitable. It has made a larger or smaller contribution to the "nut" of $2,480,000. If a large enough number of titles make large enough contributions to more than cover that nut, there will be a profit to the company, but to assign any part of the profit to any one title is a doubtful exercise in logic and a pointless one in practice.

It might be interesting to look more closely at some of the costs. Publishers are very much concerned, with good reason, with the danger of growing fixed costs. Such costs do have a way of accreting painlessly, without calling too much attention to themselves, and their effect can be devastating. The actual publisher of our example was shocked, when the figures were presented in this manner, at how high his fixed costs were. However, fixed costs are not in themselves bad.

To avoid the fixed cost of a sales force on salary, a publisher may have a sales force on commission or may use free-lance commission reps so that his selling costs are directly related to sales. Leaving aside the possible difference in productivity among these alternatives, it is clearly better to tie sales costs to sales when sales are at the low end and to accept sales costs as fixed when sales are at the high end. The same is true in comparing the use of outside computer and warehousing services with the fixed cost of internal facilities. The advantages of control and flexibility in one's own facilities cannot be ignored, but neither can the cost of such advantages.

Royalties may be too high or too low, but the percentage they happen to be of sales will not give any indication of which. They may be too low if frugality in setting royalty rates is keeping good authors away. They may, in that case, be a low percentage of an unnecessarily low sales total. If they are too high because many author's advances are not earned, the proper way to reduce them may not be lower advances or royalty rates but a greater selling effort.

Plant cost is worth a closer look. It shows in Figure 4 as a variable cost (8 percent), which, actually, it is not. It represents the cost of setting type, making color separations, and all the other one-time costs in the production of a book. While it is a fixed cost for any one book, it is a variable one in relation to the overall publishing program, depending on the number and nature of the books on the publisher's list, but it could not be shown that way on the graph. Plant cost tends to go up as a total as the number of titles (and presumably sales) goes up, but not necessarily in proportion. If the publisher sells smaller quantities of more titles, plant cost will tend to be a larger percentage of his cost than if he sells larger quantities of fewer titles. But plant cost depends on the specific book as well. A title with a lot of color and complicated composition will require more plant investment than one with no color and simple composition.

Plant has yet another dimension: the cost of the publisher's "tools" for manufacturing each book. Once the type is set and the color illustrations are prepared, the jacket design and printing plates paid for, etc., copies can be produced at will and, broadly speaking, in any quantity. The publisher must make this investment in every title for the privilege of having finished books.

The publisher's backlist represents a plant investment made in previous years that is still generating sales. But the productivity of that investment and, therefore, its value are depreciating as the titles age and sales of the backlist decay.

□ *We shall have more to say about plant cost related to individual titles and even individual copies. One point is pertinent here. Each publisher has an accounting policy for "writing off" the plant cost of each title for income tax purposes. It may be written off immediately, or on publication day, or over three years, or over 5000 copies, etc. This uniform accounting policy does not (and should not) correspond to what happens to the true value of the plant investment on each title. That will depend, in an essentially unpredictable way, on the life of that book, how many copies it sells, how long it continues to sell, etc.*

The sale of backlist titles declines at various different rates. Some, like Kahlil Gibran's *The Prophet,* seems not to decline at all or even to increase in sales as time goes on. Although the pattern of sales for any particular title may be erratic and unpredictable, the trend for a large enough group of backlist titles belonging to a particular publisher is likely to be more coherent, more uniform. If the sale of a group of titles (perhaps 50 or 100) is charted over several years, individual titles will show variations, but the entire group will probably show a steady decline in sales, possibly accelerating slightly. The rate of decline will depend on a number of factors, including the way the sales force sells the backlist as well as on the titles themselves. If this decline were, say, 10 percent each year, well within the range of experience in the industry, it tells the publisher that his investment in the backlist plant is eroding at 10 percent each year unless he does something to replenish it. Depending upon the size of the backlist and the rate of decay, the publisher can estimate how much he should be investing in plant costs each publishing season on titles likely to go on the backlist to keep his backlist sales steady.

□ *The sale of backlist titles proved a useful meter for measuring the effectiveness of changes in the sales force at Doubleday during the period 1955–57. A group of approximately 50 backlist titles, the aggregate sales of which had declined almost uniformly at 10 percent per year for several years, experienced a* 35 percent increase *in sales in the first year of the reorganized sales force. The sale of these titles continued to rise less steeply for a time before leveling out and beginning, again, to decline.*

Of course, plant investment is no more than a very rough indicator. Moreover, sales are not in proportion to plant investment. A small plant investment may account for a large percentage of the sales. Poorly selected titles might be adding high plant investment and modest sales. Yet it is useful for management to have even a rough measure of the erosion of the backlist sales and to be aware that this decay should be replaced each year just to stay even. It would help management greatly in planning its editorial strategy if it were aware of the degree to which the current publishing program is causing the backlist to grow or decline and the added effort needed, if any, to bolster the backlist.

Every new title requires plant investment, of course, whether it joins the backlist, or dies on the frontlist.

In the example shown in Figure 4, the company's investment in plant for that year was $640,000, which at a sales level of $8 million worked out to 8 percent of sales. That number was almost certainly not planned or budgeted. It just happened. Publishers make decisions book by book, essentially in isolation, and the total of that year's individual decisions added up to a plant investment of $640,000.

Although the decisions are made book by book, it would not have been crazy for management to say to the editorial director: "We are going to give you a budget of $640,000 this year for plant. And in general terms, this is what we want the investment to produce over and above what will result from previous plant investment."

The key point here is not the amount of plant costs or of putting a limit on the plant investment (which should be avoided if possible), but the recognition that publishing management should be trying to fit book-by-book decisions into an overall strategy so they stop being simply book-by-book decisions.

It is here that we experience the second major failure of traditional trade book publishing accounting. The first is the lack of useful financial models of the overall enterprise. The accounting department almost never supplies information in a form likely to stimulate consideration of the relation of fixed and variable costs to the decisions of operating management, such as are suggested by our simple chart. And we have only scratched the surface of how such information can be made useful.

The first failure of accounting is what it does *not* supply. The second is what it *does* supply: a superabundance of information directing management's attention to the title-by-title decisions, presumably aimed at enabling it to make those decisions more effectively.

In the process of twisting and contorting the numbers so that each title will somehow recreate the economics of the entire publishing business, the accountants have introduced fallacies that result in bad management decisions if they are accepted and then logically applied.

"Title accounting" is virtually universal in book publishing. Because some costs, like the fixed overhead figure in Figure 4, cannot be assigned to particular titles, they are allocated by some sort of formula. So, for example, 40 percent of sales receipts may be charged against each title to cover the fixed and variable overheads and occasionally other items.

By assigning arbitrarily allocated overhead costs to each title in addition to the costs that really belong to it, the publisher believes he can project the economics of the publication of any particular title by making a few decisions and a few assumptions. From the physical specifications, the production manager can determine the plant and manufacturing costs fairly precisely. The editor knows the cost of author's royalty even more precisely, and he can decide the retail price and assume a level of sale (very imprecisely). From these figures, a projection of income and expenditure (including the catchall "overhead") can be made that suggests the economic value of that title on the publisher's list.

The detailed projection has the appearance of being very precise. It is usually prepared by the sponsoring or the managing editor. The editor supplies the production manager with a detailed description of the physical book and an estimate of the number of copies he expects will be sold. The production manager, usually in consultation with the probable suppliers, then estimates the cost of producing the book in that quantity (or in a range of quantities). In some houses, this estimate is supplied to the fourth decimal place.

The estimated cost per copy usually determines the tentative retail price (about which we will have much more to say), and the retail price, in turn, depending on the average discount, determines the anticipated revenue per copy. It is on revenue that the calculation of overhead is based. Whatever overhead percentage the publisher uses— 40, 45, 50—is subtracted from this theoretical revenue per copy figure, and the balance is expected to cover plant and manufacturing costs, royalty, and profit. In some cases, the specific advertising appropriation to be charged against the book will also be subtracted from revenue per copy; in others, advertising is included in the overhead.

In practice, the procedure is generally as follows: The editor decides he would like to do the book and believes it will sell 10,000 copies. He describes the proposed book to the production manager in sufficient detail that the physical specifications can be determined. In due time, the production manager reports that the plant costs—book design, setting type, making plates, jacket design and plates, color separations (if any), and, in some houses, some of the editorial costs, such as copyediting and proofreading—will be $15,000. In addition, the cost for paper, printing, and binding will be $2.00 per copy for a run of 10,000 copies. The plant cost of $15,000 comes to $1.50 per copy on 10,000, so the total cost of manufacturing is $3.50 per copy.

If this publisher uses the not-unusual formula of five and one half times manufacturing cost to determine the retail price, the tentative price of the book will be $19.95 (it calculates to $19.25).

If that is the retail price, further calculations might be as follows:

Revenue, per copy, at 43% discount	$11.37
Overhead at 40% of income	4.55
Available after overhead	6.82
Manufacturing cost per copy	3.50
	3.32
Royalty per copy, at 10% of retail price	2.00
Profit	$ 1.32

Such calculations are the basis on which most publishers determine whether to publish the book, what its retail price will be, and, frequently, even what the printing quantity will be. When, on rare occasions, the logic of extrapolating all these numbers from the unit cost is challenged, the justification offered is that the cost of manufacturing the book is the most reliable number in publishing, so it should surprise no one if that is the number on which all other calculations are based.

Neat. But it overlooks something all of us were taught in high school. When several numbers are multiplied, the reliability of the result is determined by the *least* reliable number, not by the most reliable one. The sales predictions, for example, are frequently wrong. I have yet to meet the man who can predict ("guess" is more accurate) the sale of three titles in a row within 10 percent of the actual result. Overhead percentages are wrong almost as frequently. My high school math teacher would smile at the earnestness with which the unit manufacturing costs are figured to the fourth decimal place—and, of course, the unit costs themselves are wrong because they ignore the likelihood that not all the copies will be sold.

In most publishing houses, such a projection (favorable, of course) must be submitted to whatever authority in the company makes the decision to publish.

If the projection is attractive and the title is published, the accounting department will set up an account for that title and prepare periodic "profit and loss" statements for that title.

The method is loaded with booby traps of all sorts. First of all, it puts a large part of the cost into the gray area of overhead. Overhead *per title or per copy,* if there really is such a thing, depends on how many titles are published and how many copies are sold. As the publisher keeps turning down projects because they cannot (or it is predicted that they cannot) bring in the required 40 percent overhead, his actual total overhead costs remain, so the overhead percentage on the projects he has decided to publish climbs.

But even if the overhead, by some miracle, remained the same percentage of sales from year to year, the overhead concept does not help the publisher make better decisions. Obscuring the economic factors at work on any particular title by insisting that from 35 to 60 percent of the costs, depending on the publisher, have already been assigned to the book can hardly help sharpen the publisher's judgment. The larger the percentage of any title's overall cost that is determined by some vague allocation not related specifically to that title, the less responsive will be any decisions on its real pros or cons. One need only imagine making the overhead 100 percent, in which case making a decision on any title would be completely impossible. One title may, in fact, require more of the publisher's overhead than another, and this may change the true probability of profit for that title, but the figures won't show it.

The nature of the numbers tends to obscure the value of the project. The projected profits are usually expressed "per copy," but an impressive profit "per copy" can be a small total amount on a small project, hardly worth the managerial time and energy it will need, whereas an apparent break-even result on a large project may, in fact, be contributing substantially to overhead costs.

The title-by-title judgment does not direct management's attention sufficiently to the overall position of the publishing program. In Figure 4, the overhead of $2,480,000 is covered by sales of $8 million. If the backlist is to supply $4 million of that, then new publications have to produce $4 million (within the constraints of the budgets for plant, manufacturing, royalty, etc.). How much of that $4 million is already assured as we examine this next book proposal? Are we well along, or are we going to have to accept some projects that may be solid but contribute less than their quota to the overhead?

Publishers who bother to compare the actual results with the earlier projections discover that *this method does not work.* The books that actually sell their hoped-for quantity are a minority of the titles published. The variance is in both directions, although, because of the need to show a hopeful projection to break through the barriers to publication, most of the errors are in overstated sales. The errors of *understated* sales do not cost the publisher any money (the book sold more copies than the projection assumed), but what do they imply about the projects that were rejected, for which no history can exist? How many of those rejections were due to understated sales?

The wide difference between actual and projected sales that will be found in the records of every trade publisher will invariably reveal some interesting points:

1. The prediction of sales by title is highly unreliable.
2. The title accounting system frequently tempts the publisher to compound a publishing error (in itself a minor cost) by printing the exaggerated number of copies demanded by the projection rather than the modest number demanded by the market.

   □ *This temptation is particularly strong in companies where typesetting and other plant costs are included in "unit costs" (as they usually are), so that a slight difference in quantity of books manufactured seems to (but really does not) make a big difference in cost per copy.*

3. The temptation to overprint frequently further compounds the error by having the sales department place exaggerated quantities in advance (usually with wholesalers), which come back later as returns to make the publishing error still more costly.

These traps are obvious from even the most cursory analysis. What is not so obvious is that this system also tempts the publisher to make an error in fixing the retail price. The projection looks so much better if the retail price is high enough to cover the costs at the predicted sales level; but, as it turns out, the high retail price may assure that sales never actually reach that level.

The publisher would do much better with a more realistic method of evaluating prospective titles, dealing with specific costs relating directly to that project, estimating the risks, evaluating the return on the time money is invested, relating the project to the overall budget for sales and overhead recovery, and to a plan for building a list, and so on.

Although it would certainly not solve all the difficulties in judging new projects, the publisher would see the project in better perspective by using gross numbers rather than unit costs. For example, a proposal to publish a book at $14.95 that is expected to sell about 25,000 copies might look like this:

Direct editorial cost	$ 5,000
Plant cost	8,000
Manufacturing	37,500
Royalty, at 10% of retail	37,375
(10% x $14.95 x 25,000 copies)	
Variable overhead	19,175
Total cost	$107,050
Revenue at 43% discount	213,040
(57% x $14.95 x 25,000 copies)	
Margin for overhead and profit	$105,990

To arrive at some indication of risk, the publisher can calculate the out-of-pocket break-even point. Since royalty is paid only on copies that are sold, we can omit royalty from costs and subtract it from per copy revenue on the copies sold. At an average discount of 43 percent and a royalty of 10 percent, each copy sold at $14.95 yields $7.03. The total cost, excluding the royalty, to produce 25,000 copies is $69,675 ($107,050 − $37,375 = $69,675). Dividing total cost by revenue per copy ($69,675 ÷ $7.03) shows that we will recover these costs when 9916 copies are sold. How confident are we that 9916 is a safe sales projection, even if 25,000 is not? Or would it be wiser to plan on printing 15,000, which would bring the break-even point down to 7782 copies?

The project may be of interest only if a 25,000-copy sale is likely, but that interest might be reinforced if the cost of possible failure can be held down.

If the editorial department is being controlled by an investment budget (as suggested in Chapter 10, on editorial management), it may be pertinent that this title will use $50,375 for editorial and plant out of the department's budget. The predicted margin of $105,990 suggests a contribution of $2.10 per dollar of editorial budget. Is that satisfactory? How large a contribution must each dollar return in order for the department to meet its goals? How much of the budget has already been committed?

There are other considerations, of course. How quickly are the books expected to sell? What does that indicate about return on investment? How well does the title fit the objective for the overall list?

None of this will make the sales prediction more accurate. Every judgment about a projected title is subject to the reliability of that prediction. Nevertheless, the approach suggested here, particularly in calculating break-even points as an indication of risk and matching each project against the editorial budget (the criteria for acceptable contribution per dollar of investment must be developed separately for each publisher), will give the publisher a better basis for judging the desirability of the project than the usual evaluation form does.

The concept of title accounting leads to a whole substrate of fallacies that carry this concept down to the single copy of each title, which is usually called unit cost. It may have a valid use for calculating cost of goods sold for tax purposes, but it is no tool for publishing management.

For example, being a fixed cost for each title independent of the number of copies printed, the plant cost cannot be logically apportioned among the copies of that title, no matter how much the accountants insist on it. And they *do* insist on it in varying ways. The most popular way is to divide the total plant cost for each title by the quantity of the first printing, assigning the resulting "plant cost per copy" to the manufacturing cost of each copy of that printing. On the books with large first printings, the plant cost per copy may be small enough that this accounting aberration is of little consequence; but since most books have modest (and some have minuscule) first printings, the accounting distortions do cause mischief.

Having assigned a portion of the plant cost to each copy of the book, accountants like to keep track of how much of it has been paid for by the book's sales. Since most titles do not sell out their first printings (which is not the fault of the accounting department), most books do not "earn out" the plant cost by accounting definitions.

□ *Someone outside publishing will find it hard to believe that this allocation of plant cost over the first printing* frequently *leads to the following: The sales prediction for a book may be very uncertain, arguing in favor of doing a smaller first printing and running the risk of the small additional cost of a second printing (if it should turn out to be necessary) rather than the much larger risk of having far too many books. The winning argument against the wiser course is: "If we do a smaller printing, our plant cost per copy will be too high."*

There may be a publishing house somewhere in which the accountants are told to stick the plant cost elsewhere, but I don't know of one. The practice of assigning a portion of the plant cost to each copy of the book until it is "recovered" seems universal.

This exercise, aside from helping to keep the accounting department larger than it need be, has the misleading effect of suggesting that the sale of one book is more profitable than another when in fact they have the same real margins.

For example, two $10 titles may each have a royalty cost of $1 a copy, manufacturing of $1, and plant (so says the accounting department) of $1. Revenue to the publisher from the bookseller is $6 per copy (discount equals 40 percent). After Title A has "earned its plant," the accounting department says its margin is $4 per copy ($6 minus royalty and manufacturing), while slower-selling Title B has a margin of only $3 ($6 minus royalty and manufacturing *and* plant). But the company is neither better nor worse off whether the book sold is Title A or Title B; the effect on total profit is *exactly the same.*

Actually, plant cost is a matter of concern only when the title is being considered for publication and its "profitability" is being forecast. *All* costs, including plant, are very pertinent to that consideration. Plant does not belong in a consideration of the retail price, as we shall see, and it has no value tied to the cost accounting of any title. Once the decision to publish is made, the plant cost for any title joins the total plant cost for all titles as a kind of collective burden for all to bear cooperatively. From the point of view of the business, it makes no difference whether the plant for all the titles (or for that matter, *any* fixed cost) is "paid out" by fantastic sales of one of the titles or equally by less fantastic sales of many titles.

In addition to being misleading, unit cost is expensive to calculate, not in advance, when it is a simple matter of dividing one number (estimated total manufacturing cost) by another (number of copies), but afterward, when the invoices begin to arrive. The publisher sets up a complicated accounting apparatus to follow each expenditure and to assign it to a particular printing of a particular title.

When an invoice spans several titles, the total is painstakingly divided among the titles and each amount, no matter how small, is directed to its proper niche in the proper column of the proper title. If a title's costs are "closed out" prematurely and a new charge arrives, the unit costs are recalculated and adjusting entries made in the numberless places where the erroneous figure had been posted. The amount of detail is immense.

□ *In larger publishing houses, where the cash flow concerns of top management rarely penetrate to lower levels, it is not at all unusual to have the accounting department pressure the production department to "get those invoices in" so the unit costs can be calculated earlier. The publisher's cost in interest on the money used in paying bills earlier than he needs to might be forgivable if the labors of the accountants resulted in something useful.*

Although the use of the theoretical unit cost, calculated in advance, frequently does lead to bad decisions, it turns out that, paradoxically, the *actual* unit cost doesn't matter, which is fortunate, because it is frequently wrong. It is not surprising, with all this minute detail being posted by accountants who do not know one title from another, let alone one manufacturing operation from another, that there are so many errors. Many might be caught if anyone in the operating end of the business needed these figures for anything useful and had occasion to examine them. But since the figures almost never go outside the accounting department, they are almost never corrected. My own experience in examining accounting records suggests that, at least in medium to large publishing houses, about one third of the unit costs are incorrect.

It would be far less expensive in the size of the accounting staff and would give management more accurate unit costs if the publisher used an internal "standard cost" system, assigning unit costs to each book without tracking down each penny on each invoice to its precise title.

Although the actual unit costs are frequently wrong and always useless, the theoretical unit costs, those calculated from the production manager's estimates before the book is published and before it is produced, appear to be, as we have said, the most useful (more accurately, the most *used*) numbers in publishing.

The publishing world is so full of uncertainties and unpredictable shifts and changes that it is easy to see why publishers try to extract as much value as possible from the one apparently solid fact they can count on. The unit cost seems firm and reliable in an uncertain world. It is simple to understand and to calculate. It is easy to determine, even months in advance, how many dollars will be spent for typesetting, paper, printing, binding, and auxiliary items to produce X number of copies of a particular title. Dividing those dollars by X number of copies results in a number that pretends to be the cost of producing one copy. That number opens the way to endless misleading extrapolations.

What is wrong with the unit cost and the way publishers use it?

First of all, it is not really the unit cost. In all its uses and in all the ways the publisher thinks about it, the implication is that the unit cost is the cost of the product being *sold*. But the publisher in fact uses the unit cost of the copy being *manufactured*. The difference may seem a quibble, and could be in many other industries, but the overflowing remainder tables argue eloquently that the distinction is a real one in publishing. If the publisher prints 10,000 copies at a cost of $10,000 and sells 5000 copies, was the unit cost $1 or $2? Which one is the cost of each copy sold?

Or consider the actual case of my friend Bob's book, the one that got such favorable reviews. The publisher says he printed 10,000 copies. Sales came to a net of approximately 400 copies. Never mind asking why the publisher printed 10,000—or, closer to Bob's heart, asking how he managed to sell only 400 copies in the face of those glowing reviews. The fact remains that the unit cost was *twenty-five times* higher than the publisher had calculated. Certainly this case is so extreme as to be a caricature, and it does overstate the argument. But it is true that the number of copies sold *almost never* equals the number of copies of the first printing. Actual unit cost *almost never* equals predicted unit cost.

Second, unit costs differ greatly in character. They may be similar or even the same in form, but very different in fact. Consider two books, each of which has a unit cost of $1. For Book A, the dollar consists of 80 cents for plant and 20 cents for manufacturing; for Book B, the plant cost is 20 cents and the manufacturing cost is 80 cents. After the plant cost is recovered, each additional copy sold of Book A is worth four copies sold of Book B. Indeed, it is perfectly possible that the sale of 10,000 copies of Book A will result in more profit than the sale of 20,000 copies of Book B, but the publisher's arithmetic does not show that. Is Book A's unit cost of $1 equal to Book B's unit cost of $1?

And should such costs be used interchangeably in a publisher's calculations?

Third, unit cost tends to focus attention on things that matter a little while diverting attention from things that matter a lot. Consider, for example, one production manager who struggled with a title showing a unit cost 3 cents too high to fit the formula for retail price. His boss suggested using cheaper paper and cloth and considered reducing the author's royalty by the stubborn 3 cents. Since the quantity being printed was 1000, all this executive time was spent to deal with a $30 problem. In the same publishing house, a printing of 200,000 copies of a college economics textbook (no less) was being planned. A slight change in the plan would have reduced the unit cost by 7 cents. The production manager of the college department declined to make the change because the unit cost was "well within the budget" for the retail price. And the vice president in charge agreed. There went $14,000 down the drain. This was (and is) a highly successful publishing house, but *not* through clever use of unit costs.

Unit cost obscures important matters in other ways. The unit cost (and unit profit) calculation does not take proper account of costs beyond manufacturing that should influence management's decision. Is the project big enough to justify the inevitable overhead? How quickly will the financial investment be recovered? How have the risks been calculated?

Fourth, unit cost accounting assumes unit overhead. In this kind of accounting (and thinking), each copy of each book pays its share of the overhead based on unit cost or retail price. In the example above, except for the cost of money and some warehouse space, the true total overhead on the 1000-copy printing was approximately the same as the total overhead on the 200,000-copy printing. (The 1000-copy printing actually consumed more executive time and talent.) Yet the unit cost system would charge two hundred times as much overhead against the second book as against the first one.

Finally, unit cost, even when it is unit cost, should not be the basis for fixing retail price. The retail price of any commodity should depend more on the value the buyer places on the product than on the cost to the producer.

In an industry as varied and personal as publishing, so central a process as determining the retail price for a book varies greatly with each publisher. Yet it is astonishing that the common denominator of almost all the variations is some calculation based on unit manufacturing cost. Even worse, the plant cost is almost always included as part of the manufacturing cost.

The calculations do vary. Some publishers multiply manufacturing cost plus royalty by two, or two and one half, or multiply manufacturing cost alone by five and one half, etc.

I remember that at Viking, when I first came into publishing in 1946, the formula was two times manufacturing cost plus royalty. It seemed so smooth. As a little boy, when my mother took me shopping for socks and I did not know my size, the store owner would have me make a fist. If the sole of the sock went exactly around my fist, it was the right size. Well, I thought, book publishers have developed their own fist-and-sock shortcut to solving a complicated problem—until I really began to think about it. Except for the publisher's very questionable assumption that unit manufacturing cost is the only solid number available, it is hard to work one's way back through the logic that developed this fist-and-sock solution.

As I have pointed out, the unit manufacturing cost that is used to calculate the retail price is *not* the unit manufacturing cost of the copies sold. It is the predicted cost per copy of the number produced, which is *almost never* the number of copies sold. Nor does it take into account other costs, such as advertising and promotion, which vary greatly from title to title.

Why should price be based on cost? One can understand the reluctance of a publisher to sell any book below cost, but why always the same ratio to cost? Why should a book that is popular, and therefore sought after, and which will be printed in large quantities and therefore at a lower cost, carry a lower retail price? Why should a publisher with an inefficient production department charge more than a publisher with an efficient one?

The cost of manufacturing the book is, after all, the cost of manufacturing the container, *the package,* in which the author's words and ideas are delivered. How can a publisher, who enjoys pointing with pride to the cultural contributions made by books, who looks upon himself as someone to whom ideas are sacred, how can he ignore completely the value or desirability or popularity of the ideas he is selling and charge according to the cost of the container?

What happened to all the fine talk about "every book is different"?

During all my years in publishing, I have not met a single person who can justify in a manner satisfactory to me (or to himself) the logic of pricing books according to manufacturing cost. It simply makes no sense.

It would be as though I demanded a da Vinci price for the result of my amateur attempts at oil painting because the amount of paint, the size of the canvas, the cost of the frame, etc., for my painting were the same as those for the Mona Lisa. The comparison seems ridiculous only because it is extreme. In fact, no one has yet bought a book because of the physical cost of the raw materials and the cost of processing them. Every book is bought because its desirability relates favorably to its retail price for the person who buys it.

What is the purpose of the retail price? The usual purpose is to make the greatest profit possible on the item being sold. Since "profit" cannot be properly applied to one book on a publisher's list, it is perhaps better to say: to recover the maximum margin over costs, that margin then being available to pay plant and general fixed costs and, perhaps, contribute to company profits. Any other price will be less financially advantageous to the publisher.

Sometimes the objective in setting retail price may be different from the maximum immediate financial reward. On occasion it may be to get the widest possible audience for the book, perhaps because of its political or social message, to prepare the public for the author's next and potentially more successful book, because the "profit" is to come from a forthcoming movie, or for a variety of possible reasons.

There are all sorts of legitimate goals (even for a calculating businessman) other than maximum immediate financial return. Even so, it is very useful to know which retail price would bring the maximum return so that the cost of selecting a different price can be approximated.

And it would seem desirable to avoid reducing the potential return by inadvertently selecting a price higher than the most appropriate one.

□ *We cannot overlook some hard-nosed business reasons for occasionally selecting a* higher *price: if an important book club wants a higher retail price so that its "member's price" will have greater bargain appeal, for instance, or if the goal is to exaggerate the price reduction on a planned phony remainder. In such cases, the decision on price would be based on the combined "profit" from all the marketing channels.*

As we have said, if financial advantage is not the objective, once he determines the best price, the publisher need not use it. The present sock-over-fist formulas in publishing are intended to make money, not give books away.

If the retail price is intended to bring the publisher the maximum return for that book, it is at least as much related to how much people want that book as it is to how much it cost to make. Thank goodness! Otherwise, the author would be irrelevant.

Books may cost exactly the same to manufacture, but one may be able to carry a higher retail price because more people want it or want it more intensely. Whatever sale one title may have at $5.00 might go down 50 percent if the price is $6.00, whereas another title may lose only 5 percent of its sales potential with a similar price increase.

But manufacturing costs do differ, so the advantages of price increases are not the same even for titles with similar sales sensitivity. In one case, raising the retail price to $6.00 may increase the per-copy margin of revenue over direct cost only slightly; in the other, the margin might double.

It should be underlined that we are not concerned with the difference in *sales* at different retail prices but the difference in the publisher's *margins* on those sales. These margins depend on the cost of manufacturing the book, the royalty rate, and the cost of variable overheads that should properly be charged against each sale. The conceptual difference between sales and margin on sales is critical. Frequently a publisher would lose money on a larger volume of sales at a lower price and make substantial profit on a smaller volume at a higher price.

The retail price that will bring in the highest profit for any particular book depends, therefore, on the balance of two factors: the difference at each step in price between the cost of producing the book and the revenue at that price and the attraction of the book (or its converse, buyer resistance) at each step in price. For example, if the difference between cost and revenue is very small, a higher price may increase that difference sufficiently to more than compensate for a very substantial reduction in sale. Or, if the attraction of the title to potential buyers is very sensitive to the retail price, a small increase in price may reduce sales to more than wipe out any income advantage per copy.

The manufacturing cost of the book, as a total figure or per copy, tells us nothing about the value of either of these two factors nor how the balance between them will change at different retail prices.

How does one measure or gauge public response? Is it not possible to publish the book at different prices before it is published to see what the sales will be at each price? Obviously not. One must project the public reaction without an actual test on each title. (This difficulty is not a good reason for discarding valid criteria and applying invalid ones.)

The nature of the exercise will become clearer by example.

Let us imagine a book that had $12,000 in plant cost and will cost $1.40 per copy for paper, printing and binding. The royalty is 15 percent of the retail price. The variable overheads (billing and shipping, etc.) are 60 cents per copy.

□ *The $1.40 cost will vary somewhat with differences in the number of books being made. We ignore this real difference because it is truly small in relation to the retail price differences and would not affect the answer enough to matter. Also, we want a solution that is independent of number of copies to be sold because we know from experience that we cannot trust the publisher's prediction of sale.*

For the publisher who determines retail price by multiplying the manufacturing cost, assume that the expected sale (and the expected first printing) is about 10,000 copies. That would make the manufacturing cost $2.60 per copy ($1.20 per copy share of the plant cost of $12,000 on 10,000 copies, plus the $1.40 per copy for paper, printing, and binding). The multiplier recommended by publishers varies from about five times to as much as seven or eight times. Let us assume that our publisher uses a multiplier of five and one half.

The retail price, by the sock-over-fist system, would therefore be $15.00 (5.5 x $2.60 = $14.30). Now let us see how the marginal income calculation presents the choice to the publisher.

If the retail price were $15.00, the publisher would receive $8.55, assuming his average discount to stores and wholesalers is 43 percent. Against the $8.55, he would have the following costs:

Printing/binding	$1.40
Royalty	2.25
Variable overheads	.60
Total costs	$4.25

This leaves $4.30 margin per copy from which to pay plant costs for that title and to contribute something to the company overhead.

At a retail price of $18.00, the publisher's revenue would be $10.26, and his costs would be:

Printing/binding	$1.40
Royalty	2.70
Variable overheads	.60
Total costs	$4.70

This leaves a net margin of $5.56 per copy.

On the other hand, at a retail price of $11.00, his revenue would be $6.27; his costs, $3.65; and his net margin, $2.62.

We could make similar calculations at other retail prices, but this is enough to illustrate the point. What these numbers tell us is this:

The margin at each retail price is the money available (after paying for the physical book and the royalty) from which to pay plant costs, overhead, and, in a good year, profit. The margin for each copy multiplied by the number of copies sold equals the total margin from that title. The object is to make the number (total copies sold times margin per copy) as large as possible.

If we divide the margin at the $15.00 retail price ($4.30) by the margin at the $11.00 retail price ($2.62), the result is 1.64, which means we must sell 64 percent more copies at $11.00 than we do at $15.00 to get the same total dollars of margin. If we believe sales at $11.00 will be *more* than 64 percent higher than sales at $15.00, we should set the price at $11.00.

Dividing the margin at $15.00 ($4.30) by the margin at $18.00 ($5.56) gives us .77, which means that at $18.00 retail, 77 percent of the sale at $15.00 will give us the same total dollars of margin. If we believe that going to $18.00 will lose us more than 23 percent of the sale we would get at $15.00, we should stick with $15.00.

Of course, one cannot know in advance how many copies a book will sell (although the sock-over-fist system *depends* on that forecast), but it is interesting to put hypothetical numbers in our example to see how costly the sock-over-fist pricing method can be.

Let us assume that going to $18.00 retail would lose us 10 percent of the sales at $15.00 retail. Based on the above calculations, we would set the price at $18.00, but the average publisher, using his multiplier of five and one half, would have no reason to question his system, so he would price the book at $15.00. Let us assume, as he does, that the sale at $15.00 is 10,000 copies.

The margin at $15.00, which is $4.30 times 10,000, equals $43,000.

The margin at $18.00, which is $5.56 times 9,000, equals $50,040.

Our sock-over-fist publisher has just lost $7040, which is 16.4 percent of the margin he did make at the $15.00 retail price.

The multiplier system assumes that if manufacturing costs go up 10 percent, the retail price goes up 10 percent; if costs double, the price doubles. And if by some miracle the costs can be reduced, the price should be reduced accordingly. (That is why the unfortunate production manager is under constant pressure.) Worst of all, the multiplier system assumes that two titles with the same manufacturing cost should have the same retail price, without any regard to how much customers may want each title and how demand would go up or down with differences in price.

As we see it, if the best retail price is some predetermined multiple of the manufacturing cost, it is *completely accidental*. And if that multiple happens to be right for one book, it is almost certainly wrong for the next book because it is unlikely that the next book will have exactly the same variation in market acceptability at different retail prices.

The multiplier method of retail pricing is wrong in just about every aspect. It uses the wrong cost for the book since it includes plant cost. This is wrong conceptually because plant is a fixed cost, and no fixed costs of any kind belong in a consideration of retail price. But it is also wrong because it forces the publisher, completely unnecessarily, to try the highly risky business of guessing how many copies he will sell. Since his guess is almost always wrong, it simply compounds the error.

The multiplier method is also wrong because it makes no attempt to measure the marginal income at each price, so it applies the same retail price to two titles that cost the same to manufacture even though the attraction of the two books may be very different.

The income lost in a typical trade book publishing house through faulty pricing is, in my opinion, enormous. I am sure it is several times the typical publisher's annual profit. The errors are in both directions. Books are *overpriced and underpriced*. Each way reduces profit.

The same logic that we used for selecting retail price can help the publisher with a question that arises frequently these days: hardcover or paperback? It does not, by itself, answer the question because there are other considerations, as we shall see in a moment, but it provides essential information.

Assume that the manufacturing cost (excluding plant) would be $1.40 per copy in hardcover and 70 cents in paperback. The retail price in hardcover would be $14.95, with a royalty of 10 percent. It would be $7.95 in paperback, with a royalty rate of 6 percent. The average discount for hardcover would be 43 percent, for paper, 45 percent. The variable overhead would be 50 cents in either case. The two formats compare as follows:

	Hardcover	Paperback
Manufacturing cost	$1.40	$ .70
Royalty	1.50	.48
Variable overhead	.50	.50
Total	$3.40	$1.68
Income from sales	8.52	4.37
Margin	$5.12	$2.69

The margin from the hardcover ($5.12) per copy divided by the margin from the paperback ($2.69) is 1.90, showing that the paperback must sell almost twice as well (90 percent better) to return the same margin to the publisher. If he believes it will and issues the book as a paperback, he may do well, but the author may not. Dividing the author's royalty for the hardcover ($1.50) by that for the paperback (48 cents) shows that the paperback must sell 3.125 times better than the hardcover for him to come out even.

The hardcover-paperback decision is, however, not as straightforward as this simple calculation shows. Because the margin per copy is so much greater in hardcover, the publisher can afford to spend much more per copy on promotion to launch the title initially. And promotion tends to reduce the importance of price in the customer's decision. The publisher must also consider that whereas he can issue a trade paperback following the hardcover edition, the reverse is very rarely possible and even more rarely effective.

The decision therefore requires some thought about the book itself, the nature of the probable audience, the promotion required, and other factors. The comparison of margin in each format would be an essential part of this thinking.

We have already suggested that the usual treatment of overhead costs —allocating them in some theoretical and arbitrary way to each copy of each book—undermines management's judgment in deciding what to publish and in determining retail price. The failure by most accounting departments to appreciate the ways in which the overhead should influence publishing decisions works mischief in other ways as well.

Management may assume, for example, that because sales commissions are 6 percent of sales, and an increase in sales of $1 results in additional sales commission of 6 cents, so also, because overhead is 40 percent (if that is the figure) of sales, an increase in sales of $1 results in additional overhead of 40 cents.

Let us consider an imaginary example, which is actually adapted from a real case. A mythical publisher has a big advantage over other publishers. Being imaginary, he can predict in advance how many copies of each new book he will sell and be guided accordingly. He prints only as many copies as he needs.

This mythical publisher publishes two kinds of books—profitable and unprofitable—each at $10.00 retail. His overhead, including advertising, is 40 percent. His accounting department, which watches every title like a hawk, is able to report that for a given year, his profitable titles each sold 7000 copies; the figures on each of those titles looked like this:

Plant cost	$ 5,000
Manufacturing @ $1.25/copy	8,750
Royalty @ 10%	7,000
Overhead @ 40%	15,680
Total cost	$36,430
Income on 7000 copies at	
44% average discount	39,200
Profit	$2,770 per title

The unprofitable titles each sold only 4000 copies, and the accounting figures showed:

Plant cost	$ 5,000
Manufacturing @ $1.25/copy	5,000
Royalty @ 10%	4,000
Overhead @ 40%	8,960
Total cost	$22,960
Income on 4000 copies at	
44% average discount	22,400
Clear loss	$560 per title

Our imaginary publisher showed a modest profit for the year of $82,500, publishing fifty profitable and one hundred unprofitable titles.

The publisher hoped to be taken over by a conglomerate at a multiple of profits, so he wanted to improve his profitability. He called a meeting of his editorial department and showed them the accounting department figures before having a realistic, heart-to-heart talk. No more subsidizing the weak books. He was sick of it. "Every book has to stand on its own feet." He wanted them to get tough and publish only the winners. "There are too many books published, anyway."

With his help, in the following year the editors eliminated every unprofitable title, publishing only fifty profitable titles.

Now the real nature of overhead becomes clear.

Overhead is composed of variable items (like advertising and sales commissions), which change with reasonable changes in sales, and fixed items (like real estate taxes, depreciation, and executive salaries), which do not normally change very much with sales volume. For our imaginary publisher, as with real publishers, the variable part of the overhead amounted to 18 percent and the fixed part to 22 percent of the 40 percent overhead total.

Before he told those dreamers in the editorial department the hard facts of business life, the annual figures for the company looked like this:

Plant (150 titles)	$ 750,000
Manufacturing cost (100 unprofitable)	500,000
Manufacturing cost (50 profitable)	437,500
Royalty (100 unprofitable)	400,000
Royalty (50 profitable)	350,000
Overhead	1,680,000
Total costs	$4,117,500
Income (150 titles)	4,200,000
Profit for year	$ 82,500

After the elimination of all the unprofitable titles, the following year's figures looked like this:

Plant (50 profitable titles)	$ 250,000
Manufacturing cost	437,500
Royalty	350,000
Overhead	1,307,500
Total costs	$2,345,000
Income (50 titles)	1,960,000
Loss for year	$ 385,000

And, horrors, the overhead, which the accountants swore was 40 percent, was now more than 65 percent. Now, if management and the editorial department continued to allow themselves to be guided by the accounting department, they would henceforth choose only titles that earned a 65 percent overhead, so that the following year the overhead would reach 85 percent.

Obviously, the title accounting figures did not accurately reflect the situation. When all the books that lose money are eliminated, you expect the profit to go up, not down.

Perhaps if the figures on the 7000-copy "profitable" titles had been presented like this, they would have made more sense:

Plant cost	$ 5,000
Manufacturing @ $1.25/copy	8,750
Royalty @ 10%	7,000
Advertising (8% of the total variable overhead of 18%)	3,750
Variable overhead @ 10%	3,920
Total cost	$28,420
Income on 7000 copies at	
44% discount	39,200
Contribution to fixed costs	$10,780

In a similar manner, the 4000-copy "unprofitable" titles would look like this:

Plant cost	$ 5,000
Manufacturing @ $1.25/copy	5,000
Royalty @ 10%	4,000
Advertising	1,485
Variable overhead @ 10%	2,240
Total cost	$17,725
Income on 4000 copies at 44% discount	22,400
Contribution to fixed costs	$ 4,675

The fixed overhead for the year was $924,000. This *happened* (I stress *happened*) to be 22 percent of the income, so that with the variable 10 percent and the advertising of 8 percent, the total overhead as defined by the accounting department did amount to 40 percent.

The two classes of titles could have been considered this way:

50 titles making a contribution of $10,780 each	$ 539,000
100 titles making a contribution of $4675 each	467,500
Total contribution by published titles	$ 1,006,500
Total fixed overhead for year	924,000
Profit	$ 82,500

With the figures presented in this manner, our imaginary management could not possibly make such a fantastic blunder. If they eliminated a 7000-copy title, they would expect profit to go down by $10,780 (which is how much "contribution" would be lost). If they eliminated a 4000-copy title, profit would go down only $4675, but they would know it was going *down,* not up. Adding titles would increase profit, $10,780 per 7000-copy title, $4675 per 4000-copy title.

These figures make it clear *in advance* that dropping the hundred poorer titles would reduce profits by $467,500, so it would never become management strategy.

Of course, any statement from the accounting department assigning a "profit" of whatever amount to any title is suspect on its face. If the income from the sale of a title fails to cover the costs—plant, royalty, manufacturing, advertising, and variable overhead—there is no question that that title lost money. But supposing it did cover costs with something left over, can we really (meaning usefully) say that it was profitable?

In our imaginary publishing house, were the fifty "profitable" titles really profitable? If so, why didn't they remain profitable when we dropped the "unprofitable" ones?

If the accountant says, "This title shows a loss of $560," we are entitled to ask, "If we hadn't published it, would we have been $560 richer?"

The answer, it turns out, is no. If we hadn't published it, we would have been $4675 poorer. We have a right to wonder how our accounting system defines "profit" and "loss."

Contrary to our publishing accountants, it is simply *not possible* to make a useful statement about the amount of profit or loss on any one title without also saying something about every title published that year.

□ *Physicists would not find such a notion shocking. In their business, it is called Heisenberg's Uncertainty Principle.*

Any publishing accounting that presumes to assign some measure of profitability to any particular title without reference to all the other facts of that publishing year—or decade, perhaps—cannot possibly correspond to reality and can only mislead management.

The accountant who tells management that the overhead for 1980 was 40 cents for every dollar of income is simply stating that dividing the total dollars in that year's overhead (as defined by the accounting department) by the year's sales resulted in a quotient of 0.40. If he did the arithmetic correctly, his statement is undeniable.

But how useful is that number? If it leads to making bad decisions, it is not very useful.

As I have said, our imaginary publisher is not terribly imaginary. I know a publisher who reduced the publishing program in two trade departments as a direct result of his accounting department's analysis along these very lines, which recommended reducing the number of "unprofitable" titles. His profit in those two departments went *down* just a little short of $100,000 a year. As a result of similar cuts in other areas, he managed to raise his overhead from 40 to 49 percent. That case is *real*.

One can say in favor of this approach, despite the obvious error in judgment, that it was at least an attempt to apply an editorial strategy rather than permit the editorial program to be whatever happened to result each year from unrelated title-by-title decisions.

Management should indeed look closely at title-by-title decisions— though management deserves better information for such decisions than it usually gets from its accountants. But an editorial program is much more than a collection of independent decisions, to publish or not to publish. The publisher needs information that will lead to a sound editorial strategy to guide the title-by-title decisions.

The need for a policy, a strategy, a program, applies in other departments as well.

In sales, management must not allow its strategy to be simply the result of all the decisions made by title. The year's total expenditure for advertising and promotion will be equal to the sum of the expenditures for advertising and promotion for each title, but that is not how it should happen.

Advertising, promotion, and publicity are sales tools, as are the discount schedule and the sales force. The object of spending a dollar in any of these activities is to get more than a dollar in margin back. In the case of the sales force, the return is expected across the entire list, whereas an ad in the *New York Times Book Review* is expected to bring it back on the specific title or titles featured.

Measuring the effect of the selling effort is not easy. Some ways to do so are suggested in Chapter 6, on sales. The techniques need a great deal of development and will, in any case, never give better than approximate results. Nevertheless, it is useful to keep the concept very much in mind. Even with crude measurement, the publisher is likely to conclude that a reallocation of his spending will improve results. How many salesmen can be added if the advertising and promotion budget is cut by 25 percent? How much more can be done in promotion if the sales force is reduced by 25 percent?

It is important to see that controlling the economic forces on a book-by-book basis is inadequate—and particularly inadequate if the book-by-book figures supplied to management are misleading. Only information that reflects the real balance of the pertinent variables and enables management to forecast, even approximately, the results of each decision is really useful. The title-by-title accounting methods should be adapted to bring the figures closer to this ideal.

Even beyond that, management must handle its tactical decisions— in editorial, sales, promotion, or wherever—in the context of a conscious overall strategy that these decisions are intended to promote. Such strategies must take account of the economic forces throughout the business, even throughout the industry. It is bad enough for management to contend with chance and the unknowns of the world outside the publishing house. It should not be handicapped by contending with unknowns within the company itself.

13

Production Management

FEW PUBLISHERS manufacture books, for the necessary equipment would require a huge capital investment. Moreover, an efficient plant produces books in huge quantities, far greater than the needs of any except the six or seven largest publishers.

Publishers (with the one outstanding exception of Doubleday) purchase the printing and binding of their books from specialized book manufacturing plants. The work is frequently fragmented. Type may be set by one supplier for a book to be printed by a second and bound by a third, though the printing and binding steps are frequently the work of one plant. Jackets, covers, endpapers, and illustrative inserts may be printed elsewhere and shipped to the binder to be combined with the printed text.

Catering to the publishers' need are hundreds of competitive suppliers of both materials—paper, binding cloth, paperback cover stock—and fabrication—typesetting, printing, binding. Dealing with these suppliers is a primary function of the production manager.

Depending upon the organization of the particular house, the production manager may also be responsible for designing the book and sometimes for copyediting. His responsibilities generally include developing the physical specifications for each book, selecting suppliers for the material and the manufacturing operations to produce the book, preparing advance estimates of the costs, and working out a detailed schedule that shows when each step will occur and when finished books will be delivered to the warehouse. Finally, he must see that all these steps take place as scheduled.

To most publishers, the ideal production manager understands the technicalities of manufacturing, can keep myriads of details straight and properly related to each other, and knows how to buy frugally. Since the production manager spends approximately 40 cents of every dollar spent by the firm, one would expect him to be high in the councils of the company. That is seldom the case. In many publishing houses, the production manager is considered a technician rather than a manager. When he *is* only a technician, it is because his superiors fail to see the potential for management in the production function and to demand performance at a higher level.

Publishing houses generally handle the production of each book individually. Suppliers are chosen for each book by criteria that vary from publisher to publisher. Once they are selected, cost estimates and manufacturing schedules are constructed and the production department leads each book through the steps from manuscript to the last binding machine.

By competitive bidding or through his knowledge of his suppliers' price structures, the production manager is expected to manufacture each book at the lowest possible cost. It is almost impossible for the publisher to determine whether each book is, in fact, being manufactured at the lowest cost because step-by-step and book-by-book purchasing makes accurate auditing impractical. It would require an army of auditors to review each decision against each of the several alternatives for each decision in the light of several criteria: price, quality, schedule, and future relationships. (Such an audit would cost more than the book production itself.)

In most companies, the publisher makes himself vulnerable by giving the responsibility to approve the final invoice for payment to the production manager (who has already selected the supplier, estimated the cost, and placed the order). This is almost a textbook example of how *not* to control purchasing. Yet, with a policy of buying production book by book, it is hard to see how the publisher can do anything else.

It's bad enough not to have control over production expenditures. It's worse to imagine you have it when you don't. I met recently with the controller of the publishing division of a large conglomerate to discuss fiscal controls of production. "Our control is very tight," he said. "Our production manager submits cost estimates in advance. When all the costs are in, if they vary significantly from the cost estimate, the production manager has to explain the variation." If this man were in charge of a bank, I'd take my money out fast.

The planning and design of each book, whether by the designer or the production manager or the two together, involve deciding in detail how the book will look and how it will be made. This work is guided by the purpose of the book, its anticipated audience, the available manufacturing facilities, the production budget, and the personal predilections of the author, editor, designer, and production manager.

The trim size has to be determined: generally a smaller size for the book that is all text so it will sit comfortably in the hand, a somewhat larger size for the one that must display pictures effectively. The paper must be selected: perhaps an easy-on-the-eyes cream shade for the reading book and a bright blue-white for showing photographs to best advantage. The choice of type face and size may be less deliberate, though it will take into account the approximate number of pages the publisher wants in the finished book. The typographical details have to be specified: how to set chapter titles, footnotes, quotations in text, etc. There are literally hundreds of such decisions to make in order for the production of the book to proceed.

The production of each book falls into two distinct stages, and in many publishing houses, the responsibility for each of them is separately assigned. The first stage includes copyediting, typesetting, proofreading, color separation, if any, and page makeup to bring the book to the point when printing plates are ready to be made. The second stage consists of the selection and purchasing of text paper, printing, and binding.

The printing and binding of books seems to most publishers a simple matter to specify and even simpler to purchase. The specifications are far less complicated than those for composition, and the price quotations are easier to understand. The idea by which the production manager is driven seems simple and logically unassailable. Buy the printing and binding of *each book* at the lowest possible cost, and the result will be the lowest possible total cost for *all the books.*

It is simple but not unassailable, for *it is not true.* Buying the production of each book individually, even at the lowest possible price, will *guarantee* that the total cost will *not* be the lowest possible. Book-by-book buying of printing and binding wastes both money and time.

One result of buying manufacturing book by book is the dispersion of the publisher's production among many suppliers. Specifications do differ from book to book, being suitable to different suppliers. Even when specifications are identical, different suppliers may be chosen because prices for different quantities may differ. Even when specifications and prices are identical, workloads and the ability to deliver books quickly may differ. Gradually, the publisher's books are printed and bound in a growing number of different plants. Sometimes this dispersion is deliberately planned. Among the first things I heard from well-meaning colleagues from other companies when I got my first job in publishing in 1945, as production manager at the Viking Press, was: "Don't put all your eggs in one basket."

That thought was supposed to be holy writ, not to be doubted or debated. But even without this admonition to distribute the work, the natural functioning of publishers' methods for choosing suppliers ensures that it won't all be "in one basket."

A second result of buying manufacturing book by book is the dispersion of specifications among the titles. The price for making a book 6 x 9 inches, or $6\frac{1}{8}$ x 9 or 6 x $9\frac{1}{8}$, will be almost exactly the same. If the author or the editor or the designer prefers one or another for a particular book, why not indulge him? If someone would like to have a slightly thicker or thinner, brighter or duller, or smoother or rougher paper for a particular book, why not? There is no difference in cost. Sometimes the difference in cost actually justifies the difference in specifications, such as when an inferior paper is used to hold the total cost within a budget.

Although the book buyer will probably consider the dispersion of book production among many suppliers to be an internal matter in which he can have no interest, the variety in book sizes and papers is likely to be, on the face of it, appealing. Why not have variety? Certainly, suppressing variety for the sake of uniformity would be silly. Reducing variety will, in itself, contribute nothing to production speed, efficiency, or cost. However, controlling variety (and dispersion) where it really does matter, and using that control to reduce waste, can accomplish far more for the publisher (and the customer, in retail prices) than the canniest pitting of supplier against supplier in competitive bidding.

No matter how savagely a production manager may stir up competition, the most he can get from his suppliers is their profit. They cannot give any more than that if they are to be there to bid on the next job. But the waste created by the book-by-book "managing" of production is several times greater than the book manufacturers' profit, which is, in any case, already too low for the continued health of the industry.

The principal source of waste in the printing and binding of books (in quantities ranging from 1000 to 25,000) is the adjustment of machinery between titles. Each time the work is finished on one title and starts on another for which either the trim size or the paper is different (or, of course, both), adjustments must be made on the printing press, the sewing machine, the gatherer, and on virtually every machine in the bindery without exception. On shorter runs, the time spent adjusting may equal or exceed the time spent in actual production. For such books, the need to adjust machines *doubles* the printing and binding cost. As the quantities to be produced go up, the percentage of adjustment cost to total cost goes down.

Competition tends to keep the percentage of adjustment cost high. Each book manufacturer needs a continuous flow of work. After all, many of his costs, depreciation of equipment and basic labor costs, for example, are fixed, and they continue whether there is work in the plant or not. The manufacturer is very tempted to bid competitively even on work that does not neatly fit his equipment, preferring more adjustment and slower production to no work at all.

Even if the book does fit the manufacturer's equipment, which is deliberately engineered to accept the widest range of specifications, efficient production is very unlikely. A typical short-run book manufacturer is producing books in as many as 150 different page sizes. Taking account of the differences in paper (probably fifty distinct types, colors, and textures) and variations in other specifications, the manufacturer is producing literally thousands of book varieties. Much of his valuable production time, perhaps as much as 25 to 30 percent, is devoted to simply adjusting his machines.

Here, of all places, the slogan "Every book is different" sadly applies. The difference may be less than a normal eye would discern: one sixteenth of an inch in height, paper one ten-thousandth of an inch thinner or thicker, off-white shades of paper so subtle they can only be detected by a machine. The extent of the difference does not matter; any difference requires time, sometimes a great deal of time, to make adjustments while the machine and its crew produce nothing.

Of course, in order to make all these wasteful adjustments, the manufacturer has long preferred to have machines that adjust easily. So he uses presses that print sheets of paper that cost less to change from one size of book to another or one type of paper to another than presses that print continuous paper in rolls—but sheet-fed presses print much more slowly than roll-fed presses. Moreover, sheet-fed presses require the extra expense of cutting rolls of paper into sheets so they can be fed into the press. They also require the printed sheets to go through an extra folding operation, whereas the roll-fed press, printing five times faster than the sheet-fed press, delivers the pages already folded.

After printing, we have the binding operations. The binder uses a hand-fed sewing machine because it adjusts faster, but sewing would be less expensive on an automatically fed sewing machine. He has a slow-speed bindery line because it adjusts more easily, but the slower rate makes binding cost more. He puts dust jackets on the books by hand because adjusting a jacketing machine between titles costs too much.

□ *In recent years, the high cost of sewing many books has been avoided by the use of a "perfect binding," almost a sarcastic misnaming of a process by which the pages are glued together instead of sewed. Telephone directories and mass market paperbacks are familiar examples. Perfect binding has created a whole new set of problems that are very poorly handled by the book-by-book approach to buying manufacturing. The perfect binding process could deliver a much better product, and do it more economically than it frequently does, if it were not thwarted by the individual differences among the books in size and paper.*

There are other sources of waste in book manufacturing, some too technical and involved to explain here. Together, they represent a rich vein of gold for the publisher to mine—many times bigger than the book manufacturer's entire profit—but it is a lode to which the publisher searching for the lowest cost for each book is completely oblivious.

As rising labor costs have moved more book manufacturers away from labor-intensive methods to more mechanized, high-speed equipment, the penalty for book-by-book manufacture has increased, particularly for the typical trade book produced in quantities of 5000 to 10,000. For example, in plants where machine-fed sewing machines are the only ones available, they must be used, even for short runs, though the cost of adjusting them for each new title is high. This is equally true where sewing is avoided altogether in favor of a machine-applied perfect binding, though hand-fed sewing would have been less expensive for shorter runs.

Similarly in the printing step. Where the manufacturer has converted to web presses to be more competitive on long-run books, he has introduced cost handicaps for the shorter runs. Web presses, though they use less expensive paper, tend, particularly on short runs, to spoil a great deal and to do it less predictably. The result is higher production costs.

Some titles are booby-trapped in this situation. The first printing may clearly be less expensive on a web press, for instance, but subsequent smaller reprints may suffer, and the book may be retired as an active title because the high cost of small reprints cannot be tolerated.

The inexorable movement of book technology away from hand operations and easily adjusted simple machines toward more complicated, more expensive, and speedier machines has actually increased the penalty for book-by-book manufacture because these machines take longer and cost much more to adjust between books.

Because the need to adjust the machines arises from the *publisher's* specifications and the *publisher's* decision on who is to manufacture each book, it is the *publisher alone* who can control the time lost in adjusting machines.

If the book manufacturer had two titles to manufacture to identical size on identical paper—no matter how wildly different the editorial content or the colors and design of the jacket—the second title could be made without adjusting some of the machines. The printing press would require no adjustment at all. Machines that depend on the number of pages in the book, or its thickness, might need adjustment. If there were several such titles manufactured together, some would even go through those machines without adjustment.

This cannot work, of course, if the specifications differ, nor if the books of identical specifications are in different manufacturing plants. Nor can it work, it must be pointed out, if the publisher allows the manufacturer to put some other work into the middle of the ganged run because the manufacturer has a diplomatic problem with another customer.

There is another very substantial source of waste—spoilage, which requires cooperation between manufacturer and publisher to control, but it is certain nothing will begin to happen without strong initiative by the publisher. But spoilage is poorly understood and virtually ignored by publishing management. Yet spoilage—*unnecessary* spoilage, over and above the inevitable spoilage of material in producing the book—can account for a substantial portion of the publisher's production cost, perhaps as much as his production manager can save for him by estimating and reestimating costs from competing manufacturers.

Spoilage is a broad term used to describe the material (paper, cloth, binding board, etc.) that is spoiled, damaged, discarded, in the manufacture of the book. This material is supplied by the publisher, or at least charged to him, so he is concerned about how much is used. He is, theoretically, entitled to bill back to the manufacturer the cost of any "excessive" use of the publisher's material. Unfortunately, it is not possible to state, in advance, exactly what will go wrong at each stage of manufacture. If the same title is run several times, the spoilage will differ each time. The only thing that is certain is that some spoilage is inevitable. The only practical understanding between publisher and supplier is that spoilage will be "reasonable."

Many years ago, the Book Manufacturers Institute, a trade association, produced a schedule of permitted spoilages for printing and binding depending upon quantities and other factors. The schedule was generous to protect the manufacturer against publishers' claims for excessive spoilage. Not surprisingly, it was a cause of contention between publishers and manufacturers. It eventually fell into disuse, and the situation reverted to the "reasonable" spoilage allowance.

Although the manufacturers' proposed spoilage allowances were flawed, that was not the principal problem. Counterproposals by publishers' production managers seemed unreasonable from the other direction. The simple fact is that a schedule of allowable spoilage, to be applied *book by book,* is a practical impossibility.

By its nature, spoilage can only be measured as an average, over many operations and many books. A printing press that spoils 2 percent of the sheets passing through it, for instance, does not uniformly spoil every fiftieth sheet. Several thousand sheets may go through perfectly, and then the spoilage may be 15 percent on the next several hundred. The accident of which publisher's book went through the press at which moment would result in very different spoilage costs for the two books and the two publishers.

This necessarily broad approximation of the boundaries of permissible spoilage tends to discourage publishers from attempting to obtain reimbursement for excessive spoilage except in rare, extremely flagrant cases. In any situation short of that, an arbitrator is more likely to be sympathetic to the manufacturer than the publisher. Of course, charging for spoilage would not be nearly so rewarding as reducing spoilage—even below "reasonable" levels.

Functionally, there are at least three distinct kinds of spoilage. We have already discussed the first one: the damage to material that occurs at each machine or hand operation in the manufacturing process. This "operating" spoilage occurs in two ways. The first, make-ready spoilage, is the material spoiled in adjusting the machine from book to book. Whether the machine is a printing press, a folder, a casing-in machine (applying the hard cover to the book), or any other, the make-ready spoilage depends on the complexity of the machine, its operating condition, the skill of the operator, and the amount of adjustment required. For example, a folding machine going from one book to another book of the same size, printed on the same paper, requires no adjustment at all. The make-ready spoilage is zero.

When these two books reach the casing-in operation, because they may differ in number of pages, and therefore in thickness, the casing-in machine will require adjustment and may spoil some copies. On the other hand, by changing the sequence in which books go into the casing-in operation, two books may be selected to succeed each other that may have required adjustment of the folding machine but will *not* require adjustment of the casing-in machine.

Two parenthetical observations: At the same time that the avoidance of machine adjustment is saving the cost of make-ready spoilage, it is also saving machine time, and therefore money, for the book manufacturer—a saving that, when it occurs in the normal book-by-book buying prevalent among publishers, is *never* passed along to the publisher. Further, the saving in spoilage and machine time, for example, in folding two titles of the same size and on the same paper, is realized *only* if the one title follows immediately after the other.

Minimizing make-ready spoilage depends partly on the skill of the book manufacturer in making machine adjustments but much more on minimizing or avoiding the need for those adjustments. This is mostly under the control of the publisher, who determines the specifications of his books and which ones will be made by which manufacturers, though he cannot ensure that the manufacturer will put them through each operation in the most advantageous sequence.

The second way in which operating spoilage occurs is in processing the work after the machine has been adjusted to accept the particular book. This processing spoilage, called running spoilage, is usually relatively minor and is measured as a percentage of units going through the process. The reason that books in smaller quantities have higher percentages of spoilage is that the make-ready spoilage, which occurs at the start of each operation, is divided over fewer copies.

Running spoilage results primarily from the level of skill of the operators and the mechanical condition of the equipment. (Faulty bearings can ruin a great deal of paper going through a printing press.) Neither of these can be determined by examining a small sample of work going through at any particular moment. Chance variations create confusion in any small group of observations. The best way to determine operator skill *and* mechanical condition is through a control chart (described in Chapter 15, on computerization), which can measure the range of variation in performance as well as detect when the situation has changed significantly.

The second kind of spoilage results from uneven production of different portions of the book. The book is printed on large sheets of paper that may contain, for example, 64 pages, which are then folded into signatures of 16 or 32 pages each. (On web presses, printing from rolls of paper, the action is different, but the results are the same.) If a completed book will require 5 sheets (5 sheets times 64 pages equals 320 pages), the printer may divide the available paper by five to start with the same number of pieces for each of the five press runs. But his spoilage will be different on each run, unpredictably different, so he will not know which run will have the fewest *good* sheets until all five runs are complete.

The run that yields the fewest good sheets determines the maximum number of books that can be assembled. For example, if the manufacturer has only 4500 copies of the second sheet, he can produce no more than 4500 copies of the book even if he has 4900 copies of each of the other four sheets. On the typical book run, 5000 copies or less, this uneven delivery is the largest source of spoilage, and it is a significant source even on longer runs.

This uneven delivery, in turn, routinely causes uneven delivery between "book blocks" (the sewed and glued pages) and the "cases" (hard covers). The book manufacturer usually does not wait, before starting to make cases, to see how many complete books he will have, but estimates the number he will need. Because the publisher is paying for the material and the manufacturer is paid only for finished copies delivered, he will estimate on the high side. It is always better to be left with too many cases rather than too many blocks when the book leaves the casing-in machine.

Since spoilages are not precisely predictable, waste due to uneven delivery can be greatly reduced by moving away from title-by-title manufacturing, in which frequently the paper is bought for a particular run of a particular title. If variety in trim sizes and papers is reduced and books of similar specifications are assigned to one manufacturer, it will be possible to maintain stocks of paper against which the next title to be printed can draw. When this happens, the printer can print a precise quantity of each sheet for that book, regardless of the spoilage on any sheet. The spoilage will then be that minimum amount of paper damaged on the press, no more. The book will leave the press with the same number of copies of every page. There may be spoilage in later operations, but the principal source of spoilage through uneven delivery will have disappeared.

    □ *The publisher who does this will have to be sure to overcome years of Pavlovian conditioning in the printer. Even if a large inventory of paper is there and the printer can deliver even quantities of all sheets regardless of spoilage, I have found that, unless sternly reminded, the printer may take from the inventory the theoretical quantity that would have been purchased for the book, proceed to divide that quantity into even piles—and deliver uneven quantities as in the past.*

The third kind of spoilage results from remnants, usually of paper or cloth, left from the production of a particular title. Remnants too small to be used on any other book are frequently scrapped, though together they may represent a significant investment. At McGraw-Hill, before standardization of paper and cloth were introduced in the late 1960s, spoilage from remnants alone amounted to at least several tens of thousands of dollars a year.

Remnants, too, are the result of title-by-title buying. They may result when the quantity to be produced changes from the time paper is ordered to the time the book goes on press. Or they may occur when the printer, rather than dividing the paper into as many piles as he has sheets to print, prints a safely reduced quantity of each sheet, holding some paper in reserve against unusual spoilage. Not enough unusual spoilage produces an unusable remnant.

This kind of spoilage, unusable remnants, has been reduced by the recent practice of some paper mills of maintaining an inventory of the more popular papers on the printer's premises. Publishers draw from these stocks as the need arises, using only as many sheets as needed for that particular book and paying only for what they use. In well-managed printing plants, this practice has also reduced the spoilage that comes from printing uneven quantities of different portions of the book.

A very first step toward correcting the waste of machine adjustments and of excessive spoilage is putting together enough books of one size and on one paper to make gang runs possible if these books are all manufactured in the same plant. Small publishers can do this only to a limited degree (but still quite effectively), but can perhaps cooperate with others or have the production organized for them by book manufacturers such as Donnelley (about which more later). Getting all the people involved in the publishing house to agree to changes in specification, frequently minor and sometimes microscopic, is not easy, as I can testify from experience.

In the late 1940s and early 1950s, Doubleday produced books in two locations. The new, high-speed Hanover plant produced books in one size only, 5½ x 8¼ inches. There were three papers to choose from, and certain minimum printing quantities had to be ordered. Very few Doubleday titles were designed to meet these conditions.

Most of the publishing department's requirements were produced at the more flexible facilities at Country Life Press in Garden City (where we were producing books in more than 250 different sizes), while most of the Literary Guild and other book club work was done at Hanover.

Because the Hanover plant could produce books for slightly less than half, on the average, of their cost at Country Life Press, we tried to pick out any trade titles that would be needed in substantial quantities and could conform to the Hanover requirements. Whenever I detected such a title, I would call it to the attention of the trade department so they could consider the specifications with Hanover in mind.

Our most dramatic confrontation occurred over a very important book. Edna Ferber, the best-selling author, had left Doubleday for a number of years, but finally, after much wooing, the editorial department won her back. Her first new book, *Giant*, was an important event. A large printing was planned in a trim size of $5\frac{5}{8}$ x $8\frac{3}{8}$ inches.

We knew that if we could make the book one-eighth inch smaller in each dimension, we could produce the book at Hanover, which would reduce the cost on the first printing alone by $10,000, and we would be able to get reprints in one third the time. The saving to the company would actually be even greater because Hanover's prices had been artificially inflated whereas Garden City's were real.

The editor refused. Edna Ferber was too important. All her previous books had been $5\frac{5}{8}$ x $8\frac{3}{8}$. We could easily save $10,000, he said, only to throw away hundreds of thousands by alienating a major author who had just returned to the fold.

Reluctantly, I took the matter to Doug Black, the president, for him to mediate. He suggested that the editor explain the situation to Edna Ferber, offer to put part of the savings into additional advertising, and abide by her preference. To everyone's amazement, including mine, the editor came back from that lunch to report that Edna Ferber didn't care about the size. If another size was more convenient for us, it was perfectly agreeable to her. Discussions of trim size went much more smoothly thereafter.

A similar attempt at McGraw-Hill some years later did not fare as well. Back in the 1960s, before the evidence of the staggering cost of McGraw-Hill's laissez faire production policy resulted in the intervention of top management, I made what inroads toward standardization I could by persuasion, one title at a time. A popular trim size in McGraw-Hill's large College Division was 6 x 9 inches. A similar size used by the very much smaller Trade Division was $6\frac{1}{8}$ x $9\frac{1}{4}$ inches. If we were to standardize the sizes, it made sense that Trade should change its handful of titles rather than have College change hundreds.

Trade was about to publish a biography of Pope John XXIII, and I suggested to the general manager of Trade that perhaps this could be the first title to be shifted to the 6 x 9 size. He explained to me that "trade publishing is different from college publishing," and that the college market did not have the sophistication of the trade market, and that College could therefore accept specifications that would destroy the sale possibilities for a trade book. He could understand that *I*, being responsible for manufacturing, might be prepared to destroy this important book, or the entire prospects of the Trade Division, for the sake of some foolish production theory, but *he* would not allow it. My misguided suggestion could only result in catastrophe.

So the pope's biography was, of course, made in the $6\frac{1}{8}$ x $9\frac{1}{4}$ size, as he wished. I had the bindery cut one copy down to the 6 x 9 size. With this copy and a normal $6\frac{1}{8}$ x $9\frac{1}{4}$ book in hand, I went to the general manager of Trade and set one copy on one corner of his desk, the other on another corner.

"How do you like them?" I asked.

He looked first at one copy, then at the other.

"They look great," he said. "Are these books different in some way?"

I assured him they were different, and he searched through each book trying to figure it out. Then I took the two books and stood them together in front of him, making the slight difference in size obvious. His response was rich and colorful.

The Trade Division persisted for a long time, however, in insisting on the larger size for its books, even though that policy attributed a greater sophistication to the public in distinguishing trim size than the general manager himself possessed. Today, the Trade Division uses the 6 x 9 size, and if any sales catastrophes have occurred, no one has attributed them to the trim size.

It is a lot easier, of course, when the one who wishes to standardize is in control. When Collier Books, the paperback division at Crowell-Collier and Macmillan, was organized in the early 1960s, we needed to manufacture many titles in small quantities at low cost.

The Collier Books were planned to be identical to the standard mass market paperback. Such books were, and are, manufactured by a number of plants around the country on roll-fed presses, which produce up to 128 pages in one pass and deliver up to four signatures of 32 pages. One of the plants doing this work was J. W. Clement in Buffalo, New York (now part of the Arcata Group).

We set up certain manufacturing conditions for Collier Books at J. W. Clement. A ganged printing and binding run of at least 50 titles would begin on the first working day of each month and would continue uninterrupted until all the books were completed. (We began with 50 titles each month and soon added reprints, at which point we were printing 60, 70, or 80 titles in one gang.) Collier books would be manufactured only in these monthly gangs.

All Collier books would be multiples of 32 pages. We would use two papers only: a thinner paper for longer books and a thicker paper for shorter books.

Books would be printed in multiples of 10,000 copies. This (and the restriction to two papers) made it easy to combine the extra 32s, or 64s, from different titles into full 128-page forms to ensure that the press ran full every time; that is, each revolution of the press might be turning out pages for two titles at the same time.

J. W. Clement combined pages from different books as necessary to run the press a full 128 pages each time. They started the run on one paper and ran all the titles that required it, then changed the press over to the other paper and ran the balance of the titles. On the binding machine, they started with either the very thickest or the very thinnest book and adjusted the machine in small increments as they moved from one extreme of bulk to the other.

In consideration of this arrangement, we got the same price schedule as for Pocket Books titles produced in 100,000-copy quantities. Since the average Pocket Book run was less than 100,000, Collier Books, in 10,000-copy quantities, were costing, on the average (except for paper, which was of higher quality for Collier Books), *less* than the mass market paperbacks produced for Pocket Books.

The result for Collier Books was not only a much lower cost than a publisher making 10,000 copies should expect. We also avoided the publisher's usual hard choice: to print a cautious minimal quantity with a high cost *per copy* or to print many copies to achieve a lower cost per copy with a high *total* cost—and the danger of being left with large stocks of unsold books. The 10,000-copy initial Collier Books quantity was based on the assumption that every title would be reprinted, perhaps many times, since a total sales of 10,000 was not an attractive business prospect; each title had been chosen with the expectation that it would sell several times that many. Some titles were never reprinted, of course, but they did not represent, in 10,000 copies (of which most were certain to be sold however weak the book), an awesome manufacturing loss.

Inventories were kept low, averaging something like 5000 to 7500 copies, an unheard-of inventory level for a paperback publisher. Reprints could be produced very quickly (much more quickly than Pocket Books was able to do, for example). If a gang run was about to start, books for any reprint title could be ready in one or two weeks; if a run had just finished, books could be ready in three or four weeks. Paper was always on hand. There was no need to make a reprinting decision until copies of the previous edition were, literally, almost down to zero.

□ *Low production costs were not enough to save Collier from the precipitous retrenchment that occurred in the early 1960s, when Crowell-Collier stock plunged in value and the banks called in substantial outstanding loans. The fledgling Collier organization was dissolved and the name became an imprint in Macmillan paperback publishing.*

McGraw-Hill, where I went from Crowell-Collier in 1964, was a much more complicated situation. It had operated for many years under the policy of buying production title by title, seeking the lowest practical cost for each printing, with due regard for loyalty to long-term suppliers. Although management had also supported, over the years, the idea of standardization, there was no apparent economic advantage to standard specifications as long as the materials and manufacturing were bought individually.

The company operated under a decentralized system whereby the profit centers, each publishing division, were free to handle production to suit themselves. Production was costing the company millions more than it should. Books were taking much longer to produce than necessary. Quality, particularly in the grades of paper and binding material, was lower than it could have been for the equivalent cost. But management's attention was on other aspects of publishing. After several futile skirmishes with executives in the publishing divisions, I decided to bring the facts to the attention of top management.

To do this, I surveyed one year's production across all the divisions and presented the results, which showed a somewhat startled company management some interesting figures:

1. Books were being made in 144 trim sizes, some differing by only one sixteenth of an inch.

2. Books were being printed on 138 kinds of paper.
3. The company's manufacturing was dispersed among 55 printing plants.
4. As a result of the wide variations in paper and the dispersion of work, the company had an inventory of 679 distinct paper lots worth $1 million, but, in spite of this large investment, seven times out of ten, paper had to be specially bought to print a particular book.
5. In cases of popular trim sizes, the value of standardization was vitiated by the dispersion of the work. Books in the 6 x 9 size, for example, were printed in 40 separate pressrooms, so for practical purposes they could just as well have been in 40 sizes. The $6\frac{3}{8}$ x $9\frac{1}{4}$ size was printed in 26 plants.

□ *Publishers who may be inclined to read this with a superior smile should tally similar information on their own publications and then relate it to the* number of titles *and the* number of autonomous publishing departments *in their company.*
McGraw-Hill published 800 titles a year in twelve or thirteen publishing divisions. The number of specification variations is startling in an absolute sense, but it is relatively similar to what one will find, with very few exceptions, in any publishing house.

It was a situation that had developed over many years, but it was startling to see the results of the thousands of book-by-book decisions. A large number of trim sizes spread over a large number of manufacturing plants is not philosophically bad in itself. The disadvantage is strictly economic.

The results were startling enough, and the prospect of economic advantage attractive enough, that McGraw-Hill's management decided to overhaul its buying of manufacturing. It was decided to:

1. Limit book sizes to 12 basic sizes, with changes permitted only for truly exceptional reasons.
2. Limit papers, similarly, to 15 basic papers.
3. Assemble books of similar specifications so that those in one trim size would be manufactured in only one or, at most, two plants.
4. Make McGraw-Hill's participation in the scheduling of the company's work in each plant a condition for placing work in that plant.

The concentration of work in fewer plants put enough McGraw-Hill "eggs in one basket" to justify stationing a member of my staff permanently in one of those plants to perform a variety of functions

that smoothed production and reduced costs. He checked the arrival of
our paper and cloth, answered the plant's queries on all matters
quickly, avoiding delays or confusion, approved quality, monitored
schedules, assured prompt shipment in full carload quantities,
interpreted to my office any McGraw-Hill practices that created
avoidable problems, and so on.

Within one year, McGraw-Hill's identifiable savings on
manufacturing were running at the rate of $2.5 million annually, and
substantial additional savings were realized later. Average production
time per title was reduced by several weeks, and delivery dates were
more precisely controlled, which, among other things, aided greatly in
holding down the inventory investment in bound books.

How was this saving achieved? The average paper order went from
about 7000 pounds to about 100,000 pounds, at greatly improved
prices. At the same time, the average paper inventory investment was
decreased from $1 million to $200,000, and paper was on hand for
four printings out of five instead of fewer than two out of five.

Paper use was reduced by combining the printing of several titles
so the spoilage that is an inevitable cost of the first make-ready in
printing and binding served for eight or ten succeeding books.

The waste resulting from printing uneven quantities of each sheet
was greatly reduced. Because the printer used paper from a
theoretically endless inventory for each printing form (instead of
dividing the available paper among the forms for each book), he was
able to deliver very nearly the exact number of printed sheets needed
of each form, sharply reducing the discarding of excess signatures after
a book was gathered. For average printings at the 3000 to 4000 level,
which was typical for McGraw-Hill, the saving of paper by this minor
maneuver alone was approximately 2 percent of the total paper
consumption for each run.

Paper costs were further reduced because largely useless paper
remnants resulting from buying paper book by book were no longer
being created.

There were savings in trucking costs at every turn. Paper was
delivered to the printers in full carloads. Jackets, printed endpapers,
and similar book elements moved from fewer suppliers to fewer users
at substantial savings. All books, even urgently needed reprints of 500
or 1000 copies, arrived at the warehouse as part of densely packed full
truckloads.

Even such a small item as bulk cartons for finished books
contributed its share. The number of sizes of cartons was reduced and,

of course, they were purchased more frequently in larger, more economical quantities.

The major saving resulted, of course, from better organization of the work of printing and binding, which was made possible by the gathering of like work into fewer plants.

Printing several titles in sequence reduced the cost of machine adjustments on the press, on the gathering machine, on the sewing machine, the rounder and backer, and on the casing-in and the jacketing machines. For many book sizes, cloth and board for cases were bought already cut to size (avoiding waste), and the case-making and case-stamping machines were adjusted to go from one title to another in minutes.

Because case-making and stamping were made easy and quick, those operations could start *after* the books were gathered instead of before, so the case count could be more accurate.

The assurance of a steady flow of work in given sizes on standard papers in signatures of 32 pages made it possible to automate certain sizes (notably the popular 6 x 9 size) in such a way that the costs of folding, gathering, and sewing (a substantial part of the binding operation) were cut very nearly in half, with a small additional paper saving thrown in.

In other sizes, the ability to combine the printing of several titles using the same paper made it possible to enjoy the economies of web press printing for quantities normally completely uneconomical for these machines. The machines, which are engineered to print a book in a large quantity, thought that was what they were doing when, in fact, they were printing a combination of small quantities of several books. Paper in rolls is less expensive, and there were substantial savings in presswork and folding.

These economies, and many more that followed, were made possible by a more rational attitude toward setting physical specifications and by making the decision of where to manufacture a specific book on solid grounds of company interest rather than on a frivolous "don't put your eggs in one basket" non sequitur or on the accident of which salesman sold which production manager in what publishing division. Putting books where the manufacture of one helped reduce the costs of manufacturing another was a simple enough rule to follow.

A great deal of our success was due, however, to a (still) unique scheduling system, which we developed to control the progress of McGraw-Hill's work in the various manufacturing plants. The scheduling system actually preceded the survey of trim sizes and papers, to some degree inspired it, and certainly enabled us to move very quickly after management agreed that the situation needed correcting.

Before, book production had been scheduled in exactly the way production work is scheduled at all publishing houses: For each new book, a detailed calendar of steps was elaborated, setting down when composition would begin, when galleys would be delivered, when they would be returned, and so on, through every step in the process to the date that finished books were to be delivered to the publisher's warehouse. Similarly, for each reprint, the decision of how many copies were wanted and the most desirable delivery date were communicated to the production department, which ordered the necessary materials and manufacturing steps—paper, jackets, presswork, binding, etc.—and negotiated the date on which each step would be performed.

The schedules for new books stretched over many months, perhaps six to ten, and reprint schedules ranged from six weeks to as much as four months, depending on the size and complexity of the book. The schedule for each book was constructed by stringing out logical time blocks. Thus, if setting type required eight weeks, galleys would be ready at the end of that period, say on X date; allowing two weeks for reading meant they would be returned on X plus two weeks; then four weeks would be added to that to give the compositor time to correct and make up pages; and so on. The printer and binder were among the large number of recipients of the detailed schedule, which showed that six months or ten months hence they would receive this title to print or bind in some stated tentative quantity. The schedule indicated the time interval, usually generous and always reasonable, within which their work would have to be done. At this distance from the event, the only intelligent reaction the printer or binder could have was judging whether the time allowed for his task was enough for a book of that size and complexity. If it seemed insufficient, a different interval was negotiated. Then the schedule was filed away with the understanding, as with virtually all new book schedules from all publishing houses, that the problem would really be dealt with when the work was imminent.

Print and bind dates for reprintings were treated somewhat more urgently. Even in these cases, though, there was frequently an element of uncertainty, such as when paper would *really* arrive. And there was frequently also the lack of precision in the manufacturer's own plant schedules, which depended so much on whether some other publisher's paper or printing plates would arrive according to schedule.

For each of our supplier plants, we were only one of many customers, and by no means the most delinquent, either in slippage of schedules or in informing the supplier of these slippages. Every supplier was beset by 100 or more publishers, each demanding work to be performed at almost unpredictable times, in a bewildering variety of shapes and sizes, in a great range of number of pages and number of copies. Each publisher demanded immediate attention to his titles, making unreliable promises about when paper would be there, when the final quantity would be firmly established, or swearing that jackets or cartons or binding dies would arrive the following morning.

If, as is usually the case, the plant does not do the typesetting, it rarely knows in advance precisely when a new title will be ready to print and certainly not when it will receive an anguished call from a publisher for a reprint because he has just run out of a best-seller. The plant manager knows that even if the materials are on hand, an order he has just received for 5000 copies may at any moment be changed to 6000 or 10,000 or canceled altogether.

The only exceptions were the few plants operating giant equipment, costing hundreds of dollars per hour, which insisted on an orderly advance allocation of equipment time on a precise schedule. Such plants generally had customer service departments, which took the initiative, well in advance of printing and binding, to find out repeatedly from each publisher exactly where each project stood, how much it was delayed, what the dangers were of further delay, etc., and negotiated new and more reliable plant reservations.

For the short-run plant, the variety of work in sizes, shapes, and quantities, the uncertainty of daily work levels, the pleas by customers to give priority to an emergency order, etc., create management and scheduling problems of a very special nature. Actually, although they may have scheduling departments, not a single one of these book manufacturing plants actually schedules. What they call scheduling is actually queuing; that is, forming a line of work in front of each operation. The "scheduling" department simply sees that each operation has such a queue in front of it and polices and rearranges the order within the queue to satisfy customers' demands and to try to combine work in the most economical sequence.

In such situations, planning ahead more than a few days is virtually impossible. A frequent practice in the short-run book manufacturing plant is to plan the week's work in rough form on the preceding

Friday and to revise the plan the next Wednesday or Thursday from the debris of the changes, cancellations, and publisher emergencies. Planning in any real sense applies only two or three days ahead.

The need for the queues builds technically unnecessary delays into the schedules. The printer wants three weeks to print a book that will actually be one day's work; he needs the flexibility of manipulating the queue in front of the press and the assurance that the press will not run out of work. Similarly, the binder will want four weeks to do work that takes no more than a day and a half.

Therefore, when the publisher makes his individual book schedules, he has to allow three or four weeks for an operation like printing or binding, which might actually take only one or two days. No delivery promises from the manufacturer have any value at all, and most make no promises, until a book has actually and physically reached the queue.

At that point, the schedule made for each book months before counts for nothing. As each book reaches the printing stage, it takes its position in the queue. If the queue is of "normal" length, the day's printing work gets done in the three weeks allowed and the book is "on schedule." If the queue is long or if the book arrives late, there are problems.

The way in which a publisher can make up lost time is by getting the manufacturer to let him, as Londoners would say at a bus stop, "jump the queue" by moving his title to the head of the line. Such maneuvers are generally resisted by the manufacturer. Not only do they burden a not-too-sophisticated "scheduling department" with severe complications in keeping track of its work flow, but they invite the possibility that some other book on that queue will be delayed beyond its original schedule, creating a problem for another publisher.

One form of queue-jumping that is a nuisance to the manufacturer, but is at least ethically acceptable, is trading places in the queue among the publisher's own books. So a frequent response to the publisher's desperate plea is: "If you will take Title B three weeks later than we promised it, we can get Title A for you two weeks earlier than we now project." But even when the book to be bumped is for the same publisher, it might be for a different division or a different editor, so internal negotiation is almost always necessary before the production manager can respond to such an offer.

□ *Even though the trading of queue positions was the easiest (and sometimes the only) way to improve a bad delivery date for any book, and this was universally recognized by manufacturer and publisher as a proper transaction, it was rarely possible because of the dispersion of work. On my first job in publishing, back in 1946, the next title we had to send out was denied to the manufacturer who had gotten the previous two books because "we don't want to be competing with ourselves." The titles in question were each to be printed in a 5000-copy quantity; the plant in question produced 75,000 books each day. The notion that our three 5000-copy books—15,000 out of their monthly production of 2,000,000—would somehow create a bottleneck, or that the plant would refrain from seeking work from the other hundred publishers it served in order not to thwart our strategy, struck me as odd even in that naive period of my apprenticeship.*

It seemed to me that the only way to resolve the scheduling problems at McGraw-Hill and relieve the mounting pressure on everyone was, essentially, to take the unprecedented step of pushing the manufacturer's scheduling department out of the way and taking control ourselves of our own part of each queue. Then we could arrange the work in a sequence suitable to us and progress from queueing to actual scheduling.

The difference between scheduling and queueing is subtle but highly significant. An automobile plant or an oil refiner schedules; a machine shop or a short-run book manufacturer queues. Queueing is the only practical method when the plant does not control the preceding steps, so it cannot say with certainty that a given job will be ready for processing at a definite time. A printer who planned the work for each press on the basis of the statements by each of his publisher customers as to when paper would arrive, plates would be ready, a final decision on quantity made, etc., would go insane first and bankrupt second. The only practical course the printer can take, given the hundreds of books that will be ready for each press at some point, is to wait until each is truly ready and deal with it at that time. This creates real queues of real work waiting their turn at each step in the process.

The typical sight in a book pressroom is a stack of printing plates (the queue), usually several days' work, waiting in front of each printing press. In the bindery, there are skids of printed sheets in front of the folders, skids of folded signatures in front of the gatherers, and so on. The space in the plant devoted to these queues ("work in progress," in the parlance of the industry) is usually greater than the space devoted to getting the work done.

Scheduling also creates queues before each operation, but these are not physical queues but theoretical lists of work that will be ready for that operation at some precise time in the future and have, accordingly, been assigned a position in the queue. In scheduling, the work queue at a previous step can be reshuffled to make succeeding queues run more smoothly. For example, it is not advisable to put too many long books successively through a gathering and sewing line (where work proceeds according to number of *pages*) because it will cause a shortage of work in casing in (where work proceeds according to number of *books*) when the books reach that point. The object is to have each operation working as close to capacity as possible and to have as little "work in progress" as possible physically cluttering up the place.

In 1964, when I considered this problem on behalf of McGraw-Hill, the idea that a publisher would involve himself in the internal planning of a supplier's plant was a little wild, to say the least, but since the supplier could not control the operations preceding his own and we could, I saw no alternative. We started with our most important supplier and, after demonstrating success, worked our way through the others.

We agreed that first, all work would be scheduled for a particular week rather than a particular day and would be "on schedule" if it was completed by the end of the day on Friday. This created a weekly batch of books that could go through each manufacturing step in the sequence that would result in the least cost and smoothest work flow.

We were able to assign many of the titles to a weekly batch far in advance, and we would supply the plant each week with the latest revision of the list of our titles in weekly batches stretching far into the future. So, for example, a book just starting composition would be entered into a batch perhaps forty weeks hence. As the book progressed through the various stages of production, the title would be moved forward or back accordingly. Or titles that normally required reprinting before the beginning of the school year were entered, in advance, in the appropriate week with a tentative quantity. As the time approached, the quantity might go up or down or, if sales were disappointing, the book might drop from the list altogether. But each week, the plant would get our expectation, *as of that moment,* of when each title would be ready for actual production for approximately a full year in advance.

This told the plant's scheduling department precisely what work was projected for McGraw-Hill and precisely how much of it would be ready for each machine in the plant at the beginning of each week in the future—and, of course, how much machine time that work would require. One of the first dividends of this innovation *to the plant* was the ability to spot, far in advance, heavy and light work weeks. We were able, with very little effort, to advance or postpone books here and there with no inconvenience to McGraw-Hill, to even out the workload, or to reduce our demands when the plant was expecting a great deal of work for other publishers.

The change in the ambience of McGraw-Hill's manufacturing department was dramatic. The hysteria and tension that had previously accompanied the handling of 9000 printings a year disappeared. The phones were almost quiet. Fewer people were handling more work, but the attitude was relaxed and almost casual. Changing the delivery date of a book involved no more than moving a card on the schedule board. (The schedule boards were simply photocopied each Friday and copies sent to everyone concerned.)

Weeks were chopped from manufacturing times. There were, essentially, no queues. The press was ready to receive the book when the book was ready for the press. The same was true at the bindery.

The weekly schedules showed us precisely where and when particular types and amounts of paper and binding cloth were needed, when binding dies or jackets had to be ready. Planning was virtually effortless. Our use and purchase of materials were better planned, and our inventories, particularly where we had large volumes of work, were kept ridiculously low in comparison with previous levels.

As we gained experience, we learned to use the schedules even more effectively to cut costs as well as save time. In plants where we had work of various sizes and types, we grouped the titles into batches that could be produced together economically.

After we won McGraw-Hill management over to the idea of standard sizes and papers, the schedule boards were a helpful guide, showing how work should be reallocated among plants to make each one produce more economically. Still later, other benefits developed. It was no longer necessary or useful to issue the usual detailed printing or binding order to a plant to authorize work. Moreover, since many books were now manufactured in batches in which some steps were combined for economy, invoicing book by book became somewhat complicated. So the weekly schedule became the manufacturing order for all the titles listed on it, saving hours of typing, proofreading, and filing time, and at the same time it became the basis for a weekly invoice that was easy to check against the information in the schedule.

The McGraw-Hill staff required to handle the production of 800 new titles and 8000 reprints annually, using this system, is less than half of what it was using the conventional production system, and the situation is under incomparably tighter control. Manufacturing schedules are weeks shorter, and a missed delivery date, instead of being a common occurrence, is an extraordinary event. The savings in manufacturing cost was running about $2.5 million annually when I left McGraw-Hill in 1969. My former colleagues tell me it is considerably greater now. Why, then, is this still the only publisher who schedules his work at his suppliers? I wish I knew!

I have said it is the publisher who controls the specifications as well as the placement of his manufacturing work, so it is the publisher who must organize it to move from the waste of title-by-title buying to a more rational organization. All this may now be changing.

R. R. Donnelley, the largest printing company in the United States, has opened a plant in Harrisonburg, Virginia, designed primarily to produce on web presses and high-speed binding equipment, to standard specifications, the work normally produced by others on sheet-fed presses and low-speed binding equipment. The plant is large enough, and Donnelley rich enough, to have several parallel lines so that different standards can be processed simultaneously.

□ *Back in the 1960s, a Donnelley study group submitted a report to its management concluding that short-run book manufacturing could never be profitable and that it should not enter the field. I was then in charge of manufacturing at McGraw-Hill, and I recall an afternoon at the New York Yacht Club arguing with the Donnelley executives, who had unveiled the study to us, against its conclusions. I maintained that short-run production could be very profitable on web presses if approached imaginatively, with standardization and functional scheduling as a requirement. I do not kid myself that that discussion changed Donnelley's direction, but it is nice to see that Harrisonburg is organized almost precisely along the lines I advocated at that meeting.*

If the Harrisonburg plant develops as planned, it will offer large and small publishers an effortless opportunity to benefit from production line economies, with no need to do any organizing themselves. Because it will offer a great deal of book manufacturing capacity at very favorable prices, Harrisonburg will reduce the work available to other manufacturers; as a result, at least some existing plants are almost certainly destined to leave the scene.

The effect of Harrisonburg—beneficial for publishers, devastating for trade book manufacturers—may be blunted if Donnelley management deviates from its apparent goals or dilutes the standards, but it is hard to see why that should happen.

The production processes discussed thus far are the second group of operations involved in creating the physical book: the printing and binding. What of the first manufacturing steps: book design, copyediting, and typesetting? These activities are intertwined, but in different publishing houses the three functions may have different emphases. They are sometimes under the control of the editorial department, and the supervisor of all three may be the managing editor. Although the design function will never dictate to editorial, it is, in some houses, distinctly senior to production in the sense that typesetting conforms to the plan laid out by the designer. In the more cost-conscious houses, the designer is expected to do his work within the restrictions imposed by the most economical typesetting methods.

The organization of these operations involves a completely different perspective than the organization of printing and binding. There is no economic advantage in setting the type for several books at one time— or, for that matter, in designing several books at one time. Each title can be treated individually; indeed, each title *must* be treated individually. This is obvious in copyediting, but it is also true of design and typesetting. Two mystery novels in the same trim size, with the same number of pages, have identical printing and binding problems, but the design and composition would be different because, for example, the two books would almost certainly have a different number of words per page.

Yet, the fact that some of these manufacturing steps do not impose economic limitations on variety does not suggest that variety is desirable for its own sake or that the operations are best handled in a completely undisciplined manner.

Let us consider a key operation that is typically badly organized by publishers: typesetting. In setting type, publishers frequently use modern typesetting equipment, but they do so using the *methods* of old technologies, at great cost in time, convenience, and money.

When Gutenberg invented movable type, he created an industry in which the compositor translates into type the words of the author so that they can be reproduced in quantity on some sort of printing press. For a long time after Gutenberg, the compositor set the type one letter at a time, spacing out each line to the "full measure" before beginning the next one. Obviously, the compositor's work had to be checked, so proofreading evolved. The situation did not change in substance when movable type was replaced by movable matrices with the invention of the Linotype machine, except that the Linotype machine itself could make mistakes, even if the compositor didn't, so proofreading became, if anything, even more important.

Proofreading was essential to check not only the compositor's first step but also each subsequent step. The correction itself had to be checked, since the compositor might introduce new errors in resetting the line or the rest of the paragraph. When the corrected galleys were made into pages, even though no new typesetting was involved, the pages had to be checked to see that no lines had been dropped and that no type had been damaged, or removed and incorrectly replaced. A final check had to be made as close to presstime as possible, because errors could occur with each handling. At the very least, the final proof had to be examined for broken letters or type worn down by careless proofing.

When photographic composition of type became more common in the late 1950s, it was no longer necessary to look for broken letters (though the opaquer's brush frequently deformed photographic type), but the proofreader was still needed to search for the errors of the keyboarder and the page-maker.

The need to proofread affected the production of books in two unfortunate but virtually inescapable ways. First, it slowed down the composition process itself. Proofs had to go back to the publisher and to the author for reading. In each case, they would seldom be read immediately, so there was a delay, and an unpredictable one, in the return of each batch of proof to the compositor. Since the compositor could not possibly know exactly when the proof would come back or how extensive the corrections would be and how much time they would require, he could not know when he would resume work on that book or when he would be finished. He had no recourse except to place each returned batch of proof in a queue, awaiting its turn for attention. The result is that setting the type for a book takes weeks, more usually months, when it requires no more than days.

Proofreading has also affected typesetting by creating "author's alterations." Proof is supplied to the author so he can catch and correct the mistakes of the compositor, but they give the author (and the editor) an irresistible opportunity—to improve the work. This was the beginning of the author's alteration—the AA—whether inserted by author or editor. The compositor pays the cost of correcting his own PEs, printer's errors, but he bills the publisher for the AAs.

Over the years, the incidence of PEs has steadily declined (for good technological reasons), but AAs have just as steadily increased. The author's alteration has become so much the normal part of typesetting that many forget that giving the author one final opportunity for revising his work is *not* why proof is supplied.

There is even a kind of folkloric notion that seeing the work in a different (typographic) form is essential to the author's appreciation of his own words and results in his penciled improvements on the galleys. Nonsense. The galleys have the advantage of arriving at least some weeks (if not months) after the last time he made revisions, so he reads it from a somewhat fresher point of view. But the truth is that whenever an author looks at his work again, in manuscript, typewritten, or in type, he will see ways to make changes and improvements.

Until recently, the point would be academic. If the author must see proof anyway, there is no good way (as publishers have discovered) to restrict him to correcting printer's errors. Publishers usually include clauses in their contracts with authors that penalize the author who edits his work in proof, but these clauses do not discourage the author, nor, in most cases, are they enforced.

But now *proofreading is no longer necessary.* With the use of modern technology, it is, in fact, downright silly. In that case, does it make sense to pretend to be going through a proofreading step so the author can do later what he should have done earlier? The answer depends, of course, on the cost.

First, there is a cost in time. The need to proofread, in itself, imposes a composition schedule of months for work that could be done in two days to a week. Books that take six to eight months to produce from final manuscript to bound copy could be produced routinely in three to five weeks.

□ *Another time factor is this: In the old technology, whether hot metal or film, the compositor decides where to end each line and when to hyphenate. It is therefore desirable that one compositor, or perhaps two with similar habits, set the entire book, so the word spacing will not be noticeably different in different sections. Another reason for putting the book through one or two composing machine operators is that, particularly in hot metal, the compositor usually has only one or two fonts of a particular type. The result is that each book moves through the process slowly—since each compositor will be setting the equivalent of five to seven pages per hour and only one or two can work on the same book at a time. With modern technology, where the computer makes the end-of-line and hyphenation decisions, the typeface is a digitized program in the computer's memory, and the keyboards are a fraction of the cost of the old composing machines, the book can be given to a dozen "compositors" and set in two days. But why rush, if the author is going to take a month to read the proof and rewrite half the book?*

Second is the cost in dollars. To determine this cost, I studied the AA charges of a large book publisher. The actual payment to the compositors for author's alterations for a twelve-month period was $456,000, or approximately 15 percent of the composition cost. (Of this amount, the publisher recovered $10,000 from authors by applying the punitive clauses of his contracts.)

But the payments to the compositors were only the beginning of the publisher's costs. Proofs for reading had to be pulled by the compositor. They had to be logged in and sent to the author (who did not charge for reading them) and to the publisher's proofreader (who did). When each set came back, it had to be matched against the original and the corrections transferred. After each book was finished, the compositor's invoice had to be checked in detail against the "dead matter" to be sure that the $456,000 was paid for value received.

We calculated that all the auxiliary costs to create the opportunity to permit the publisher to pay $456,000 were worth at least another $456,000 and probably more. So, on top of a composition cost of $3,250,000, the publisher was paying as much as $1 million for the privilege of adding delays to the production of his books. Actually, the dollar cost is higher. Proper use of the new technology, which incidentally also obviates proofreading, would also substantially reduce the basic composition cost of $3,250,000 by at least 25 percent. The immediate saving to this publisher would therefore be in the area of $1.75 million. Translated into figures that can be applied to any publisher's composition costs: The elimination of proofreading and the correct use of new composition technology can be expected to reduce composition costs by twice the cost of AAs plus 25 percent of the cost of composition itself.

We are able to eliminate proofreading because by using the computer properly, we need only determine that the input—in text and in composition instructions—is correct.

    □ *A curious and potentially very embarrassing incident occurred in connection with my own advocacy of the elimination of proofreading. In 1968, I wrote an article for one of the journals of the Institute of Electrical and Electronics Engineers, explaining how the new technology could eliminate the need for proofreading, because it is almost impossible for an error to be introduced by the computer. My article was typeset by the old technology, of course, a fact that might not have occurred to all my readers, and a proof was sent for me to read. Sure enough. My statement that "shifts in responsibility make tight scheduling at each step virtually impossible" had been altered by the keyboarder's error in omitting the "f" from "shifts." It was perhaps still a defensible statement, though no longer a part of the particular point the article was making. Fortunately, I caught it, which would otherwise have been forever an unanswerable, though invalid, argument for the absolute need to proofread everything.*

Using a computer properly to set type means this: You tell the computer what words you want it to set by keyboarding the manuscript, and you tell the computer how you want the words set by giving it a series of typographic instructions. If you have given it the right words and the right instructions, you will get precisely the result you want.

Moreover, the computer will follow your instructions more faithfully than any human compositor. If you want it to "set tight," with minimum space between words (which you should, for both legibility and lower cost), you can define precisely how "tight" you want it set, something no human compositor could do without tremendous cost in time. It will hyphenate words exactly where you want them hyphenated, and you only have to tell it once. Or, if you decide to make your books easier to read by eliminating hyphenation (and justification) altogether (as we have in this book), the computer will follow those instructions to perfection.

□ *It is also the new computer technology that has made it economically practical to eliminate hyphenation, freeing the reader from the nonsensical interruption of having to fit two pieces of the word together before he can get on with it, and justification, promoting reading ease by placing the same minimal space between words instead of varying it from line to line. With the older systems, in which the human compositor made the end-of-line decisions, eliminating hyphenation and justification would substantially* increase *the cost of setting type.*

Just tell the computer what you want, *but tell it correctly,* and it will deliver exactly that.

It is no longer necessary—and it no longer makes any sense—to proofread the composed type, which comes from the computer. It is much more useful and sensible to check what has gone into the computer, since if there are any errors in the finished product, that is where they will be found. For the first time in composition, the result can be *predicted* and *controlled,* so it does not have to be examined and reexamined at each step.

If the computer keyboarding is verified, and the computer is given the rules for composition and page makeup, a book of 320 or 1000 pages can be keyboarded in a matter of a few days at most and then set in finished pages in a few minutes.

The rules for composition, which must accompany the keyboarded manuscript, are provided by the book designer (about which more later).

What of the keyboarding, and how may it be verified to take advantage of the computer's speed and versatility? There are a number of ways, so the publisher can choose the one best suited to the particular title.

One method can be provided by the compositor himself. In an article I wrote for *Publishers Weekly* in 1969, I suggested that a book might be independently keyboarded by two operators (preferably prone to different kinds of errors) and those results compared by computer, signaling whenever the keys struck by the two keyboarders differed so that the correct stroke could be selected. The errors that would get through such a system would be only those made by both keyboarders; the computer would only signal the disagreements. I suggested that this method, while not assuring complete freedom from error, would probably be more effective at stopping error than is proofreading, which is notoriously imperfect.

There are now several commercial compositors (and at least one private plant) operating this way. The evidence seems to support the belief that double keyboarding is more efficient at avoiding error than proofreading is at catching it. If this method of bypassing proofreading is used, it is essential that the author see the final copyedited version of the manuscript, or a Xerox of it, before it goes to the keyboarders.

But there are other ways to prepare material for the computer. The author may type the manuscript on word-processing typewriters that produce a magnetic record that is intelligible to the computer, or the publisher may retype it on such equipment if the author has not done so. Or the magnetic recorded version for copyediting can be created by having the author use a typewriter that can be read by an optical scanner. All the copyediting marks and the author's second thoughts can be entered on the print-out of the magnetically recorded typed version and then simply keyboarded as corrections to the magnetic record.

□ *Back in the 1960s, when I proposed to eliminate proofreading by more careful control over material in computer-readable form, suggesting that the author get involved in such a procedure was unthinkable. It seemed hard enough—and it has been—to bring the publisher along. But in the February 13, 1981, issue of* Publishers Weekly, *in an article very aptly subtitled "Some writers are moving into the electronic age a good deal faster than their publishers," Gay Courter writes about authors who are composing their books on electronic machines that produce a magnetic record that can be directly entered into a computer to produce the final book pages—except the publishers aren't using properly what the authors give them. Among the authors who are typing their scripts this way are John Hersey, Richard Condon, Harold King, Leonard Sanders, George Cherry, and Douglas Hofstadter.*

No matter how the material is prepared, the word processor or the typesetter's computer can check every word against a large dictionary and question any one that seems to be misspelled. The method is not infallible but is probably several times more accurate in catching spelling errors than a proofreader.

The programs already exist to enable the computer to catch most grammatical errors, such as plural subject and singular verb, misuse of "who" and "whom," use of the adverb for the adjective and vice versa, etc. It can also detect overlong sentences and paragraphs, excessive word repetition (and suggest synonyms), and the use of clichés. Moreover, the threshold of this "editing" activity can be set at whatever level of vigilance the human editor wishes his computer assistant to perform.

Some of these computer programs, though well developed, are not yet commercially available. When they are, they will greatly assist the human editor by identifying any violation of the rules of syntax or good usage and by defining the precise nature of the violation. The computer will, for example, be able to analyze the manuscript overnight and have a list of the problems on the editor's desk the next morning. The editor (or the author) can then decide whether any changes should be made. The use of such computer systems will not make sense for poetry or creative writing of many kinds in which the author is not obliged to accept syntactical standards.

Though it may be some time before these editing aids are available, there is no need to wait for further computer development to eliminate proofreading. That requires no more than the verification of the keyboarded material, and that capability has been at hand for many years.

Transferring the keyboarding from the compositor to the publisher or the author is not as wrenching as it may appear. It made no sense for publishers to keyboard when the keyboard was attached to a monstrously heavy, oversized device spewing molten lead or even to a slightly smaller but highly complicated and expensive photographic machine. But present keyboards are not much larger, and only slightly more expensive, than electric typewriters. Moreover, if the publisher already has word-processing typewriters (and if he has more than three typewriters in his office, he should), he needs no additional equipment at all.

If the publisher does the keyboarding, the author should see the result before the magnetic record is released for composition. The elimination of proofreading is not intended to deny the author control over his manuscript. The intent is to transfer the point of control to the material being typeset rather than the final type. This does not diminish the author's control in the slightest but permits the production process to continue unhindered, at much lower cost and considerably higher speed.

The "proofread" magnetic record can be entered, together with all the typographic instructions, directly into the compositor's computer, which will, in a matter almost of minutes, produce final film in page form, with spaces for illustrations, if any, blocked out.

If the publisher is to produce the final computer tape, or even supply a final manuscript for double keyboarding, the design decisions must accompany the manuscript or be part of the tape. This requirement may force book design to be performed more rationally than it has in the past.

Book design, except for expressions of support of artistic integrity and freedom in general, has rarely gotten serious critical attention from publishing management. Designers have worked under the friendly sponsorship, but rarely with the full understanding, of their publishing bosses.

Back in the days of letterpress ascendancy, which were coming to a close after World War II, book design was a practical craft, and book designers learned their skill very close to the typesetting machines and hand compositors and the pressrooms. These designers were concerned with manipulating the typesetting and printing processes to create attractive books, with legible, easily read pages. Accordingly, they would create title pages that were miniature tasteful posters, bindings that would grace a bookshelf—in general, books that were pleasant to hold and to read. But the artistic accomplishments of book design were supposed to be subordinated to the practical demands of the typesetting and printing processes.

If a book was to be printed from the actual type rather than from electrotype duplicate plates made from the type, it was important to choose a typeface that could best absorb, without excessive deformation, the pounding of the heavy printing press. Page numbers could not be placed where printing pressure would cause them to wear faster than the text type. The designer had to know which typefaces were on matrices that could set roman type in combination with boldface type and which could set roman with italic on a simple single-magazine machine to avoid setting the book on a more expensive mixer machine. Certain display faces were available on Ludlow machines (which cast new expendable type each time), but only up to a certain size. Setting by hand was to be avoided as it used type that was hard to replace, was more expensive, invited mixing worn type with new type, and sharply limited the choice of compositor.

Right after World War II, concern with book design seemed to be the mark of the intellectually serious publisher. Houses such as Random House, Knopf, Viking,

Houghton Mifflin, Doubleday, and Simon & Schuster paid serious attention to design. Many of the others left it to the compositor to choose the typeface and make all the other design decisions.

During the late forties and early fifties, a number of designers who had trained in schools of art and design rather than in composing rooms entered the book design field. Their work showed a shift in emphasis from the practical to the artistic and allusive aspects of book design, reflecting a philosophy that subordinated technological and economic considerations to the design.

Their exaggeration of the importance of design was also expressed in demands for greater recognition of their contribution to the finished book. I recall one meeting of the American Institute of Graphic Arts in the late forties at which several designers seriously proposed that the designer's name appear next to the author's. They argued that the design of the book was a part of the book's message and conveyed meaning that would not be evident from the author's words alone. Of course, most designers were more modest about their contribution, but the very fact that such extravagant claims could be made at a meeting of designers and production experts and not be hooted down was an unfortunate indication of where the pendulum had swung.

The new typesetting technology of the fifties and sixties seemed to free the designer from the technical constraints of hand composition and the Linotype machine. Many liberties—in range of type sizes, in placement of folios and type blocks, in use of gray (benday) tints, etc.—were taken before the advancing technology really removed the cost distinctions, and a great many books cost much more to set than they should have. In the atmosphere of speedy technical changes in typesetting, when the new developments were often only dimly understood by the designer and even by the production manager, and in a production process where price comparisons were difficult to make, the publisher's inclination was to allow the designer free rein even at substantial cost.

There was among publishers an inclination to consider book design an artistic expression, and to assume that as artists, designers were entitled to work as nearly as possible without any constraints. Designers frequently usurped the production manager's prerogative by their decisions: For example, they might effectively choose the typesetting process, or even the actual compositor, by selecting a typeface that was not available elsewhere.

I recall that back in the early fifties, when I announced to the design department at Doubleday that henceforth they would have only four text typefaces available, it was interpreted by some of them as the first step in an authoritarian takeover of the company.

Certainly book design has its artistic aspects. The general appearance of the book, the shape and "color" of the type page, the selection and arrangement of the display types, etc., are by no means beside the point. The look and heft of the book is an important part of the reading experience. But book design is functional as well, and there is a mixup of priorities when art is permitted to frustrate function.

Managements that feel that they are acting anti-intellectually or anti-artistically if they impose restraints on the designer or question the rationale for some design decisions, are wrong. A book designer is not an easel artist and is not entitled to that kind of freedom. It is very clear that an automobile is also a thing of beauty, and even clearer that beauty helps sell cars. But an automobile designer has no right, in order to create an appearance he personally finds pleasing, to design a car that pollutes, or uses excessive fuel, or is unsafe to drive. Nor does he have the right, in the name of artistic freedom, to design a fender that must be shaped by hand because it cannot be formed by machine. Similarly, a book designer's freedom to amuse himself with forms and appearances is, or should be, constrained by his obligation to produce a book that is as easy as possible to read and, in the context of the quality suitable to its purpose, as inexpensive as possible to make.

Although legibility of type is not precisely understood, the parameters are sufficiently definable. While there is considerable uncertainty, and lack of conclusive proof even where there is relative certainty, there are many guidelines on which type experts are in general agreement.

Since reading depends partly on the eye distinguishing the shape of one letter from the shape of another and, even more, the shape of one word from the shape of another word, anything that subtracts from these easily discernible differences makes it harder for the eye to see them and the mind to grasp them. Sans-serif letters are simplified to make the letters less different from each other. It also makes the shape of words less distinctive. That is probably why sans-serif type is harder to read than most of the serif faces. That difficulty, which is simply an additional straining of eye and mind to decipher the message, is not sufficiently bothersome when reading only a phrase or two; an occasional headline causes no difficulty. The difficulty of reading just a few words is minor and may be more than compensated for by the additional contrast that sans-serif provides to set the heading off from the text. Sans-serif "packs" better, which is why it is frequently used in want ads, where extensive reading of text is not a factor in any case.

If a type page is more difficult to read, such as this one, which is set in sans-serif, the reader is usually not aware of why he becomes tired quickly. He feels that perhaps the content is boring or the light is bad or that he is tired. All of this may be true, but he will almost never be conscious of the strain that the designer has gratuitously caused by setting the words in sans-serif. (See Appendix E.)

Length of line is also a factor in legibility for two reasons. First, it may affect the space between words. This is not a problem in unjustified composition because the space between words is constant no matter how wide the line. In a book that is being set with a justified right-hand edge, so that the amount of space between words must vary from line to line, a somewhat longer length for all lines softens that disadvantage because the line contains more spaces between words into which to divide the justifying space, thus making the difference in the space between words less noticeable. On the other hand, since the reader cannot really pause in the middle of a line without serious danger of losing his place, a long line may tire the reader by requiring total attention for longer periods between breaks.

Second, a line too long or too short creates problems regardless of word spacing. Too few words on a line slows the reader in the same way that hyphenation does. Hyphenation requires the reader to pause to reconstruct the divided word. In reading a longer line, the eye must travel back farther from the end of one line to find the beginning of the next, making it more likely that the eye will be momentarily confused or even begin reading the wrong line before the error is realized. If justification is used, line widths should be chosen so that the line is not so short that there will be excessive space between words. Any space beyond the minimum necessary to signal that one word has ended and another begun will slow the reader, and truly excessive space will require reading one word at a time and pausing to put them together logically. Even worse is solving the problem of excessive space by putting e x t r a   s p a c e   b e t w e e n   t h e   l e t t e r s   o f   w o r d s. The mind has then to r e c o n s t r u c t words it would otherwise recognize at a glance and then pause to put the words logically into phrases.

I do not propose to cite here all the possible pitfalls of book design or to explain all the rules within which a designer should do his work. The point is that there *are* rules that have evolved from experience and good common sense. Furthermore, they are rules that are the concern of publishing management as well as of the designer or production man. Legibility and aesthetics may have to be balanced against cost. The type line becomes less legible but also less costly as it gets longer. Cost and legibility also go down together as the type size gets smaller. At what point on the scale of cost and legibility does management wish its design to be? The answer need not be specific in dollars, but the concern of management with legibility, and quality in general as it relates to cost, should be somehow expressed to its designers.

One constraint on design, therefore, must be a set of rules, arrived at by management in consultation with design and production, that establishes the limits of quality and cost.

Another constraint must be the adoption of approaches to design that are not as costly of designers' time as the traditional one-book-at-a-time approach, nor so likely to produce bad decisions.

The title page and binding of each book may require a distinctive treatment, but the same cannot be said of the text page. The design of book after book in, for example, the 6 x 9 inch trim size requires the designer, book after book, to solve the problem of fitting 350 or 380 or 340 words on a pleasant, easily read page. The combinations of typeface, size, line length, leading, and number of lines per page that can accomplish this are virtually infinite, but all combinations are not equally satisfactory. Nor are they equally available, since some typefaces may be within easier reach than others. If the designer will spend more time and thought solving the general problem of the best way (or several ways) to get 350 words on a 6 x 9 page and the rules by which to adjust that page as the number of words goes up or down within narrow limits, he is more likely to arrive at a better solution than by solving that same problem over and over again (and differently) for each book as it comes up. Such a solution can be used on book after book until the designer develops a better one. The same approach should be taken with other problems that can be stated generally, like books with two levels of heads, or books with long or short footnotes, etc.

One of the more thoughtful and creative designers in book publishing, Stanley Rice, has attacked book design from exactly this point of view. The result of his systematic study of the design problems faced in all sorts of books is an extensive "menu" of possible solutions for each problem. Sensitive to the designer's wish for maximum freedom, Rice has provided more alternatives than any one person could possibly need. He has incorporated these alternatives into a computer program that enables the designer to choose the specifications like a diner choosing dishes in a restaurant. A systematic exploration of Rice's menu by any publisher, with his own range of design problems in mind, would result in a more restricted version, which would give that publisher's design a distinctive personality and which could be incorporated into the memory of the typesetting computer. Thereafter, the publisher's designer could indicate his choices from the menu and design only those elements in any book that require special attention *before* the manuscript goes to the keyboarders. The result would be more carefully considered solutions to recurring design problems to produce consistently high-quality design at greater speed and lower cost.

This approach does not belittle the importance of the designer to the book anymore than a collection of recipes belittles the chef's role in preparing a meal. The design rules, like the recipes, benefit because they rest on a foundation of sound principles, of experiment with reasonable alternatives, and consideration for the practical realities.

There is little doubt that, although there is some advantage in size, most publishers, large and small, can very sharply reduce the cost of production and even more sharply increase the speed. No reduction in the quality of the book is required. On the contrary, improvement in quality should be a by-product of these developments because the publisher can afford better materials and because smoothing out the production flow will allow more positive control of the manufacturing operations.

The result should be books that are more useful because they are more timely and more accessible because they are lower in price.

14

How Many Books and When?

Printing Quantities and Inventory Control

THE PRICES of trade books are unnecessarily high because they must absorb the unnecessarily high costs of a distribution system that is rife with inefficiencies and of production methods that do not take full advantage of available technology. Making books by methods that are avoidably wasteful is bad enough if you need the books. Most publishers manage to compound the waste by producing books that are not needed at all, or, if needed, are produced too late to avoid the cost of being out of stock, or are produced in quantities that tie up money while the books sit in the warehouse. This compounding of high production costs results from the general failure of publishers to refine the methods by which they decide how many copies to print and when to print them.

The publisher spends more money on manufacturing books than he does on any other commodity or activity. By far, the largest part of his business investment is sitting on skids in his warehouse. It is not surprising that a great deal of money can be wasted—or saved—whenever the publisher must decide how many copies of a book to print.

The importance of making precise printing decisions is obvious to most publishers; they are repeatedly reminded of the errors of overprinting by the list of overstock they submit to remainder dealers for bids. The errors of underprinting, which result in lost sales because the publisher is out of stock, are probably much less serious, though costly, and not nearly so obvious. An additional burden is the cost of maintaining excessive inventories of solid backlist titles because the

quantities in which they are manufactured are not determined
carefully.

Printing decisions fall into two classes. The first is the decision on a
new book, the first printing, or perhaps the second, when the expected
sales rate is the key to the answer. The second is the decision on a
backlist title, where the rate of sales can be forecast reasonably well
and the key is investing the company's money most advantageously.

Management is faced with the first type of printing decision before
publication, when the sales rate of the book is still unknown and even
the advance sale to the book trade can only be estimated. In some
publishing houses, the printing decision is part of the prepublication
financial analysis. Since the publishing plan is based on a per-copy cost,
any change from that cost, such as a different printing quantity, would
require going through the whole laborious approval process again, so
there is great reluctance to disturb the original printing decision. It's
hard to believe, but true.

In most publishing houses, management attempts to judge anew, as
late as possible, how many copies it will really need. The key piece of
information needed is the number of copies for which advance orders
will ultimately be received—the number of copies that will need to be
in the hands of wholesalers and retailers on publication day. This is not
the printing quantity; it is simply the minimum number required.
Depending on the book, its expected life, the make-ready cost of
reprinting, the lead time for reprinting, etc., the printing quantity will
be extrapolated from the advance sale.

But what will the advance sale be? At the time of printing, the
sales reps are still traveling around the country, soliciting orders from
booksellers. Some orders are already in, but these may represent as
little as 5 or 10 percent of the advance sale or even less. (For a
publisher with a merchandising plan, the problem is simplified because
he knows *exactly* how many copies of each new title he will send to
the accounts that participate in the plan even before the reps leave
the sales conference. It is necessary only to determine what the
advance sale will be to accounts not on the plan.) Generally, the
advance is estimated from the orders on hand, however scattered and
fragmentary, and from the feeling the editor and sales manager may
have about how the book will ultimately fare. In some companies, the
decision may be made by a committee; in others, it may result from
informal opinions transmitted to the publisher or business manager,
who then issues the formal order to the production department.

The best way to forecast the advance sale is to predict it
mathematically, by some *objective* method, from the orders already in.

This procedure was followed very successfully at Doubleday as long ago as 1954, and the prediction methods were developed for unusual reasons.

Some of the serious cost and scheduling problems at Country Life Press, Doubleday's wholly owned book manufacturing plant on Long Island, were caused by the failure of the publishing departments to decide early enough how many copies of each new book they would order. The production aspects were under reasonably good control. The books were ready for press in good time. But we could not go on press because publishing was not able to tell us how many copies to print. When we needed to start production to have copies by the specified shipping dates, responses from bookstores were often only just beginning to come in.

This is one of the hazards of a captive plant. A commercial printer could say, "No order; no books," or could charge a penalty high enough to get the attitude changed. We had to live with it.

In those days, invoices to bookstores were created on NCR accounting machines rather than computers. New books were shipped twice a month, so a semimonthly invoice could have fifteen or twenty titles on it. Once the invoices were prepared, we were committed to shipping every one of those titles on the same day, no matter when the publishing department finally agreed to let us print.

The result was heavy overtime work just before the books were shipped. Even so, we frequently could not complete all the runs. If publishing said 15,000 copies and we needed 11,000 to cover the invoiced orders, the plant might print 11,000, lift the job, and go back to produce the other 4000 copies two or three weeks later. Even with this practice (which resulted in higher manufacturing costs), books were ready so late that there was insufficient time for reviewers to comment, and deliveries to West Coast bookstores often arrived after publication date.

Applying discipline to the publishing side was part of my production responsibility, so Charlie Pitkin, the vice president for manufacturing at Doubleday, expected me to "get those guys straightened out." Whenever I raised the question with publishing, and I raised it often, I got substantially the same answer, which ran something like this:

"You've got to stop insisting on the convenience of the production department. You are a service department. You do not serve if you push us into printing the wrong quantity. Our sales reps are calling on the stores and the wholesalers. Until enough orders are in, we cannot estimate what the total orders will be, and the last ones won't come in until weeks *after* the first books are shipped. If we print too many, we will be remaindering the extra copies for pennies. If we print too few, the time lost getting a reprint could cost us the sales momentum that might make a best-seller."

I was invited to attend the meetings that decided quantities, and I watched how the sales manager, business manager, usually two editors, and possibly the promotion manager—an impressive collection of expensive talent—struggled to discern solid trends in the thin information they had. They might try to guess what an important customer would buy or phone a rep in the field who might have an important order not yet sent in. These meetings made it clear that the process was by no means scientific or consistent. The same sketchy collection of numbers could result in one decision today and a different one tomorrow. It wasn't blind guesswork; it was like guesswork through cataracts.

The decisions were postponed until they were working with anywhere from 30 to 50 percent of the orders by number of accounts but less than that in volume of books, because the larger accounts usually bought later. Clearly, they felt the information they had was insufficient; they resented my suggestion that they do it a few weeks earlier, with even less information.

At about that time I became interested in operations research, which is, generally, the attempt to apply mathematical methods to business (or strategic) problems. The technique of regression analysis looked as though it would be able to predict the advance sale of books to bookstores more objectively from less information than a group of high-level executives sitting around a conference table. However, I was not then and have never been a mathematician, so I asked Doug Black, president of Doubleday, if I could hire someone to experiment with regression analysis. That is how I introduced George Blagowidow, already working toward a Ph.D. in marketing at New York University, into the publishing world.

Our goal was to arrive at a printing quantity four weeks earlier than the publishing department. George began experimenting with the first 2 or 3 percent of the orders, making dry-run predictions from the earliest orders received for books published the previous year. It was soon clear that the regression analysis predictions with 2 to 5 percent of the orders were better than the executives' predictions with 30 percent of the orders. (See Appendix F.)

Very soon, the expensive committee was no longer meeting. The regression analysis was being done on an $800 Friden calculator by one person, Charles Harris—then fresh out of college, now director of the Howard University Press—who gave that entire function about one day a week.

Although printing decisions were made four to six weeks earlier, they were dramatically better in every respect. The number of out-of-stock title-days was cut in half; the average number of printings per title over the first six months of its life was cut from three to two; the excess inventory from overprinting was reduced to insignificance. We estimated that the direct out-of-pocket savings alone, in the first year, was $250,000. And, of course, the scheduling problems at Country Life Press caused by late decisions disappeared.

□ *The unexpected, indirect payoff from the prediction system came about two years later. Prediction from the sales reps' orders led us to look more closely at the orders. This in turn led to how the sales reps got the orders, the pattern of order writing for one publishing season compared to another, and the pattern of sources of orders compared to the pattern of population, income level, educational level, etc., around the country. The result was a recommendation for expanding the size of the Doubleday sales force and changes in the methods of sales management. Doug Black approved the recommendation, and Doubleday sales almost quadrupled in five years with no change in the mix, quality, or number of titles published.*

Objective forecasting of the advance sale from the analysis of the few orders received is similar to forecasting an election result from a survey of a small sample of the electorate. The pollster does not predict how any particular individual will vote, even though he may predict the pattern of voting quite accurately. Prediction deals with probability, so it is useful in estimating what the sum of the actions of a large group of buyers will be from the actions of a sample of that group. But this sample is not a reliable guide to how a particular buyer will order, so it cannot be used to predict the actions of important individual buyers who may greatly influence the final result. Estimating the orders from the few giant accounts, such as Baker & Taylor or B. Dalton, cannot be usefully attempted by mathematical extrapolation of the orders placed by other accounts. They should be separately predicted subjectively by whoever covers the account or they should be sold early enough so the actual order is in hand.

Predicting the advance by any one of several mathematical methods depends on consistency in the coverage of accounts from season to season. That is because all prediction systems are based on relating the orders received so far to the orders from the same accounts in previous seasons. Calculating the relation of those *previous orders* to *previous total advances,* the system projects the advance that would have the analogous relation to the current orders. To the extent that the accounts being sold this season differ from those sold the previous season, the prediction will lose validity.

So, to estimate the advance reliably from a scattering of early orders, it is important that the sales force cover the same accounts with each new list.

□ *There is a much more pressing reason than improving prediction to get every account covered every season—sales. Skipped accounts equal lost sales. That concept is simple enough that one would expect thorough account coverage to be the primary obligation of sales management. It is painful to say it, but it is the exceptional publisher who directs the sales force's activity to ensure that the eligible accounts are covered consistently from season to season.*

The nice thing about mathematical prediction is that it can be tested, and therefore adjusted, before it is used. Individual orders from previous seasons are in the file and can be pulled in the sequence in which they were received. Any mathematical method can be tested by going into the file, applying that method to the earliest orders, and comparing the prediction with the total advance sale that the file shows actually resulted in each case. The methods that predict successfully for the past are likely to predict successfully for the future.

Regression analysis, which is a relatively simple application of differential calculus and the method we applied at Doubleday, stands up well when tested in this way.

This technique predicts what the advance sale will be, but the decision on printing quantity does not automatically result. In the first place, the prediction is always a range rather than a specific number. Favoring the high or the low side of the range will depend on a number of factors that management must consider. For example, if it feels that the book has been oversold to the reps and is being oversold to the stores, it may favor a conservative print order, with the idea of bringing books back early from accounts where they are selling slowly to cover reorders from accounts where they are selling more rapidly, thereby reducing the danger of a heavy remainder.

The ease and speed with which the production department can get reprints will also be a factor in deciding the printing quantity. A larger safety margin of stock is needed for a book that needs three months to arrive from Hong Kong than for one that can be delivered in two weeks from Brattleboro, Vermont.

The cost of make-ready will be a factor. Make-ready includes all the costs of *getting ready* to print and *getting ready* to bind after the plant costs of composition and color separation, etc., have been covered. It can be thought of as the cost of the first copy. A book with color illustrations requires longer press preparation on a more expensive machine than one with black and white illustrations only. The cost of "run-on" copies (all those after the first copy printed and bound) on two titles may be $1 per copy. If it costs $1000 to get the first copy of one title and the other costs $200, it is clear that overprinting the first is a lesser risk than overprinting the second.

   □ *Some publishing houses use the* wrong *manufacturing cost figures and so arrive at* wrong *printing decisions. If, as is frequently done, the composition and other plant costs are included in the manufacturing cost, the cost per copy will* seem *to go down much more than it really does as the quantity manufactured goes up. This mistake in accounting logic costs many publishers lots of money.* Make-ready costs *do matter.* Plant costs *only confuse the issue.*

The expected reaction of the literary critics and the planned promotion will also be factors. If a heavy buying surge is expected on publication day, a larger safety stock above the quantity needed to fill advance orders may be a sound investment.

If the book is expected to have a long life, perhaps with a strong library sale that is usually not evident until weeks after publication, that will have to be considered in the printing decision.

Sometimes the second printing decision creates the oversupply, usually because the first printing was overcautious.

If a second printing appears necessary before publication, the best way to judge its need and determine its size is by the same methods used on the first printing. Since more orders will be in hand, the prediction should be more reliable.

This must be done with discrimination. It is important to determine whether the second printing is necessary because of faulty prediction in fixing the first printing or because of a change in the orders that arrived later. Often the publicity buildup (or unplanned growth in popular interest) starts after the reps begin their work, and they find an increasingly receptive attitude as they make their rounds. One result if the *quality* of orders has changed is that it is likely that there will soon be reorders from the accounts covered earlier, so the second printing should be a little larger to anticipate this.

The way to judge whether quality has changed is to run one regression on the first hundred orders received and another on the hundred most recent orders. If the difference in the two predictions is significant, it is a good bet that the booksellers' perception of the title has changed.

If, as is more often the case, the second printing appears to be needed after publication, the publisher should have sales information from the stores to guide his decision. In order to be truly useful, the sales record of the publisher's titles should be collected regularly over a long period, so that the sample sales figures can be related to the history of other titles.

Unfortunately, the "data collection" that the publisher typically resorts to at this point is to call a few important accounts to inquire how many copies have been sold. Without records relating previous sales in individual stores with overall sales for those titles, it is very difficult to interpret "ten copies in three weeks" in this or that account (and even more difficult to interpret "Great, it's going great!") into a need for 5000 or 10,000 copies—or perhaps none at all.

One booby trap that triggers many a useless second printing is a flurry of orders just after publication, which seem to be reorders in response to public demand but are in fact only the first advance orders from accounts that were visited late. This error occurs more frequently in publishing houses that do not adequately monitor or direct the reps' selling activity.

The publisher should have at least twenty or thirty "indicator" accounts (about two or three per rep), which are widely dispersed (but close to the reps' homes) and each large enough to sell a reasonable quantity of any important book. The reps should routinely report on the inventory of important titles so that a history of sales in those stores against total sales can guide future printing decisions.

With sales intelligence from the field, an unnecessary second printing can frequently be averted, *and* potentially lost sales retrieved, by calling books back from customers who have too many copies (and would later return them) to supply those who are out of stock.

After the exciting publication period, most books, unfortunately, turn up their toes and are laid to rest. Some titles, however, despite all that is done to kill them, survive to become part of the backlist. Those that do generally settle into fairly predictable patterns. Sales may be fairly steady through the year or seasonal. They generally deteriorate somewhat each year, but they are still reasonably predictable.

Backlist titles present reprinting problems of an entirely different type. They are generally handled within the publishing house under the functional heading of "inventory control," which includes deciding which titles should be continued, identifying for each title the time to reprint, and deciding how many to reprint. In most publishing houses, the person carrying the nominal responsibility for inventory control doesn't really make these decisions; he is kept busy sounding alarms, presenting cost estimates, and bringing information to the executives who will make the decisions.

Used in connection with the backlist, "inventory control" has a completely different meaning from the same term when it describes the book assortment in a retail store, and the nature of the problem is equally different.

The bookseller provides stock for a theoretically open, indefinite market. *Anybody* may march into the store at any time looking for any title. No one can say how many customers will, in the next moment, want a particular book, or which book it will be. The customer cannot be identified in advance. The publisher, on the other hand, supplies a closed system of accounts—bookstores and wholesalers, primarily—who are familiar to him and can give him information to guide his decisions.

The lead time for replenishment is significant. The publisher must have the books fabricated, and many factors may affect the date of delivery. The minimum printing quantity is large enough—at least hundreds, usually thousands—to involve considerable risk.

The bookseller is not filling a pipeline. If he has no inventory, there are no books belonging to him hidden somewhere in the system. The publisher may be down to zero inventory, but he may have filled the pipeline in wholesalers and retailers so thoroughly (or so unevenly) that in time, he may get back substantial numbers of copies in returns.

Inventory of specific titles is a more critical matter for the publisher. The bookseller, if he is alert, can retrieve a lost sale by suggesting another title to the customer who seeks a book that is not in the store. The publisher is not likely to benefit from substitutability; if a title is out of stock, the sale is lost.

Unfortunately, publishers do not assign sufficient importance to inventory control, so they give very little thought to developing ways to make such control more effective. On the one hand, there is generally insufficient concern about the cost of maintaining high inventories with slow turnover. On the other, there is insufficient concern over the damage done by books being out of stock. Some publishers are content to let a title stay out of stock for a while, letting orders build up, with the shortsighted notion that the more copies they can ship when the reprint edition is ultimately delivered, the quicker they will get their investment back.

No publisher I know has a rational, objective system for actively patrolling his backlist, choosing, on the basis of season or stock level, the titles that should be considered for reprinting, calculating the balance of economic factors pertinent to the decision, and deciding on printing according to the overall criteria established by top management. The requirements of such a backlist control system are easy to define and translate into reality.

One objective of any inventory system is to minimize the number of out-of-stock titles and the length of time they remain out of stock. A backlist inventory replenishment system must call attention to the title that should be considered for reprinting so the new printing can be delivered before the title runs out of stock. For each book, the likelihood of being out of stock depends, in addition to the rate at which it is selling, on the time it takes management to notice the situation, consider the options, and make the decision, plus the time it takes to reprint the book plus a margin of safety based on experience. That time is different for each book, or at least for each class of book.

Whatever factors affect the speed of production for a publisher and a title, the result is that for each title the publisher can say: "We can have a reprint, in the range of quantities appropriate to this title, in X weeks," or "We can have a reprint in X weeks at one season of the year and in Y weeks at another season of the year."

The time required to secure a reprint, including the time management needs to arrive at a decision, can be determined for each title. The rate of sale of each book can, in turn, translate any inventory level into the time available before the last copy is sold. With an appropriate allowance for "safety," this can determine the inventory level at which the inventory control system asks each title to "step forward" to be considered for reprinting. This can be done effortlessly by the computer, which can track the rise and fall in the rate of sale and continuously translate inventory *copies* into equivalent *time.*

If the time required for management to make the decision, place the orders, and have the books delivered is six weeks for a title selling on the average of 50 copies a week, the system must deal with this title when the inventory falls to 300 copies. This "reorder point" will change for this title if the period includes a seasonal variation in sales (e.g., it may sell 100 copies a week in the period before Christmas). The time required for printing the book is different at different times of the year. In some publishing houses, where several approvals are necessary, management decisions are reached more slowly during vacation periods. Thus the reorder point, always expressed in number of *books*, may have to keep shifting so that it reflects the number of weeks (or days) dictated by the situation at that moment.

The term "reorder point" is not unknown in publishing, nor is the concept. But most publishers do not translate reorder points into the time required for reprinting, and almost none keeps shifting the reorder point to reflect the different situations at different times of the year, even though the computer makes it quite simple. On the contrary, the review of possible reprinting needs is haphazard in most publishing houses. Where it has been rationalized by the establishment of reorder points—usually one of the triumphant accomplishments of the computer department—they are very rarely *reorder* points. They are rather "this title has reached an inventory level that deserves attention" points. Usually the inventory levels are approximately, but not precisely, related to rates of sale, and they are almost always high enough to be well above any genuine reorder point if anybody bothered to calculate it.

The result is that in most publishing houses, many titles are called up for review much too early. Most of them are simply given a new, lower inventory level "reorder point" signal and returned to the file. This wastes everyone's time and weakens vigilance. The use of the term "reorder point" for those "look at me" signals, which gives the publisher's inventory control the gloss of being up to date, is only a gesture, not movement, in the right direction.

Even in those publishing houses where the reorder point truly represents a calculated and carefully considered time interval translated into a number of copies under current conditions, further sophistication is desirable. Whereas a book with minor seasonal variation in sales can be handled under a procedure that continuously recalculates reorder points, it is not satisfactory for books that have sharp seasonal differences in sales. The reorder point for such a title will jump about crazily. Reprinting just after the period of heaviest use will mean tying up inventory investment for a longer period of light use—exactly the opposite of the desirable strategy.

For titles with seasonal interest, the reorder points should be determined not by inventory level but by a date on the calendar. The possibility of reprinting should be considered a certain number of weeks before the beginning of the heavy shipping season for that particular title. This review may be annual (Christmas book) or semi-annual (college texts). The question that arises when this calendar signal sounds is: "Do we have enough copies to carry us through the next seasonal peak?"

As discussed in Chapter 13, on production, inventory control is simpler and more effective if book production is under tight control. The prediction of out-of-stock dates is an approximation. A supply of books apparently sufficient for ten weeks may be exhausted in five or may last fifteen, depending upon the chance arrival or delay of a few large orders. The ability of the production department to speed up or delay the delivery of finished books right up to the last moment can reduce inventory and investment in inventory enough to be of financial importance to the company. If the publisher's stock turn is 1 (which means he has an average of one year's stock on hand), a reduction of the overlap of new stock with old by five weeks (10 percent of a year), on the average, across the list, suggests a reduction of 10 percent in the inventory investment. And that is easily done by a good production department.

More carefully identifying the best moment at which to consider reprinting each backlist title would relieve many publishing managers of the nuisance and cost of looking at the same book over and over again. Even with such a system, it is necessary to establish the criteria for deciding whether to reprint at all—that is, whether to continue the book on the list—and if so, how many to print.

Most publishers have no guidelines for making these decisions, because "every book is different." In smaller houses, management can afford the luxury (and fun) of considering each title. Even in some larger houses, such decisions may be made independently for each book at a middle management level by a department manager or a committee. In at least some of the larger houses, guidelines for keeping books in print and for deciding printing quantities are established, usually as suggestions rather than rigid rules. Many such guidelines are simple rules of thumb, like McGraw-Hill's once popular and now discarded dictum, "Print for one year, bind for six months." A more popular general publishing rule is to make one year's supply. How good are these rules? Not very.

Similarly, many publishers have a rule of thumb for continuing a backlist title in print. It may be expressed in number of copies: "Any title that does not sell at least 1000 copies [or whatever] a year will be dropped." Sometimes the rule is more realistically (though erroneously) expressed in dollars of sale: "It has to sell $5000 [or whatever] worth a year."

Neither criterion is very good. The decision on each title should depend on margins and rate of return. The decision on keeping a book in print should follow the determination of the most economical quantity to print. If printing that quantity does not produce desirable margins on money invested or a satisfactory rate of return, no printing will, and the title should be dropped.

The critical inventory control decision on backlist titles is the number of copies to print. Considering that every publisher, without exception, has more money invested in inventory than in any other part of his business, it is hard to understand the lack of thought applied by most publishers to so simple a problem.

Printing a small quantity will result in the need to print more frequently, which, in turn, will result in incurring the costs of ordering more frequently. Most ordering costs (inventory control specialists like to call them "procurement costs"), such as the cost of preparing manufacturing estimates, of the executive time spent in making buying decisions, the cost of placing purchase orders, of production department time spent in supervising and following up, receiving and accounting costs, etc., are usually substantially the same for each title being reprinted.

One procurement cost, and the most important one, varies greatly with each title. That is the cost, in the pressroom and bindery, of make-ready and make-ready spoilages—generally, the "fixed costs" of reprinting that title—which decline as a percentage of the cost of each book as the number of copies of any single printing increases.

On the other hand, printing a small quantity has the advantage of holding down the cost of money invested in inventory as well as the cost of insurance, warehousing, spoilage, and the danger of obsolescence. These "carrying costs," in contrast to procurements costs, are all costs that tend to go up (depending on the title) as the size of the printing increases and the books, as a consequence, are held for a longer period.

The procurement costs per copy—the costs of buying—go down as the quantity printed is increased, while the carrying costs—the costs of keeping the books—go up. As every textbook on inventory control emphasizes, the most advantageous quantity to manufacture or to buy (the EOQ, the economic order quantity) is the one at which these two costs are in balance, the point at which procurement costs equal carrying costs. The formula for EOQ in book publishing is developed in Appendix G.

Expressed in words, the EOQ equation, $\sqrt{\dfrac{2YP}{CI}}$, says that the most advantageous printing quantity is the square root of the quantity obtained after multiplying twice the yearly sales rate by the procurement cost and dividing the result by the product of the manufacturing cost per copy and by the annual cost of money, storage, and related costs.

It is interesting to see the effect of sales rate on EOQ.

Assume two similar titles. The cost of procurement in each case is $500; the manufacturing cost is $1 per copy; the cost of money invested is 15 percent. Title A is selling 2000 copies per year and Title B, at 20,000 copies, is doing ten times as well. The two equations look like this:

Title A: $\quad EOQ = \sqrt{\dfrac{2 \times 2000 \times 500}{1 \times .15}} = 3651$ copies

Title B: $\quad EOQ = \sqrt{\dfrac{2 \times 20,000 \times 500}{1 \times .15}} = 11,547$ copies

In the case of the slower-selling title, Title A, the best printing quantity is sufficient for twenty-two months, whereas for the faster-moving title, Title B, it is sufficient for only seven months. The example contradicts two widely accepted truths in publishing: The printing quantity does *not* go up and down proportionally to sales; one year's supply as the printing quantity is wrong *most of the time.* Over the breadth of any publisher's list, "print one year's supply" results in a frightful waste of money.

It is also interesting to see the effect of the cost of money (or inflation) on the EOQ. In the case of Title A, if the cost of investment dropped from 15 to 8 percent, the EOQ would change from 3651 copies to 5000 (or two and a half years' supply) and if it went up to 25 percent, the EOQ would drop to 2828 copies (seventeen months' supply). Not unexpectedly, as the cost of money goes up, the printing quantities should go down; as the cost of money goes down, quantities go up.

Well-managed book production can greatly influence the effectiveness of inventory control. In addition to the obvious benefit of tight control of delivery dates, a good production department will reduce make-ready and other procurement costs. For example, McGraw-Hill, using the scheduling system described in Chapter 13, in addition to reducing make-ready costs in the manufacturing operations, eliminates at least one minor procurement step and cost by not writing printing and binding orders to the suppliers. So, for example, if by superior organization the production department can reduce procurement costs from $500 (in the above examples) to $300, it will reduce the EOQ to 77 percent of the previous level.

Reducing printing quantities to 77 percent does not automatically reduce inventory investment correspondingly, though it certainly does reduce inventory. If it made it possible to reduce investment to 85 percent of the present levels, that would be a significant contribution at today's interest rates, and by putting fewer books into inventory, it would relieve some of the space pressure so common in publishers' warehouses.

Obviously, printings would not be ordered as 3651 copies or 11,547 copies. Rounding off 3651 copies to 3500 or 3750 will not undermine the value of the calculation.

What we have discussed here is the reordering problem in its very simplest form, though the principles remain valid for more complex versions. The EOQ equation applies to titles whose sales rate is fairly steady throughout the year. Calculations for titles that have seasonal sales patterns would have to reflect them. Similarly, if the optimal printing quantity will last a long time, some allowance must be made for an anticipated decline in the rate of sale.

Having calculated the most economical printing quantity, which is, by definition, the one that makes the best use of money, the publisher may decide that even the best use for this title is not good enough. It may be even more economical to have the title go out of print.

The key economic factor in this decision is neither the number of copies nor the dollars of sale. It is the dollars of margin of income over cost. In this case, cost means *cost*, without the phony accounting practice of "spreading" fixed overheads to each copy as though they were part of the cost. (Many a backlist title has been dropped, or its price increased to the point that it amounted to the same thing, because it failed to cover 40 percent in overheads. After being dropped, it covered zero.)

Royalty and manufacturing costs also affect the margin a book will produce. A title with no royalty cost (perhaps because it has still not sold enough copies to have earned out an unrealistic royalty advance) or a low manufacturing cost may continue in print because it will return high enough margins at relatively lower sales levels.

Just what the minimum contribution of any title should be will depend on the particular publishing house. A publisher with elaborate bureaucratic procedures and heavy overhead may retire a title as a nuisance that would contribute happy dollars to a smaller or trimmer company. A publisher with a very large backlist may be more willing to retire a title than a publisher carefully husbanding a small list. Yet a large backlist, supported by a merchandising plan, may give each title added value. Some of the added value will show simply as higher sales from the automatic distribution under the plan, but there is also the added attraction the plan will have for the bookseller from the simple fact that it covers a wider spectrum of his needs, even if some of the titles sell slowly.

The financial contribution of each title can be a part of the inventory control computer file for that title, so the research is not required each time and the calculations need not be repeated each time the computer reminds management that it is time to reprint again.

Very few publishers bother to do the EOQ calculation in determining reprinting quantities, though it takes no more than a minute on a pocket calculator. The costs of this shortsightedness differ with each publisher and with each title on his list, but they are no doubt considerable. One of them is the management time and effort involved in making the reprinting decisions. It takes many knowledgeable people a lot of time to make all those mistakes!

15

Computerization, Management Information, and Odds and Ends

THE HEAD OF THE publishing division of a large American company remarked to me recently: "We have as much computer capacity as NASA had to send a man to the moon, but if I want something done on a computer reliably and quickly, well, I prefer an outside service."

Computers can do two things well. One is decreasing the load of paperwork by permitting one entry to be stored and used as frequently as needed for a wide variety of clerical and accounting procedures. Publishers in general have managed, after some years of difficult and painful adaptation, to get their computers to handle the clerical work, rarely well, but frequently acceptably.

Because the computer can sort and do complicated calculations with lightning speed, it can always provide an up-to-the-minute analysis of how the business is functioning. It can measure management's performance and the performance of those who report to it. It can measure the effect of forces amenable to management's control so that they can be manipulated to the best advantage. The use of the computer for such purposes in book publishing is close to zero.

Coping with the clerical complications peculiar to publishing has been a constant problem for everyone involved. This burden seems to have grown geometrically as publishing has grown in number of titles, number of publishers, and number of stores.

The publishers, the creators of much of the confusion, have been able to apply computer technology to their clerical routines, thereby avoiding being smothered by a human swarm of paper pushers. Smaller publishers have computer service bureaus that can, under a contract, prepare invoices and maintain records of sales, inventories, accounts receivable, and other essential business information. Booksellers, except for the chains and a few brave pioneers, are still largely denied these advantages.

Publishing has probably passed through the worst of the disruptions caused by the introduction of the computer, but the computer still evokes some negative reaction among authors, booksellers, and even publishers whenever it is mentioned. Some of the early computer catastrophes were monstrous and laughable, including publishing houses completely incapable of making shipments for weeks and sometimes even months, unable to issue any invoices or statements, because their records were irretrievably lost in the electronic guts of their new miracle machines. Companies that delayed their computerization, with their colleagues' catastrophes before them, avoided this nightmare by better advance planning of the computer installation and more cautious conversions. All the companies that lived through that changeover have, by this time, managed to work out their problems.

The particular problems that created those early crises differed with each publishing house. The only generalization that may explain the extraordinary consistency of these crises is the natural chaos and the charming insistence on individuality that prevail in book publishing. Many managements resisted the pleading of their computer advisers to set up more rigid rules of operation, to reduce the number of exceptions that required managerial intervention, to establish consistent rules in areas that were being handled differently by different people at different times. This resistance sometimes resulted in very expensive computer systems that worked, more often in systems at reasonable cost that did not work well.

In keeping with the stubborn individuality in publishing, computer systems differ somewhat from one house to another, no two being the same. Some are more economical to operate than others and some provide more trustworthy information. Today it can be said at least that all the computer systems "work": Books get shipped; customers get invoices; inventory records are reliable; authors are paid properly and on time; delinquent accounts are identified.

Virtually without exception, where computer systems have been installed in publishing houses, it has been in response to the needs of the accounting department and its order-fulfillment section. The heart of each of these systems is one or another form of billing and shipping. The computer creates the invoice and automatically creates (the feature that usually intrigued the financial vice president the most) all of the auxiliary records that rely upon this information: bringing customers' accounts up to date; adjusting the book inventory to subtract the copies shipped; entering the sale on the author's royalty statement; updating the sales figures for the title; adjusting the cost of sales accounting; etc. As the number of titles, accounts, and the complexity of discounts increased, the computer has simplified the life of the accounting department to some degree.

But the computer has not uniformly worked well for publishers. In some cases, the costs of preparing an invoice are now so high that many publishers resist orders that they were once happy to process manually but that they reckon (probably wrongly) actually cost money in the computer system. It is a fact that some publishers ship two or three weeks after receiving an order and that a cumbersome system, into which the computer has been fitted, is at least partly to blame.

In some areas, however, the higher cost results from the failure to design the system to fulfill the tasks it must perform. Some 20 to 30 percent of the orders a typical trade book publisher processes each day are for one copy of one book. I know of no computer system that was designed with that in mind. The typical publisher "gets 80 percent of his business from 20 percent of the accounts" or some approximation of that. I know of no computer system that was designed with that in mind.

More important than these defects in details, I believe it can be fairly said that in its application of computers, the publishing industry has badly missed the boat. The boat in this case is using the computer in its most talented capacity: the ability to analyze great masses of information to enhance the effectiveness of management and the breadth of areas that management can control.

Even where the computer does its accounting job efficiently and inexpensively, I know of no publishing houses in which the computer is supplying management in general, and sales management in particular, with the kinds of operating analyses that it certainly could supply because it has much or all of the necessary information as a by-product of its billing and shipping activities.

The failure of the computer as a tool of management is the fault of neither the machine nor the computer technicians. The computer does not supply operating information because such information has not been sought by management. If there had been a strong desire for analytical information, it would have been supplied, though expensively and inadequately, under the manual system, and it would have been made part of the criteria by which the computer systems were designed and installed. Unfortunately, because these considerations played no part in the initial designs of any of these systems, most of the computers presently operating cannot easily supply management analyses without extensive additional programming.

Because, as we have noted, the computer was introduced to help cope with the rising tide of clerical detail, it is usually under the control of the accounting department or the financial vice president. Even in the few cases where it has a quasi-independent status, reporting to the head of the house, it is kept well insulated from the operating managers. So it continues to be an accounting machine, producing mountains of records, many of them useless or unused, sometimes misleading while seeming tremendously impressive.

Paradoxically, publishing management needs the computer for the same reasons accounting insisted on installing it: The complexity and great mass of seemingly random detail simply cannot be handled adequately by hand.

The computer can also become a powerful tool for shortcutting work as well as for analysis and control. It can be programmed to perform all the routine work in book design. In the production department, it can create the cost estimates, develop and control the schedules, write purchase orders, etc. In the editorial department, it can keep track of individual productivity, analyze proposals against the company's financial criteria, etc.

We can suggest tools that a director of marketing should want and let this suggest the kinds of analyses that an editorial director, a financial director, or the head of the business might find it useful to have.

For example, as we have already explained, the computer can translate the rate and pattern of sales of each title into a projection that can alert management whenever the stock of that title reaches the point at which there is just enough time to get a reprint before stock is exhausted. It can then advise management, in view of the current interest rates and other costs, how many copies to reprint to make the best use of working capital. In the period directly after the sales conference, it can determine which accounts have been sold the forthcoming titles and which have been missed. It can compare the quality of selling among the reps, on both new books and the backlist.

As orders for new books come in, it can project the probable advance sale for each title and revise that projection based on the newest data, so that management can be confident it is selling and printing the right quantity. The computer can distinguish, from the pattern of a rep's orders, the subjective judgment each rep has made about each title, so management can correct misconceptions or weaknesses early in the selling season.

The computer can analyze the cost-effectiveness of discount schedules and of special offers like "one free in ten" or prepublication prices. It can distinguish the difference in the quality of returns of unsold copies by sales territory to help management control returns.

The travel plan and the account visiting plan for each sales territory will probably be developed manually, although the computer can do it. Thereafter, the computer can keep track of how faithfully the plan is followed. It can analyze the nature of the orders it receives from the various sales reps and present sales management with a report card for each one, showing his performance against a variety of criteria.

The number of copies of any new book going into any bookstore should be expected to relate in some way to the sale of previous similar titles in that very same bookstore. This relation is what is arrived at, theoretically, in the negotiation between the publisher's rep and the bookseller. However, their grasp of the historical information is sketchy at best, and the circumstances under which the dialogue usually takes place do not encourage unbiased and unhurried weighing of whatever evidence is perceived. At the very least, the publisher's computer has a record of the shipment and returns to that bookstore of each of *that publisher's* previous titles.

Each book is, of course, truly different from every other book, and public taste and willingness to buy change continuously. Yet extrapolation from previous experience is several orders of magnitude more reliable than the give and take in hundreds of thousands of uncontrollable negotiations between sales reps and booksellers. And, though it may be a deflating revelation to an author, books that may differ in content, style, and literary merit may have very similar selling profiles.

The similarity (and variety) of selling profiles will reveal itself in a study of the sales history of previous titles, as will the characteristics that count in the book and the store. Some titles may be so "different" that previous experience will offer no useful guide, but it is very likely that sales history will usually be a reliable indicator.

It is absolutely and completely practical, and almost childishly simple, to send the computer in most publishing houses back to previous sales experience to write a "suggested order" for every title on the publisher's list for each store the sales rep is going to visit. The computer would use the historical information to strike the best balance between the danger of oversupply and returns versus undersupply and being out of stock. And the computer could change that balance according to changes in the cost of money or of handling returns. This would enable the sales rep to place on the table before the store buyer an objectively calculated order to serve at the very least as the starting point for the selling conversation.

□ *Since the computer has no ego and human beings have a great deal, the computer's calculation might initially be presented as "simply a starting point" from which the superior intelligences of the sales rep and the bookseller could begin their work. In time, the human beings would learn by experience, particularly as the computer itself improved by experience, that the computer's suggestions were pretty good after all.*

Publishers who have relied heavily on wholesalers do not have the complete sales history of each of their books at each retail location in their computer records. For those publishers, an analysis based on their sales directly to booksellers would understate the needs for the bookstores who have been using wholesalers. (Sales would be understated for two reasons. First, because the publisher's files would not show the books actually supplied to the store by the wholesalers; second, because of the sales lost through booksellers' reliance on wholesalers, as we have already discussed.) That would be a minor handicap, which would, moreover, correct itself in a season or two. Even before the change in selling methods provided better sales records and forecasts, the smaller initial orders where the computer understated sales would be easily corrected by secondary and tertiary shipments triggered by keeping track of bookstore sales *after* publication.

I am not suggesting that the computer can write the perfect advance order for each bookstore. Obviously, neither a computer nor any human being can do any such thing. The computer will occasionally write crazy orders, sending many copies when none are needed and vice versa. (At least some of these will be manifestly crazy and therefore correctable by the sales rep.) However, considering all the accounts that must order books, it can write orders so much better than those that now result from negotiations between reps and booksellers that the benefits to publishers and retailers must be projected in the millions of dollars.

The computer can also help a sales manager judge how successfully he is extracting sales from each piece of geography. As we have already explained, the sales that a publisher may expect in Houston, Texas, or Albany, New York, depend on a number of factors, including the nature of his list and the degree to which his titles appeal to some narrow field of interest, e.g., music, juveniles, etc., or satisfy a broader spectrum. The more general the range of publications and prices and the larger the list, the more sales will approach the same ratio, in Houston and Albany, to the population or income level in those two cities.

For publishers whose output is more specialized, the relative potential of sales is measured by some other yardstick, or combination of yardsticks, which measures the quantity of the specialized interest in that community. This might be the number of college students enrolled in social science courses, the population between the ages of X and Y, the number and economic status of families with children in elementary school, and so on.

The computer can be used in the first place to determine which of these independent variables are reasonably good indicators of the relative potential sales of the publisher's list. The computer can do this, not by a priori notions, but by actually comparing the strength of the indicator with the strength of the sales. The computer may reveal that there is no valid indicator or combination of indicators—a very unlikely result. But when the computer finds an indicator, it can continue to refine it and make it increasingly more useful.

Having gotten this far, the computer can now tell sales management how its effort is functioning in various cities and in various parts of the country, indicating where performance is below par. The poor performance may be because the sales rep in that area is less competent, because he is being asked to cover more geography or more of the potential market than other reps, because of unusual activity by a competitor, or for other reasons that can be ascertained by closer examination. But that examination would never occur without the analysis to indicate that there is a sales situation that is not following the normal pattern.

The comparison of sales to some measure of potential cannot be done simply from the information already in the computer. The computer must be fed the demographic data for the various parts of the country in which sales are being made. But these data are collected by various government bureaus and are readily available, so this detail is a relatively routine chore.

Almost every publisher has a list of accounts that he expects his sales force to call on with each new list. Unfortunately, few publishing houses keep accurate track of whether these calls and these sales are being made. It would be very easy for the computer to keep track of the salesmen's visits and to alert management in good time whenever accounts or cities are being skipped. As we suggested earlier, the computer could analyze the orders resulting from these visits against a variety of criteria. It could then project from these orders the probable size of the advance sale. This would give management an early indication of whether the goals it has set are likely to be met. This would reduce the current horrendously high cost of wasteful first printings, decided with insufficiently sophisticated analysis.

The computer can also be used effectively to analyze, in advance, the effects of proposed changes in retail prices, sales policies, discount schedules, number of titles published, distribution of titles over the calendar year, and a host of other marketing strategy possibilities for which the logical considerations are perfectly clear but that involve a number of complicated, interacting variables.

The possibilities are almost limitless, but they depend on management learning what the tool can do by using it, trying it in one way and then another, to develop both its versatility and management's confidence in its use.

Unfortunately, the computer is typically *not* used to do these things, perhaps because line management is not eager enough to manage (and in many publishing houses, insufficiently motivated), perhaps because top management is too concerned with the cost of such tools, and because the computer is usually in the hands of accountants who have little interest and little appreciation for operating problems.

Two disadvantages frequently created by the presence, prestige, and the paper-generating power of the computer are the undigestible outpourings of raw "information" and the increased authority assigned to pedestrian accounting thinking wrapped in computer reports.

The volume of "reports" the computer can spew out, sorting and summarizing perfectly ordinary information in a variety of perfectly ordinary ways, is prodigious. The month is a convenient unit of time for the accountant (though probably not at all helpful to the operating manager), so it is often arbitrarily designated as the interval for these reports. Their frequency and sheer weight have a deadening effect. Whereas it was exciting years ago to be able to demonstrate the extraordinary power of the computer by producing a list of every bookstore that bought *Lady Chatterley's Lover* in a given month and how many copies each store took, now the sales manager's eyes glaze over long before he picks up the report from his In basket and deposits it immediately on his shelf. Monthly reports continue to spew out of these machines long after anyone can remember who suggested that particular cut through the information file or why it seemed a good idea at the time. The recipients keep the bulky printouts for a month or two, and then throw them away to make room for the unending flow.

The information loses some of its value because the useful nuggets are so often buried in pages of relentless detail. The lulling similarity of the data month after month tends to dull the analytical sensitivity of the recipients. Although the accounting department may need regularity, the information provided to operating management would be more useful in many cases if it were provided less frequently and when requested rather than on a regular schedule.

The computer contains a gigantic file and has a fantastic ability to sort, recombine, manipulate, subtotal, and total information in the file. Supplying operating management with complete monthly reports in all their detail is, in a sense, handing the file over to management one month at a time so *it* can do the sorting, recombining, and manipulating, which, of course, it can't.

An attempt to respond to this difficulty and to provide analysis as well as information is evident in the move in larger organizations to set up so-called MIS (management information systems) departments. Generally, these departments are firmly under the control of financial management and think like financial managers rather than operators. The result is that MIS frequently becomes less a tool of operating management than a tool for financial management to guide (more accurately, to prod) managers.

It's really too bad, because the technology has developed in the direction of making decentralization of computer capacity extremely practical. In the early days, centralized control of the computer was essential, and the accounting department was the natural choice to control its use. Today it is perfectly practical, even if a single large company computer is centrally located, for each department to have its own computer files coupled to the central company files, with facilities for manipulating its data and producing its own reports.

While this alone would not immediately transform the computer into a management tool, it would be a big step toward helping operating management learn how to use data effectively. Continuing to have accountants supply data to operators in a form convenient and understandable to accountants and slanted by the fallacies that accounting thinking brings to operating problems simply puts off the day that operating managers will use the computer creatively for their own purposes.

The computer, unfortunately, gives prestige and authority to whatever comes out of it. Too often the computer has enhanced the authority of the accounting department without giving it greater insight. Title accounting and unit cost accounting, for example, are as fallacious as ever, but they are more impressive coming out of the computer.

On the other hand, the computer can make it easy to use statistical mathematics to analyze and control a great variety of activities that would otherwise appear too random and confused for management to deal with in any organized, systematic way.

Today, with the proper program in the computer, an advance sales prediction can be made instantly, on demand, as frequently as sales or production management wants to check its position. And, of course, the ease of producing similar analyses of all sorts of information, going far beyond the simple advance order analysis, means that operating management can use the computer to get an understanding of seemingly patternless masses of raw data that can be rendered meaningful only by statistical methods.

Production management may want to study the spoilage of the publisher's paper in printing plants, either comparing manufacturers' performance or looking for changes in pattern. Warehouse management may want to know whether the daily rate of shipment, or the level of service, is improving. Sales management may want to examine the order-writing performance among the reps and in detail for a particular rep. It may want to know when the sales rate of a lead title in sample stores indicates a true change in sales level, not just a normal fluctuation. The computer makes all this easy.

One very important by-product of the use of statistical methods is the development of tools (or, rather, their adaptation from other industries) for determining when the activity being observed is changing in some way that is more than just chance variation. This can be done by using the "control chart," or "quality control chart," developed in industry for completely different purposes.

It was discovered long ago that a printing press, or a paper-making machine, or an automobile assembly line does not produce at a uniform, steady rate. The rate varies within some range—a range that

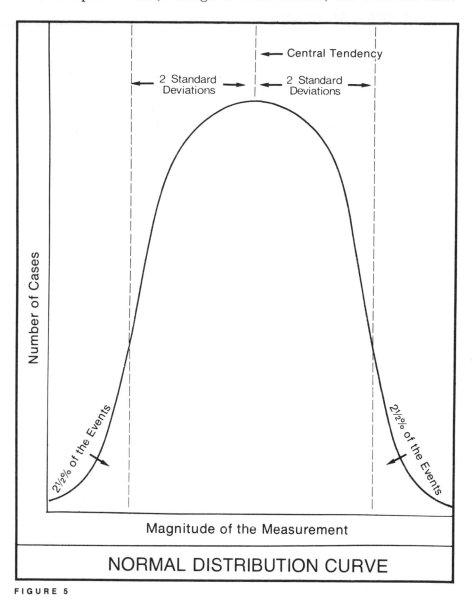

NORMAL DISTRIBUTION CURVE

FIGURE 5

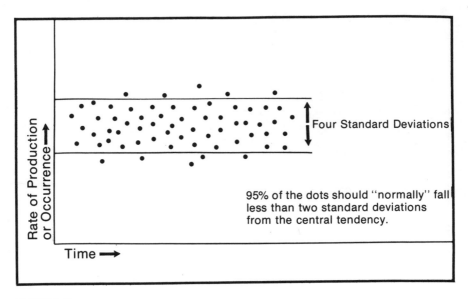

FIGURE 6

depends on the machine, the work being put through it, the crew, and other factors—but from day to day and even moment to moment, there is some variation, in some situations considerable variation.

The existence of this inevitable variation presents a problem. How is the manager of any production operation to know when the variation is normal, "chance" variation and when it is due to some actual change—the gradual deterioration of the machine or a deliberate slowdown by the crew?

For example, if your thermostat is set at 80 degrees Fahrenheit, the actual temperature may vary between 78 and 82 degrees. This variation is due to the sensitivity of the thermostat, the lag inherent in the heating system, the wind outside, the configuration of the house, the location of the thermostat, and other factors. And the variation in some houses will be naturally greater than in others. If you adjust the thermostat every time the thermometer does not register exactly 80 degrees, you will drive yourself and the heating system crazy and cause even greater fluctuations. However, when something does go wrong, such as a progressive deterioration in the boiler or the thermostat, it will reveal itself (among other ways) in these very fluctuations in temperature. How do you distinguish one from the other?

The answer is the control chart. The control chart for any operation is constructed from the history of previous performance: production per hour or per shift. The past production will be distributed over what statisticians call a normal distribution curve (see Figure 5). The curve may be very broad if the chance factors are many and powerful, narrow if the chance factors exert less influence. In any case, the variation will range on both sides of a central axis. In a normal distribution, 95 percent of the points will be within two "standard deviations" of the central axis, the standard deviations being larger for a broad curve than for a narrow curve, but in either case, precisely calculable.

The result is a chart (see Figure 6), for each situation to be "controlled," into which the production rates can be posted. So long as the variables operate normally, nineteen out of every twenty points (95 percent) will fall within the boundaries of the two standard deviations, plus and minus. When more than one point in twenty falls outside those lines, management has reason to look for some causal change in the factors at work.

The normal distribution and the control charts have another important use. The broader the distribution (the wider the normal distribution curve), the more chance factors are influencing the result.

(In Chapter 10, on editorial management, the graph for the decisions by the editorial committee indicates a situation in which *all* the factors are chance. Anything so extreme is hard to find outside a table of random numbers.) The more that chance controls, the less management controls. One objective of management is to reduce the influence of chance and increase the influence of deliberate control. It can measure its success in doing this (improving machine maintenance, better training of crews, better selection of titles, etc.) by the degree to which it narrows the range of the normal distribution and brings the lines (on Figure 6, for instance) at the distance of two standard deviations closer to each other. It is a kind of management report card.

There are a number of ways in which a control chart can be used in publishing. During the period of advance selling, if regression analysis is used to predict a total advance, the mathematics that supplies the prediction also results in the calculation of the standard deviation. This postulates a pattern of incoming orders around the predicted line. If more than 5 percent of the orders fall more than two standard deviations from the predicted line, then the situation that gave rise to the prediction has changed.

Similarly, after publication, the random variations in the daily receipt of orders need not confuse management or cause any uneasiness because they can be identified as random, and a meaningful change in the order pattern can be detected with ease.

One of the accusations of backwardness that outsiders (and some insiders) frequently level at publishing in general is its failure to do "market testing," or "market research."

Market research is a broad term, covering different activities undertaken for different purposes. One purpose of market research is to determine the potential customers for a projected product before the product is put on the market and to tailor the product and its advertising to suit the characteristics of those potential customers. This may be done for a new soap, a new magazine, or some other ambitious new product aimed at broad sections of the buying public.

It is possible that research of this kind would be helpful in launching best-sellers of the type produced by Irving Wallace or Robert Ludlum, and it's even remotely possible that the research would help the authors craft the plot or develop the characters. It's not a very attractive idea and highly unlikely to revolutionize the best-seller industry.

Such research would certainly make sense in connection with a project for a new dictionary or thesaurus, or for any similar tool aimed at a wide audience, the purchase of which is likely to be made thoughtfully and deliberately.

Still, thank goodness, the distinguishing characteristic of book publishing is that it produces a large variety of products, each of which appeals to small numbers of people. Some observers (and, sad to say, some practitioners) mistake this central characteristic of the book as some sort of defect. They deplore the small quantities in which books sell and would like all the books published to be best-sellers.

It has been a central purpose of this book to point out the inefficiencies, waste, and ineptitude of our trade book distribution system. The poor sales performance of virtually every trade book published, including the best-sellers, results from the failure of this system to put the book within reach of its audience. *Every* book should sell more copies than it does. But the effect of the long overdue improvement in book distribution, if it ever happens, will not be and *should not be* to make most books into best-sellers. On the contrary, better distribution is most likely to encourage many more titles selling at modest levels. Whether or not that improvement happens, the aim of editorial departments, even under today's conditions, should not be to concentrate on selecting and nurturing best-sellers.

Such a focus would result in a gigantic economic catastrophe for publishing and an even greater cultural catastrophe for America. The fact that the book is the only medium that makes it possible to communicate with small audiences, sometimes specialized, sometimes not, is book publishing's greatest source of strength as well as its chief contribution to the health of our democratic culture.

For economic and social reasons, we need to find for each book the greatest portion of its market that we possibly can, but that will not necessarily turn it into a best-seller. It is easy to visualize the modest size of the market when we can clearly define the small potential audience, as with a book on growing tropical fruit in northern climates or on exercises for handicapped children. It is not so obvious with books that have a less readily defined market, such as first novels, spiritual self-help, folk medicine, political exhortations, etc. These too, except when struck by best-seller lightning, perform their function by reaching a modest audience sufficient to make each an economically sound publishing venture.

□ *What is truly economically sound is somewhat distorted by bad publishing practice, which inflates overhead costs and creates expensive waste in overprintings and returns, and bad accounting practice, which misstates the publishing results. Whereas most publishers would probably consider the sale of 10,000 copies the threshold to economic acceptability, the number could be in the neighborhood of 3000 copies, which, with more efficient distribution, should be much easier to attain than it is today.*

But, if the product is to be marketed to 5000, 10,000, or even 25,000 potential customers in a population of many, many millions, how effective can traditional market research be? Even to discover whether these 5000 or 25,000 potential customers exist would require sampling large sections of many millions of people at considerable cost even before there would be an opportunity to study the potential customers in detail.

The smaller the specific audience, the more expensive and difficult is the market research, particularly if that audience is largely undifferentiated, as it would be for a first novel. A publisher issuing 50 or 100 titles each year, pleased to be publishing a variety of titles for a variety of audiences, would be driven to distraction, if not to bankruptcy, if he tried to research the market for each title.

There is the further problem of the additional time required to go through even the most unsophisticated research program before the publication of any book. Mistaken publishing, production, and distribution procedures already seriously circumscribe the marketability of books by the delays they introduce between the manuscript and the reader. Unless the research delivers spectacular insights, further delay can only do serious harm. We need to find ways of getting the author to his readers more quickly to make the medium more effective as a communicator, so the book conveys ideas as effectively as it stores them.

But, of course, contrary to the critics' charge, the publisher does rely on useful, though rough-and-ready market research: the experience of his previous publications and what he can observe of the competition. He can extrapolate from these experiences to an expectation for the proposed title. There is nothing unreasonable or illogical in drawing conclusions from this practical information rather than from information specifically gathered for a new editorial project. On the contrary, the actual experience has the virtue of being real rather than "let's suppose."

The publisher's experience would be even more useful if he took the trouble to analyze, with greater sophistication, the hundreds of thousands of orders, reorders, and returns already in his files. They would tell him much more precisely the marketing lessons of his publishing history.

This brings us to another, more decisive reason to view with great caution the type of market research outsiders so often recommend. Market research in other industries has a tremendous advantage in that the producer is solidly connected to his market through a reliable distribution system. Whether it is shoes, soap, or breakfast cereal, if an audience large enough to support some new product or style variation is detected by market research, the distribution channel will reach it.

Supposing the publisher discovers, through research, that there are 25,000 or 125,000 or 525,000 prime customers for a book on some subject, or by some writer, or whatever; how can he be sure he will reach them? Through distribution-by-negotiation, with all its accidental permutations and combinations of conversations (or lack of them) between reps and booksellers? With the additional accidents of store display, clerks' ignorance, premature returns?

We all know that two identical books (certainly at a level below best-seller sales and perhaps at that level as well) might be published at approximately the same time and reach widely different markets both in numbers and in description. Separate the publication dates by a month or two and the probability of such a difference in sales is markedly increased. Does the same book have different markets? No. But our distribution is so inefficient at reaching the market for even the ordinary book that it is hard to predict what part of it, and how much of it, the book will reach. What is the point of studying the patient's reflexes when the shinbone is not connected to the anklebone?

On virtually every subject, including market research, the discussion cannot escape the central fact, and the central problem, of trade book publishing: Book distribution is inefficient, chaotic, and unpredictable—all the other problems and shortcomings in publishing are minor in comparison.

It is certainly true that 3000 (or, at the very most, 5000) copies sold of almost any book should be sufficient for it to break even. (If your accountant tells you otherwise, fire him.) If a country of our size, with our level of literacy and general education and with our standard of living, cannot produce 5000 buyers for almost any book that has passed a publisher's editorial department, a business committee, and other devices that the publisher uses to try to stop marginal publishing projects from reaching his catalogue—if after all this examination, reexamination, and heavy financial analysis, a mere 5000 buyers cannot be found, that in itself is a complete indictment of the system of book distribution.

It is possible to imagine a trade book publishing industry producing titles in such overabundance, and covering such a wide variety of special subjects, that some of the books would be of so little interest that there would be reasonable doubt that 5000 buyers actually exist. That is not the case today, when the inadequate sales levels are due, not to an inadequate market, but to the inadequate means of reaching it.

It may be tempting to hope that the inefficiencies of book distribution can be circumvented by some sort of "market testing," but there is no serious reason to believe it can happen.

The International Standard Book Numbers (ISBNs), which are already used by almost all publishers to identify each title, and the standard store numbers, which are gradually coming into use to identify each retailer, are creating a situation that could profoundly change how books are billed and shipped to bookstores. It would be a change that, contrary to most of the recent and potential developments in the industry, would actually help the smaller publisher.

Currently, each publisher assigns his *own* identifying code to each of his customers. As publishers replace their own identifiers with the new standard identifying numbers, it will become easy for any group of publishers to combine their billing and shipping, sending to the bookstore all their books in one combined shipment and even on one combined invoice.

Billing and shipping for several publishers at once occurs now in a very limited way when smaller publishers operate under a distribution agreement with larger ones. It requires that the publishers' books be sold together and the orders come into the warehouse on one order, which may be under separate headings for different publishers. In such cases, the participating "distributee" must accept the sales services of the larger publisher, as well as the billing and shipping services, for the system to function. He must also accept an approximate allocation of money as the distributing publisher collects from the bookstores.

With the use of standard bookstore numbers, a distributor, who need not be a publisher at all—it could be an independent warehousing and fulfillment service, a book manufacturer offering that service, a wholesaler transforming the nature of book wholesaling—can combine shipments to booksellers no matter how the order was received or from whom. This is important for any publisher who wishes to have the advantages of combined invoicing and shipping but wants to retain the advantage of controlling his own selling effort.

There is another, seemingly minor, development that strongly supports the practicality of such combined billing and shipping. Under the present distribution arrangements, the distributor has no way of precisely relating the payments, as they come in from bookstores and wholesalers, to the titles and the publishers to whom those payments belong. As a result, the distributor approximates the amount due each publisher, based on that publisher's percentage of the total sales and on the distributor's rate of collection. To protect himself against overpayment, the distributor holds back a portion of each publisher's theoretical receipts. But the system, in addition to penalizing the distributee, whose income is being deliberately slowed, may actually jeopardize the distributor as well, since he may discover that his "average" withholding of receipts has resulted in his severely underpaying one publisher but overpaying another.

There is now at least one computerized billing service that can determine precisely the books that each bookstore payment covers. (I know, because it was developed specifically for me.) There is no longer any need for the publisher to accept the distributor's approximation. The receipts from customers can be allocated exactly to the proper title (and, of course, the publisher), and, moreover, each publisher can know precisely how many copies of each title have been billed but not yet paid for, so he can know precisely about his own accounts receivable. It is also possible for each publisher in such a combined fulfillment system to maintain his own separate discount schedule.

The fulfillment service would work something like this: The service would operate a warehouse, an order department to receive and edit orders and enter them into the computer, a credit and collection department, and a customer service department to answer queries from bookstores and wholesalers. The computer would combine any shipments going to the same bookstore and would combine invoices into a single monthly statement, even if the orders in the course of the month were not received close enough to be shipped together. Depending on the size of the operation and the policies of the participating publishers, the probability of combining could be increased by "pulsing" the order processing to each geographic location. That is, shipments to San Francisco could go every Friday, or every Monday, Wednesday, and Friday. It is likely that such pulsing would actually speed receipt of books in San Francisco on the average because some combined shipments would go as single truck shipments, which travel faster than several postal shipments, or because the distributor would find it economical to combine all the packages to San Francisco in one trailerload, to be broken down and distributed there by United Parcel Service. As such a fulfillment service is used and expanded, it will become more useful, more effective, and less expensive.

The benefit to the bookseller is the considerable reduction in clerical burden. There would be fewer shipments to open and check in, fewer invoices, and simpler communication with fewer customer service departments. There would also be a substantial saving in shipping cost, though this might become the publisher's economy if we get to the point of publishers paying freight. The publisher would benefit from lower fulfillment costs, less reluctance on the part of the bookseller to place an order, and, perhaps more important, surer collection of bills. It is to be expected that the larger the combination of publishers represented in the combined fulfillment and the correspondingly more attractive their titles, the greater likelihood that booksellers will be careful not to put themselves on credit hold by delaying payment.

A service of this kind operating on behalf of university presses could change the ratio of wholesaler to retailer sales sufficiently to improve their financial results radically. A fulfillment service for such publishers would also encourage ordering because the bookseller, aware that the university press itself is more likely to be in stock than the wholesaler is, would have a greater expectation of prompt fulfillment than he does when ordering from even the larger wholesalers.

It is perfectly reasonable to expect that such a fulfillment service, dispensing books of general publishers in sufficient volume, would find it economical to establish two or three satellite warehouses (operated from the one central computer) around the country. If each warehouse is operated on a simple statistical inventory control system, its stock can be kept very small, to be replenished strictly by scheduled trailerloads. It could guarantee the local retailer surer service than any wholesaler can supply, and the advantage to the publisher of the retailer discount over the wholesaler discount would more than cover the cost of the local operation.

Such a fulfillment service would by no means (not in *our* publishing society, thank goodness!) include all publishers. It is likely that there will be several such systems, coming into being very quickly after the first pioneer has proved that the idea works. No matter. Each such consolidation will represent a saving for booksellers and publishers, and will help expand the availability of books to the public by encouraging possible newcomers to the retailing field by the prospect that the clerical burdens of bookselling will not be unbearable. Even if the consolidation of fulfillment results only in reducing the number of shippers of books from 450 to 50, it will be a remarkable improvement from which all except wholesalers will benefit. It may actually (and this is a desirable objective indeed) encourage an increase in the number of publishers by simplifying for small publishers what is now a costly complication.

16

Conclusion

THERE IS NO LONGER very much doubt that trade book publishing is suffering from more than its share of our present economic malaise. The mass marketer's spurning of reprint publishing is already being felt. Meeting the economic pinch by cutting overhead and publishing programs has brought temporary relief here and there, but some publishers have already passed through that palliation to realize that they are now worse off than before.

After what has been said in these pages, it may seem hardly possible to find the obligatory optimistic note to strike in the final chapter. Yet I believe that it is precisely the unrelenting pressure of publishing's new economic problems that will force some publishers to abandon traditional responses and experiment with new approaches more appropriate to the magnitude of the problem.

The immediate future for trade book publishing *in general* is bleak, but the future for any trade book publisher *in particular* lies in whatever that particular publisher does to swim upstream.

It takes only a few pioneers to demonstrate a new set of truths from which many can extract the benefits. The directions in which trade publishing must go to correct its weaknesses are not mysterious. The key to success is the same as it is for every consumer industry: efficient, pervasive, inexpensive distribution. Granted that the complications inherent in books make distribution more difficult for publishing than it is for any other consumer product; that simply makes the need more urgent while it raises the level of ingenuity needed to fill it.

Many of my suggestions for improving the distribution of books, which seemed so outlandish and impossible when they were proposed twenty-five years ago, seem much less radical today. In the interim they have, in one form or another, been tried and found to work reasonably well. Today we have a bookseller demanding that each publisher take responsibility for selecting his own books for that store. It may turn out to be the very step we need to move us through the looking glass into rational book distribution.

Whether the remarkable initiative taken by the Turners of Under Cover Books does it or not, I am convinced that the basic proposals suggested here for a better organization of book distribution will be commonplace in a few years. Once publishers feel the need to reexamine the assumptions underlying distribution-by-negotiation, changes will quickly follow. It may take nothing more than two or three publishers discovering, in assuming responsibility for their books at Under Cover, that they have greatly increased their volume of sales in that store and just as greatly reduced their returns.

Once publishers and booksellers have tasted the advantages of rational distribution, it will spread rapidly. It does not seem too far-fetched to suggest that some of the larger publishers will someday make publisher control of inventory a condition for doing business with a book retailer. When he has learned that out-of-stocks and heavy returns are not an unavoidable burden in trade book distribution, the publisher may not wish to tolerate those costs for the privilege of supplying a few eccentric booksellers trying to perpetuate tradition.

The introduction of rational, publisher-controlled and publisher-responsible distribution implies other desirable consequences. Improving the profitability of bookselling and reducing the drudgery as well as the uncertainty will expand the number of retail bookstores. Moving more books through stores by better control of inventory in the increased number of stores will mean a very significant increase in the number of books sold.

Distribution controlled by the publisher will reduce the shameful waste resulting from the present need to guess how many copies will be needed on publication day. The publisher will know, before the presses start to roll, exactly how many copies will be going to the bookstores, and he will have a fairly firm notion of what should be held in reserve. Reprints will be based on the sound knowledge of how many books are in stock in exactly which stores and how fast they are moving out.

The reduction in production waste and in the waste of handling and processing returns, together with the efficiencies in order processing, warehousing, shipping, and all the activities concerned with distribution, should lead to a reduction in the retail price of books. Even at half their present levels, book prices will give publishers much greater margins than they now enjoy.

Lower retail prices should reduce the attraction, and sensible printing and distribution should reduce the need, for remaindering. That may disappoint those customers who regularly outsmart the book distribution system by carefully watching the remainder tables. Their compensation will be generally lower retail prices and wider availability of more titles.

When it is no longer necessary for the publisher's sales force to fan out across the country months before publication to plead for orders or to be elaborately prepped for that task at a semi-annual sales conference, other sources of waste will be eliminated. How many copies to send to each store will be decided when the book exists, close to the time it will be put on sale, instead of as a result of a debate months earlier, when the climate into which it will be shipped can only be projected.

Since books will not need to be "sold" months in advance, catalogue closings and sales conference dates will no longer interfere with allowing each title to be published on the schedule that suits it best. Whether a book appears weeks or years after the manuscript is ready will be determined by management's judgment of the most effective timing for that book.

Once publisher control of bookstore inventory demonstrates that some publishers—even a few—can substantially improve sales and stock turnover, every publisher will be required to learn how. Implicit in the whole idea of having each publisher responsible for his own titles in the store is that the publishers will be in competition, or as Joel Turner of Under Cover Books said to me, "We are putting the publishers on commission."

It is not reasonable to expect that the store will allow the publisher who delivers a poor return the same budget and freedom as it allows one who delivers a high return. Nor is it reasonable that the successful publisher will fail to remind the bookseller that he deserves more generous treatment. If, in fact, publisher control of store inventory does spread beyond the single case of Under Cover Books, as I think it must, publishers will have to become much more sophisticated about how to ensure a higher return on the store's investment.

In the course of acquiring such sophistication, publishers will learn two important lessons. The first is that a title should be kept alive as long as possible. With the drying up of the paperback reprint market, that will not be hard to accept, though it will require breaking some old habits and learning some new techniques.

The second is that the contrast between the books showing high sales and those showing low sales will be much less than it is now. This will happen despite the fact that "best-sellers" will actually sell better; the improvement in the lesser books will be much more dramatic.

The combination of these lessons may wean management away from the best-seller syndrome that is now so prevalent: the notion that profitability can be attained by publishing fewer, more popular books and replacing them frequently. It is more likely that editors will be asked to supply broader lists that appeal to more diverse interests. With the break-even point for any single book much lower, and the average level of sale much higher, the intense, misdirected pressures that now weigh upon editors should be very much reduced.

Will more titles be published? I think they will, although the change may simply result in longer life for the titles that are published. On the one hand, the number of new titles may decline. The fact that some books—like cookbooks, gardening books, etc.—live longer will tend to establish them more firmly and discourage the appearance of similar titles with no clear advantages. But on the other hand, because the inventory system and the extension of the network of stores will permit many more titles to be available at any one time, there may be an increase in number of titles. Certainly, a lower break-even point and a reduction in the uncertainties of publishing would encourage more titles.

If the distribution system is improved by shifting from negotiation to publisher control of inventory, is it likely to be accompanied by parallel improvements in accounting methods and the organization of book production? Probably not. The changes in distribution are easier for publishers to see; and in a sense, they are being pushed into them. Moreover, the move is more likely to become widespread because the results are clearly visible and because pressures to adapt to the change will develop rapidly.

By contrast, even if a publisher should develop a better accounting method or more economical production, it is unlikely that other publishers would even know about it, and there would certainly be no pressure on them to follow suit.

The likelihood is that if the expected improvements in distribution occur, the prosperity they will generate for the publishers who pioneer them will have the same narcotic effect that paperback royalties had until they were withdrawn. If the pressure to improve accounting or production (or any other function) diminishes because the pressure on profits diminishes, they will not be improved. In this respect, management in publishing does not differ greatly from management in any other industry.

The long-term prospects for trade publishing seem bright, partly because the short-term prospects are so dismal and because the remedies, though radical, are evident. Nevertheless, the adjustment is likely to be painful and probably not fast enough. There will be casualties, and they will probably include old and honored houses, too set in their ways to adapt readily to the profound changes taking place.

But when the adjustment is made, if developments move in the direction that seems so likely, trade publishing should find itself on a new and very much higher plateau that is much more comfortable for everyone—authors, publishers, booksellers, and the reading public.

Appendixes

The Current Profitability
of Bookstores

The American Booksellers Association engaged Booz, Allen &
Hamilton in 1977 to conduct a survey of its member stores to study
and report on their financial and business operations, including their
profitability. The stores studied ranged in annual sales volume from
$50,000 to $1 million.

Some of the stores, particularly the smaller ones, reported a profit
without deducting a salary for the owner-manager. When the survey
adjusted its figures to provide for such a salary, the profit frequently
became a loss. The range of return on sales ran from a loss of 4.5
percent for the least profitable group of stores to a profit of 12.1
percent for the most profitable.

The survey arrived at some average figures for all the participating
stores. The cost of books, including delivery cost, averaged 64.8
percent. Expenses for salaries, rent, advertising, etc., came to 32.7
percent. The average profit was 2.5 percent.

Since the cost of goods averaged 64.8 percent, the average effective
discount on sales reported by the survey was 35.2 percent. This
represents a markup over the average cost of goods of 54.32 cents for
every dollar of cost. The average number of turns of stock was
reported to be 3.32; therefore each dollar of inventory, on the average,
produced 3.32 times 54.32 cents, or $1.8034 of gross margin annually.
It is from this average gross margin that the store paid its expenses,
amounting to 32.7 percent of sales, and had 2.5 percent of sales
remaining as profit.

The annual inventory turnover of 3.32 means that the store sold in
a year 3.32 times the value of the books it had (on the average)
available for sale—which were, of course, being replenished constantly,

replacing not only the books that were sold, but also those that were returned to publishers.

Since the turnover was 3.32, the store had an average inventory for each dollar of sales of 30.12 cents ($1 divided by 3.32) at retail value, which was 19.52 cents (30.12 multiplied by 64.8 percent) at cost to the store. The 2.5 percent profit on sales (that is, 2.5 cents profit per dollar of sales) was, in fact, a profit of 12.8 percent on the average inventory investment of 19.52 cents per dollar of retail sales, which sounds considerably less tragic than the same profit expressed as 2.5 percent on sales and is a much more useful measure. In effect, the bookseller earned a profit of 12.8 cents on every dollar he had invested in inventory.

In the Booz, Allen survey, and in our extrapolations from it, the value of the interest on the inventory investment has been ignored. Including the cost of the money invested in inventory (a perfectly legitimate and virtually unavoidable expense) would substantially reduce the bookstore profit as calculated from the survey. (An interest rate of 12.8 percent would, of course, wipe the profit out completely.)

The survey does not attempt to study the difficulties faced by the bookseller in what seems to outsiders to be a simple retail business.

Inventory Control
in Bookstores

Let us look more closely at some aspects of inventory control to see
what the bookseller is up against.

According to the classical explanations of inventory control, the
retail manager chooses a stock level for each item (SKU, or
stockkeeping unit), depending on its rate of sale and his cost of placing
buying orders. The less often he orders, the larger the inventory he
must carry, increasing the cost of his investment. He chooses an
inventory level that will just balance the cost of ordering against the
cost of investment. Such an inventory level is adjusted whenever
changes in the sales rate or in the costs of ordering or carrying
inventory alter that balance.

The reorder *date* for any single item of inventory will depend on
how long it takes to place the order and how much time will elapse,
on the average, before the merchandise will be received. That, in turn,
will depend on the distance from the source of supply, the shipping
method used, and the speed of the supplier's order-processing
procedures. Since all of these factors can only be approximated, the
reorder date will be chosen so that, on average, the replenishment
stock arrives *before* the last unit of the stock is sold. How much earlier
will depend on how damaging the retailer feels it will be to be out of
stock of that particular item.

The reorder *quantity* will depend on the cost of the investment,
which is heavily influenced by the rate at which it is sold, balanced
against the cost in clerical time, discount disadvantages, etc. of placing
orders more frequently.

Obviously, the slope of the sales line, the rate at which the item
will sell (we are ordering for the future, not the past), is critical to

determining when to reorder and how many copies to reorder. One key element, therefore, in any inventory control method is knowing the *future* rate of sale.

IBM suggests that "the most important step to be taken in deciding whether to order a new supply" (or, I suggest, even the first supply) "of a particular SKU is to obtain an accurate forecast of the future sales of that SKU."

How does one know future sales? One way, and virtually the only way available to a retailer, is to study previous sales of the same item and project those sales into the future.

Classical inventory control systems, including those offered by IBM, make sense *only* because they use statistical projections of present and past sales of each SKU to determine probable future sales of that SKU. Then, based on the expected future sales, the control systems choose the most profitable balance of inventory level and reorder pattern.

Unfortunately, the classical methods cannot be applied to books, *store by store*, because the rate of sale of any title (except for a rare 2 or 3 percent of titles) never reaches levels that permit valid statistical projection. That is why an inventory control system, if it is to operate at all, must use the sales data from many stores. Though a bookseller chain can theoretically use its own sales data for this purpose (though none do so yet), the independent bookseller must depend upon the publisher to provide such a service.

Relating Sales Territories to Sales Force by SMSA

SMSAs (Standard Metropolitan Statistical Areas), which define where people live and spend their money, should be the building blocks for assembling or dividing sales territories rather than the arbitrary and frequently irrelevant government divisions such as states and major cities, which are commonly used. A great deal of economic and demographic information is available for the SMSAs, making them very convenient for planning coverage, analyzing workloads, measuring results, etc. Except when the SMSA is itself larger than a sales territory should be (metropolitan New York, for example), an SMSA should never be divided between territories, although many SMSAs cross state lines. Since, except for special accounts based in a rural area, there is almost no business outside SMSAs, a sales territory can be defined by the SMSAs it includes.

Population is not the only characteristic—perhaps not even the most important one—of the market areas covered by the sales force. There are a number of demographic factors, called independent variables in this context, that may be reliable indicators of the potential for book sales: that is, the relative variation in one, or a combination, of these variables may correspond to the relative variation in potential book sales.

These variables are "independent" because they exist outside anything the publisher does, and they vary without any influence from the publisher or his activity. But they do describe and assign some numerical value (like number of adult inhabitants, total dollars of retail sales) to a characteristic of each SMSA (and the market as a whole, for that matter), which may relate to the SMSA's potential for the publisher's books.

We can start by testing population (or general retail sales, or purchasing power) in each SMSA compared to the publisher's sales in that area. Some indexes combine several variables (population, personal income, and educational level, for example) to give a single number. Obviously, some of these independent variables will have little or no relationship to the factors that influence book buyers; others will have such a relationship in varying degrees. Nothing, except the actual sale of books, will have a perfectly corresponding relationship to book sales.

The degree to which any one of these variables indicates the relative potential for the sales of the publisher's books among the SMSAs does not have to be accepted on faith or on a subjective judgment of the logic of the relationship. It can be measured. The publisher may think that educational level is the best indicator. It is easy enough to find out.

The mathematical procedure called regression analysis (which is discussed in greater detail in Chapter 14, on determining printing quantities) measures the degree to which any one (or combination) of these independent variables corresponds to the variation in sales among SMSAs. This degree of correspondence is called the correlation. The variable that shows the closest correspondence can then be used to indicate the relative potential of each SMSA for the purchase of that publisher's books. The actual mathematical value of the correlation tells the publisher how strongly he can rely on the independent variable.

Detecting which, if any, of these independent variables has such a relation to potential sales can tell a sales manager how to assign his available sales strength. (And, jumping ahead a little, it does not take too much imagination to see that the ratio of the publisher's *actual* sales in each SMSA to the magnitude of the independent variable in that area is one indicator of how effective the sales effort is in that particular market region compared to others.)

The index of retail sales (or whichever index is found to correlate best) provides sales management with an approximation of the relative potential for book sales for each SMSA and for each territory. Sales time cannot be allocated simply in a ratio to the potential sale in each geographical area. Allowance must be made for the time required to cover the extraordinarily large account (a wholesaler or the headquarters of a large chain) that happens to be located in that area but is not related to the calculated potential.

Allowance must also be made for the travel time required, which may vary widely from one part of the country to another. Sales management may decide that Arizona requires 50 percent travel time; Wyoming, 70 percent; and New York City, none at all. In that case, the potential assigned per sales rep day should be half in Arizona what it is in New York City.

After making these allowances, the tentative territories (corresponding to the number of reps available) can be adjusted so that the *effective* selling time per unit of potential is approximately the same for each territory. The territory's lines may need to be further adjusted (by trading SMSAs among adjoining territories) so that the total sales force's travel time, taking into account the residence of each rep, is minimal.

That gives you the territories.

The next focus is each individual territory. The sales manager with a commission sales force will be able to do as little here as he could in delineating territories, but if the reps work for him alone, he should welcome both the responsibility and the opportunity.

Within each territory, each SMSA represents some percentage of the total potential for that territory. The SMSA that represents 10 percent should get 10 percent of the available selling time, the one that represents 20 percent should get 20 percent, and so on. This is, of course, the time available after allowing for the large accounts and for travel.

Such a simplistic approach to allocating time is a perfectly good way to start. However, sales management should be alert to the need for more sophisticated formulas, which will only become evident after some years of supervised sales force activity and some rather subtle mathematical analysis of the results. I suspect the analysis may well show the best strategy to be the opposite of the a priori one: to get maximum results from a sales force larger than the absolute minimum, more time per unit of potential should be given to the areas of lower potential rather than the areas of higher potential.

Applying the percentages to the number of available days gives you the number of days of selling time that should be assigned to each SMSA. The result is the gross division of time and effort within each territory.

It is then a simple and straightforward exercise to allocate time to each locality—even to each account—and, matching that allocation against a calendar and a map, to determine exactly when each account should be visited. Obviously, such a detailed plan can be easily amended to suit changes in the potential, in the size of accounts, and even for the rep's personal needs or preferences.

Calculating Optimum Sales Force Size

The first step is to determine sales to retailers, including the branch stores of all chains, by SMSA (Standard Metropolitan Statistical Area). To increase the validity of these numbers, wholesaler sales should be allocated as nearly as possible to the SMSAs of the retailers to whom the wholesaler sells the books (ignoring wholesaler library business). What we want to know, as nearly as possible, is the sale to consumers in each geographical location (SMSA).

The next step is to relate these sales by SMSA to the independent variable, such as population, retail sales, etc., which shows, by correlation analysis, the most sensitivity to the publisher's sales. The SMSAs can then be ranked in descending order based on the ratio of the publisher's actual sales volume to the independent variable. This measures how completely the potential sales in each SMSA is being translated into actual sales.

On the list of SMSAs, enter the amount of sales time given to that SMSA, expressed as "number of store visits."

The next step is to break the list of SMSAs into four groups; for instance:

Group 1. Top 10 percent of the SMSAs
Group 2. Second 20 percent
Group 3. Third 30 percent
Group 4. Remaining 40 percent

For each group, total the sales, the independent variable, and the number of store visits. Calculate, from these totals, the ratio of sales per unit of independent variable and the ratio of number of store visits per unit of independent variable.

Sales per unit will be in descending order from Group 1 through

Group 4. If the sales effort is truly effective (meaning that the more effort, the more sales), the "store visits" per unit will also generally be in descending order, though there may not be a strict one-to-one correspondence with each SMSA.

Now, for each group below Group 1, calculate the additional "store visits" that would be required to make the coverage per unit of potential equal to the average coverage of the next higher group, and the sales that would result if the sales per unit equaled the average sales per unit of the bottom half of the next higher group.

This is a conservative measure of the additional sales that can be expected from additional coverage. If the marginal return on these sales (that is, the return above manufacturing costs, royalties, costs for billing and shipping, etc.) is more than the cost of the manpower needed for these additional store visits, then expansion of the sales force will be profitable.

Although my experience has proved the above calculation to be useful, I believe it might be even more precise first to stratify the SMSAs according to size into two or three segments, and then to do the calculations I have described within each segment.

In calculating the "store visits per additional rep" to translate the number of additional visits into number of additional reps, it should be remembered that adding reps results in less travel time for the existing reps, which will increase their total visits and decrease their travel expenses.

Typesetting and Type Design

In 1965, when I was in charge of book manufacturing at McGraw-Hill, I proposed to management that the company commission the design of a new typeface, to be created cooperatively by a type designer and an eminent psychologist. My idea was rejected; while the matter is not the most pressing one in book publishing, the rationale behind it may be of interest.

The design of typefaces is influenced by subjective factors such as taste, general aesthetic standards, and our familiarity with the letter forms as well as the nature and level of industrial development and the specific materials and tools available to the printing industry. It was easier and more natural for the monks working on parchment to move from letter to letter without lifting the pen from the surface (except to replenish ink or to signal the end of a word), so letters tended to be joined in ligatures. Thus *st* and *ct* were usually written as one character, as were the more familiar *ff* and *ffi*. The nature of the writing implements and of the irregular parchment resulted in coarse, heavy letters.

When Gutenberg introduced typecasting technology, he retained the appearance of the scribes' work (he was, in effect, counterfeiting it), by casting type in the two-letter and three-letter combinations that the scribes' use of the pen favored. Because he wet the paper to get better ink penetration and adhesion, it was easy for him to obtain the coarse and heavy result he wanted.

The development of smoother papers and better inks and inking methods, and the skills in the working of metal and the etching of fine designs which were a by-product of gunsmithing, made possible the new finer and more delicate typefaces designed by Baskerville, Didot, Bodoni, and others.

The invention of the Linotype machine, and the use of the much softer metal associated with it, forced a number of changes. The number of channels in a Linotype "magazine," which holds the molds for the letters to be cast, is limited. That argued against yielding channels for ligatures. As a result, the only ligatures retained were *fi*, *ff*, *fl*, *ffl*, and *ffi*. Worse than that, since each letter was an individual brass mold into which the molten lead was poured, each mold had a brass wall on either side of it to contain the lead. The wall had to be thick enough to withstand the pressure of the molten metal as well as the rough treatment the mold received in its circuits through the typecasting process. The minimum distance between any two letters within a word (except the three ligatures) became the thickness of the two brass side walls that separated them. This pushing apart of the letters had never been necessary before and was one reason that Monotype composition, though more expensive, was favored by many for a long time over Linotype.

The fast casting method and the use of a soft lead alloy, which does not lend itself to fine detail and needs a certain coarseness of line to withstand the pounding of the larger and heavier printing presses then being introduced, required that the thin strokes of any letter be not overly thin and that the open spaces, the "counters"—in the lower-case *e* or *a*, for example—be large enough that, even though shallow, they would not fill in with ink and paper dust when on the press. These were the demands of Linotype composition and letterpress printing.

Even though today the composition is photographic and the printing is probably offset, the Linotype-letterpress appearance continues to be copied at the expense of legibility. If you will look closely at the letters in a newspaper, magazine, or book, you will see that the letters are farther apart than they need to be to perform their function. That is because the photographic type continues to be designed to *look* like Linotype, even though imitation confers no advantage on the type or the reader. Space between the letters makes no contribution to legibility. On the contrary, the space detracts from legibility by making each word longer and by encouraging the eye to break the word into its individual letters, which results in forcing the brain to reconstruct the word instead of recognizing it by its shape the way fast readers normally do.

But our technology has reached the point, both in typesetting and in printing, that it no longer insists on putting excessive space between letters, nor does it require excessively open counters on the letters themselves. There are no more molds, no more molten lead alloys, no more sculptured letters receiving and transferring ink. Letters can be separate, or touch, or even overlap at will. The white portion of a letter can be as small as the point of a needle and print cleanly without filling up. In short, we can design our typefaces for utility— which means principally for legibility and ease of reading—rather than to conform to the limitations imposed by technology. And since we live in an age that requires each of us to ingest increasingly more information that comes to us in printed form, even a modest improvement in our reading efficiency should be worth some effort.

Fortunately, redesigning type to make it more legible also tends to make the letters narrower on the average (not shorter) as well as bring them closer together. "Condensed" typefaces have been designed many times, but these faces, based on the old technology, are unpleasant distortions of the normal types. Redesigning the letters and reducing the wasted space between them should be done in a way that does not call attention to itself by a distorted look to the type.

In 1965, my experiments convinced me that a skilled type designer, working with a psychologist to measure the effect of the changes on the reader's speed and awareness of any "strangeness" in the type, would be able to compress type by at least 15 percent in width while increasing reading speed. I estimated that the cost of producing such a typeface, including the testing steps, would be not more than $75,000. If a typeface compressed a mere 10 percent were used only on McGraw-Hill's longer books in 1965, the saving in printing plates, paper, printing, and binding would have been at least $200,000 annually. The real benefit would have been, however, not in increased profit at McGraw-Hill but increased speed and ease of reading for the people who read its books.

Projecting Advance Sale
with Regression Analysis

Essentially, regression analysis compares the earliest orders received for the current title with the orders from these same accounts that were received for previously published similar titles and then draws a mathematical analogy between the relation of the previous orders to the previous total advances and the present orders to the present expected advance. First, the analysis applied to the historical file tells us whether the analogy is a good one; that is, it determines how consistently previous orders from these accounts have related to the total of advance orders on previous titles (which it tells us through a number called the "coefficient of correlation"). If the relationship has been sufficiently consistent, the regression analysis predicts what the total advance will be, by further analogy, from the current orders on hand.

As much as possible, the previously published titles chosen to develop the regression analysis "analogy" should be those that bear at least a general resemblance to the title currently being sold. It is obvious that the pattern of sale of a mystery story will be very different from the one for a book on gardening (even if the total advance sale is the same), and that a book on gardening in the tropics will not be helpful for a book on how to insulate greenhouses.

Although the regression line is mathematically calculated rather than graphically derived, the way in which regression provides a prediction can best be explained by means of a graph (see Figure 7 on page 394).

When prediction of advance sale is needed, the orders already on hand (which might be from 50 of the ultimate 2000 accounts) are examined and the sales records consulted to see what those accounts,

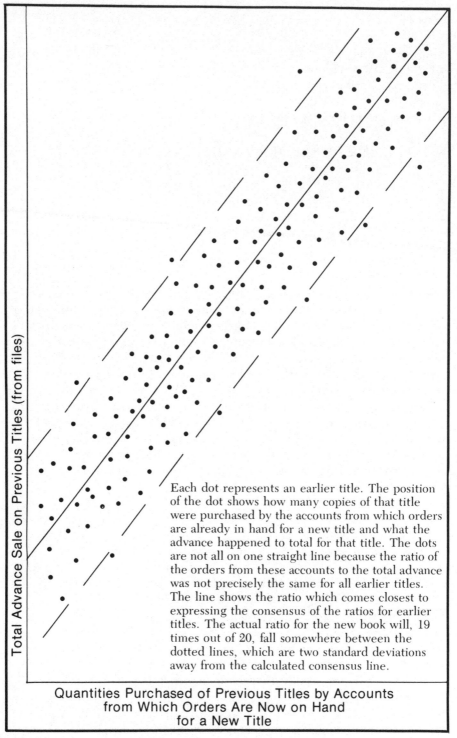

Each dot represents an earlier title. The position of the dot shows how many copies of that title were purchased by the accounts from which orders are already in hand for a new title and what the advance happened to total for that title. The dots are not all on one straight line because the ratio of the orders from these accounts to the total advance was not precisely the same for all earlier titles. The line shows the ratio which comes closest to expressing the consensus of the ratios for earlier titles. The actual ratio for the new book will, 19 times out of 20, fall somewhere between the dotted lines, which are two standard deviations away from the calculated consensus line.

Quantities Purchased of Previous Titles by Accounts from Which Orders Are Now on Hand for a New Title

Total Advance Sale on Previous Titles (from files)

FIGURE 7

combined, bought of earlier titles, and what the total advance for each of those earlier titles was. Each dot on Figure 7 represents that information on one previous title. If these accounts are going to be useful predictors of the total advance, the dots will tend to group themselves somewhat vaguely but nevertheless discernibly around a central line, the regression line, which represents the mathematical "consensus" of the dots. The degree to which the dots cluster around that line (the degree to which the consensus truly represents the commonality of the relation of their purchases to the total advance purchases) is the coefficient of correlation. The coefficient of correlation would be 1 if all the dots were on the regression line. The advance for the new title could then be confidently expected to be right on that line.

The spread of dots around the line, which results in a coefficient of correlation less than 1, is one measure of the uncertainty of the prediction. The degree to which the dots scatter around the line is expressed by a mathematical quantity called the "standard deviation:" Ninety-five percent of the dots fall within two standard deviations above and below the regression line, shown by the dashes on the graph.

The regression measures how consistently the accounts from which the orders are already in hand have predicted previous advances. If these sample accounts were relatively consistent, the advance can be predicted with 95 percent certainty within narrow limits; if not, the predicted advance will be stated more broadly. For example, depending on the sample of orders, the prediction for one title may be 10,000 copies plus or minus 1500 copies (meaning that the probability is 95 percent that the advance will be between 8500 and 11,500 copies) and on another title 10,000 copies plus or minus 300.

Determining the Economic Order Quantity

The ideal quantity to order (the Economic Order Quantity) is the one at which the cost of procuring the books equals the cost of maintaining them in inventory. Procurement costs (ordering, make-ready, etc.) are constant for any particular title, regardless of the quantity printed. We can simply lump those costs and express them by the letter P.

The carrying costs *do* vary with the quantity printed. The number of books held in inventory, assuming a fairly steady rate of sale, will be, on the average, for the life of the quantity produced, half the number of books printed. (The average equals the number at the start, all the books, plus the number at the end, none of the books, divided by 2.) The cost of carrying these books equals their average number (EOQ over 2) multiplied by the unit manufacturing cost of each copy (C), excluding make-ready cost (which is in our procurement cost), multiplied by the annual percentage cost (I) of the average investment in inventory, which includes interest, warehousing, spoilage, etc., but making allowance for the reverse effect of inflation, and all of this multiplied by the number of years (T) it will take to sell out the printed quantity at the expected rate of sale.

Expressed mathematically, that looks like:

$$P = \frac{EOQ}{2} \times C \times I \times T$$

which becomes:

$$P = \frac{EOQ \times C \times I \times T}{2}$$

T, as we have said, is the number of years it will take to sell out the reprint edition. It can be expressed another way: the reprint quantity, the EOQ (economic order quantity), divided by Y, the number of copies being sold per year, or EOQ/Y.

If we substitute EOQ/Y for T, the equation becomes:

$$P = \frac{EOQ \times C \times I \times EOQ}{2 \times Y}$$

or:

$$P = \frac{EOQ \times C \times I \times EOQ}{2Y}$$

or:

$$P = \frac{EOQ^2 \times CI}{2Y}$$

Since it is EOQ we are interested in, we want it on the left of the equal sign, so

$$EOQ^2 = \frac{2YP}{CI}$$

and, finally:

$$EOQ = \sqrt{\frac{2YP}{CI}}$$